June 6th, 1998

Bought @ VanDusen Garden Show. Spent wonderful day with Edna Allan.

HERITAGE PERENNIALS

Perennial Gardening Guide

JOHN M. VALLEAU

Heritage Perennials
Perennial Gardening Guide

John M. Valleau
Edited by John D. Schroeder

Published in Canada by
Valleybrook International Ventures Inc.
Abbotsford, British Columbia

Third Edition, May 1998

Canadian Cataloguing in Publication Data

Valleau, John M., 1962–
        Perennial gardening guide: the authoritative
North American guide to over 1500 varieties of
perennials, ferns, grasses and herbs

3rd ed.
Includes bibliographical references and index.
ISBN 0-9699483-1-X

        1. Perennials 2. Perennials—Pictorial works.
I. Schroeder, John D. (John David), 1956– II. Title.

SB434.V34 1998   635.9'32   C98-900650-6

Foreword

As a grower of perennials for many years, it is gratifying to see how interest has grown in these plants over time. Judging by the number of magazine articles and books about perennials everywhere, interest in this diverse and tremendous group of plants has never been greater.

What is equally satisfying is to see the constant introduction of new and rediscovered perennials to the gardening public. Of course, not everything new is necessarily better but there is nothing more exciting to a compulsive plant collector than a great new item that has not been seen before.

Our goal in publishing this best selling guide is to provide concise and accurate information in a useful and entertaining fashion about perennials which are readily available in North America. Considering that the first two editions were bestsellers, John Valleau has succeeded in using his extensive experience as a horticulturist and plant collector in achieving just that.

It gives me great pleasure to confidently recommend this book to both beginning gardeners and those who have room for 'just one more plant' in their garden. Please use this book as your guide to selecting and growing the right plants, both old standards and new introductions, to thrive in your garden.

John Schroeder
President, Valleybrook Gardens Ltd.

This book is dedicated to the memory of my late partner,
Warren Hartman (1942–1998). His keen designer's eye somehow
managed to saddle my unbridled passion for plant collecting.
Together we made The Tangled Garden.

Introduction

Gardening with perennials has suddenly become a passion for a whole generation of people that, for the most part, weren't even gardening just a few short years ago. It's all part of that nesting thing we keep hearing about: Baby Boomers with more leisure time, two incomes and the need to make their surroundings beautiful. But, what I really see happening lately is so much more than middle-aged couples with pretty yards. People of all ages, all over North America are taking those *yards* and turning them into the wonderful, personal spaces that we call *gardens*.

Because of its personal nature, varying climates and that mysterious thing we call *fashion*, a real garden is awfully hard to define. To me the main difference between a yard and a garden is defined by how the owner perceives it. It's the difference between the act of gardening being a chore or being a pleasurable activity. It's the difference between planting because you have to (keeping up with the Joneses) or gardening for yourself. It matters little whether the plants themselves are the newest and latest cutting-edge specimens or more common and familiar flowers handed over from neighbors and friends, because the plants alone will never make a garden. The kind of special magic that makes a true garden can happen only with the efforts of a gardener who is inspired.

How do we become inspired gardeners? Only by opening our eyes to see other gardens, public or private, large or small, in person, in books and magazines, on television, or even on the world wide web. Sometimes happy accidents will happen in a garden, self-sown seedlings will create unusual combinations of plants that we would never have considered planting together. As gardeners we must be open to these acts of nature, prepared to let the garden happen a little all by itself, yet with a restraining hand available for when it too a little carried away. Most important, is to banish the concept that the garden can ever be *finished*! Perennials, more than any other group of garden plants, offer you the key to a garden that is in a constant state of change, every single day of the year.

Anyone can learn about the *science* of gardening — how much sun or shade, how far apart, when to do this or that. This book is full of information about all those type of things. The *art* of gardening is much more elusive, and something that I truly hope you can find here as well. If even one person is inspired by this book to plant a Verbascum at the front edge of the border, make a butterfly garden, or grow some perennials in a hanging basket, then I will consider my efforts a success. My goal is to help inspire your perennial gardening, to perhaps share an idea or two and maybe someday be able to visit your garden and glean an idea or two to add to my own inspirations and dreams.

John Valleau

Acknowledgements

Photographs used in this book are primarily from Valleybrook International Ventures Inc.'s comprehensive image bank. Photographers include: John Schroeder, John Valleau, Geoff Lewis, Greg Baxter, Maureen Newman and Jackie Mays. Additional photographs supplied by: Ewan McKenzie, Bruce McDonald, Steven Still, Adrian Bloom, Lynne Milnes, Paddy Wales, Sharon Hubbard and Blooms of Bressingham North America. Garden photographs include the gardens of Adrian Bloom, Rob Proctor and Sue Lee.

Front cover photograph: Paddy Wales – UBC Botanical Garden
Back cover photograph: John Schroeder

The author and publisher would like to thank all who shared their insight and experience through the quotations used throughout this book. Their entertaining and insightful comments add immeasurably in creating an enjoyable reference book.

As well, thanks are due to Edward Kehler, designer and producer, for the numerous late nights required to get this book done on time.

A word about Heritage Perennials...

For over 15 years, Heritage Perennials have been growing some of the finest perennials in North America. First available in the western USA and Canada, they are now sold at leading garden centers throughout Canada, the Pacific Northwest and Northeast USA. Heritage Perennials are produced by Valleybrook Gardens Ltd., a family owned farm, and are grown in distinctive blue pots, hence the slogan, 'The Best Perennials come out of the Blue'.

All the plants listed in this guide are grown by Heritage Perennials, although all varieties might not be available at one time or at one location. This list, while comprehensive, won't include every variety available since new varieties are always coming onto the market.

Additional information about Heritage Perennials can be found on the Internet at www.perennials.com. Additional copies of this book can be found at your local garden center or bookstore, ordered directly from our website, or by writing to:

	Heritage Perennials
In Canada:	P.O. Box 8000-454, Abbotsford, BC V2S 6H1
In USA:	P.O. Box 8000-454, Sumas, WA 98295

Table of Contents

Perennials

In the early days of European settlement, perennial flowers were grown in almost every North American garden. After World War II, however, perennials gradually fell out of favour; foundation evergreen plantings, flowering trees and shrubs, masses of annuals and groundcovers swept us off our feet for a few decades. In the last ten years or so, many home gardeners have had a craving for something more. More than a carpet of petunias or impatiens, more than another spreading juniper, even more than a bed of hybrid tea roses. And for many, perennials have become the perfect answer.

Because there is such a vast array of perennials to choose from, it would be difficult for any gardener to become bored of using them. For the addicted perennial gardener, the possibilities become endless. Planning, arranging, planting, taking notes, rearranging again and again, these are the joys and challenges of perennial gardening. Indeed, most perennial fanatics would agree that the border is never truly finished; there is always a new idea waiting to be tried.

Beginning gardeners, please don't be scared off! One of the best things about perennial gardening is that it can be tailored to suit your needs, experience, and even your budget. No need to convert your whole lawn into an English-style border. Start with your current landscaping as a base, and try to figure out a way of integrating perennials into what is already there.

A few basics

Let's do a little review of a few gardening basics:

ANNUALS are plants that complete their life cycle within one year. Examples: marigolds, petunias, impatiens, zinnias.

BIENNIALS usually need two years to bloom, set seed and die. Sometimes they get mixed up and take one year or even three years to do this. Examples: sweet william, forget-me-not, foxglove, canterbury bells.

PERENNIALS generally live for several years, though some are longer-lived than others. This varies a lot, depending on your climate, soil conditions, insects or diseases, and the plant in question. Herbaceous is a word used to describe plants that do not develop woody stems. Most of our garden perennials therefore fall into the category of herbaceous perennials. This is to distinguish them from trees and shrubs.

Perennial benefits

No matter what your garden situation, there are a number of perennials available that will adapt to the conditions you already have. There are perennials for sun, shade, clay, sand, wet or dry soil, hot or cold climates, and everything in between.

Perennials flowers appear in every colour of the rainbow, as well as black, white and brown! No matter what colour scheme you can think up, there will be a perennial available to match. Just as important, the range of form and texture among perennials is quite diverse. Low, spreading carpets, medium rounded bushes and tall spiky spires are all available from among the ranks. Texture ranges from fine and feathery to bold and glossy.

Perennials can provide you with a much broader selection of plant material to choose from when planning your landscape. Not using perennials in our gardens would be like not decorating the walls of a room. We would be ignoring the endless possibilities of colour, texture, and the changing seasons.

And they are a good investment. Not only do they provide you with most of the same benefits as annuals, they even come back! And they get bigger. Within a few years many varieties will need to be lifted and divided, and what an excellent opportunity that is to share or trade with friends and neighbours. One healthy, large clump of Summer Phlox can be divided into ten or more pieces, so you can easily see an increase in value right there in your own garden.

For people with a limited amount of time available to garden, some of the more rugged and carefree perennials will fit very nicely into a low-maintenance scheme.

Perennial misconceptions

One misconception about perennials is that they will somehow magically take care of themselves. In most cases this is not true. They will still need help both in getting established, and in staying healthy and vigorous.

This means regular watering, weeding, trimming back or pruning, dividing, transplanting, fertilizing, and sometimes dealing with pests or diseases. This might sound like a lot of work, but compared to growing and maintaining a healthy lawn it can actually amount to much less.

Creative gardening with perennials

Back at the turn of the century, the British developed the perennial garden concept, borrowing ideas from the quaint country cottage gardens and refining them into the herbaceous border, an impressive thing indeed! Twenty feet deep by two hundred feet long would have been an average-sized border in that age of cheap labour and wealthy estate owners. The English-style border, with its grand scale and lavish use of colour, is more or less relegated to large parks and botanical gardens in modern times.

Few of us have the space, energy, time, or money necessary to recreate this effect successfully in our own gardens. So instead, we must figure out a way of incorporating perennials into the smaller gardens of today.

There are several other ways of using perennials besides the classic perennial border. Renowned British plantsman Alan Bloom pioneered the concept of island beds, which can be viewed from all sides. By putting taller plants in the centre, and gradually shorter ones towards the outside edge, this sort of bed provides its own backdrop. Maintenance is fairly easy, as the bed can be reached from all sides.

A shaded site with lots of deciduous trees is the perfect spot for a woodland garden, combining shade-loving perennials with spring-blooming bulbs, and low shade-tolerant flowering shrubs. Ferns, hostas and daffodils would all do very nicely here.

Container gardening with perennials is a relatively new idea. In milder areas perennials may be left in the pots for the winter, and in colder areas either sink the pots in the ground, or remove plants to the garden in late fall.

Mass plantings of perennials are very effective around large office buildings and other public areas. They create a large block of colour and texture, and are especially good flowing around or among trees and shrubs. This ground-cover effect can be easily adapted to the low-maintenance residential garden.

Many people like to enjoy their flowers indoors, and most perennials will last at least a few days when cut, some for well over a week! A special garden for cut flowers might be worth considering if you don't like to pick the flowers from other areas of your garden.

Symbols Key

- ☼ Full Sun
- ☼ Part Shade
- ● Full Shade
- △ Alpine
- ✂ Good Cut Flower
- ▲ Evergreen
- ∿ Groundcover
- 🦋 Attracts Butterflies
- 🦅 Attracts Hummingbirds
- ⚱ Suitable for Containers
- 🕸 Drought Tolerant

How to plant perennials

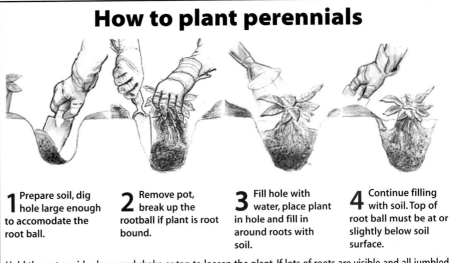

1 Prepare soil, dig hole large enough to accomodate the root ball.

2 Remove pot, break up the rootball if plant is root bound.

3 Fill hole with water, place plant in hole and fill in around roots with soil.

4 Continue filling with soil. Top of root ball must be at or slightly below soil surface.

Hold the pot upside-down and shake or tap to loosen the plant. If lots of roots are visible and all jumbled together, the plant may be rootbound. If so, the root ball must be disturbed to force new, healthy root growth. Using a sharp knife, slice up the bottom 2cm (1") of roots and rough up the sides of the ball with your fingers. Make sure the soil in the pot is moist. Planting a dry root ball makes it very difficult to provide sufficient water.

With a spade or trowel, open up a hole deep enough to accommodate the root ball. For best planting results, use the "puddling method." Fill the hole with water, place the plant upright in the hole and fill in around the roots with soil. Pat the soil to thoroughly mix the soil and water. This helps to eliminate any air pockets around the roots and ensures sufficient moisture for growth. Be sure the root ball surface is at or just slightly below the garden soil surface. After planting, spread a mulch to a depth of 2–5cm (1–2").

Perhaps the best way of using perennials though, is in a more integrated kind of scheme, one that mixes them together with flowering bulbs, shrubs, trees, evergreens, ornamental grasses, herbs, annuals, and perhaps even vegetables! The resulting pot-pourri of plants is often referred to as the mixed border. By mixing in woody plants with perennials, the garden has a real backbone or shape all year round, something that might otherwise be lacking in a garden that uses only perennials.

Getting started

Look at the basic landscape that you already have, and try to determine what the good and bad elements are. Removing any diseased trees or shrubs might be a good place to start. Changing the line of a sidewalk or the shape of a planting might be all that is required. A basic book on landscaping will come in very handy at this point.

Rather than look at your entire yard, try to focus in on just a few spots that could use some improvement. If you re-work a few areas each year, it won't take very long at all to see a marked difference in your whole garden.

Look for spots that seem to need brightening up at certain times of the year. For example, maybe you have an area with a lot of tulips or daffodils already planted, and the dying foliage is an eyesore in May and June. Consider planting summer-blooming perennials among the bulbs; Coreopsis 'Moonbeam', Babies breath (Gypsophila), or Monkshood (Aconitum) would all be effective.

Maybe you have a narrow area beside the house that gets hot and dries out quickly. This sounds like a good spot for Hens-and-chicks (Sempervivum) or dwarf Stonecrops (Sedum) of various kinds. Either will look much better than bare dirt, and will actually thrive in that hot, harsh environment.

Think ahead

The hardest part about designing with perennials is planning for colour over an extended season. Although certain varieties will bloom for many weeks on end, most perennials bloom for three to four weeks at the most. If all the varieties in your garden begin blooming in early June, there won't likely be much colour left by September.

Check the blooming information under each plant listing, or check plant tags at your garden centre. This will help you to choose combinations that bloom at the same or different times, depending on the design you have in mind.

Ideally, a good selection of different perennials will give you colour somewhere in the garden from early April to late October. Learning which varieties bloom at what time is part of the challenge of perennial gardening. Take a good

Hardiness Zones

Use this table to help determine which plants are suitable for your winter conditions. Any plant with your zone number or lower should be suitable.

If you are in doubt be sure to ask your local garden centre staff.

Zone	Minimum Winter Temp.	
	°F	°C
1	Below -50	Below -46
2	-50 to -40	-46 to -40
3	-40 to -30	-40 to -34
4	-30 to -20	-34 to -29
5	-20 to -10	-29 to -23
6	-10 to 0	-23 to -18
7	0 to 10	-18 to -12
8	10 to 20	-12 to -7
9	20 to 30	-7 to -1
10	30 to 40	-1 to 4

Use this information as a general guide for selecting suitable plants for your area. Many other factors affect overwintering of perennials. Some of these factors include: reliability and depth of snow cover, soil moisture levels, and site-specific micro-climates.

look around your neighbourhood this year. Try to take notes about when plants that appeal to you put on their best display. It is only one step further to begin combining different varieties together in clever ways that perhaps nobody ever thought of before!

Plan in threes

When looking for an attractive combination of plants, one of the most successful methods is to think in threes. For example, maybe you have a nice big clump of old-fashioned pink Bleedingheart (Dicentra); let's try to combine two other plants with it that will look attractive at the same time. Perhaps you might add a nice clump of blue Siberian Iris, which has tall, grassy leaves, and maybe a clump or two of white-edged Hosta down at the front. Notice that the Hosta does not bloom at the same time, but still adds interest with its variegated leaves.

Planting a combination of three plants together can easily lend itself to all sorts of interesting designs. Try to imagine combinations of herbs, perennials and annuals, for example; no need to just stick to perennials alone. This little trick can easily be adapted to container gardening as well.

So, before digging up that chunk of lawn to install an English herbaceous border, just ask yourself if that commitment of time, energy, and money is what you really want. If perennials are new to you, we recommend starting out in a small way first, and slowly adding to your perennial display. After all, you can always dig up the lawn next year.

Selecting and planting perennials

When buying perennials, look for fresh, healthy-looking plants that appear vigorous and ready to grow. Avoid overgrown, rootbound plants and any that have insects or diseases.

When to Plant

Spring is the ideal time to plant container-grown perennials. They have a chance to get well established before the heat of summer arrives. Spring is also a good time to divide or transplant most types of perennials that you may already have in your garden. Peonies, Iris and Oriental Poppies should not be divided in the spring. However they can be planted from containers all season long.

Summer planting can be very successful, as long as plants are not allowed to dry out. Watering is especially important if the weather is hot and dry. Transplanting or dividing perennials already established in your garden is not recommended during the summer, except for Bearded Iris, which should be divided only in July or August.

Fall planting is highly recommended in most areas. Early-blooming varieties will put on a colourful display in spring if planted in the fall. Dividing or moving established perennials in the fall is usually very successful.

Winter frosts may "heave" fall planted perennials. Check them in late winter, and if any have popped out of the ground, gently press them back in place.

Preparing your soil

Most perennials grow best in a deep, rich, well-drained soil. Check the tag for specific soil or site requirements. Properly preparing your soil is the single most important step to having healthy, successful gardens.

Dry, sandy soils can be improved by adding plenty of organic matter, such as compost, moistened peat moss or composted manure. Dig the area to a depth of at least 8 inches, preferably with a fork or spade.

Heavy clay soils need to be opened by adding plenty of organic matter, along with perlite or coarse sand.

Few perennials do well in wet, poorly drained soils. Consider building raised beds or installing drainage tubing if you have a soggy garden area. If you are not prepared to do this, choose perennials which do well under these conditions.

Weeds

The planting area must be free of perennial weeds, especially spreading types like Canada Thistle and Couch or Quack Grass. Ask your garden centre how these can be eliminated. Annual weeds are easily controlled by hand weeding.

Mulching around your plants will help to control weeds, and will keep roots cool and moist. Choose a mulching material that is organic and weed free, such as bark, cocoa beans or shredded leaves.

Watering

If these planting instructions are followed, no more watering should be required for a week or so. This will of course depend on temperature, rainfall etc. Otherwise, water plants immediately after planting and once a week or so for the first two weeks, unless the weather is rainy. Summer plantings may require more frequent watering, especially during periods of drought.

Fertilizing

Perennials may be fertilized with either a liquid or a slow-release granular-type fertilizer. Ask your garden centre to recommend a good product. If your soil is fertile and well-prepared to begin with, no additional fertilizing should be necessary the first year, although incorporating some bone meal at planting is often helpful.

Established perennial beds benefit from a yearly spring application of slow-release fertilizer or compost.

Maintaining perennials

This guide on perennials will help you to learn about some of the special things that should be done to your plants, such as staking, cutting back and controlling any diseases or pests. Ask your garden centre which other books they recommend for additional information you may require.

Here are some general guidelines for maintaining perennials:

- Prune off any dead tops in late winter or early spring.
- Remove dead flowers to encourage repeat blooming.
- Water during drought if possible; early morning is best.
- Clip back scruffy looking plants to promote fresh, attractive growth.
- Control pests and diseases as soon as noticed to avoid spreading the problem to other plants.
- Stake Peony, Delphinium, Summer Phlox and other tall plants early to avoid wind damage later.
- Divide perennials when the centre of the plant begins to die out with age.

Acaena caesiiglauca

Acanthus mollis

Achillea × 'Anthea'

Achillea 'Walter Funke'

ACAENA
(Sheepburr, New Zealand Burr) ☀ ◔

A unique and under-used group of low-growing groundcovers from the southern hemisphere, valued for their dense, spreading carpet of evergreen foliage, and colourful burr-shaped seed heads which appear in late summer. Although these are usually planted in rock gardens, they grow quickly and can sometimes smother out choicer alpines. Good cover plants in combination with early spring flowering bulbs. All are drought tolerant once established, and don't mind poor soils.

HEIGHT/SPREAD:	10cm (4")/30–60cm (1–2')
LOCATION:	Well-drained soil. Tolerates poor soil. Dislikes wet soil.
BLOOMS:	June–August
USES:	△﹏▲🌿 Fast spreader

'Blue Haze'   ZONES 6–9
Attractive blue-green leaves, much larger than *A. microphylla*. Many stems of brown burrs in the fall.

> "One that I have most often met… has quite tiny glaucous pinnate foliage borne on longish scrambling stems that can rise into and intermingle with any foot- or 18-inch-tall plant or shrub they happen to be near." – Christopher Lloyd, *Foliage Plants*

caesiiglauca   ZONES 5–9
(Silver-leaf New Zealand Burr) Silvery-blue leaves with a soft, downy texture. Reddish burrs. One of the best forms, and reported to be less invasive. Not widely tested yet for hardiness but worth a try to Zone 4.

microphylla   ZONES 3–9
(Bronze-leaf New Zealand Burr) Good low carpeter. Unusual bronzy-green foliage and showy copper-red burrs. The toughest species, great for between paving stones! Spreads quickly.

ACANTHUS
(Bear's-Breeches) ☀ ◔

Bold specimen plants, very popular with landscape designers. When grown in borders or containers these form large leafy clumps with a tropical flair. Exotic upright spikes of light pink flowers appear throughout the summer months. Choose a well-protected area as they can be damaged by late spring frosts. In colder areas plant in tubs for easy overwintering indoors. Where hardy, these can spread to form a large patch.

> "Bear's breeches,…with its thick mounds of long, jagged leaves, easily dominates a borderful of smaller foliage, even without its head-high stems of tubular, mauvy flowers." – Ann Lovejoy, *The American Mixed Border*

SPREAD:	90cm (3')
LOCATION:	Well-drained soil. Dislikes winter wet
BLOOMS:	July–August
USES:	✂◄♥ Dried Flower, Specimen, Borders

hungaricus   ZONES 6–9
(Hungarian Bear's-Breeches) (*A. balcanus*) Definitely one of the hardiest forms, this has spiny leaves with a thistly appearance, olive-green in colour. Flower spikes are held well above the foliage and are superb for cutting, if you can bring yourself to do it. HEIGHT: 90–120cm (3–4')

mollis   ZONES 7–9
(Common Bear's-Breeches) The most well-known species, with large, glossy and deeply-lobed leaves. Mauve-pink flowers, vigorous habit. Excellent cut flower. Use a winter mulch in Zone 6. HEIGHT: 90–150cm (3–5')

Achillea 'Terra Cotta'

ACHILLEA
(Yarrow) ☀

The Yarrows are among the best perennials for hot and dry locations, providing good colour throughout the summer months, and even tolerating poor soils. All but the shortest varieties are superb for cutting, used fresh or dried. Divide and replant clumps every two years.

× 'Anthea'   ZONES 2–9
A newer hybrid, bred by Alan Bloom of Bressingham Gardens, an offspring of a cross with 'Moonshine'. Plants are upright with intensely silver foliage on a bushy, non-spreading clump. The large flower clusters open primrose yellow fading to cream, blooming continually all season if faded flowers are removed.

HEIGHT/SPREAD:	30–45cm (12–18")/30cm (12")
LOCATION:	Average well-drained soil.
BLOOMS:	June–September
USES:	✂▲♥🌿 Dried Flower, Borders, Massing

filipendulina   ZONES 2–9
(Fern-Leaf Yarrow) Forms an upright clump of ferny green leaves with large clusters of golden-yellow flowers on tall stems. Good for massing. Flowers are superb for drying. Very drought-tolerant.

HEIGHT/SPREAD:	90–150cm (3–5')/45cm (18")
LOCATION:	Well-drained soil. Heat tolerant.
BLOOMS:	June–September
USES:	✂🌿 Dried Flower, Borders

× lewisii 'King Edward'
See under *A. tomentosa*.

millefolium Hybrids   ZONES 2–9
(Common Yarrow) A catch-all group that includes a number of older selections as well as some outstanding newer hybrids that have been mostly developed in Germany for the cut-flower trade. All selections sport good-sized clusters of flowers held above ferny green foliage. Inclined to spread, but may be useful as a groundcover on slopes. Dead-head or clip back hard after blooming to force a second flush. Very drought-tolerant.

HEIGHT/SPREAD:	45–70cm (18–30")/60cm (24")
LOCATION:	Well-drained soil. Heat tolerant.
BLOOMS:	June–September
USES:	✂✦❄ Dried Flower, Borders

'Apple Blossom' ('Apfelblute') Large clusters of lilac-pink flowers. HEIGHT: 90cm (3')

'Christel' Gorgeous new clear magenta-pink selection. Outstanding!

'Heidi' Clear pink flowers, compact form.

'Hoffnung' ('Great Expectations') Primrose yellow flowers tinged with peach. Compact habit.

'Lavender Beauty' Unusual pastel lavender-pink flowers.

'Paprika' Cherry-red, gold centered flowers, fading to light pink and creamy yellow.

'Red Beauty' Deep crimson-red clusters. Still the best deep red!

'Summer Pastels' A seed-grown mix of the various colours above, including also some beautiful shades of wine, salmon and creamy white. An All-American Award winner.

'Terra Cotta' New selection with gorgeous salmon-pink flowers that age to rusty terra cotta orange. HEIGHT: 75cm (30")

'Walter Funke' Brick-red flowers with a yellow eye.

× 'Moonshine'   ZONES 2–9

An outstanding early hybrid by Alan Bloom of Bressingham Gardens. Valued for its summer-long display of rich canary-yellow flowers held in large clusters above silvery-grey leaves. Non-spreading habit. Combines well with ornamental grasses. Remove faded flowers for continual bloom. Still one of the best perennials of all time. Moderately drought-tolerant

HEIGHT/SPREAD:	45–60cm (18–24")/30cm (12")
LOCATION:	Average well-drained soil.
BLOOMS:	June–September
USES:	✂◀▼❄ Dried Flower, Massing, Borders

ptarmica 'Dwarf Ballerina'   ZONES 1–9

(Double White Yarrow) Airy sprays of fluffy white flowers similar to Baby's Breath. Compact form of an old-fashioned favorite. Inclined to spread.

HEIGHT/SPREAD:	30–45cm (12–18")/45–60cm (18–24")
LOCATION:	Average to moist soil. Heat tolerant.
BLOOMS:	June–July
USES:	✂<❄ Dried Flower, Massing, Borders

tomentosa   ZONES 2–9

(Woolly Yarrow) Carpet-forming, with short stems of lemon-yellow flowers in early spring. Easy rock garden plant. Clip off the flowers after they fade. Very drought-tolerant. **A. × lewisii 'King Edward'** has a similar habit, with heads of soft primrose-yellow flowers.

HEIGHT/SPREAD:	20cm (8")/30cm (12")
LOCATION:	Well-drained soil.
BLOOMS:	May–July
USES:	▲〰❄ Edging, Borders

ACONITUM
(Monkshood) ☼ ◖

Tall, sturdy perennials, these look their best in larger borders. Showy spikes of flowers appear during the summer or fall and are beautiful for cutting. They prefer a cool, moisture-retentive soil. All Monkshoods are extremely poisonous!

SPREAD:	60cm (2')
LOCATION:	Cool, moist, well-drained soil.
USES:	✂ Borders

× cammarum   ZONES 2–9

(Hybrid Monkshood) Good, sturdy spikes of flowers, summer-blooming types.

'Bicolor' (Bicolor Monkshood) Flowers are an attractive violet-blue and white combination. HEIGHT: 90–120cm (3–4')

'Bressingham Spire' One of the best forms. Compact stems don't require staking. Deep violet-blue flowers from midsummer through the fall. HEIGHT: 90cm (3')

× carmichaelii 'Arendsii'   ZONES 2–9

(Autumn Monkshood) Incredible tall spikes of bright blue hooded flowers, appearing in mid to late fall and lasting until hard frost. Superb for cutting! HEIGHT: 120–180cm (4–6')

> "Even after the first snows fly, this plant stands tall and stately, in full, rich bloom with its leaves still glossy and green. It's a true friend to the northern gardener."
> – Cathy Forgie, Zone 4

lamarckii   ZONES 2–9

(Yellow Monkshood) (= *A. pyrenaicum*) Unusual creamy-yellow flowers. Just as easy to grow as the blue-flowered forms, flowering in the summer. HEIGHT: 60–120cm (2–4')

napellus   ZONES 2–9

(Blue Monkshood) Deep blue helmet-shaped flowers. Old-fashioned favorite, also a summer bloomer. HEIGHT: 120–150cm (4–5')

'Carneum' A unique selection with pale rose-pink flowers. Similar in stature to the regular blue form, and a lovely contrast to it in the border. Flowers may fade during hot weather.

septentrionale 'Ivorine'   ZONES 2–9

Another Bressingham Gardens selection bred by Alan Bloom. Neat, compact variety. Ivory-white flowers in short spikes. Earlier blooming. The best of the white forms. HEIGHT: 60–90cm (2–3')

AEGOPODIUM
(Goat's foot, Snow-on-the-Mountain, Bishop's Weed, Goutweed) ◖ ●

podagraria 'Variegatum'   ZONES 1–9

Perhaps an overly well-known groundcover, with green and white variegated foliage. Quickly forms a solid patch, even in poor soil. Difficult to eradicate once established. Dislikes hot sun. Recommended for pots and containers, or where it can spread without becoming a problem. Clip off the flower stems for best appearance. Extremely drought-tolerant.

> "If you are moving away from neighbours that you can't stand, plant this on the property line just before you go. You can rest assured you will have gotten even for every wrong, no matter how great."
> – Val Ward, Zone 5

HEIGHT/SPREAD:	30cm (12")/30–60cm (12–24")
LOCATION:	Tolerates most soils.
BLOOMS:	Flowers usually removed
USES:	〰▼❄ Invasive! Use carefully

AGAPANTHUS
(African Lily, Lily-of-the-Nile) ☼ ◖

Magnificent, exotic plants from South Africa, valued for their large flower heads. Excellent container plants, especially in colder regions where plants may be easily overwintered indoors. May be hardy in Zones 6–7 with sufficient winter protection. Superb cut flower.

Achillea 'Moonshine'

Aconitum napellus

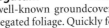

Aconitum × cammarum 'Bicolor'

Agapanthus Hybrid

Agastache 'Pink Panther'

Ajuga reptans

Ajuga reptans 'Burgundy Glow'

Ajuga reptans 'Catlin's Giant'

Hybrids ZONES 8–9

The result of extensive breeding in England resulting in many good selections with increased hardiness and deeper colours, in shades of blue through to white.

SPREAD: 30–60cm (12–24")
LOCATION: Well-drained soil.
BLOOMS: July–September
USES: ✂✿❦ Borders, Massing

'Bressingham White' Large growing plant with pure white flowers. Another Bressingham Gardens introduction. HEIGHT: 90cm (36")

'Lilliput' Excellent container plant. Dwarf, compact habit, bright blue trumpet flowers. HEIGHT: 45cm (18")

AGASTACHE
(Anise-Hyssop) ☼ ☽

foeniculum ZONES 2–9

Selection of a North American wildflower, native to sunny prairies and meadows. Tall wands of pale violet or white flowers appear summer through fall, and are a favorite of bees and butterflies. Good for cutting. Entire plant has a pleasant anise fragrance and can be used to make a soothing tea. (see also under Anise-Hyssop in the HERB chapter)

SPREAD: 60–90cm (2–3')
LOCATION: Average well-drained soil.
BLOOMS: July–September
USES: ✂❦ Wildflower, Dried Flower, Borders, Herb gardens

'Blue Fortune' A new hybrid selection bred in Holland, with a compact habit and terrific display of deep violet flowers. Terrific for cutting! HEIGHT: 60–90cm (2–3')

'Fragrant Delight' Taller selection with mauve flowers. HEIGHT: 90–120cm (3–4')

Hybrids ZONES 6–9

A wonderful new group of garden plants developed in recent years using several species native to the south-western US. Because of this parentage, these all hate having cold, wet feet in the winter and require perfect drainage. Because they perform so well the first year, these make terrific flowering plants for pots and tubs, or could be included in the herb garden for their fragrance.

SPREAD: 30–60cm (1–2')
LOCATION: Average well-drained soil. Avoid wet feet.
BLOOMS: July–September
USES: ✂❦⚘ Containers, Tubs, Borders, Herb gardens

'Apricot Sunrise' Clear apricot-orange flowers, grey-green fragrant foliage. HEIGHT: 45–60cm (18–24")

'Pink Panther' Bronzy-green foliage, long spikes of rose-pink flowers. HEIGHT: 75–120cm (30–48")

AJANIA
(Silver & Gold Chrysanthemum) ☼ ☽

pacifica ZONES 5–9

(Formerly *Chrysanthemum pacificum*) Bushy mounds of toothed green foliage, attractively edged with silver. Yellow button flowers will appear very late fall if the season is long and warm, in some areas blooming into December. Also a superb container plant, either kept bushy or trained into a standard. 'Pink Ice' is a new selection, introduced by Tony Avent of Plant Delights Nursery. Yellow button flowers are surrounded by a row of pale pink petals.

HEIGHT/SPREAD: 30–60 cm (1–2')/30–60 cm (1–2')
LOCATION: Average well-drained soil.
BLOOMS: October–November
USES: ✂❦ Edging, Borders

AJUGA
(Carpet Bugle, Bugleweed) ☽ ●

Widely used as a groundcover for shady areas. Most types are fast-spreading but easy to control, forming a low mat of rounded leaves. Showy spikes of flowers appear in late spring. There are a great number of varieties available.

genevensis ZONES 2–9

(Geneva Bugle) Spikes of bright blue flowers, thick mat of green foliage, the hardiest form.

HEIGHT/SPREAD: 15–20cm (6–8")/30–45cm (12–18")
LOCATION: Prefers moist soil.
BLOOMS: May–June
USES: ⚘▲❦ Edging

'Pink Beauty' Soft-pink flowers, held on more upright spikes. Long blooming season. Not as hardy as the blue form, Zone 5.

'Mini Crisp Red' ZONES 3–9

(sometimes incorrectly listed as 'Metallica Crispa') A most unusual form, the deep-red leaves are crimped and crinkled like spinach, very compact and congested. This form is extremely slow compared to the other varieties. Can be used in a rockery with no fear of invasion. Almost black winter colour. Short spikes of blue flowers. Choice.

> "Looks like a cross between spinach and brains — shiny crinkled leaves suffused with deep purple form a non-invasive clump that seems to do equally well in sun or shade. Impossible to walk by without bending to see what it feels like. Short spikes of blue bugles in late spring are a welcome bonus."
> – Larry Davidson, Zone 5

HEIGHT/SPREAD: 5–10cm (2–4")/20–30cm (8–12")
LOCATION: Prefers moist, well-drained soil.
BLOOMS: May–June
USES: ▲△⚘▲❦ Edging

reptans ZONES 3–9

(Common Bugle) Fast-spreading mats, bright blue flowers in spring. Among the many selections are some outstanding forms with unusual foliage colouring. The deep red types are especially dramatic when massed below green or gold-leaved shrubs.

HEIGHT/SPREAD: 15cm (6")/30–45cm (12–18")
LOCATION: Prefers moist soil.
BLOOMS: May–June
USES: ⚘▲❦ Edging

'Braunherz' ('Bronze Heart') Newer German variety. Glossy deep purple-bronze leaves, contrasting deep blue flowers. The best dark leaved form.

'Bronze Beauty' Popular older bronze-leaved variety. Bright blue flowers.

'Burgundy Glow' Brightly-coloured leaves, variegated with scarlet, cream, and green. Bright blue flowers. Good fall colour. Rogue out any reverting shoots regularly.

'Catlin's Giant' Unusually tall spikes of blue flowers, huge bronzy leaves. Inclined to clump at first, later forming a solid patch. Excellent for edging! HEIGHT: 15–30cm (6–12")

'Pat's Selection' A new selection, a little bit like 'Burgundy Glow' with tri-colored foliage in bronze and pink, with a hint of creamy-white. Puckered appearance.

'Purple Torch' Bright green foliage, tall spikes of lavender-pink flowers. Bronze winter colour.

'Ruffled Lace' Fabulous new discovery! Deep, rich burgundy-purple colour and a crispy appearance.

ALCEA
(Hollyhock) ☼

rosea
ZONES 2–9

These tall spikes of crepe-textured flowers have been grown in gardens for centuries. Best at the back of a sunny border with medium-sized plants in front to hide the bare lower stems. Usually biennial, the plants will readily self-seed if allowed. Leaf rust may be a problem, particularly with the double types; either ignore it or try using a systemic fungicide. Cutting plants back immediately after flowering may encourage them to return for another year. Said to attract hummingbirds.

> "For many years, I preferred the fat doubles but now find them congested and graceless next to the simple singles, perhaps because of the comment that doubles look 'like those toilet paper decorations on wedding cars'— enough to put one off any flower." – Patrick Lima, *The Harrowsmith Perennial Garden*

HEIGHT/SPREAD:	150–210cm (5–7')/30cm (12")
LOCATION:	Average well-drained soil.
BLOOMS:	July–August
USES:	✄<➤ Borders

'Chater's Doubles' Large double ruffled blooms, like Kleenex™ flowers. Generally available in mixed colours or sometimes separately in shades of maroon, rose, pink, scarlet, white, and yellow.

'Nigra' Unique single maroon-black flowers.

'Powderpuff Mix' More compact in habit, with fully double blooms in a complete range of mixed colours. Sometimes treated as an annual. **HEIGHT:** 120–150cm (4–5')

Single Mix (*A. ficifolia* hybrids) The single-flowered forms of Hollyhock have a certain grace and charm that is totally lacking in the double types. They are generally not as badly affected by leaf rust, with an overall tougher constitution. Said to be the easiest to establish, with more of a perennial habit. Flowers are available in a whole range of pastel shades.

ALCHEMILLA
(Lady's Mantle) ☼ ◐

Popular plants for edging, these form a mound of rounded leaves with billowing sprays of yellow-green flowers. Sometimes mass planted as a groundcover. They adapt to most garden conditions.

alpina
ZONES 2–9

(Alpine Lady's Mantle) Compact grower. Silvery leaves, buff-coloured flowers.

HEIGHT/SPREAD:	15cm (6")/30cm (12")
LOCATION:	Well-drained soil.
BLOOMS:	June–August
USES:	◭〜✄❦ Edging, Borders

ellenbeckii
ZONES 5–9

(Creeping Lady's Mantle) Tiny, pleated leaves, plants spreading to form a low mat. Excellent rock garden selection or useful for edging paths. Sprays of chartreuse flowers in summer, held in among the leaves.

HEIGHT/SPREAD:	10cm (4")/30cm (12")
LOCATION:	Well-drained soil.
BLOOMS:	June–August
USES:	◭〜✄❦ Edging, Containers

mollis
ZONES 2–9

Scalloped green leaves, covered in a soft down. Flowers and foliage are good for cutting. Self-seeds readily.

> "A totally 60's plant! Airy sprays of chartreuse flowers rising high above velvety grey-green leaves like bee-hive hairdos atop prom queens in lime-green minidresses!" – Dr. Duncan Himmelman, Zone 3

> "Its leaves are like an umbrella turned inside out and they are hairy, holding raindrops in their centre, but with a light-reflecting air bubble trapped underneath, that winks and sparkles with contagious glee." – Christopher Lloyd, *Foliage Plants*

HEIGHT/SPREAD:	30–45cm (12–18")/45–60cm (18–24")
LOCATION:	Well-drained soil.
BLOOMS:	June–August
USES:	◭〜✄❦ Edging, Borders

ALLIUM
(Flowering Onion) ☼ ◐

A useful and under-used group of flowering perennials, offering a wide range of heights and colours for the sunny border. Flowers are arranged in a ball-shaped cluster, the taller varieties making excellent cut flowers.

schoenoprasum
ZONES 1–9

(Chives) A familiar plant to most gardeners, but too often relegated to the herb garden or vegetable patch, rather than being included with other flowering perennials. Beautiful when combined with late tulips! See also the HERB chapter under Chives.

HEIGHT/SPREAD:	30cm (12")/30cm (12")
LOCATION:	Average well-drained soil.
BLOOMS:	May–June
USES:	✄❦〜 Borders, Herb gardens

'Album' Clean snow-white flowers, a most unusual form that is seldom seen.

'Forescate' (Giant Chives) A select variety with extra large rose-purple balls of flowers.

senescens 'Glaucum'
ZONES 3–9

(Pink Curly Onion) Unique blue-green leaves twisting out from the base in a spiral. Small clusters of pink flowers in late summer. Nice edging or rockery variety.

HEIGHT/SPREAD:	15–30cm (6–12")/30cm (12")
LOCATION:	Well-drained soil.
BLOOMS:	July–September
USES:	◭〜 Edging, Borders

ALTHAEA
See ALCEA.

ALYSSUM
(Mountain Alyssum) ☼

Popular plants growing on walls or among rocks. The species A. saxatile is now listed under AURINIA.

montanum
ZONES 2–9

(Mountain Alyssum) A low, spring-blooming species for the rock garden. Compact silvery mats are smothered by fragrant lemon-yellow flowers. Easy to please. Good for edging borders as well as in rock gardens or walls.

HEIGHT/SPREAD:	10–15cm (4–6")/30cm (12")
LOCATION:	Lean, well-drained soil.
BLOOMS:	April–June
USES:	◭▲❦ Edging, Walls

Alcea 'Single Mix'

Alchemilla alpina

Alchemilla mollis

Allium schoenoprasum

Amsonia tabernaemontana

Anemone japonica – Mixed Border

Anemone 'Hadspen Abundance'

Anemone sylvestris

AMSONIA
(Blue Star) ☼ ◐

Little-known perennials that are mostly native to North America, and ideally suited to the border or wildflower meadow. Flowers are pale blue stars. All are long-lived.

hubrechtii   ZONES 5–9
(Arkansas Blue Star) Unique in its display of feathery-textured foliage, making an upright bushy clump. Yellow fall colour is truly outstanding. Steel-blue flowers appear in early summer.

HEIGHT/SPREAD:	90–120cm (3–4')/90cm (3')
LOCATION:	Average to moist, rich soil.
BLOOMS:	May–July
USES:	✂ Wildflower, Borders

tabernaemontana   ZONES 3–9
Slightly coarser in habit, forming an arching clump of green leaves, with clusters of light blue starry flowers in late spring and early summer. Useful for cutting.

HEIGHT/SPREAD:	60–90cm (2–3')/60–90cm (2–3')
LOCATION:	Average to moist, rich soil.
BLOOMS:	May–July
USES:	✂ Wildflower, Borders

ANACYCLUS
(Mt. Atlas Daisy) ☼

pyrethrum depressus   ZONES 4–9
Unique daisy flowers, white on the front, red on the back. Forms a low clump of ferny foliage. Good rock garden plant, blooming over a long season. Fairly drought-tolerant.

HEIGHT/SPREAD:	10cm (4")/20–30cm (8–12")
LOCATION:	Well-drained soil. Dislikes winter wet.
BLOOMS:	May–July
USES:	▲ ⚘ Walls, Slopes

ANAPHALIS
(Pearly Everlasting) ☼

margaritacea   ZONES 2–9
A native wildflower, often gathered and dried as an everlasting. Flowers are clusters of white buttons, contrasting nicely with the grey foliage. Good border plant, although somewhat invasive. Moderately drought-tolerant. Attracts butterflies.

HEIGHT/SPREAD:	30–90cm (12–36")/30cm (12")
LOCATION:	Well-drained soil. Drought tolerant.
BLOOMS:	July–September
USES:	✂ ⚘ 🦋 Borders, Edging

ANEMONE
(Windflower) ☼ ◐

A large group of hardy perennials, many of easy garden culture. By far the most widely known are the fall-blooming hybrid Japanese Anemones, but there are also other species that flower in spring or summer.

× hybrida   ZONES 5–9
(Japanese Anemone) Outstanding plants for the late summer and fall garden. The branching stems of poppy-like flowers are superb for cutting. These will spread to form a solid patch. Good low-maintenance perennial. Mulch well for the first winter.

> "No plant of autumn brings more joy than Japanese anemones. They look wonderful if given a spot all to themselves in front of shrubbery, but they also associate very well with ferns growing at their feet." – Allen Lacy,
> *The Garden in Autumn*

HEIGHT/SPREAD:	60–150cm (2–5')/60cm (24")
LOCATION:	Rich, moist to damp soil.
BLOOMS:	August–October
USES:	∿ Massing, Borders

'Alice' Semi-double, light pink flowers. Compact. HEIGHT: 60cm (24")

'Hadspen Abundance' Free-blooming deep rose-pink, semi-double petals. HEIGHT: 60cm (2')

'Honorine Jobert' Large, single white flowers, an excellent old variety. HEIGHT: 90–120cm (3–4')

> "'Honerine Jobert' is a priceless classic of a perennial for your garden. Place it in the semi-shade against a darker backdrop and the substantial white blossoms will just glow!" – Suzette McDonnell, Zone 6

hupehensis japonica A forerunner of the modern hybrids, with single and semi-double flowers in a range of pink shades through white. Grown from seed, and variable. HEIGHT: 75–90cm (30–36")

'Margarete' Double pink flowers. HEIGHT: 90cm (36")

'Pamina' Deep rose-red flowers, one of the darkest. HEIGHT: 60–90cm (24–36")

'Prince Henry' Small, deep rose semidouble flowers. HEIGHT: 90cm (36")

'Queen Charlotte' Pink, semidouble flowers. HEIGHT: 90cm (36")

'September Charm' Large silvery-pink, single flowers. HEIGHT: 60–90cm (24–36")

'Whirlwind' Semidouble white flowers. HEIGHT: 90–120cm (3–4')

× lesseri   ZONES 5–9
An early summer-blooming hybrid with glowing rose-red flowers, glossy foliage. Often reblooms in the fall if cut back. This is a slower growing, non-invasive species.

HEIGHT/SPREAD:	30–45cm (12–18")/30cm (12")
LOCATION:	Deep, well-drained soil.
BLOOMS:	May–June
USES:	✂ Woodland gardens, Borders

pulsatilla
See PULSATILLA.

sylvestris   ZONES 2–9
(Snowdrop Anemone) Delicate nodding white flowers in late spring and intermittently throughout the summer. Quickly spreads to form a dense patch, suitable for use as a groundcover. Good cover for spring bulbs.

> "How does one deal with a plant that's as rampant as it is beautiful? In my garden, I've paired *Anemone sylvestris* with Sweet Woodruff. True, they're both fighting for dominance — but was there ever a more glorious battlefield?" – Kevin Ward, Zone 5

HEIGHT/SPREAD:	30–45cm (12–18")/30–60cm (12–24")
LOCATION:	Average to moist soil.
BLOOMS:	May–June
USES:	∿ ✂ Massing, Borders

tomentosa 'Robustissima'   ZONES 4–9
(Grapeleaf Anemone) Similar to a pink Japanese Anemone, but even more vigorous and hardier. Upright clumps of deep green foliage remain attractive from spring to late fall. Light pink single flowers are held on branching stalks well above the leaves. One of the showiest perennials for the late summer and fall garden. Plants will quickly spread to form a large patch.

HEIGHT/SPREAD:	90–120cm (3–4')/60cm (2')
LOCATION:	Average to moist well-drained soil.
BLOOMS:	August–September
USES:	Massing, Borders

ANGELICA
(Angelica) ☼ ☽

gigas   ZONES 4–9
(Red-flowered Angelica, Purple Parsnip) A bold-leafed perennial that forms a medium-sized clump of coarse green leaves. Large umbels of crimson-red flowers are held on tall stems for several weeks in mid-summer. Always commands attention in the garden. Inclined to be biennial. Should be allowed to self-sow.

HEIGHT/SPREAD:	90–120cm (3–4")/60cm (24")
LOCATION:	Prefers a rich, moist soil.
BLOOMS:	July–August
USES:	Borders, Tubs

ANTENNARIA
(Cat's-Paw, Pussytoes) ☼ ☽

dioica 'Rubra'   ZONES 1–9
(Pink Pussy-Toes) Forms a dense carpet of silver-grey foliage. Clusters of rosy-pink flowers appear in late spring. An extremely drought-tolerant groundcover deserving wider use. Trim flower stems off after blooming. Native North American wildflower.

HEIGHT/SPREAD:	10–15cm (4–6")/30cm (12")
LOCATION:	Well-drained soil. Withstands drought.
BLOOMS:	May–June
USES:	Between paving stones

ANTHEMIS
(Marguerite) ☼

Hardy, showy members of the Daisy family. Best used as filler plants in hot sunny perennial borders. Though short-lived they will usually self-seed to form a large patch. Excellent for cutting. Trim plants back hard after the first flush of flowers.

× hybrida 'Kelwayi'   ZONES 2–9
(Golden Marguerite) (Formerly listed as *A. tinctoria*) A profusion of yellow flowers all summer long.

HEIGHT/SPREAD:	60–90cm (24–36")/30–45cm (12–18")
LOCATION:	Well-drained soil. Moderately drought-tolerant.
BLOOMS:	June–August
USES:	Borders, Meadows

sancti-johannis   ZONES 2–9
(Orange Marguerite) Bright orange daisies with yellow centres.

HEIGHT/SPREAD:	60cm (24")/30–45cm (12–18")
LOCATION:	Well-drained soil. Moderately drought-tolerant.
BLOOMS:	June–August
USES:	Borders, Meadows

ANTIRRHINUM
(Perennial Snapdragon) ☼ ☽

braun-blanquetii   ZONES 5–9
(Yellow Perennial Snapdragon) Practically a non-stop bloomer, even in warm summer areas. Short spikes of cool creamy-yellow flowers with a darker yellow throat. Plants form a low, bushy mound. Said to be short-lived but readily self-sows.

HEIGHT/SPREAD:	30–50cm (12–20")/45–60cm (18–24")
LOCATION:	Average well-drained soil.
BLOOMS:	June–September
USES:	Borders, Pots

Aquilegia 'McKana's Giants'

AQUILEGIA
(Columbine) ☼ ☽
Popular, old-fashioned perennials, available in a variety of sizes and colours. Both the flowers and ferny foliage are good for cutting. In many regions the Columbine Leaf Miner will spoil the appearance of the leaves in June; simply cut the plants back to encourage clean new growth.

alpina   ZONES 2–9
(Alpine Columbine) Bright blue flowers, nice compact form. Good choice for rock gardens.

HEIGHT/SPREAD:	30–45cm (12–18")/30cm (12")
LOCATION:	Average to moist soil.
BLOOMS:	May–June
USES:	Borders, Woodland gardens

canadensis   ZONES 2–9
(Wild Red Columbine) Delicate brick-red flowers with yellow centres. Excellent in a woodland setting. A North American native wildflower.

> "An absolute boon to neglectful gardeners such as myself — the original, pampered plant expired post haste — yet its progeny continue to proliferate in the most inhospitable cracks and crevices of the fieldstone retaining wall." – Kevin Ward, Zone 5

HEIGHT/SPREAD:	60–75cm (24–30")/30cm (12")
LOCATION:	Average to moist soil.
BLOOMS:	May–June
USES:	Borders, Woodland gardens

chrysantha   ZONES 2–9
(Golden Columbine) Large golden-yellow flowers with long spurs, long blooming season. Mildew-resistant. Said to rebloom if dead-headed. A North American native wildflower.

HEIGHT/SPREAD:	75–105cm (30–42")/30cm (12")
LOCATION:	Average to moist soil.
BLOOMS:	May–June
USES:	Borders, Woodland gardens

flabellata   ZONES 2–9
(Japanese Fan Columbine) A truly dwarf Columbine with large, waxy flowers in blue or white. Beautiful in rockeries. Especially handsome blue-green leaves.

HEIGHT/SPREAD:	20–30cm (8–12")/20cm (8")
LOCATION:	Average to moist soil.
BLOOMS:	May–June
USES:	Walls, Edging

Angelica gigas

Anthemis × *hybrida* 'Kelwayi'

Aquilegia canadensis

Aquilegia chrysantha

Aquilegia vulgaris

Aquilegia 'Nora Barlow'

Arabis caucasica 'Snow Ball'

Arctanthemum arcticum 'Red Chimo'

Hybrid Strains   ZONES 2–9

By far these are the most widely grown Columbines, their large pastel flowers usually have long tails or spurs that create an effect like a flying bird. Plants are vigorous and, although fairly short-lived, these will no doubt seed themselves around a bit. They will readily cross with any other Columbine species resulting in surprising new colours and forms.

> "In their numerous colours they blend or contrast well with Bearded Irises, Catmint, Lupins and Oriental Poppies."
> – Graham Stuart Thomas,
> *Perennial Garden Plants*

SPREAD:	30cm (12")
LOCATION:	Average to moist soil.
BLOOMS:	May–June
USES:	✂ ➤ Borders, Woodland gardens

'Crimson Star' Bright crimson flowers with a white corolla, long spurs. HEIGHT: 60–90cm (24–36")

'Dragonfly Hybrids' Full colour range in a mixture of blue, yellow, white, pink and red. Compact plants. HEIGHT: 45–60cm (18–24")

'McKana's Giants' Large, showy flowers in a wide mixture of pastel shades. Long spurs, widely flaring trumpets. HEIGHT: 75cm (30")

vulgaris   ZONES 2–9

(Granny's Bonnet) An old cottage-garden form with small, frilly rounded flowers in a range of colours. Especially nice are the dark maroon, blue and violet shades that always seem to appear. These self-seed quite nicely.

SPREAD:	30cm (12")
LOCATION:	Average to moist soil.
BLOOMS:	May–June
USES:	✂ ➤ Borders, Woodland gardens

'Leprechaun Gold' Boldly variegated foliage sets this one apart! Leaves are streaked and blotched with chartreuse yellow and green, with rich deep-purple flowers. HEIGHT: 70cm (28")

'Nora Barlow' Wide-open, fully double quilled flowers in a unique combination of red, pink, and green. Totally unlike any other variety, looking more like a miniature dahlia! HEIGHT: 70cm (28")

'Plena' Mixture of double forms. Eventually singles will also appear among the seedlings that develop in your garden. HEIGHT: 50–60cm (20–24")

ARABIS
(Wall Cress, Rock Cress) ☼

Popular spring-flowering perennials, often seen cascading over rock gardens and walls. Plants form a dense carpet of leaves, smothered with flowers for several weeks. All are evergreen. Said to attract butterflies.

blepharophylla 'Spring Charm'   ZONES 5–9

('Frühlingszauber') Carmine-red flower spikes on a compact clump. Very bright and showy. A short-lived variety, will sometimes self-seed. Needs excellent drainage. Fairly drought-tolerant.

HEIGHT/SPREAD:	15cm (6")/15–20cm (6–8")
LOCATION:	Well-drained soil.
BLOOMS:	April–June
USES:	▲▼🦋 Walls, Slopes

caucasica   ZONES 3–9

The old-fashioned type, so widely planted in rockeries. Prune back immediately after blooming to keep plants compact and attractive. Several forms of this are widely available. Fairly drought-tolerant.

HEIGHT/SPREAD:	20cm (8")/30–60cm (12–24")
LOCATION:	Well-drained soil.
BLOOMS:	April–June
USES:	▲⋀▲▼🦋 Walls, Slopes, Edging

'Compinkie' Rosy-pink flowers, non-fading. Try it with blue Hyacinths.

'Plena' Fully double sterile white flowers, blooming much longer than other forms. Outstanding!

'Snow Ball' Very dwarf, compact strain. Flowers pure white.

'Variegata' Green leaves are strongly edged with creamy-white. Looks attractive throughout the year. White flowers. Rogue out any plain green shoots before they take over. Needs excellent drainage.

ferdinandi-coburgi   ZONES 3–9

Very low alpine variety, slowly forming a low mat of attractively variegated leaves with white flowers in spring. There is more than one colour form of this available. An excellent and easy alpine! Fairly drought-tolerant.

HEIGHT/SPREAD:	10cm (4")/15–20cm (6–8")
LOCATION:	Well-drained soil.
BLOOMS:	April–June
USES:	▲⋀▲▼🦋 Walls, Slopes

'Old Gold' A newer yellow and green variegated form, especially bright in spring.

'Variegata' Reliable white and green variegation, with hints of pink in the winter.

> "In my garden this is an easy care plant which lights up and contrasts well with semi-dwarf bearded Iris and Blue Oat Grass." – Bruce Zimmerman, Zone 6

× sturii   ZONES 3–9

(Hybrid Creeping Wall Cress) Makes a very tight low mat of glossy green leaves, studded with large white flowers. One of the best varieties available. Especially useful as a groundcover for a smaller areas. Fairly drought-tolerant.

HEIGHT/SPREAD:	10cm (4")/30cm (12")
LOCATION:	Well-drained soil.
BLOOMS:	April–June
USES:	▲⋀▲▼🦋 Walls, Slopes

ARCTANTHEMUM
(Arctic Daisy) ☼

arcticum 'Red Chimo'   ZONES 4–9

(Formerly included under *Chrysanthemum*) Recent Canadian selection. Plants form a cushion-shaped mound of fresh green leaves, absolutely smothered by large rose-pink daisies in late summer and early fall. Outstanding new border or rock garden perennial. Divide every two to three years to maintain vigour.

HEIGHT/SPREAD:	30–40cm (12–16")/60cm (24")
LOCATION:	Well-drained soil.
BLOOMS:	August–September
USES:	✂ Borders

ARENARIA
(Sandwort) ☼

montana   ZONES 2–9

(Mountain Sandwort) Very classy alpine, like a refined *Cerastium*. Large white flowers cover the compact green mat of leaves. Not at all invasive. Needs good drainage.

HEIGHT/SPREAD:	10cm (4")/30cm (12")
LOCATION:	Well-drained soil.
BLOOMS:	May–June
USES:	▲ Walls, Slopes

ARMERIA
(Thrift, Sea Pink) ☼

Their ball-shaped flower clusters make for a showy display, complemented by narrow grassy foliage. Shorter varieties have long been used to edge perennial beds, and in the rockery. Flowers eventually fade into papery everlastings.

'Formosa Hybrids'   ZONES 2–9
(Large Thrift) A taller border strain, large balls of flowers in shades of carmine, pink or white. Useful for cutting, fresh or dried.

HEIGHT/SPREAD: 30–60cm (12–24")/30cm (12")
LOCATION: Well-drained soil.
BLOOMS: June–August
USES: ✄ Dried Flower, Borders

juniperifolia   ZONES 2–9
(Spanish Thrift) A true alpine species. Forms a very dense tuft or bun of needle-like green leaves. Soft pink flowers are held just above the leaves. Best planted in a scree or trough garden where it can easily be seen and admired.

HEIGHT/SPREAD: 5–10cm (2–4")/15cm (6")
LOCATION: Well-drained soil, scree.
BLOOMS: May–June
USES: Walls, Troughs

maritima   ZONES 2–9
(Common Thrift) Easy and rewarding rock garden plants. Flowers are showy over a long period. Low grassy tufts of evergreen leaves. Tolerant of seaside conditions. Very drought-tolerant.

HEIGHT/SPREAD: 10–15cm (4–6")/30cm (12")
LOCATION: Well-drained soil.
BLOOMS: April–June
USES: Walls, Edging

'Alba' Pure white pompom flowers.

'Dusseldorf Pride' Rosy-red balls, remove faded flowers for continued blooming.

Artemesia stelleriana 'Silver Brocade'

ARTEMISIA
(Wormwood, Silver Sage) ☼ ◑

These are valued for their silvery-grey foliage, which can be most effective in the landscape. A surprisingly wide range of heights and textures are displayed among the various types, making them suitable for many different purposes. With a couple of exceptions they are all drought and heat tolerant, preferring a well-drained site. The flowers are insignificant unless otherwise noted.

> "Every garden needs all the artemisias they can get. *A. lactiflora* 'Guizho' is one of the best screening plants I know. Any of the other silver foliaged forms can knit together a border in a sophisticated way and they require zero maintenance. The perfect plant." – Marjorie Harris, Zone 5

abrotanum   ZONES 2–9
(Southernwood) Spicy-fragrant, bright green ferny foliage forming a bushy, upright clump. Plant this near a gate or entranceway so the fruity scent can be enjoyed each time someone brushes by. Will slowly spread to form a patch, but not invasive. Attractive foliage for the border, and excellent for cutting. Often benefits from a midsummer clip.

HEIGHT/SPREAD: 60–120cm (2–4')/60–90cm (2–3')
LOCATION: Well-drained soil.
USES: ✄ Borders, Herb gardens

×'Huntingdon'   ZONES 5–9
A near-shrubby hybrid. Similar foliage to 'Powis Castle' but easily twice the size, forming a loose upright bush of silvery-grey. Grows fabulously well at the West coast and likely over a much wider area. Plants should be cut back to 15cm (6") in early spring to encourage fresh growth. Very drought-tolerant.

HEIGHT/SPREAD: 90–120cm (3–4')/90–120cm (3–4')
LOCATION: Well-drained soil.
USES: ✄ Specimen, Borders

lactiflora   ZONES 3–9
(White Mugwort) Outstanding for its showy plumes of creamy-white flowers that appear in late summer. Highly recommended as a cut flower! An excellent background plant for a late season display. Definitely prefers a moist site.

HEIGHT/SPREAD: 1.2–1.5m (4–6')/60–90cm (24–36")
BLOOMS: August–October
USES: ✄ Dried flower, Borders, Specimen

'Guizho' A unique new selection, with red-brown stems and ferny black-green leaves, pleasantly musk-scented. The showy sprays of creamy-white flowers are a lovely contrast. Introduced by Bressingham Gardens. This cultivar may possibly be a hybrid or different species.

> "A show stopper in the garden that people are always surprised is an Artemisia. A first-rate clump former with dissected purple foliage, topped with mounds of contrasting creamy-white flowers that last well into fall. Even more stunning when placed with blue or variegated foliage plants." – Larry Davidson, Zone 5

ludoviciana   ZONES 4–9
(Silver Sage) A species native to the plains of North America. The foliage is exceptionally effective, the leaves entire rather than ferny, and strongly silver-grey in colour. Plants are bushy and upright, spreading at the roots to form a patch or large clump, and doing so rather quickly in light sandy soils. Good drought and heat tolerance, generally remaining attractive throughout the season. The species itself is seldom available but there are several excellent selections, all useful for cutting fresh or drying. Extremely drought-tolerant.

SPREAD: 60–75cm (24–30")
LOCATION: Well-drained soil.
BLOOMS: August–September
USES: Massing, Borders

Armeria juniperifolia

Artemisia ×'Huntingdon'

Artemisia ludoviciana 'Silver Frost'

Artemisia ×'Powis Castle'

Artemisia ludoviciana 'Valerie Finnis'

Arum italicum

Aruncus dioicus

Asarum europaeum

'Silver Frost' Completely unlike the other types listed here, this form has extremely narrow leaves and a light, feathery appearance. Excellent for cutting! HEIGHT: 45–60cm (18–24")

'Silver King' Intensely grey leaves and stems, followed by a mist of fine-textured silver-white flowers that give a cloud-like effect. A vigorous selection hardy to Zone 2. HEIGHT: 75–90cm (30–36")

'Valerie Finnis' Like a compact version of 'Silver King', with very wide silvery leaves, and a less invasive habit. Some say this is the best grey foliage plant available. HEIGHT: 45–60cm (18–24")

pontica   ZONES 4–9
(Roman Wormwood) A ground-covering species, with grey-green filigree leaves. Very feathery in appearance. Good choice for containers. Can be fairly invasive, particularly in lighter soils. Site carefully. Very drought-tolerant.

HEIGHT/SPREAD:	30cm (12")/30–60cm (12–24")
LOCATION:	Well-drained soil.
USES:	☼ ❦ ❦ Borders, Massing

× 'Powis Castle'   ZONES 6–9
Makes a bushy, upright clump of feathery, silver-grey leaves. An excellent non-invasive variety for the border, sometimes clipped to form a low hedge. Plants should be cut back to 15cm (6") in early spring to encourage fresh growth. Non-blooming. This selection is proving to be hardier than we first expected. Very drought-tolerant.

> "The arrival of *Artemisia* 'Powis Castle' on the scene a few decades ago was a great event." – Christopher Lloyd,
> *Christopher Lloyd's Flower Garden*

HEIGHT/SPREAD:	60–70cm (24–30")/60–70cm (24–30")
LOCATION:	Well-drained soil.
USES:	❦ ❦ Massing, Borders

schmidtiana 'Silver Mound'   ZONES 1–9
Perhaps the most popular grey-leaved perennial of all time. The feathery silver-grey leaves form a beautiful compact dome. Valuable as a rock garden plant, accent, or edging. Plants should be ruthlessly clipped back hard (to 2 inches!) when they begin to flower (mid to late June), otherwise they will melt out, get floppy and generally look like the dog slept on them. Fresh new growth will appear in about two weeks. Very drought-tolerant.

HEIGHT/SPREAD:	30cm (12")/30–45cm (12–18")
LOCATION:	Well-drained soil.
USES:	❦ ❦ Edging, Borders, Massing

stelleriana 'Silver Brocade'   ZONES 2–9
A low, compact selection, fairly similar in appearance to Dusty Miller, with scalloped silvery-white foliage. Excellent for edging, groundcover, pots and hanging baskets. Evergreen in milder regions. Trim plants back in early spring and again in midsummer to encourage fresh growth. Introduced by the University of British Columbia Botanical Garden.

> "With its fabulous gray-white foliage use it for transitions and contrasts with red, pink, purple, blue or plain boring white. Just a great border edger." – Bruce Zimmerman, Zone 6

HEIGHT/SPREAD:	15–30cm (6–12")/60–75cm (24–30")
USES:	❦ ❦ Massing, Edging

ARUM
(Arum) ☼ ●

italicum   ZONES 5–9
(Italian Arum) A unique and wonderful plant for the woodland garden. Large exotic arrow-head shaped leaves make an appearance in the fall, remaining throughout the winter only to disappear by late spring. Creamy-white flowers push out of the ground in May, followed by clusters of bright orange berries in the summer. A plant for all seasons! Appreciates some shelter from winter winds.

HEIGHT/SPREAD:	30cm (12")/30cm (12")
LOCATION:	Rich moist woodland soil.
BLOOMS:	April–May
USES:	❦ ❦ Woodland borders

ARUNCUS
(Goat's Beard) ☼
Moisture-loving plants, well suited to waterside or woodland plantings. All have creamy-white plumes of flowers in summer, and attractive lacy foliage, somewhat resembling Astilbes.

aethusifolius   ZONES 2–9
(Dwarf Korean Goat's Beard) The miniature of the genus. A delicate mound of crispy green leaves, with short forked spikelets of creamy white flowers. Good rock garden plant.

> "Plant Dwarf Korean Goat's Beard alongside a path in afternoon shade, and you won't be able to resist bending down to stroke its dense mounds of foliage every time you walk by! This well-behaved perennial is an ideal candidate for 'control-freaks' who insist on neat and tidy gardens at all times." – Kevin Ward, Zone 5

HEIGHT/SPREAD:	20–30cm (8–12")/30cm (12")
LOCATION:	Rich, moist soil.
BLOOMS:	June–July
USES:	❦ ❦ Woodland borders

dioicus   ZONES 2–9
(Giant Goat's Beard) A rather monstrous border plant, spectacular in flower with its enormous creamy plumes the size of your head. Elegant lacy leaves form a very dense and bushy clump. This plant demands space. Inclined to sulk in hot summer areas unless planted at the waterside or in peaty, moist soil. Cut plants back in summer if they look untidy.

> "...flowers with the main flush of shrub roses and is a lovely companion for them." – Graham Stuart Thomas,
> *Perennial Garden Plants*

HEIGHT/SPREAD:	1.2–1.8m (4–6')/90cm (3')
LOCATION:	Rich, moist soil.
BLOOMS:	June–July
USES:	Dried Flower, Waterside, Borders

'Kneiffii' Leaves are finely cut, resembling a green Japanese Maple, setting off the creamy-white flowers. A more reasonable size for the smaller garden. Beautiful beside a tiny pool. Increased by division only. HEIGHT: 90cm (3')

ASARUM
(Wild Ginger) ☼ ●

europaeum   ZONES 2–9
(European Wild Ginger) A choice woodlander, much sought after by plant connoisseurs, but usually in limited worldwide supply. The rounded

leaves are dark green and brightly polished. This is a texture plant, contrasting beautifully against lacy ferns. Will slowly form a first-class groundcover for a small area and will even self-seed if you are very lucky! Evergreen in Zones 8–9.

"Shines in the shade in every way."
– Bruce Zimmerman, Zone 6

HEIGHT/SPREAD:	15cm (6")/30cm (12")
LOCATION:	Moist rich woodland soil.
USES:	▲△⋀⋅▲ Woodland border, Edging

Asclepias tuberosa

ASCLEPIAS
(Milkweed) ☼

Not all the members of this genus are weedy, and a few are excellent summer-blooming perennials for the sunny border. Flowers are extremely attractive to butterflies. The species in cultivation are mostly native North American wildflowers.

tuberosa   ZONES 4–9
(Butterfly Weed) Native to eastern North America where the clusters of bright orange flowers appear in early summer. Modern seed strains often include red and yellow forms as well. The Monarch butterfly depends entirely on this plant for its food source. Plants prefer a well-drained, sandy or gravelly site. Flowers are good for cutting, the immature seed pods are also cut and dried for floral arranging. Removing faded flowers will encourage continual blooming. Butterfly milkweed comes up very late in the spring. Very drought-tolerant.

"Vibrant! Audacious! Hot! Asclepias tuberosa will spice up your summer perennial show and the transitional fall colors of the seed pods are a definite bonus!" – Suzette McDonnell, Zone 6

HEIGHT/SPREAD:	60–90cm (2–3')/60cm (2')
LOCATION:	Well-drained sandy soil.
BLOOMS:	July–August
USES:	✄⋖⋇ Borders, Meadows

ASTER
(Aster, Michaelmas Daisy) ☼

Reliable, showy plants for a late summer and fall display, with a wide range of flower colours and plant heights to choose from. The different varieties all have similar daisy-style flowers, and plenty of them! The modern varieties are mostly descended from common roadside species, selected over the years for improved form, colour and disease resistance.

Aster 'White Opal'

In general, taller cultivars should be staked by midsummer to prevent flopping. Pinching or pruning plants back by half (before July 1st) will encourage dense, compact growth and more flowers. Plants will grow best in a rich moist soil — too dry a location will invariably lead to problems with unsightly powdery mildew on the leaves. Early frosts may damage the flowers in Zones 2–4, but in years with a mild fall the display is so wonderful that it's usually worth chancing. All cultivars are excellent for cutting.

alpinus   ZONES 2–9
(Alpine Aster) An unusual exception in this group, these low-growing plants put on a bright display of single golden-eyed daisies in late spring. Ideal for the border front or rock garden. They are not long-lived but often will self-seed if conditions are to their liking.

HEIGHT/SPREAD:	20–25cm (8–10")/20–30cm (8–12")
LOCATION:	Well-drained soil.
BLOOMS:	May–June
USES:	▲△⋇⋖ Walls, Edging

'Dark Beauty' Dark violet-blue.

'Happy End' Rose-pink flowers, compact.

amellus 'Violet Queen'   ZONES 4–9
From Europe comes this summer and fall bloomer, with sprays of large violet-purple daisies, with a yellow eye.

HEIGHT/SPREAD:	45–60cm (18–24")/45cm (18")
LOCATION:	Average to moist well-drained soil.
BLOOMS:	July–October
USES:	⋇⋖⋘ Borders

divaricatus   ZONES 4–9
(White Wood Aster) A wild North American species, widely grown in Europe. Medium-size starry white flowers are held on branching purple-black stems. Plants are shade-tolerant, attractive grouped among shrubs where they can spread. May require pinching. Tolerant of dry soil.

HEIGHT/SPREAD:	45–90cm (18–36")/45cm (18")
LOCATION:	Average to dry well-drained soil.
BLOOMS:	August–October
USES:	⋇⋖⋘ Borders, Woodland gardens

Dumosus Hybrids   ZONES 3–9
A group of compact hybrid selections, ideal for the front of a sunny border. When well grown the plants form a dome or cushion of colour in the fall. As these are heavy feeders, fertilize in spring and midsummer and keep plants well watered. Divide every year or two, and watch for signs of powdery mildew.

SPREAD:	30cm (12")
LOCATION:	Rich, moist soil.
BLOOMS:	August–October
USES:	⋇⋖⋘ Borders, Edging

'Alert' Deep crimson red. HEIGHT: 30cm (12")

Aster alpinus 'Happy End'

Aster amellus 'Violet Queen'

Aster 'Alma Potschke'

Aster 'Professor Kippenburg'

Aster n.a. 'Purple Dome'

Aster pringlei 'Monte Cassino'

Aster n.b. 'Royal Ruby'

Aster × frikartii 'Flora's Delight'

'Audrey' Mauve-blue. Excellent. HEIGHT: 30cm (12")

'Lady-in-Blue' Semi-double, blue. HEIGHT: 25cm (10")

'Little Pink Beauty' Semi-double, bright pink. HEIGHT: 40cm (16")

'Professor Kippenburg' Clear bright blue, semi-double. HEIGHT: 40cm (16")

'White Opal' White flowers. HEIGHT: 30–40cm (12–16")

ericoides 'Pink Cloud'   ZONES 3–9
(Heath Aster) Bushy mounded habit, with tiny leaves and clouds of starry pastel-pink flowers. Nice filler flower for the garden or for cutting. Quite mildew resistant, tolerant of drier sites.

HEIGHT/SPREAD:	75–90cm (30–36")/60cm (24")
LOCATION:	Average to moist well-drained soil.
BLOOMS:	August–October
USES:	✄ ꕷ Borders, Meadow gardens

× frikartii   ZONES 5–9
A hybrid group of Asters with a habit of blooming non-stop from summer through fall. Mildew resistant. Planting before midsummer is recommended. Inclined to be a little temperamental, but good drainage in winter is the key!

SPREAD:	60–90cm (24–36")
LOCATION:	Average well-drained soil.
BLOOMS:	July–October
USES:	✄ ꕷ Borders, Meadow gardens

'Flora's Delight' Lovely lilac-mauve single flowers with a yellow eye. Introduced by Blooms of Bressingham. Excellent. HEIGHT: 45cm (18")

'Mönch' Lavender-blue flowers, a strong bloomer over a very long season. An excellent taller variety. HEIGHT: 75cm (30")

> "Plant this softly colored aster near to silver-gray *Artemisia* 'Powis Castle', mix it with pastel pink and pale powder-blue flowers and edge the bed with gray felted leaves of *Stachys olympica* 'Silver Carpet'."
> – Penelope Hobhouse,
> *Colour in Your Garden*

laevis 'Bluebird'   ZONES 4–9
A new introduction from Mt. Cuba in Delaware. Features strong upright red stems loaded with single violet-blue daisies in late summer. Reported to be mildew-free and tolerant of most soils. Also does not need staking if grown in full sun.

HEIGHT/SPREAD:	90–120cm (3–4')/70cm (30")
LOCATION:	Average to moist well-drained soil.
BLOOMS:	August–October
USES:	✄ ꕷ Borders, Meadow gardens

lateriflorus 'Prince'   ZONES 4–9
Unusual dusky plum-purple foliage contrasts beautifully with the flowers, which are tiny white stars with a raspberry-red eye. Erect, mounding habit.

> "Dark stems densely covered with tiny purple leaves form a large tight bun which erupts in the fall with a myriad of small flowers with hot pink centers and minute petals of the palest pink. Electric!"
> – Larry Davidson, Zone 5

HEIGHT/SPREAD:	75–90cm (30–36")/70cm (30")
LOCATION:	Average to moist well-drained soil.
BLOOMS:	August–October
USES:	✄ ꕷ Borders, Meadow gardens

novae-angliae   ZONES 2–9
(New England Aster) Some of the best cutting types are in this group. The taller growing cultivars form large clumps of upright branching stems that will require staking, and are best used behind other plants as the lower leaves may wither early. Tolerant of wet soils. Watch for mildew.

SPREAD:	45cm (18")
LOCATION:	Rich, moist soil.
BLOOMS:	August–October
USES:	✄ ꕷ Wildflower, Borders, Meadow gardens

'Alma Potschke' Warm, glowing salmon-pink. One of the best asters. HEIGHT: 100cm (40")

'Pink Winner' Medium pink, tall habit. HEIGHT: 90cm (36")

'Purple Dome' Compact habit. Masses of deep purple flowers. A recent introduction from the Mt. Cuba Centre in Delaware. HEIGHT: 45cm (18")

'September Ruby' Deep ruby red. HEIGHT: 120cm (4')

novi-belgii   ZONES 3–9
(New York Aster) This species in one of the parents of the dwarf Dumosus hybrids. Selections of the true New York Aster are medium to tall in habit, preferring moist, rich soils and a sunny exposure. Powdery mildew can be problematic. Divide every year or two.

SPREAD:	30–45cm (12–18")
LOCATION:	Rich, moist soil.
BLOOMS:	August–October
USES:	✄ ꕷ Wildflower, Borders, Meadow gardens

'Coombe Rosemary' Outstanding double violet-purple flowers. HEIGHT: 90cm (36")

'Diana' Good medium-size variety. Clear rose-pink flowers. HEIGHT: 45–60cm (18–24")

'Royal Ruby' Deep red, semi-double. A selection by Alan Bloom of Bressingham Gardens. HEIGHT: 50cm (20")

'Winston Churchill' Bright red, single. Early bloomer. HEIGHT: 45cm (18")

oblongifolius 'Raydon's Favorite' ZONES 4–9
Superb new introduction, a very late bloomer that is literally smothered in violet-blue single flowers. Upright, bushy habit and no signs of mildew!

HEIGHT/SPREAD:	70–90cm (30–36")/70cm (30")
LOCATION:	Average to moist well-drained soil.
BLOOMS:	September–October
USES:	✄ ꕷ Borders, Meadow gardens

pringlei 'Monte Cassino'   ZONES 4–9
Widely grown in Europe and imported year-round for use by commercial florists. Only recently introduced to gardens however, but proving to be one of the best border forms in existence. The sturdy, upright clumps of tiny green leaves have a delicate texture all season long, developing nice bronzy tones in late fall. Masses of small starry white flowers go on blooming for several weeks, well into late fall. Seems tolerant of average to moist conditions.

HEIGHT/SPREAD:	75–120cm (30–48")/45cm (18")
LOCATION:	Rich, moist soil.
BLOOMS:	September–October
USES:	✄ ꕷ Borders, Meadow gardens

sedifolius 'Nanus'   ZONES 2–9
(Rhone Aster) Clouds of starry blue, yellow-centred flowers. Has a delicate billowing appearance in the border. Always a reliable bloomer on the prairies. Mildew resistant.

HEIGHT/SPREAD:	45–60cm (18–24")/30cm (12")
LOCATION:	Average to moist soil.
BLOOMS:	August–October
USES:	✄ ꕷ Borders, Meadow gardens

vimineus 'Lovely'   ZONES 4–9
Brand new selection that forms a tall, upright bush. Masses of small starry lilac-pink flowers in early fall. Mildew-free. Excellent for cutting. Really shows promise in the border!

HEIGHT/SPREAD:	90–120cm (3–4′)/70cm (30″)
LOCATION:	Average to moist soil.
BLOOMS:	September–October
USES:	✄ ❦ Borders, Meadow gardens

ASTILBE
(Astilbe, False Spirea) ☼ ●

Considered the Queen of Flowers for shady areas, their fluffy plumes are a familiar sight in the summer garden. With the many new varieties available there is a much wider selection of flower and leaf colour, plant form, and blooming time than ever before. The Astilbe season can easily be extended by choosing varieties that bloom at different times.

All cultivars share the same need for a rich moist soil free of tree root competition, and a partly shaded location. Astilbes will also tolerate full sun in cool summer regions. The taller types in particular are heavy feeders; they should be lifted and divided every two to three years, also fertilized in early spring and again after blooming. Remove faded flowers spikes and any tired-looking leaves throughout the season.

> "Why does no one expound upon the winter interest of Astilbe? Surely, if the wizened seed-pods of *Iris sibirica* merit glowing praise, the 'freeze-dried' plumes of Astilbe should be held in reverence!"
> – Kevin Ward, Zone 5

× arendsii Hybrids   ZONES 3–9
(Garden Astilbe) Large showy flower spikes appear over upright mounds of elegant, lacy foliage. Complex breeding has resulted in many modern varieties, offering flowers in the complete range from clear white to cream, rose, peach, pink, red and magenta.

SPREAD:	60–75cm (24–30″)
LOCATION:	Moist, rich, well-prepared soil.
BLOOMS:	June–August
USES:	✄ Borders, Woodland gardens

'Amethyst' Violet-rose, erect habit. Green foliage. Mid-season. HEIGHT: 90cm (36″)

'Bressingham Beauty' Rich pink, long lasting. Green foliage. Raised by Alan Bloom of Bressingham Gardens. Mid-season. HEIGHT: 100cm (40″)

'Diamant' ('Diamond') Tall selection with pure white plumes that are long and somewhat diamond shaped. Mid-season. HEIGHT: 90cm (36″)

'Elizabeth Bloom' A new compact selection from Bressingham Gardens. Large plumes of rich pink flowers over vigorous green foliage. Mid-season. HEIGHT: 60cm (24″)

'Fanal' Bronzy-red foliage in spring, later becoming green. Narrow spikes of deep red. Extremely popular selection. Early. HEIGHT: 55cm (22″)

'Glut' ('Glow') Dark scarlet-red spikes with a rosy cast. Airy plumes. Foliage is bronze in spring. Mid-season. HEIGHT: 70cm (30″)

'Granat' Deep ruby flowers, fading to pink. Large panicles. Mid-season. HEIGHT: 90cm (36″)

'Snowdrift' Selected by Alan Bloom for the especially clear snow-white flowers. Green foliage. Good compact habit. Early. HEIGHT: 60cm (24″)

chinensis   ZONES 3–9
(Chinese Astilbe) These have very dense, lacy foliage. Plants will spread somewhat to form a patch, the shorter varieties are excellent for massing as a groundcover. Because they bloom after most of the Garden Astilbes, the *chinensis* selections are useful for extending the season into late summer.

SPREAD:	30cm (12″)
LOCATION:	Average to moist well-drained soil.
BLOOMS:	August–September
USES:	⛰❦✄❦

'Finale' Bright pink flowers, held just above the leaves. Late. HEIGHT: 40cm (16″)

'Intermezzo' Salmon pink flowers, more upright habit. Late. HEIGHT: 50–60cm (20–24″)

'Pumila' Makes a low, vigorous spreading patch, the best type for general groundcover purposes. Rose-purple flowers in short spikes. Will tolerate a fair bit of sun or dry shade. Undemanding. Very late. HEIGHT: 25cm (10″)

'Purple Lance' ('Purpurlanze') A tall form with large spears of bright purple-red flowers. Late. HEIGHT: 90cm (36″)

'Superba' (Formerly listed as *A. taquetii* 'Superba') Lavender-magenta flowers, held in a long, narrow spike. Late. HEIGHT: 100cm (40″)

× crispa   ZONES 4–9
A newer group of hybrids, all with unusual dark green, crispy foliage. Compact in habit, these are excellent for the border front, edging, and in the shady rock garden.

SPREAD:	30cm (12″)
LOCATION:	Moist to average well-drained soil.
BLOOMS:	July–August
USES:	⛰ Woodland garden, Edging

'Perkeo' Short spikes of light pink flowers. HEIGHT: 15–20cm (6–8″)

glaberrima saxatilis   ZONES 4–9
A true gem, this is a tiny dwarf variety for rock gardens or edging. Dark green glossy foliage with short stems of shell-pink flowers, blooming late in the Astilbe season.

HEIGHT/SPREAD:	10–20cm (4–8″)/20cm (8″)
LOCATION:	Moist to average well-drained soil.
BLOOMS:	July–August
USES:	⛰ Woodland garden, Edging

> "For anyone who has a deserved fondness for the simplicifolia hybrid Astilbes, then this is one not to miss. The diminutive, glossy green foliage catches the eye as it unfurls in the spring and more than holds its own throughout the season, but one is particularly rewarded when the short spikes of candyfloss-pink blooms open in high summer." – Cathy Forgie, Zone 4

japonica Hybrids   ZONES 3–9
Quite similar to the × *arendsii* Hybrids, this group for the most part have large pyramidal-shaped plumes and vibrant coloration, blooming towards the middle of summer. Good vigour and a full habit of growth make them an excellent choice.

SPREAD:	60–75cm (24–30″)
LOCATION:	Moist, rich, well-prepared soil.
BLOOMS:	June–July
USES:	✄ Borders, Woodland gardens

'Peach Blossom' Delicate peach-pink, glossy green foliage. Early. HEIGHT: 50cm (20″)

simplicifolia Hybrids   ZONES 3–9
Another distinct group of hybrid *Astilbe*, mostly developed in recent years by British and German breeders. Most of these have a compact habit, the foliage generally not as lacy as other types, but richer in colour. Well suited to massed plantings, providing colour in late summer when it is so often lacking in shade gardens.

Astilbe chinensis 'Finale'

Astilbe chinensis 'Purple Lance'

Astilbe simplicifolia 'Hennie Graafland'

Astilbe × arendsii 'Elizabeth Bloom'

Astrantia major – White Form

Astrantia major – Pink Form

Astrantia major 'Rubra'

Astrantia maxima

LOCATION:	Moist, rich well-drained soil.
BLOOMS:	July–August
USES:	⌂⋀⋙⚹◀♥ Edging, Woodland gardens

'**Aphrodite**' Beautiful bright rose-red panicles. Somewhat coarse foliage. Late. HEIGHT: 30cm (12")

'**Hennie Graafland**' Like a taller, more vigorous version of 'Sprite', delicate arching sprays of light pink flowers. HEIGHT: 45cm (18")

'**Sprite**' An excellent selection bred by Alan Bloom of Bressingham Gardens. Spikes of delicate shell-pink flowers held above the dark bronzy-green leaves. Clumps are dense and compact. Outstanding shade garden plant! A former *Perennial Plant of the Year*. HEIGHT: 25cm (10")

'**William Buchanan**' Dwarf hybrid with crimson-tinged leaves. Creamy-white flowers. Late. HEIGHT: 20–30cm (8–12")

thunbergii Hybrids   ZONES 3–9
Differs from the × arendsii Hybrids in blooming later and typically the large panicles of bloom have an arching, weeping appearance. These are tall.

SPREAD:	60–75cm (24–30")
LOCATION:	Moist, rich, well-prepared soil.
BLOOMS:	July–August
USES:	⚹◀ Borders, Woodland gardens

'**Professor van der Weilen**' Huge drooping plumes of white flowers. Large mounding habit. HEIGHT: 120cm (48")

ASTILBOIDES
(Rodgersia) ☼ ◑

tabularis   ZONES 3–9
(Shieldleaf Rodgersia) (formerly listed as *Rodgersia tabularis*) A bold-leaved perennial for the woodland or bog garden. Produces very large round umbrella-like leaves. Big plumes of creamy flowers resemble Astilbe, appearing in early summer.

HEIGHT/SPREAD:	90–120cm (3–4')/60–90cm (2–3')
LOCATION:	Rich, moist soil.
BLOOMS:	June–July
USES:	⚹◀ Dried Flower, Borders, Waterside

ASTRANTIA
(Masterwort) ☼ ◑
Adored by floral designers for their unique umbels of starry flowers, a bit like a refined Queen-Anne's-Lace in effect, but not at all weedy in habit. Especially nice as a filler in moist, shady borders. Dead-heading is recommended to avoid self-seeding.

carniolica 'Rubra'   ZONES 4–9
(Dwarf Red Masterwort) A compact species for the front of the border. This selection has rich maroon-red flowers, surrounded by green bracts. Lacy green foliage.

HEIGHT/SPREAD:	30–45cm (12–18")/45cm (18")
LOCATION:	Prefers a moist, rich soil.
BLOOMS:	June–August
USES:	⚹◀ Borders, Woodland

major   ZONES 4–9
(Great Masterwort) A variable species, with good-sized umbels of greenish-white flowers with a distinctive, showy collar or bract that ranges in colour from white through green to rose-red. Loose clumps of dark-green compound leaves. Likes to self-seed. Blooms over a long season.

HEIGHT/SPREAD:	75cm (30")/45cm (18")
LOCATION:	Prefers a moist, rich soil.
BLOOMS:	June–August
USES:	⚹◀ Borders, Woodland

'**Lars**' Good dark red selection with an especially long blooming-season.

'**Rubra**' Flower bracts are various shades of red through pink. Showy!

maxima   ZONES 4–9
(Large Masterwort) Large rose-pink or white flowers, surrounded by sharp pinkish-green bracts. Individual flowers look a bit like a *Scabiosa*. Considered by some to be the most beautiful species. Plants spread quickly underground, forming a patch.

HEIGHT/SPREAD:	45–60cm (18–24")/45cm (18")
LOCATION:	Prefers a moist, rich soil.
BLOOMS:	June–August
USES:	⚹◀ Borders, Woodland

Aubrieta 'Whitewell Gem'

AUBRIETA
(Rock Cress) ☼ ◑

Hybrids   ZONES 4–8
Popular rock garden plant, smothered with brightly coloured flowers in spring. The grey-green carpet of leaves will cascade over sunny banks or walls. Seed-grown colour forms will show some variation; buy plants in flower if you require a specific shade. Shear plants back lightly after flowering to keep them compact.

HEIGHT/SPREAD:	10–15cm (4–6")/30–60cm (12–24")
LOCATION:	Well-drained soil among cool rocks.
BLOOMS:	April–June
USES:	⌂⋀⋙▲ Walls, Slopes

'**Argenteo-variegata**' Leaves are strongly variegated with creamy-yellow and green. Purple flowers. Be sure to remove any all-green sections.

'**Blue Carpet**' Various shades of blue.

'**Dr. Mules**' Especially good deep violet-purple form. May rebloom in fall.

'**Red Carpet**' Red to rose flowers.

'**Whitewell Gem**' Velvety purple to violet.

AURINIA
(Basket-of-Gold, Perennial Alyssum) ☼

saxatilis   ZONES 3–9
(formerly *Alyssum saxatile*) A springtime favorite, forming fairly large mounds of good silver-grey foliage with contrasting yellow flowers. Especially nice on slopes or walls. Fairly drought-tolerant.

HEIGHT/SPREAD:	20–30cm (8–12")/30–60cm (12–24")
LOCATION:	Lean, well-drained soil.
BLOOMS:	April–June
USES:	⌂⋀⋙▲⚹ Edging, Walls

'**Citrina**' Like 'Compacta' but in a pale sulphur-yellow shade, an easier colour to design with.

'**Compacta**' (Basket-of-Gold) Profuse, bright yellow flowers. The most popular variety.

'**Dudley Nevill Variegated**' Primrose-yellow flowers, beautiful green and cream variegated leaves. Remove any all-green shoots. This variety seems to require perfect drainage. Grown from cuttings.

'**Sunny Border Apricot**' Pale apricot-yellow flowers.

BAPTISIA
(False Indigo, Wild Indigo) ☼

Cousins to the Lupines, with similar spikes of pea-like flowers in late spring. These are sturdy wildflowers native to the prairies of North America. Easy to grow in average sunny border conditions, the plants are long-lived but resent being disturbed once established. Consider these as a substitute if you have not succeeded in growing Lupines.

australis   ZONES 2–9
(Blue Wild Indigo) Short spikes of deep blue flowers, followed by attractive curly black seed pods that are sometimes used for dried arrangements. Dark green foliage forms a dense bushy mound. Moderately drought-tolerant.

> "Attention 'back-to-the-earth' parents! Not only does *Baptisia australis* fix nitrogen in the soil, its dried seed pods make very satisfactory rattles to amuse the leaders of tomorrow!" – Kevin Ward, Zone 5

HEIGHT/SPREAD: 90–120cm (3–4')/90cm (3')
LOCATION: Average well-drained soil.
BLOOMS: May–June
USES: ✂ ⚘ Wildflower, Borders, Meadows

BELLIS
(English Daisy) ☼ ◐

perennis   ZONES 3–9
Widely used for bedding with spring-blooming bulbs, English Daisies are an old-fashioned favorite, usually treated as a biennial or short-lived perennial. They will sometimes self-seed. These perform best in coastal climates.

SPREAD: 15cm (6")
LOCATION: Well-drained soil. Dislikes hot weather.
BLOOMS: April–June
USES: ✂ Massing, Edging

'Monstrosa' Flowers are double and extra large, in shades of white, pink or red, with distinctive quilled petals. HEIGHT: 20cm (8")

'Pomponette' Smaller button-type flowers in profusion. Compact habit. Shades pink, red and white. HEIGHT: 10cm (4")

BERGENIA
(Bergenia, Pig-squeak) ☼ ◐

cordifolia   ZONES 2–9
(Heartleaf Bergenia) Reliably evergreen in most climates, the large glossy leaves take on rich bronzy-red tones throughout the fall and winter months. Clusters of nodding pink flowers rise above in early spring, and both these and the leaves are valuable for cutting. At their best when mass planted. Tolerant of a wide range of soils and conditions, including dry shade. Many selections and hybrids of this species have been made.

> "The plant can look very presentable...sandwiched between the edge of a border and something taller than itself behind, under whose skirts the bergenia can investigate." – Christopher Lloyd, *Foliage Plants*

HEIGHT/SPREAD: 30–45cm (12–18")/60cm (24")
LOCATION: Average to moist soil.
BLOOMS: April–June
USES: △△◑▲✂ Massing, Edging, Borders

'Baby Doll' Baby-pink flowers, very freely flowering. HEIGHT: 30cm (12")

'Bressingham Ruby' Winter colour is deep burnished maroon. Rose-red flowers. Green foliage in summer. A Blooms of Bressingham selection. HEIGHT: 35cm (14")

'Bressingham White' Robust growth, snowy white flowers fading to pink. Early-blooming. HEIGHT: 30cm (12")

'Perfect' Lilac-red flowers, large bronze tinged leaves. HEIGHT: 30cm (12")

BLETILLA
(Hardy Orchid) ◐

striata   ZONES 5–9
(Chinese Ground Orchid) Arching sprays of magenta-pink flowers rise over slender, pleated leaves. This easy-to-grow deciduous orchid is a treasure for the shady rock garden. Also reported to tolerate sunny locations with regular moisture. May be overwintered indoors in colder regions.

HEIGHT/SPREAD: 30cm (12")/20–30cm (8–12")
LOCATION: Prefers a cool, woodland soil.
BLOOMS: May–June
USES: △◑✂⚘ Woodland gardens

Boltonia asteroides 'Snowbank'

BOLTONIA
(Boltonia) ☼ ◐

asteroides   ZONES 4–9
(Bolton's Aster) Similar in effect to a tall fall-blooming *Aster* or Michaelmas Daisy. Billowing clouds of small daisies appear in late summer and fall. Foliage remains disease free. Nice background plant for borders, growing especially big and tall in moist, rich soils. Good for cutting. North American wildflower. The selections below are more commonly grown over the species.

HEIGHT/SPREAD: 90–120cm (3–4')/90cm (3')
LOCATION: Average well-drained soil.
BLOOMS: August–October
USES: ✂ Borders, Meadows

'Pink Beauty' Pale pink flowers, somewhat loose habit. Found by Edith Edelman in North Carolina.

> "Performing on a garden scale as a few springs of Baby's Breath do in a bouquet, this is one of those rare tall plants that I value for its very ability to flop and require no staking." – Cathy Forgie, Zone 4

'Snowbank' Masses of white daisies, good bushy habit.

Aurinia saxatilis 'Citrina'

A. saxatilis 'Dudley Nevill Variegated'

Baptisia australis

Bergenia 'Bressingham Ruby'

Brunnera macrophylla

Brunnera macrophylla 'Variegata'

Calamintha nepeta nepeta

Campanula carpatica 'White Clips'

BRUNNERA
(Siberian Bugloss) ☼ ◐ ●

macrophylla   ZONES 2–9
Low clumps of heart-shaped leaves produce upright stems of blue Forget-me-not flowers for many weeks. Lovely woodland plant for moist, shady sites. A true perennial.

> "A drift of dark blue at the back of a shrubbery or under the canopy of a silver-leaf weeping pear is unforgettable."
> – Penelope Hobhouse,
> *Colour in Your Garden*

HEIGHT/SPREAD: 30–45cm (12–18")/45cm (18")
LOCATION: Prefers a rich moist soil.
BLOOMS: April–June
USES: ⋔⅏⤝ Massing, Woodland gardens

'Langtrees' Green leaves with unusual aluminum spots arranged in a V-shaped pattern.

'Variegata' Absolutely stunning foliage, boldly blotched and edged in creamy-white. This needs full shade or the leaves will scorch. A *must* for the collector!

BUDDLEIA
(Butterfly Bush) ☼

Truly these are shrubs, attaining a large size in mild winter areas. In colder regions the woody stems often die back severely, regrowing again from the base and flowering on new wood in late summer. Many gardeners just treat Buddleia like a perennial, cutting them back to 15cm (6") every spring. By pruning them this way the flowers are on shorter stems where they can be easily seen at eye level, and associate nicely with other perennials in the fall border. The long wands of flowers are fragrant and attract butterflies and hummingbirds like crazy!

davidii   ZONES 5–9
This species has given rise to numerous modern selections, some of them naturally compact and well suited to border use. There is an excellent range of colours to choose from. Great for cutting. Moderately drought-tolerant.

HEIGHT/SPREAD: .9–2.4m (3–8')/.9–1.2m (3–4')
LOCATION: Average well-drained soil.
BLOOMS: July–October
USES: ⅊⋓➤ⵗ Borders

'Black Knight' The deepest midnight blue flowers. Tall.

'Dartmoor' Unusual for its branching flower spikes, in a lovely soft lilac-purple shade.

'Harlequin' Gorgeous variegated creamy-yellow and green leaves, magenta-red flowers. Fairly compact. Seems to be a little less hardy. Be sure to remove any all-green shoots if they appear.

'Lochinch' Stunning silvery-grey foliage, setting off a display of lavender-blue flowers, each with a tiny orange eye. Outstanding!

'Nanho Blue' Naturally compact. Silver foliage, deep blue flowers.

'Nanho Purple' Similar to above, dark purple spikes.

'Pink Delight' Good clear pink flowers, tall.

'Royal Red' Fairly compact habit, rich magenta-red flower spikes.

'Summer Beauty' Terrific new selection. Very large wands of deep pink flowers.

'White Profusion' Silvery-white flowers, tall.

CALAMINTHA
(Calamint) ☼ ◐

nepeta nepeta   ZONES 4–9
(= *C. nepetoides*) Good choice for edging pathways, where the minty-fragrant foliage will be brushed on passing. Tiny pale lilac flowers are produced abundantly on upright stalks. Nice frontal plant for the late summer border. Long blooming season. Not at all invasive.

> "An imperturbable little plant with a long flowering season, and a delicious minty odour when crushed."
> – Graham Stuart Thomas,
> *Perennial Garden Plants*

HEIGHT/SPREAD: 30cm (12")/30–45cm (12–18")
LOCATION: Well-drained soil.
BLOOMS: July–October
USES: ⋔ Massing, Edging

Caltha palustris 'Plena'

CALTHA
(Marsh Marigold) ☼ ◐

palustris   ZONES 2–9
Native wildflowers over most of the northern hemisphere, and much loved for their showy single buttercup flowers that grace streamsides and other wet places in early spring. They grow best in a rich moist soil that never dries out, but will adapt to moist border conditions. There are a couple of selections that are sometimes available.

HEIGHT/SPREAD: 15–30cm (6–12")/30cm (12")
LOCATION: Rich constantly moist soil.
BLOOMS: April–May
USES: ⏏⅏ Waterside, Moist areas

'Alba' Compact mound, early pure white flowers.

'Plena' Perfectly double golden buttercups.

CAMPANULA
(Bellflower) ☼ ◐

One of the most popular groups of perennials, ranging in height from low creeping alpines to tall stately spikes for the back of a border. Their bell-shaped flowers seem to have a universal appeal, usually blue in colour, but sometimes ranging to lavender, violet, rose or white. Most of the taller varieties are excellent for cutting. All prefer a sunny exposure, although many types are tolerant of partial shade.

alliariifolia   ZONES 3–9
(Spurred Bellflower) Creamy-white bells hang from arching stems for several weeks. Medium-sized plant for the border or woodland edge. A true perennial.

HEIGHT/SPREAD:	45–60cm (18–24″)/45cm (18″)
LOCATION:	Average well-drained soil.
BLOOMS:	June–August
USES:	✄ Border, Woodland garden

Campanula × 'Birch Hybrid'

× 'Birch Hybrid'   ZONES 4–9

Outstanding variety, trailing stems are smothered with nodding purple-blue flowers. Choice rock garden plant, blooming all summer long. Not invasive.

HEIGHT/SPREAD:	10–15cm (4–6″)/30cm (12″)
LOCATION:	Well-drained soil.
BLOOMS:	June–September
USES:	▲〰☙ Walls, Slopes

carpatica   ZONES 2–9

(Carpathian Bellflower) Compact rounded clumps bearing large, upturned cup-shaped flowers in various shades, blooming over a long period. Excellent for edging, also happy growing among rocks.

HEIGHT/SPREAD:	15–20cm (6–9″)/30cm (12″)
LOCATION:	Average well-drained soil.
BLOOMS:	June–September
USES:	▲☙ Edging, Borders

'Blue Clips' Medium blue shades.

'White Clips' White flowers.

'Chewton Joy' Later blooming, pale dusky blue flowers with darker blue margins.

cochleariifolia   ZONES 2–9

(Fairy Thimble) (formerly *C. pusilla*) Forms a low creeping mat with an abundant display of little nodding bells in summer. Very easy alpine plant, attractive growing in cracks and crevices or between patio stones.

HEIGHT/SPREAD:	10cm (4″)/15–30cm (6–12″)
LOCATION:	Well-drained soil.
BLOOMS:	June–August
USES:	▲〰☙ Walls, Troughs

'Blue Tit' Especially deep blue flowers.

'Dickson's Gold'   ZONES 4–9

An exciting, unique form, similar to *C. poscharskyana*, but with bright golden-green leaves and loose clusters of bright blue flowers. Good rock garden specimen, appreciating protection from hot sun. Nearly evergreen.

HEIGHT/SPREAD:	15cm (6″)/15–30cm (6–12″)
LOCATION:	Average well-drained soil.
BLOOMS:	June–August
USES:	▲☙ Troughs, Edging

'Elizabeth'   ZONES 4–9

A hybrid form, similar to *C. takesimana* in habit, but with arching stems of large drooping raspberry-pink bells.

HEIGHT/SPREAD:	60cm (24″)/45cm (18″)
LOCATION:	Average well-drained soil.
BLOOMS:	June–August
USES:	✄☙ Borders

glomerata 'Superba'   ZONES 2–9

(Clustered Bellflower) Rich violet-purple flowers in large clusters. Good choice for a lightly shaded border. Clumps should be divided frequently. Very popular for early summer colour. May need a trim after blooming. **'Acaulis'** is a nice dwarf selection useful for edging. HEIGHT: 20cm (8″)

> "Campanula should be used more often.
> My favorite is the *glomerata* 'Superba',
> which offers a profusion of colour even in
> a sunny area. I use it often as a cut flowers
> and find friends are amazed when told it
> is a bellflower."
> – Dr. Virginia Hildebrandt, Zone 5

HEIGHT/SPREAD:	45–60cm (18–24″)/45–60cm (18–24″)
LOCATION:	Average well-drained soil.
BLOOMS:	June–July
USES:	✄ Borders, Woodland, Meadows

'Kent Belle'   ZONES 4–9

Vigorous new hybrid featuring tall arching stems of dangling rich violet-purple bells. Discovered in a British garden. May need staking.

HEIGHT/SPREAD:	90–150cm (3–5′)/60cm (24″)
LOCATION:	Average well-drained soil.
BLOOMS:	June–August
USES:	✄☙ Borders

lactiflora   ZONES 4–9

(Milky Bellflower) Generally this is a tall border plant, but some of the newer compact varieties are excellent for frontal positions. Their large clusters of starry flowers bloom for many weeks. Best in part shade.

SPREAD:	30cm (12″)
LOCATION:	Prefers a cool, moist soil.
BLOOMS:	June–September
USES:	✄ Borders, Woodland

'Loddon Anna' Tall-growing selection with clusters of flesh-pink flowers in summer. Excellent for cutting. HEIGHT: 120–150cm (4–5′)

'Pouffe' Bushy green mounds with clouds of lavender-blue flowers. An early Alan Bloom selection. HEIGHT: 25–45cm (10–18″)

'Prichard's Variety' Lavender-blue flowers on sturdy, upright stems. HEIGHT: 90cm (36″)

'White Pouffe' White counterpart to 'Pouffe' with the same compact habit. HEIGHT: 25–45cm (10–18″)

medium   ZONES 2–9

(Canterbury Bells, Cup-and-Saucer) Old-fashioned cottage-garden plants, valued for their showy display in early summer. Huge bell-shaped flowers are held on upright spikes, in shades of rose, pink, blue, lilac, through white. The regular single-flowered form is charming, but the double form has bizarre cup-and-saucer style flowers that are a hit with kids! Superb for cutting. Biennial, sometimes self-seeding.

HEIGHT/SPREAD:	60–90cm (24–36″)/30cm (12″)
LOCATION:	Well-drained soil.
BLOOMS:	June–July
USES:	✄ Bedding, Massing

persicifolia   ZONES 2–9

(Peach-leaved Bellflower) Flowers are large blue or white bells, arranged on strong stems that are excellent for cutting. Blooms over a long period. Old-fashioned cottage garden perennial. Often self-seeds. Still one of the easiest and most rewarding perennials.

Campanula 'Dickson's Gold'

Campanula 'Elizabeth'

Campanula glomerata 'Superba'

Campanula 'Kent Belle'

Campanula persicifolia

Campanula persicifolia 'Chettle Charm'

Campanula rotundifolia 'Olympica'

Caryopteris × *clandonensis* 'Dark Knight'

HEIGHT/SPREAD: 60–90cm (24–36″)/30–45cm (12–18″)
LOCATION: Average well-drained soil.
BLOOMS: June–August
USES: ✂❦ Borders

'Chettle Charm' Brand new in North America, a new selection from Blooms of Bressingham. Palest porcelain-blue flowers, shot with darker violet-blue along the petal edges. Outstanding in the pastel border! HEIGHT: 90cm (3′)

poscharskyana   ZONES 2–9
(Serbian Bellflower) Trailing rockery plant, smothered with starry lavender-blue flowers. Spreads fairly quickly, so keep this away from delicate alpines. Useful as a groundcover, or try it in containers. Grows well in part shade.

> "This old-fashioned cottage-garden plant is a gem. It is a vigorous creeper and very compact, perfect for clambering amongst Oriental Poppies, then conveniently filling in as they disappear after blooming. It is a great groundcover and also excellent in containers."
> – Ellen Eisenberg, Zone 5

HEIGHT/SPREAD: 10–15cm (4–6″)/30–45cm (12–18″)
LOCATION: Average well-drained soil.
BLOOMS: May–July
USES: ▲⋀❦ Walls, Slopes

'E.H. Frost' Flowers are porcelain white with a pale blue eye. Long-blooming.

punctata 'Wedding Bells'   ZONES 4–9
Unusual double flowers in a hose-in-hose arrangement (one flower inside another). Petals are clear white on the outside, heavily spotted with deep red on the inside. This species is inclined to spread.

HEIGHT/SPREAD: 45cm (18″)/45–60cm (18–24″)
LOCATION: Average well-drained soil.
BLOOMS: June–July
USES: ✂❦ Borders

rotundifolia 'Olympica'   ZONES 2–9
(Bluebell of Scotland) Airy masses of nodding lavender-blue flowers. Performs best in cool-summer areas. Delightful native North American wildflower. Terrific cut flower.

HEIGHT/SPREAD: 30cm (12″)/30cm (12″)
LOCATION: Average to lean well-drained soil.
BLOOMS: June–September
USES: ▲✂ Borders, Meadows

takesimana   ZONES 4–9
(Korean Bellflower) Forms a spreading clump, with arching stems of large dangling bells. Flowers are pale lilac, with dark maroon spots on the inside. Tolerant of dry shade.

> "No plant this easy to cultivate should evoke such praise from gardeners and non-gardeners alike! Give it rich soil and a few hours of morning sun, then sit back and prepare yourself for the barrage of compliments." – Kevin Ward, Zone 5

HEIGHT/SPREAD: 45–60cm (18–24″)/30cm (12″)
LOCATION: Average well-drained soil.
BLOOMS: June–August
USES: ✂ Borders, Woodland garden

trachelium 'Bernice'   ZONES 4–9
New double-flowered border selection from England. Wide-open bells of medium purple, held on arching stems.

> "Dainty yet striking! One of the best of all the double Campanulas. Non-flopping two foot stems are filled with hanging pale violet-blue, paper-like, double fairy bells with the ends of the petals upturned."
> – Larry Davidson, Zone 5

HEIGHT/SPREAD: 60cm (24″)/30–45cm (12–18″)
LOCATION: Average well-drained soil.
BLOOMS: June–July
USES: ✂❦ Borders

CARYOPTERIS
(Bluebeard, Blue Spirea) ☼

× clandonensis   ZONES 5–9
Although actually a woody shrub, this is usually cut back each spring to 15cm (6″) and treated more like a perennial, blooming in the fall on new wood. Upright stems hold clusters of fragrant blue flowers from late summer on. This colour is welcome in the fall border as a contrast to the many types of yellow daisies blooming at the end of the season. Several selections have been made. Planting before midsummer is recommended. Fairly drought-tolerant, also said to be a butterfly magnet.

HEIGHT/SPREAD: 60–90cm (2–3′)/60–75cm (24–30″)
LOCATION: Well-drained soil.
BLOOMS: August–October
USES: ✂❦❦ Borders, Massing

'Dark Knight' One of the darkest forms, rich deep-purple flowers.

'Longwood Blue' Sky-blue flowers, silver-grey leaves. Floriferous.

'Worcester Gold' Bright blue flowers contrasting against golden-green foliage. Unusual!

CASSIA
See SENNA.

CATANANCHE
(Cupid's Dart) ☼

caerulea   ZONES 3–9
Papery lavender-blue flowers with a maroon eye. Plant forms a neat, slender clump of grey-green leaves. Moderately drought-tolerant. Short-lived, but will usually re-seed itself freely. Excellent for cutting, fresh or dried.

> "Mingled with some grey foliage to give them rather better furnishing — *Artemisia stelleriana*, for instance — they give a long-lasting summer picture."
> – Graham Stuart Thomas,
> *Perennial Garden Plants*

HEIGHT/SPREAD: 60cm (24″)/30cm (12″)
LOCATION: Well-drained soil. Dislikes winter wet.
BLOOMS: June–August
USES: ✂❦ Borders

Centaurea hypoleuca 'John Coutts'

CENTAUREA
(Perennial Cornflower) ☼

Sturdy, handsome perennials for planting in the border. Brightly coloured thistle-shaped blooms are long-lasting cut flowers. All types benefit from a hard shearing back after blooming. Reliable and long-lived.

dealbata   ZONES 3–9
(Persian Cornflower) Rosy-purple flowers in early summer. Foliage is grey-green, handsomely lobed.

HEIGHT/SPREAD: 45–75cm (18–30")/60cm (24")
LOCATION: Average well-drained soil.
BLOOMS: June–July
USES: ✂ Borders

hypoleuca 'John Coutts'   ZONES 3–9
An especially attractive form with finely-lobed greyish foliage and masses of clear pink flowers over a long season. This will usually rebloom in the fall if deadheaded. Excellent for massing in the border.

HEIGHT/SPREAD: 60–75cm (24–30")/60cm (24")
LOCATION: Average well-drained soil.
BLOOMS: June–August
USES: ✂ Borders, Massing

macrocephala   ZONES 2–9
(Globe Centaurea) Showy, golden-yellow flowers on stiffly upright stems. Nice at the back of a border. Superb for cutting, fresh or dried.

HEIGHT/SPREAD: 90–120cm (3–4')/60cm (24")
LOCATION: Average well-drained soil.
BLOOMS: June–August
USES: ✂ Borders

montana   ZONES 2–9
(Perennial Bachelor's Button) Cornflower-blue blossoms are an old-fashioned favorite. Nice filler plant towards the front of a border. Will usually rebloom in the fall if cut back. Very drought-tolerant. Inclined to self-seed prolifically.

HEIGHT/SPREAD: 30–60cm (12–24")/60cm (24")
LOCATION: Average well-drained soil.
BLOOMS: May–June
USES: ✂ 🐝 Borders

CENTRANTHUS
(Red Valerian) ☼

ruber   ZONES 4–9
An old-fashioned cut flower, back by popular demand. Large rounded clusters of rosy-red, fragrant flowers for many weeks. Plants are upright and bushy. Short-lived, but will self-seed. Moderately drought-tolerant.

HEIGHT/SPREAD: 30–90cm (1–3')/30–45cm (12–18")
LOCATION: Average to poor well-drained soil.
BLOOMS: June–September
USES: ✂ 🐝 Borders, Slopes, Walls

CEPHALARIA
(Giant Scabious) ☼

alpina
See SCABIOSA *alpina*.

gigantea   ZONES 3–9
Pale yellow pincushion flowers, similar in shape to *Scabiosa* but on a very tall, open upright bush. Nice subject for the back of a moist border. Plants will be more bushy and compact if pinched in May or June. May need staking. Good for cutting.

> "A striking companion for Delphinium 'Black Knight,' the luminous yellow blooms are similar in shape to Scabiosa, but are held on wiry stems up to seven feet above the coarse foliage."
> – Kevin Ward, Zone 5

HEIGHT/SPREAD: 1.5–1.8m (5–6')/60–90cm (2–3')
LOCATION: Prefers a rich moist soil.
BLOOMS: June–September
USES: ✂ Borders

CERASTIUM
(Snow-in-Summer) ☼

tomentosum   ZONES 1–9
(Snow-in-Summer) Vigorous, spreading mat of bright grey leaves, smothered with white flowers in early summer. Spreads quickly, often used as a groundcover on sunny slopes. Sometimes invasive. Not recommended for rock gardens! Very drought-tolerant. Shear plants back after blooming to keep them dense and compact.

HEIGHT/SPREAD: 15–30cm (6–12")/60cm (24")
LOCATION: Well-drained soil.
BLOOMS: May–June
USES: ∿▲🐝 Slopes, Walls

CERATOSTIGMA
(Blue Leadwort, Plumbago) ☼ ◑

plumbaginoides   ZONES 5–9
An unusual low perennial, valuable for fall display. Flowers are brilliant blue, foliage turns from green to maroon red in late fall. Nice as a ground cover or at the front of the border. Needs a winter mulch in colder areas. Planting before midsummer is strongly recommended.

> "Although slow to emerge in spring the dark blue flowers and reddening foliage in the cooler weather make it worth the wait!" – Ellen M. Talmage, Zone 7

HEIGHT/SPREAD: 20–30cm (8–12")/45cm (18")
LOCATION: Well-drained soil. Dislikes winter wet.
BLOOMS: August–October
USES: ▲∿ Massing, Edging, Borders

CHEIRANTHUS
See ERYSIMUM.

CHELONE
(Turtlehead) ☼ ◑

obliqua   ZONES 3–9
(Pink Turtlehead) Stiff spikes of rose-pink flowers, blooming over a long period. Excellent for cutting. Nice waterside plant, also does well in the border. A North American native wildflower. Outstanding for fall flower colour! There is also a beautiful white form known simply as 'Alba'.

Centaurea montana

Centranthus ruber

Cerastium tomentosum

Ceratostigma plumbaginoides

Chelone obliqua

Chrysanthemum × rubellum 'Clara Curtis'

Chrysanthemum × rubellum 'Mary Stoker'

Chrysanthemum 'Morden Delight'

"An all-time favorite. 'Pink Turtlehead' may be apropos — but 'Snapdragon on Steroids' strikes closer to the mark. Pair it with Astilbe and/or Siberian Iris for 'winter interest' that would make Rosemary Verey sit up and take note!"
— Kevin Ward, Zone 5

HEIGHT/SPREAD:	60–90cm (24–36")/60cm (24")
LOCATION:	Moist to wet rich soil.
BLOOMS:	August–October
USES:	✄ 🦋 Borders, Waterside

CHIASTOPHYLLUM
(Cotyledon) ☽

oppositifolium   ZONES 5–9
Dangling chains of yellow flowers, succulent green leaves like a *Sedum*. Will cascade nicely over rocks and walls. An unusual, easy alpine plant for a shaded rock garden.

HEIGHT/SPREAD:	15cm (6")/30cm (12")
LOCATION:	Well-drained soil. Dislikes hot sun.
BLOOMS:	June–July
USES:	▲☽ Edging, Walls

CHRYSANTHEMUM
(Daisy, Chrysanthemum) ☀ ☽

In recent years this group has been split up into several new genera, but finally the botanists have been convinced to keep the old familiar "garden mums" here, listed under Chrysanthemum. Other types are listed elsewhere in the guide, see below for the new names.

coccineum
See TANACETUM.

Hybrids   ZONES 5–9
(Hybrid Garden Mum) (was briefly *Dendranthema indica*, but once again restored!) Unlike the typical modern garden mums, these are vigorous old varieties that have stood the test of time, only recently making it back into commercial production. Plants spread to form a clump, and should be divided every year or two to maintain vigour. Pinch as for regular garden mums.

SPREAD:	60cm (24")
LOCATION:	Well-drained soil.
BLOOMS:	September–November
USES:	✄ Borders

'Mei-Kyo' Small deep lavender-rose double flowers with a yellow centre. Late. HEIGHT: 60cm (2')

Morden Series A nice range of compact mums with excellent hardiness, bred by Agriculture Canada in Morden Manitoba in the 1960's and 70's. All are fairly compact and cushion-like in habit, with double flowers. 'Morden Cameo' – creamy-white, 'Morden Canary' – bright yellow, 'Morden Candy' – bright pink, 'Morden Delight' – bronzy-red, 'Morden Eldorado' – golden-yellow, 'Morden Fiesta' – vibrant mauve-purple, 'Morden Garnet' – deep red. Zones 3–4. HEIGHT: 60cm (24").

'Sheffield' (a.k.a. 'Hillside Pink') Light pink single daisy flowers. HEIGHT: 70cm (28")

nipponicum
see NIPPONANTHEMUM.

pacificum
see AJANIA.

parthenium
see TANACETUM.

× rubellum   ZONES 4–9
(was briefly moved to *Dendranthema zawadskii*) Large, fragrant single daisies are held in loose sprays. Plants form a densely branching clump. Easy and reliable border plant, blooming several weeks ahead of fall mums. Plants will be more compact if pinched back by half in early June. Very few selections from this hybrid group are still in existence.

HEIGHT/SPREAD:	60–75cm (24–30")/60cm (24")
LOCATION:	Average well-drained soil.
BLOOMS:	July–September
USES:	✄ ☽ 🦋 Borders

'Clara Curtis' Large, deep-pink single flowers.

"The 'Mum' for those who despise the over-blown appearance of traditional fall Mums! Clara's strength is in her understated elegance — a 'painted daisy' for the autumn — an ideal compliment to those late blooming English Daisies."
— Kevin Ward, Zone 5

'Mary Stoker' Golden-apricot flowers, fading to peach.

× superbum
see LEUCANTHEMUM.

weyrichii   ZONES 3–9
(was briefly *Dendranthema weyrichii*) A low, creeping species, in effect like a dwarf garden mum. Flowers are large yellow-centred single daisies. These usually bloom in early fall.

SPREAD:	45cm (18")
LOCATION:	Well-drained soil
BLOOMS:	September–October
USES:	▲☽✄ ☽ 🦋 Edging, Massing

'Pink Bomb' Large rosy-pink flowers. HEIGHT: 25cm (9")

'White Bomb' Creamy-white flowers, fading to pale pink. Excellent vigour. HEIGHT: 30cm (12")

CHRYSOGONUM
(Golden Star) ☽ ●

virginianum   ZONES 5–9
This is a useful little groundcover, tolerating shady locations, and spreading to form a low patch of green foliage, studded with yellow star-shaped flowers for many weeks. A native North American wildflower. Appreciates a site sheltered from winds.

HEIGHT/SPREAD:	15–30cm (6–12")/30cm (12")
LOCATION:	Moist, well-drained soil.
BLOOMS:	May–July
USES:	〰 Borders, Woodland gardens

CIMICIFUGA
(Bugbane) ☼ ☽

Some of the more interesting and unusual forms of Bugbane are starting to become available here in North America, although they will likely always be in short supply! The lacy clumps of foliage are not unlike Astilbe, but flowers are held on tall stems, in a bottle-brush spike. Good for late summer and fall interest. All types prefer a rich, moist humusy soil and a woodland setting. Avoid disturbing established clumps.

SPREAD:	60–75cm (24–30")
LOCATION:	Likes a rich, moist soil. Dislikes greedy tree roots.
BLOOMS:	August–September
USES:	✄ Wildflower, Borders, Massing

acerina   ZONES 4–9
(Compact Bugbane) A compact species, similar to *C. racemosa*. Sturdy clumps of lacy foliage and wiry stems of white bottle-brush flowers. HEIGHT: 75–90cm (30–36")

racemosa   ZONES 3–9
(Black Snakeroot) Tall spikes of ivory-white flowers in late summer. Fruit capsules remain attractive into early winter. A wild flower native to eastern North America. HEIGHT: 90–150cm (3–5')

> "This engaging species is undeniably a 'must-have' for the back of the shade border. Those slender, veritably anorexic spikes of pure white flowers send shivers up the spine, just as the malodorous scent of the flowers rushes the hand to cover the nose — look, but don't smell."
> – Dr. Duncan Himmelman, Zone 3

ramosa 'Atropurpurea'   ZONES 4–9
(Purple-leaf Bugbane) Unusual and exotic foliage, forming a medium-sized clump of dark purple, lacy leaves. An eye-catching contrast to the tall spikes of creamy-white flowers. Move this up to the front of the border for all to see! HEIGHT: 1.5–2.1m (5–7')

'Brunette' An even darker form, with black-purple leaves and fragrant pale pink flowers. A terribly exciting collector's plant, finally available in reasonable supply!

> "After I'd sold a few, I compulsively removed them from the benches and put them in the ground. I couldn't help myself. When they came into bud, the practical voice in me said, 'Nip the buds — go for the root growth.' I couldn't. But that little act of rebellion rewarded me with plants of a magnificent dark purple topped with the most incredibly scented blush-pink brushes of bloom, the aroma luring me to my visual reward from quite a distance. This is a must-have plant." – Cathy Forgie, Zone 4

simplex 'White Pearl'   ZONES 3–9
(Kamchatka Bugbane) Tall bottlebrush spikes of creamy-white flowers are held above light green, lacy leaves. Nice background plant for the fall border, and excellent for cutting. Later to flower than the other species, September–October. HEIGHT: 90–120cm (3–4')

> "A necessity if you're going to get an "A" in Shade Gardening. Architectural yet delicate spires illuminate the summer garden. Large compound leaves easily fill a three foot space so leave plenty of elbow room." – Bobbie Schwarz, Zone 5

CLEMATIS
(Clematis) ☼ ☽

Although the flashy, large-flowered hybrid types are great old favorites, the smaller flow-ered varieties listed here are valuable garden plants as well, and are deserving of wider use. Some of these are woody climbing vines, oth-ers sprawling perennials that die back to the ground each year, leaning on the nearest shrub or stake in the border for a little support.

heracleifolia 'Davidiana'   ZONES 3–9
(Blue Bush Clematis) Not a climbing type, but more of a vigorous bush that dies back nearly to the ground each year, but usually requires the support of a nearby shrub or stake that it can clamber up. Flowers are like clusters of fragrant blue hyacinths, appearing in late summer. Unusual!

HEIGHT/SPREAD:	90cm (3')/60cm (2')
LOCATION:	Prefers a rich, moist soil.
BLOOMS:	August–September
USES:	✄ Borders

integrifolia   ZONES 2–9
(Solitary Clematis) Not a climbing vine, but a bor-der perennial that forms a sort of sprawling clump. Nodding, urn-shaped flowers are rich indigo blue, followed by fluffy seed heads. Plant this where it can sprawl up or over a shrub, or plan on staking it. Cut back to the ground in spring.

HEIGHT/SPREAD:	60–90cm (2–3')/60cm (2')
LOCATION:	Prefers a rich, moist soil.
BLOOMS:	July–August
USES:	✄ Borders

× jouiniana 'Mrs. Robert Brydon'   ZONES 4–9
Another herbaceous type, dying back nearly to the ground each winter. Extremely vigorous upright habit, clouds of the palest blue starry flowers in late sum-mer. Needs to be tied to a tall stake, fence or trellis, or allowed to scramble through a shrub.

HEIGHT/SPREAD:	2m (6–7')/60cm (2')
LOCATION:	Prefers a rich, moist soil.
BLOOMS:	July–September
USES:	✄ Borders

× 'Prairie Traveler's Joy'   ZONES 1–9
Very hardy hybrid developed by the late Dr. Frank Skinner in northern Manitoba. Sprays of starry white flowers bloom throughout the summer, fol-lowed by fluffy seed heads. Vigorous to the point of being aggressive. Mow or prune back hard every two or three years. Use as either a hardy climber or sprawl-ing groundcover. Very drought-tolerant.

HEIGHT/SPREAD:	30cm–5m (1–15')/90cm (3')
LOCATION:	Average well-drained soil.
BLOOMS:	June–September
USES:	⋀ ❦ Climbing vine

recta 'Purpurea'   ZONES 2–9
(Ground Clematis) Another herbaceous species, this requires some support to be at its best, though it is not really a climbing vine. Rich maroon-purple leaves are featured, with a good display of fragrant little white star flowers in summer. Silvery seed heads are attractive in fall.

HEIGHT/SPREAD:	90–120cm (3–4')/60cm (2')
LOCATION:	Prefers a rich, moist soil.
BLOOMS:	June–July
USES:	✄ Borders

Cimicifuga acerina

Cimicifuga racemosa

Cimicifuga racemosa 'Brunette'

Clematis integrifolia

tangutica   ZONES 2–9

(Golden Clematis) Bright yellow bell-shaped flowers through the summer and fall, followed by large feathery puffs. Excellent cover for difficult areas with poor soil, or trained as a climbing vine.

HEIGHT/SPREAD:	30cm–5m (1–15')/90cm (3')
LOCATION:	Average well-drained soil.
BLOOMS:	July–September
USES:	⋔☂ Climbing vine

CODONOPSIS
(Bonnet Bellflower) ☼ ◐

clematidea   ZONES 3–9

A semi-sprawling plant that can be quite showy when planted on a bank or wall so the flowers can be viewed from below. Flowers are large light blue bells, with dramatic purple and orange patterns on the inside. Plants have a mysterious fragrance when in bloom.

HEIGHT/SPREAD:	30–45cm (12–18")/60cm (24")
LOCATION:	Well-drained soil.
BLOOMS:	June–August
USES:	⛰ Walls, Slopes

CONVALLARIA
(Lily-of-the-Valley) ◐ ●

majalis   ZONES 1–9

Fragrant, white bell-shaped flowers. A sturdy groundcover for difficult shady sites, even under trees. Old-fashioned cut-flower. All parts of this plant are poisonous, especially the red berries. **'Rosea'** is a very old form with small pale-pink flowers, hard to find!

> "Lily-of-the-valley must not be forgotten, for though we grow it in greater quantity in reserve ground for cutting and in woodland, yet its beautiful foliage and sweetest of sweet bloom must be near the front edge of this border also."
> – Gertrude Jekyll, *Wood and Garden*

HEIGHT/SPREAD:	15cm (6")/30cm (12")
LOCATION:	Average to moist soil.
BLOOMS:	April–May
USES:	⋔✄ Woodland gardens

Coreopsis auriculata 'Nana'

COREOPSIS
(Tickseed) ☼

Bright yellow daisy-like flowers characterize this popular group of plants. All bloom constantly from midsummer to frost, particularly when fading flowers are removed. Good for cutting. The original species are all native North American wildflowers.

auriculata 'Nana'   ZONES 4–9

(Maysville Daisy) A long-lived dwarf variety, ideal for edging or in the rock garden. Plants give a showy display of single orange-yellow flowers in late spring. May repeat bloom if deadheaded.

HEIGHT/SPREAD:	15–25cm (6–9")/30cm (12")
LOCATION:	Average to moist well-drained soil.
BLOOMS:	May–July
USES:	⛰✄☂ Edging, Borders

grandiflora   ZONES 4–9

(Large-flowered Coreopsis) Large, golden-yellow flowers, blooming for many weeks in the summer. Both single and double flowered forms are available as well as a good range of heights. Hybrids between this species and *C. lanceolata* have produced many of the modern selections. These all have a tendency to bloom themselves to death; removing the flower stems from about early September on will encourage plants to form overwintering leaves rather than going to seed and wearing themselves out. Outstanding cut flowers.

SPREAD:	30cm (12")
LOCATION:	Prefers a rich, moist soil.
BLOOMS:	June–September
USES:	✄✿ Borders, Massing

'Baby Sun' Single flowers. HEIGHT: 30–50cm (12–20")

'Double Sunburst' Fluffy double flowers. HEIGHT: 75–90cm (30–36")

'Early Sunrise' Semi-double, award winner. HEIGHT: 45–60cm (18–24")

'Goldfink' Miniature single flowers, true dwarf. Must be grown by vegetative means. HEIGHT: 20–25cm (8–10")

rosea 'American Dream'   ZONES 3–9

(Pink Flowered Coreopsis) Formerly listed simply as *C. rosea*. Charming plant for edging or massing. Low, airy mounds of green leaves are studded with bright rose-pink daisies. Plants are vigorous and spreading, to be used with caution in the border. Prefers a moist soil.

HEIGHT/SPREAD:	30–45cm (12–18")/30–45cm (12–18")
LOCATION:	Average to moist soil.
BLOOMS:	June–September
USES:	✄⋔☂ Massing, Borders

tripteris   ZONES 4–9

(Giant Coreopsis) The giant of the species, forming an upright clump that bursts into bloom in late summer through fall. Flowers are large butter-yellow daisies held in sprays. Attractive to butterflies, and birds apparently like to eat the seeds.

HEIGHT/SPREAD:	1.5–2.4m (6–8')/75cm (30")
LOCATION:	Average to moist soil.
BLOOMS:	July–September
USES:	✄✿ Borders, Meadows

verticillata   ZONES 3–9

(Thread-leaved Coreopsis) Truly among the best garden perennials available. Plants form an airy dome of narrow leaves, covered with starry flowers for many weeks. Can be mass planted as a groundcover. Excellent for combining with ornamental grasses. Generally long-lived and carefree. Very drought-tolerant.

> "For bright pure colour a group of this fine daisy is hard to beat. Grow it next to dark reds, bright orange curtonis or crocosmia with sword-like leaf contrast, or associate it with a pale yellow × *Solidaster luteus*." – Penelope Hobhouse, *Colour in Your Garden*

SPREAD:	30–45cm (12–18")
LOCATION:	Average well-drained soil.
BLOOMS:	June–September
USES:	✄☂🌿 Massing, Borders

'Golden Gain' New free-flowering selection from Blooms of Bressingham. Golden-yellow flowers, good compact habit. HEIGHT: 60cm (24")

'Golden Showers' (a.k.a. 'Grandiflora') Large golden-yellow flowers. Vigorous. HEIGHT: 60–75cm (24–30")

'Moonbeam' Unusual pale yellow flowers. Deservedly popular, and perhaps one of the all-time best perennials, blending in nicely with pastel colour schemes. Not always long-lived, however, and very late to make an appearance in spring. A former *Perennial Plant of the Year.* HEIGHT: 45–60cm (18–24")

'Zagreb' Especially compact form. Bright chrome-yellow flowers, similar to 'Golden Showers'. HEIGHT: 30cm (12")

CORONILLA
(Crown Vetch) ☼

varia   **ZONES 3–9**
Widely used as a groundcover on roadsides and other difficult sunny sites, valued for its ability to fix nitrogen from the air, improving the soil. Rose-pink clover-like flowers bloom all summer. Very aggressive, unsuitable for most garden situations. Extremely drought-tolerant.

HEIGHT/SPREAD: 30–60cm (12–24")/60cm (24")
LOCATION: Very tolerant of poor soils.
BLOOMS: June–August
USES: ⋏⋇ Roadsides, Slopes

CORYDALIS
(Fumitory, Corydalis) ☼
Related to the familiar Bleedingheart, these have similar ferny foliage, and upright stems of delicate showy flowers. They appreciate a cool, moisture-retentive but well-drained soil, perhaps at the edge of a woodland.

flexuosa   **ZONES 5–9**
(Blue Corydalis) Lacy blue-green foliage with arching stems of the most incredible sky-blue, fragrant flowers over a long season. A recent arrival from China, and worth a try in any partly shaded rockery. Flowering is intermittent from spring to fall, although these have a tendency to go summer-dormant if the weather is hot and humid.

HEIGHT/SPREAD: 20–30cm (8–12")/30cm (12")
LOCATION: Rich, moist well-drained soil.
BLOOMS: May–October
USES: ⋏▲♥⋇ Edging, Walls

'Blue Panda' Clear sky-blue, that elusive Himalayan blue-poppy colour!

> "In *The Harrowsmith Perennial Garden*, Patrick Lima advised pairing the blue *Polemonium caeruleum* with the yellow *Corydalis lutea* — so when I found myself in possession of the yellow *Polemonium pauciflorum*, I couldn't resist teaming it up with the blue *Corydalis* 'Blue Panda'. Forgive my botanical dyslexia Patrick — but it still works beautifully!"
> – Kevin Ward, Zone 5

'China Blue' More vigorous habit, slightly paler blue flowers.

lutea   **ZONES 4–9**
(Golden Corydalis) A charming little plant for a rock wall or slope, with pretty yellow locket-shaped flowers for months! The fresh green leaves make a low ferny mound. In a partly shaded cool site this will happily self-seed all over the place.

> "No better companion for Jacob's ladder [*Polemonium*] could be found than a foreground planting of *Corydalis luteus*."
> – Patrick Lima,
> *The Harrowsmith Perennial Garden*

HEIGHT/SPREAD: 20–30cm (8–12")/30cm (12")
LOCATION: Prefers a moist, well-drained soil.
BLOOMS: May–September
USES: ⋏▲♥ Walls, Borders

COSMOS
(Cosmos) ☼

atrosanguineus   **ZONES 7–9**
(Chocolate Cosmos) This plant has quickly become a hit. The large dark maroon-red flowers are distinctively chocolate-scented on warm days. Good for cutting. Plants form a tuberous root which can be lifted and stored indoors like a Dahlia, so this can even be grown in colder regions! The easiest way to grow this is in a large pot, just bring it into the basement in the winter.

HEIGHT/SPREAD: 45–75cm (18–30")/30cm (12")
LOCATION: Well-drained soil.
BLOOMS: June–September
USES: ✂◄♥ Borders

COTULA
See LEPTINELLA.

COTYLEDON
See CHIASTOPHYLLUM.

CRAMBE
(Sea Kale) ☼

cordifolia   **ZONES 5–9**
(Heartleaf Seakale, Colewort) A most bizarre and unusual plant, something like a Baby's Breath crossed with a cabbage! Huge green leaves are deeply lobed and form a large mound. Clouds of tiny star-shaped flowers are held above on tall stalks in early summer. An interesting specimen plant for the larger border. Very long-lived.

> "…with its huge rough cabbage-shaped leaves and tall stems of cloud-like white flowers, is a wonderful perennial. It flowers early, needs no staking, and contributes architectural quality, so often lacking in flowering border plants. "
> – Penelope Hobhouse,
> *Colour in Your Garden*

HEIGHT/SPREAD: 120–180cm (4–6')/120cm (4')
LOCATION: Well-drained soil.
BLOOMS: June–July
USES: ✂ Specimen, Borders

maritima   **ZONES 4–9**
(Blue Seakale) Although this species forms sprays of off-white flowers, it really is grown more for the fantastic powdery-blue foliage. Leaves are large and cabbage-like, forming a rounded clump. Especially good in dry xeriscape situations.

HEIGHT/SPREAD: 60–70cm (24–30")/60cm (2')
LOCATION: Well-drained soil.
BLOOMS: June–July
USES: ⋇♥ Specimen, Dry borders

CROCOSMIA
(Crocosmia, Montbretia) ☼
Becoming popular both for gardens and as a cut flower. Recent breeding work has greatly increased the selection of heights and flower colours and generally improved hardiness.

Corydalis flexuosa 'China Blue'

Corydalis lutea

Cosmos atrosanguineus

Crambe maritima

Crocosmia 'Emberglow'

Crocosmia 'Jenny Bloom'

Delosperma cooperi

Delosperma nubigenum

Upright clumps of sword-shaped leaves produce arching stems of brilliant nodding funnel flowers from midsummer on, the effect a bit like some kind of exotic gladiola.

In Zones 1–4 the fleshy roots may be over-wintered indoors like Canna lilies, and this is well worth the effort. Divide plants every 2–3 years for best blooming. A deep winter mulch is recommended in Zones 5–7, or wherever snowcover is unreliable. Superb cut flowers.

Hybrids: ZONES 5–9

Although our zoning may seem optimistic, there are gardeners in both Zones 5 and 6 that are succeeding with Crocosmia outside. Reliable snowcover and/or a deep mulch of leaves in winter appears to be the key to success in these regions. An addition, planting before the end of June would be well advised.

SPREAD: 30cm (12")
LOCATION: Average well-drained soil.
BLOOMS: July–September
USES: ✄❀ Borders, Massing

> [re: Crocosmia 'Lucifer'] "If you want a brilliant splash of colour in your garden, one that makes people stop in their tracks and ask 'What's that!', plant this beauty. The glorious flower spikes stand three feet tall in good conditions and almost glow. Very dramatic and eye-catching."
> – Margaret Burke, Zone 6

'Bressingham Beacon' Beautiful orange and yellow bicolour raised by Alan Bloom. HEIGHT: 100cm (40")

'Emberglow' Very large flowers, burnt orange-red. An older Alan Bloom selection. HEIGHT: 75cm (30")

'Jenny Bloom' A newer deep yellow hybrid by Alan Bloom. HEIGHT: 100cm (40")

'Lucifer' Brilliant flame-red. The most famous of the older Alan Bloom hybrids. HEIGHT: 120cm (4')

CRYPTOTAENIA
(Mitsuba, Japanese Parsley) ☽

japonica 'Atropurpurea'   ZONES 4–9

(Purple-leaved Mitsuba) An interesting new foliage plant that is attractive as well as edible! Related to parsley, the leaves are divided and somewhat ferny in texture, in a beautiful shade of bronzy-purple. Add this to the list of 'black' leaved plants. Umbels of pale pink flowers appear in summer. Excellent companion to gold-leaved Hostas. Inclined to self-sow. Plants can be cut back after blooming to encourage fresh new growth. Use leaves like regular parsley.

HEIGHT/SPREAD: 40–60cm (16–24")/30cm (12")
LOCATION: Prefers a rich, moist soil.
BLOOMS: June–July
USES: ✄❀ Borders

CYCLAMEN
(Hardy Cyclamen) ☽

hederifolium   ZONES 5–9

Suited to a shady rockery or woodland area, these form low clumps of ivy-shaped green leaves with intricate grey and bronzy patterning. The little pink or white rocket-shaped flowers appear in early fall, followed by the leaves. Clumps remain evergreen for the winter, going dormant during the heat of summer. Large corms develop underground. These resent overhead watering in the summer, so are best paired up with plants that are fairly drought tolerant. Excellent under trees and shrubs, these often begin to self-seed.

> "Hardy Cyclamen wintered over in an eastern bed and under some spruce trees at our home near Guelph. I was delighted that it could take our winters and enjoy the heart-shaped leaves and rocket-like flowers, which seem to brighten up the out of the ways corners."
> – Dr. Virginia Hildebrandt, Zone 5

HEIGHT/SPREAD: 10–15cm (4–6")/15–20cm (6–8")
LOCATION: Very well-drained soil.
BLOOMS: September–October.
USES: ◭▲❦❀ Woodland gardens

DARMERA
(Umbrella Plant) ☼ ☽

peltata   ZONES 5–9

(formerly *Peltiphyllum peltatum*) An interesting waterside plant, with large round rhubarb-like leaves that form a wide clump. Bizarre clusters of pink flowers appear before the leaves in early spring. In effect like a small *Gunnera* but far hardier. This is a wildflower native to southern Oregon.

HEIGHT/SPREAD: 90–120cm (3–4')/90cm (3')
LOCATION: Rich, constantly moist soil.
BLOOMS: April–May
USES: Waterside, Specimen

DELOSPERMA
(Hardy Ice plant) ☼

Spreading, succulent plants similar in effect to Sedum. Flowers are single stars, studding the evergreen mat of leaves. These require very good drainage, especially in wet winter regions. Best on a slope or gravelly rock garden. Drought-tolerant.

cooperi   ZONES 6–9

(Purple Ice Plant) Blooms all summer long with magenta-purple daisy-like flowers. Intolerant of wet soil, and usually treated as an annual in the eastern part of the continent. Foliage develops good red fall and winter colour. Much used as a groundcover in the south-western U.S. Very drought-tolerant.

HEIGHT/SPREAD: 5–10cm (2–4")/30–60cm (12–24")
LOCATION: Very well-drained soil.
BLOOMS: June–September.
USES: ◭〰▲❦❀ Slopes

nubigenum   ZONES 3–9

(Yellow Ice Plant) Low weed-proof mat of green foliage, turning bronze-red in cold weather. Flowers are bright yellow, mostly in late spring. Reliably hardy, much more tolerant of wet soils and extended cold than the Purple Ice Plant. Worth considering as a lawn substitute. Very drought-tolerant.

HEIGHT/SPREAD: 5–10cm (2–4")/30–60cm (12–24")
LOCATION: Average to very well-drained soil.
BLOOMS: May–June.
USES: ◭〰▲❦❀ Slopes

DELPHINIUM
(Delphinium, Larkspur) ☼

One of the classic garden perennials, so important to the traditional English-style herbaceous summer border. We are all familiar with the taller types, with their stately spires of colour. However, the smaller-flowered larkspur-style varieties are also excellent border plants, so useful for cutting, and often succeeding in hot humid climates where the taller forms do not.

All types need a rich, moist but well-drained soil and full sun. Taller types are especially heavy feeders, so they should be fertilized regularly. Removing faded flowers will encourage repeat blooming; cut taller varieties back to 10cm (4″) after flowering, shorter types need only to be dead-headed. Staking of the larger forms in late May will help to prevent damage by strong winds at flowering time.

> "…we wind stout cord from stake to stake and tie the plant in at several ascending levels, but not so tightly as to give it a Scarlet O'Hara waist. Support is the goal, not strangulation." – Patrick Lima, *The Harrowsmith Perennial Garden*

× belladonna   ZONES 2–9

Larkspur-style flowers held in a loosely-branching spikes, rather than in a solitary one. These are in various shades of blue and white, and are excellent for cutting. Good repeat bloomer if dead-headed. Not as long-lived as the Elatum hybrids.

HEIGHT/SPREAD: 90–120cm (3–4′)/45cm (18″)
LOCATION: Rich, average to moist soil.
BLOOMS: June–August.
USES: ✄ Borders

× 'Connecticut Yankee'   ZONES 2–9

Also with larkspur-type flowers on compact, bushy plants that require no staking. These are more suited to a smaller garden, with an extended season of bloom. Flowers are in mixed shades of white, blue, lavender and purple.

HEIGHT/SPREAD: 60–75cm (24–30″)/60cm (24″)
LOCATION: Rich, average to moist soil.
BLOOMS: July–September
USES: ✄ Borders

Elatum Hybrids   ZONES 2–9

(Pacific Giant Hybrids) (*D.* × *cultorum*) These tall colourful spikes of double flowers can be the backbone for the early summer border. Flowers often have a contrasting centre or "bee". Plan to renew plantings every three years, otherwise the plants will get woody and begin to decline. Fall flowering is usually good if plants are trimmed back after the summer flush is over. Many seed strains have been developed in a wide range of separate colours.

> "Blue Delphiniums are a must in the garden. They remind me of the blue sky, on a cloudy miserable day." – John Vandenberg, Zone 6

HEIGHT/SPREAD: 120–180cm (4–6′)/60cm (2′)
LOCATION: Rich, average to moist soil.
BLOOMS: June–July, fall.
USES: ✄ Borders

'Astolat' Lavender pink, dark bee.

'Black Knight' Deep midnight violet, the darkest.

'Blue Bird' Clear medium blue, white bee.

'Blue Fountain' Compact, windproof strain in a good range of colours, including blue, lavender, rose and white. HEIGHT: 75–90cm (30–36″)

'Blue Jay' Medium blue, dark bee.

'Camelliard' Lavender blue shades.

'Galahad' Pure white.

'Guinevere' Lavender-pink with white bee.

'King Arthur' Royal violet with white bee.

'Summer Skies' Light blue, white bee.

grandiflorum 'Blue Elf'   ZONES 2–9

Totally unlike the taller forms already listed, these form dwarf bushy mounds, covered with large brilliant blue flowers all summer and fall. Excellent for edging or massing. Although short-lived, these put on such a spectacular show that they are worth using even as a bedding annual. Sometimes self-seeds. 'Blue Mirror' is very similar, with electric-blue flowers, to 40cm (16″) tall.

> "If you think 'pink and blue' is cute but tired, pair 'Blue Elf' with *Lychnis coronaria*. Pastel it's not — spectacular it is!" – Kevin Ward, Zone 5

HEIGHT/SPREAD: 30cm (12″)/30cm (12″)
LOCATION: Average to moist well-drained soil.
BLOOMS: June–September.
USES: △▲♥✄➤ Borders, Edging

nudicaule   ZONES 6–9

(Orange Larkspur) Unusual species native to California, with a nice display of bright orange-red flowers. Most effective when several are planted closely together in a group. Short-lived, best treated as an annual in wetter areas. Needs perfect drainage in winter. Drought-tolerant.

HEIGHT/SPREAD: 30–60cm (12–24″)/30cm (12″)
LOCATION: Very well-drained.
BLOOMS: June–August.
USES: △✄♥🌱 Wildflower, Borders

DENDRANTHEMA
See CHRYSANTHEMUM.

Dianthus × 'Spotty'

DIANTHUS
(Pinks) ☼

A large and diverse group of plants, including Carnations and Sweet William. Many forms are low growing, well-suited to rock gardens or for edging. Divide all but the alpine types every two years to keep plants vigorous and young. Most are evergreen. Cushion-forming Dianthus will benefit from a little clean up after flowering, removing flower stems and giving a light trim to the foliage.

× allwoodii   ZONES 2–9

(Border Pinks) A hybrid group that includes many of the older varieties with fragrant flowers that were once so popular for edging. Generally a little taller and more sturdy than the *D. gratianopolitanus* types.

SPREAD: 20–30cm (8–12″)
LOCATION: Average well-drained soil.
BLOOMS: May–July
USES: ✄<△▲♥ Edging, Walls, Borders

Delphinium 'Blue Bird'

Delphinium 'Blue Jay'

Delphinium 'King Arthur'

Delphinium 'Summer Skies'

Dianthus barbatus – Double Mix

Dianthus gratianopolitanus 'Bath's Pink'

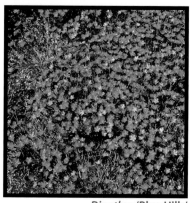
Dianthus 'Blue Hills'

Diascia 'Coral Belle'

'Frosty Fire' Deep ruby-red fringed flowers. Bright silver-blue foliage. an outstanding form! HEIGHT: 15–20cm (6–8")

'Oakington' An older introduction from Blooms of Bressingham. Double light pink flowers. HEIGHT: 15cm (6")

'Painted Beauty' Taller variety, branching stems of lavender-rose flowers with burgundy streaks. HEIGHT: 20–30cm (8–12")

alpinus   ZONES 3–9
(Alpine Pink) Very dwarf rock-garden type. Grassy clumps of leaves and large, single hot-pink flowers. Appreciates a little afternoon shade.

HEIGHT/SPREAD:	5cm (2")/15cm (6")
LOCATION:	Well-drained, moist soil.
BLOOMS:	May–June.
USES:	⛰▲🏺 Scree, Troughs

barbatus   ZONES 2–9
(Sweet William) Classic cottage garden plant. Large showy clusters of flowers, blooming all summer if dead-headed regularly. A biennial or short-lived perennial, but will usually self-seed freely. Taller types make excellent cut flowers. There are several mixed seed strains available in both single and double-flowering forms, with varying heights and in colours ranging from shades of red, pink, and salmon, through to white.

HEIGHT/SPREAD:	15–60cm (6–24")/20–30cm (8–12")
LOCATION:	Average well-drained soil.
BLOOMS:	May–August.
USES:	⛰〰▲🏺✂ Edging, Borders

caryophyllus 'Grenadin Series'   ZONES 4–9
(Hardy Carnation) Ever popular as cut-flowers. These are not long-lived and benefit from yearly division to keep the plants thriving. A thick mulch will help to bring them through cold winters. Their large, fragrant double flowers appear throughout the summer in a good range of colours, including shades of pink, red, white, and soft yellow. Blooms reliably as an annual in cold areas.

HEIGHT/SPREAD:	30–45cm (12–18")/30cm (12")
LOCATION:	Well-drained soil. Dislikes hot summers.
BLOOMS:	June–September.
USES:	✂ Borders

deltoides   ZONES 2–9
(Maiden Pinks) Low, spreading mats of foliage are smothered by small single flowers in summer. Good edging plants. Will often self-seed. Several colour strains are available.

HEIGHT/SPREAD:	15–20cm (6–8")/30–45cm (12–18")
LOCATION:	Average well-drained soil.
BLOOMS:	June–August
USES:	⛰〰▲🏺 Edging, Borders

'Albus' Green foliage, white flowers.

'Brilliant' Fresh green leaves and cherry-red flowers.

'Flashing Light' Ruby-red flowers, bronzy leaves.

'Zing Rose' Deep rose-red flowers, green leaves, fairly upright habit. Repeat bloomer. Likely a hybrid.

gratianopolitanus   ZONES 2–9
(Cheddar Pinks) These have been grown in gardens for centuries, and a large number of named cultivars exist. All form a low cushion of grassy foliage, usually tinted grey or steel blue. Flowers are sweetly scented, the taller varieties excellent for cutting. Popular for edging and rock gardens, and outstanding growing in or over walls.

SPREAD:	20–30cm (8–12")
LOCATION:	Average well-drained soil.
BLOOMS:	May–July
USES:	✂⛰▲🏺 Edging, Walls, Borders

'Bath's Pink' An especially vigorous new selection. Fringed soft-pink flowers in great numbers. Widely reported to be tolerant of warm, humid conditions. Steel-blue leaves. HEIGHT: 15cm (6")

'Blue Hills' Silvery-blue foliage, single rose-pink flowers. HEIGHT: 15cm (6")

'Bourbon' Tight, compact mounds with single dark-pink flowers. HEIGHT: 7cm (3")

'Dottie' Fringed single white flowers with a crimson eye. Compact green clump. An offspring of 'Spotty'. HEIGHT: 10cm (4")

'Mountain Mist' Exceptionally blue foliage, dusty-rose flowers. Heat tolerant selection. HEIGHT: 20–30cm (8–12")

'Royal Midget' Semi-double deep pink flowers, tight habit. HEIGHT: 10–15cm (4–6")

'Spotty' Bluish leaves, unusual cerise-red flowers with white spots. HEIGHT: 15–20cm (6–8")

'Tiny Rubies' Tiny, double rose-pink flowers. Extremely compact mounds of olive-green leaves. Best in a rock garden. Very fragrant. HEIGHT: 10cm (4")

'Whatfield Mini' Shell-pink single flowers, nice tight habit. HEIGHT: 10–15cm (4–6")

knappii   ZONES 3–9
(Yellow Pinks) Open, upright habit. Flowers are pale yellow, blooming over several weeks. Good for cutting. Short-lived but self-seeds prolifically.

HEIGHT/SPREAD:	45cm (18")/30cm (12")
LOCATION:	Average well-drained soil.
BLOOMS:	May–June
USES:	✂ Borders

plumarius 'Spring Beauty'   ZONES 3–9
(Cottage Pinks, Clove Pinks) Blue-grey, grassy foliage forms a wide, handsome clump. Flowers are like small clove-scented carnations with fringed petals, in a mixture of pink, rose, salmon and white. A true cottage garden perennial. Excellent for edging. Fairly drought-tolerant. Grown from seed and inclined to be variable.

HEIGHT/SPREAD:	30cm (12")/30cm (12")
LOCATION:	Average well-drained soil.
BLOOMS:	May–June
USES:	✂⛰▲🏺🌱 Edging, Walls, Borders

Diascia 'Salmon Supreme'

DIASCIA
(Twinspur) ☀ ◐

These are widely grown in England, but relatively new to North American gardens. Plants will bloom all summer long, with a showy display of bright pink flowers. Worth a try in containers or hanging baskets. Best treated as half-hardy, even in mild West coast gardens.

"Their small, spurred flowers of rose or coral or coppery salmon bring zest to an excess of pastels, and they have a knack for putting themselves into stunning combinations." – Ann Lovejoy, *The American Mixed Border*

Hybrids   ZONES 7–9
Vigorous selections, all these form a low spreading clump of fresh green leaves, with clusters of bright flowers all summer long. Terrific for weaving through the front of a border.

HEIGHT/SPREAD:	15–20cm (6–8")/30cm (12")
LOCATION:	Well-drained soil. Dislikes winter wet.
BLOOMS:	June–September
USES:	⚠☀ Edging, Baskets, Borders

'Blackthorn Apricot' Gorgeous shade of pale apricot pink. Unusual!

'Coral Belle' Deep coral flowers, compact.

'Langthorn's Lavender' Small lavender-pink blooms.

'Ruby Field' Deep pink flowers, lilac cast.

'Salmon Supreme' Excellent form in an interesting coppery-salmon shade.

Dicentra spectabilis

DICENTRA
(Bleedingheart) ☼ ●
Much-loved shade garden plants, although most Dicentra will also tolerate full sun if they have adequate moisture. The various types all have the same classic heart-shaped flowers. Divide dwarf varieties every three years to maintain vigour. All are excellent for cutting.

eximia   ZONES 3–9
(Fringed Bleedingheart) Native to eastern North America. Flowers are light pink over delicate ferny leaves. Similar in effect to 'Luxuriant' but more delicate. A nice little woodlander. Prefers bright shade. May go summer dormant during droughts.

HEIGHT/SPREAD:	20–30cm (8–12")/30cm (12")
LOCATION:	Rich, moist well-drained soil.
BLOOMS:	May–July
USES:	⚠☀ Massing, Woodland garden

'Alba' Milky-white flowers, light green leaves.

'Stuart Boothman' Bright pink flowers and powdery blue-green foliage.

formosa Hybrids   ZONES 2–9
(Fern-leaf Bleedingheart).Vigorous dwarf fern-leaved selections, excellent in a wide range of shade or part-shade situations. Foliage makes a lacy mound, flowers are held well above on arching stems. Long-blooming.

HEIGHT/SPREAD:	30cm (12")/30cm (12")
LOCATION:	Well-drained soil.
BLOOMS:	May–August
USES:	⚠☀ Borders, Massing

'Adrian Bloom' Dark green leaves with deep reddish-pink flowers. Outstanding. Selected by Blooms of Bressingham.

'Langtrees' (Formerly listed as 'Pearl Drops') Powdery blue-grey leaves and delicate ivory-white flowers with a pink tip.

'Luxurient' Cherry-pink flowers bloom continually above clumps of ferny green foliage. An older selection, but still excellent.

'Snowflakes' New selection from England. Lacy green foliage and upright stems of dangling white flowers. Good vigour.

spectabilis   ZONES 2–9
(Old-fashioned Bleedingheart) An old favorite from everyone's childhood, with the familiar drooping chains of pink hearts on a large, bushy mound. Often goes dormant by late summer, especially in hot climates, so be sure to plant something in front that will get big later in the season. In cool-summer areas cut plants back to 10cm (4") after blooming to encourage fresh new growth. The white form **'Alba'** is a refreshing change from the pink, and they look especially nice together.

"I would rate the white bleeding heart as one of the loveliest and most elegant perennials we grow. If its foliage lasted until fall, it would be the perfect plant."
– Patrick Lima,
The Harrowsmith Perennial Garden

HEIGHT/SPREAD:	60–90cm (2–3')/60cm (24")
LOCATION:	Rich, moist well-drained soil.
BLOOMS:	May–June
USES:	☀ Borders, Woodland gardens

DICTAMNUS
(Gas Plant) ☼

albus   ZONES 2–9
(Formerly *D. fraxinella*) Truly a superb plant for the sunny border, where it will form a large green clump with spikes of white flowers (**'Albiflorus'**) in the early summer. The old tale about the flowers giving off a flammable gas is true; I tried lighting it on fire once and it worked! Spectacular once established in the garden, these always look rather pathetic for the first year or two until they take hold, so be patient. Very long-lived. Resents being disturbed. The form **'Purpureus'** has soft mauve-pink flowers with darker veins.

"Dictamnus is a favorite of mine – it distinguishes a garden. I love the quote from Prince's catalogue 1831 (New York): *'this plant exhales inflammable gas'*. One gets the image of a fire-breathing dragon, but it has never even lit up for me!"
– Denise Adams, Zone 5

HEIGHT/SPREAD:	60–90cm (2–3')/60cm (2')
LOCATION:	Average well-drained soil.
BLOOMS:	June–July
USES:	☀ Borders

DIGITALIS
(Foxglove) ☼ ☼
These showy spikes of large, dangling tubular flowers are a classic sight in the early summer border. They grow best in a woodland setting but adapt well to border conditions. Dead-

Dicentra 'Adrian Bloom'

Dicentra 'Langtrees'

Dictamnus albus 'Purpureus'

Digitalis purpurea 'Foxy'

Digitalis 'Apricot Beauty'

Dodecatheon meadia

Doronicum orientale 'Magnificum'

Echinacea purpurea 'Magnus'

heading will encourage continual blooms. All types will self-seed.

grandiflora   ZONES 2–9

(Yellow Foxglove) (= *D. ambigua*) Short wind-proof spikes of pale butter-yellow flowers. Excellent for cutting. Good repeat blooms in the fall. A true perennial type, long-lived.

> "So, you just got *Polemonium* 'Brise d'Anjou'? Set it off to perfection with Yellow Foxglove and *Hosta* 'Regal Splendor'. Trust me, that's what that Jekyll woman would have done!"
> – Kevin Ward, Zone 5

HEIGHT/SPREAD:	60–90cm (2–3')/30cm (12")
LOCATION:	Moist, well-drained soil.
BLOOMS:	June–August
USES:	✂ Borders, Woodland gardens

× mertonensis   ZONES 4–9

(Pink Foxglove) A perennial variety, compact in habit, with spikes of large deep-pink flowers. Excellent foliage. Divide plants every two years to maintain vigour.

HEIGHT/SPREAD:	90cm (3')/30–45cm (12–18")
LOCATION:	Moist, well-drained soil.
BLOOMS:	June–July
USES:	✂ Borders, Woodland gardens

purpurea   ZONES 4–9

(Common Foxglove) Very showy in bloom, with stately spikes of large bell flowers. Requires an evenly moist soil. Biennial, but usually self-seeding. Various seed strains are available; in the garden these will often revert back to magenta-purple after several years of self-seeding.

> "The spectacle of those erect spires of spotted purple flowers can stop the hearts of many passers-by — and thank God, since *Digitalis* is known to possess the ability to restart it!"
> – Dr. Duncan Himmelman, Zone 3

SPREAD:	30–45cm (12–18")
LOCATION:	Moist, well-drained soil.
BLOOMS:	May–July
USES:	✂ Borders, Woodland gardens

'Apricot Beauty' Unusual soft apricot-pink flowers. HEIGHT: 120cm (4')

'Excelsior Hybrids' Mixed shades of white, rose, pink, and lavender. Very large flowers, very colourful. HEIGHT: 120–150cm (4–5')

'Foxy' Bright mix of colours, compact plants. HEIGHT: 90cm (36")

DODECATHEON
(Shooting Star) ☼ ◑

meadia   ZONES 2–9

Delicate umbels of flowers rise up from a flat rosette of leaves. Flowers are rose-pink with a yellow band, cyclamen-shaped. Plants usually go dormant by midsummer, so mark the area well to avoid digging them out! Nice companions to various *Primula*. A native North American wildflower.

HEIGHT/SPREAD:	30cm (12")/15cm (6")
LOCATION:	Likes a rich, moist soil.
BLOOMS:	May–June
USES:	▲△✂ Woodland gardens

DORONICUM
(Leopard's Bane) ☼ ◑

orientale 'Magnificum'   ZONES 2–9

(= *D. caucasicum*) These large perky yellow daisies bloom in mid-spring, combining so nicely with tulips or tall blue Forget-me-nots. Plants usually go dormant and leave a gap by midsummer. Great for cutting. Tolerant of woodland conditions.

> "A sparkling spring picture has golden alyssum (where it thrives) and candytuft in the foreground, a mass of soft orange tulips behind and, still farther back, leopard's bane, the first of the garden's daisies to bloom." – Patrick Lima, *The Harrowsmith Perennial Garden*

HEIGHT/SPREAD:	50cm (20")/30cm (12")
LOCATION:	Average to moist well-drained soil.
BLOOMS:	April–June
USES:	✂ Borders, Woodland gardens.

ECHINACEA
(Purple Coneflower) ☼

Similar to Rudbeckia, highly valued for their large brightly-coloured daisies. Each flower has a prominent central brown cone, the petals often drooping down attractively. These make a rich display in the border and are also excellent for cutting, the seed-heads used in dried arrangements. Plants bloom over a long season, standing up well to summer heat and humidity. A favorite of butterflies! Native North American wildflower.

purpurea   ZONES 3–9

The most common garden species. In recent years breeders have developed more compact strains that bloom over a longer season. Flowers are available not only in the regular purple, but also in a handsome white form with an unusual greenish-brown cone. Very drought-tolerant.

> "…purple coneflower loves full sun and good drainage and is practically a weed if given these basic requirements. I highly recommend it for naturalization."
> – Dr. Virginia Hildebrandt, Zone 5

HEIGHT/SPREAD:	75–120cm (30–48")/45–60cm (18–24")
LOCATION:	Average well-drained soil.
BLOOMS:	July–September
USES:	✂🦋🕊 Borders, Meadows

'Magnus' A selected seed strain. The flower petals are reddish-purple and stick straight out, rather than drooping downwards. Compact habit. HEIGHT: 70cm (30"). Chosen as the 1998 Perennial Plant of the Year.

ECHINOPS
(Globe Thistle) ☼

ritro   ZONES 2–9

Globular, metallic-blue flowers are excellent for cutting, fresh or dried. Tall, thistly-looking plants are dramatic at the back of the border. Not invasive. May require staking in rich soils.

"Globe thistles…with their needle-studded flower balls poised on long stalks like so many vegetable maces, have a strong garden presence. Even when out of bloom, their great, toothed leaves, rich green backed with gray, rise powerfully amid shrubby looking peony foliage and grassy daylilies" – Ann Lovejoy, *The American Mixed Border*

HEIGHT/SPREAD: 90–120cm (3–4')/60cm (24")
LOCATION: Average to moist well-drained soil.
BLOOMS: June–September
USES: ✂ 🐝 Borders, Specimen.

'Vietch's Blue' Smaller flower heads, in a lighter blue shade.
HEIGHT: 120cm (4')

Epimedium × rubrum

EPIMEDIUM
(Barrenwort) ◐ ●

Hybrids　　　　　　　ZONES 4–9
Valued for their unusual semi-evergreen foliage. Leaves often become bronzy in cold weather. Superb as a slow-spreading groundcover for shady areas. Short sprays of starry flowers appear in spring, looking like tiny Columbines. Varieties are either clumping or spreading in habit, so choose according to the site requirements. Trim off any tired-looking foliage in early spring before the new growth begins. Slightly drought-tolerant.

HEIGHT/SPREAD: 20–30cm (8–12")/30cm (12")
LOCATION: Rich, moist woodland soil.
BLOOMS: April–May
USES: 🔺▲〰️🌿 Woodland garden, Borders

grandiflorum 'Lilafee' Very compact selection but vigorous. Leaves tinged purple at first, flowers are deep violet-purple. Deciduous.

× *perralchicum* 'Fröhnleiten' Compact variety. Bright yellow flowers, bronzy marbled foliage. Spreading habit. Evergreen.

pubigerum 'Orangekönigin' Evergreen. Pale orange flowers. Clumping habit.

× *rubrum* Smallish red flowers. Showy. Spreading habit. Deciduous.

"…a wonderful plant for all-season interest. Makes a thick clump. Good in damp shade with a multitude of airy red flowers in early spring, with red-edged leaves that turn bronzy-red in fall. Cut the old foliage down in March before the new growth starts." – Anna Leggatt, Zone 5

× *versicolor* 'Sulphureum' Light primrose-yellow flowers. Clumping habit. Deciduous.

× *youngianum* 'Niveum' Pure-white flowers. Clumping habit. Deciduous.

× *youngianum* 'Roseum' Lilac-rose flowers. Clumping habit. Deciduous.

EREMURUS
(Foxtail Lily) ☀
These tall spires of lily-like flowers are a spectacular sight. Since the foliage dies back at flowering time, it is a good idea to plant something of medium height at the base to hide the fact. Try these in a sunny, very well-drained location. Protect from late-spring frosts.

stenophyllus　　　　ZONES 5–9
A more reasonable height for the smaller garden. Flowers open dark yellow, fading to an attractive burnt orange, usually with multiple stems. Also good for cutting. Plants are long-lived and easier than the taller species.

HEIGHT/SPREAD: 90–150cm (3–5')/60cm (2')
LOCATION: Very well-drained soil.
BLOOMS: June–July
USES: ✂ Borders

ERIGERON
(Fleabane Daisy) ☀
Sprays of small daisies, quite similar to the fall-blooming Asters, but blooming through the summer months. Reliable, tough plants mostly for a sunny border or cutting garden.

compositus　　　　　ZONES 1–9
(Alpine Fleabane) An exception to the taller types, with compact silvery filigree foliage, and pale lavender-blue flowers. An easy little alpine native to the Rocky Mountains. Will self-seed into cracks and walls. Very drought-tolerant.

HEIGHT/SPREAD: 10cm (4")/10–15cm (4–6")
LOCATION: Needs a well-drained soil.
BLOOMS: April–June
USES: ▲🌿🌿 Troughs

Border Varieties　　　ZONES 2–9
Valuable cut flowers, good display of colour in the summer border. Divide clumps every 2–3 years or they will become woody. Inclined to be floppy if planted in too rich a soil. May need staking. Shear plants back after blooming to promote a second flush in the fall.

HEIGHT/SPREAD: 50–60cm (20–24")/30–60cm (12–24")
LOCATION: Average well-drained soil.
BLOOMS: June–August
USES: ✂ Borders, Cutting garden

× 'Pink Jewel' Bright pink to rose flowers. Compact.

× 'Prosperity' Large single lavender-blue flowers.

speciosus macranthus Deep lilac blue flowers.

ERODIUM
(Heronsbill) ☀
Closely related to the hardy Geraniums, these are long-flowering plants for the alpine garden or trough. Plants seem to resent wet winters, and are not always reliably hardy, but worth a little extra effort to grow as they are so showy. In colder areas these are well worth trying as annuals for their constant colour.

Epimedium × perralchicum 'Fröhnleiten'

Epimedium × youngianum 'Niveum'

Erigeron speciosus macranthus

Erodium × variable 'Bishop's Form'

Eryngium giganteum

Eryngium planum

Erysimum × 'Bowles Mauve'

Eupatorium rugosum 'Chocolate'

petraeum glandulosum　　　ZONES 4–9

(Fragrant Heronsbill) A tough species that seems to be reliably hardy over a wide area, especially if grown in a well-drained rock garden. Mats of olive-green ferny foliage and large orchid-like flowers, pale lavender with wine-purple markings. Blooms all season.

HEIGHT/SPREAD:　15–20cm (6–8")/30–45cm (12–18")
LOCATION:　　　Well-drained gravelly soil.
BLOOMS:　　　　May–September
USES:　　　　　△▽ Walls, Edging

× variabile　　　ZONES 7–9

(Dwarf Heronsbill) Like a miniature hardy *Geranium*, with a show of dainty flowers all season long. Forms a low clump. Excellent in a pot, indoors or out.

HEIGHT/SPREAD:　10cm (4")/15–30cm (6–12")
LOCATION:　　　Well-drained gravelly soil.
BLOOMS:　　　　May–September
USES:　　　　　△▲▽ Troughs, Edging

'Album' White flowers with a tiny pink stripe.
'Bishop's Form' Bright pink flowers, very cheery.

ERYNGIUM
(Sea Holly) ☼

Open umbels of steel-blue, prickly flowers are a favorite for cutting and drying. Tolerant of hot, dry sites and high salt soils. Attractive in the border and generally well-behaved. Most are very drought-tolerant.

> "Not everyone's cup of tea, Sea Holly's spiny nature is admittedly not an easy one to incorporate into the well-mannered border. So, don't use it there!! Plan to use Sea Holly and its kin in those surly and malicious borders designed to keep cats and small dogs at bay. As a bonus, cut them, dry them and use them in your favorite Halloween bouquets!"
> – Dr. Duncan Himmelman, Zone 3

amethystinum　　　ZONES 2–9

(Amethyst Sea Holly) Branching stems of small metallic-blue flowers in profusion. Nice filler plant. Drought tolerant.

HEIGHT/SPREAD:　75–90cm (30–36")/45cm (18")
LOCATION:　　　Poor to average well-drained soil.
BLOOMS:　　　　July–August
USES:　　　　　✂ 🎴 Dried Flower, Borders

giganteum　　　ZONES 4–9

(Miss Willmott's Ghost) Unique among Sea Hollies, this species has very large silvery-grey flower bracts, and is suberb for drying. Plants generally behave as self-seeding biennials. British plantswoman Ellen Willmott, it is said, used to secretly scatter seeds of this whenever she went visiting other people's gardens.

HEIGHT/SPREAD:　75–90cm (30–36")/30cm (12")
LOCATION:　　　Average well-drained soil.
BLOOMS:　　　　June–August
USES:　　　　　✂ 🎴 Dried Flower, Specimen, Borders

planum　　　ZONES 2–9

(Blue Sea Holly) One of the hardiest species, and a reliable long-lived plant for the border. Umbels of small steel-blue flowers are fine for drying. Will spread to form a small patch.

> "At last — a 'spoonful of sugar' for those orange Lilies you can't bear to uproot!!"
> – Kevin Ward, Zone 5

HEIGHT/SPREAD:　75–90cm (30–36")/30cm (12")
LOCATION:　　　Average well-drained soil.
BLOOMS:　　　　July–August
USES:　　　　　✂ 🎴 Dried Flower, Borders

yuccifolium　　　ZONES 4–9

(Rattlesnake Master) A species native to North America, and quite different from the other Sea Hollies listed. Evergreen leaves are arranged at the base like a yucca plant, with tall stems of creamy-green golf-ball shaped flowers. Very unusual for cutting.

> "The stiff, spiky rosettes of our native rattlesnake master…do indeed mimic gray-blue yuccas, though the flowers that open in small sprays above their four-foot stems look more like frosted white thistles than the open, creamy bells of true yuccas." – Ann Lovejoy,
> *The American Mixed Border*

HEIGHT/SPREAD:　90–120cm (3–4')/30cm (12")
LOCATION:　　　Average well-drained soil.
BLOOMS:　　　　July–September
USES:　　　　　✂ 🎴 Dried Flower, Specimen, Borders

ERYSIMUM
(Wallflower) ☼

Formerly listed as Cheiranthus. *Best known are the spring-blooming Wallflowers, often used for massing with bulbs. All types have sweetly-fragrant flowers.*

asperum　　　ZONES 3–9

(Siberian Wallflower) (formerly listed as *Cheiranthus allionii*) Often mass planted with tulips, these late-spring bloomers will hide that unsightly shriveling bulb foliage. Usually treated as a biennial, they will freely self-seed in a favorable location, especially in well-drained gravelly soils. The loose spikes of flowers are typically bright yellow or orange.

HEIGHT/SPREAD:　30–60cm (12–24")/20cm (8")
LOCATION:　　　Well-drained soil.
BLOOMS:　　　　May–July
USES:　　　　　✂ 🎴 Bedding, Naturalizing

× 'Bowles Mauve'　　　ZONES 6–9

Shrubby, upright plant, evergreen in milder regions. Handsome grey-green leaves nicely set off the profuse clusters of mauve flowers. This blooms over a long season, sometimes all winter at the West coast. Plants develop a woody base and should be sheared back to 15cm (6") in midsummer to promote fall flowering. In colder regions this performs well as a container plant.

HEIGHT/SPREAD:　60–75cm (24–30")/45cm (18")
LOCATION:　　　Well-drained soil.
BLOOMS:　　　　May–October
USES:　　　　　✂▼🎴 Specimen, Borders

linifolium 'Variegatum'　　　ZONES 7–9

Similar to the shrubby 'Bowle's Mauve' in habit, this variety is valued for its handsome cream and green variegated foliage. Flowers are mauve and brown. Best used as a container plant in most areas. Shear back to 15cm (6") in midsummer where hardy.

HEIGHT/SPREAD:　30–60cm (12–24")/30cm (12")
LOCATION:　　　Well-drained soil.
BLOOMS:　　　　May–October
USES:　　　　　✂▼🎴 Specimen, Borders

EUPATORIUM
(Boneset) ☼ ◐

With increasing frequency these hardy, reliable plants are showing up in perennial gardens from coast to coast. They can provide welcome colour and structure to late summer and fall schemes. Most are selections of native North American wildflowers.

cannabinum 'Plenum'   ZONES 3–9

(Hemp Agrimony) Loose heads of double mauve-purple flowers. Used in Europe as a long-lasting commercial cut-flower. Coarse bright-green fragrant foliage.

HEIGHT/SPREAD:	120cm (4')/60cm (2')
LOCATION:	Rich, moist to wet soil.
BLOOMS:	July–August
USES:	✄ 🦋 Borders

maculatum   ZONES 4–9

(Joe-Pye Weed) (Formerly listed as *E. purpureum*) Often described as an architectural plant. This forms a very large clump, with big umbrella-like heads of rosy-purple flowers in late summer and fall. Stems are purple in colour, with whorls of bold leaves. An excellent choice for a late-summer specimen plants! Butterflies love this.

> "I look forward as eagerly to the first appearance of Joe Pye Weed in early August as I do to the first snowdrop in late winter. It too is a harbinger, but a harbinger of fall." – Allen Lacy,
> *The Garden in Autumn*

> "The Joe Pye Weed, with its showy swags of violet blooms, will be happiest if you never let the soil dry out. It loves the sun, but needs daily drinks of water to avoid seasonal parchment 'burn-out' of the leaves." – Joan Nicks, Zone 6

HEIGHT/SPREAD:	2.1–3m (7–10')/90cm (3')
LOCATION:	Rich, moist to wet soil.
BLOOMS:	August–October
USES:	✄ 🦋 Specimen, Borders

'Atropurpureum' The classic form, with purple stems and dark rose-purple flowers.

'Gateway' A little more compact in habit, huge flower clusters. HEIGHT: 1.5–1.8m (5–6')

> "Leave it to the English to take one of our weeds and return it to us as an aristocrat. In late summer from stout dark purple stems emerge massive heads of pink flowers — a very dramatic focal point. Also makes a striking dried flower."
> – Larry Davidson, Zone 5

rugosum   ZONES 3–9

(Boneset, White Snakeroot) Quite unlike the taller purple Joe-Pye Weeds, this is a species of medium texture that forms a fairly large bushy mound. The clusters of pure white flowers look very much like annual ageratum. This is an easy border perennial, and the flowers are excellent for cutting. Tolerates dry shade.

HEIGHT/SPREAD:	90–120cm (3–4')/75cm (30")
LOCATION:	Moist to average well-drained soil.
BLOOMS:	August–September.
USES:	✄ 🦋 Borders

'Chocolate' Brand new selection with exceptionally dark bronze-purple foliage, later becoming dark green at flowering time. Blooms a little later than the species. An exciting discovery!

> "You eventually get an ice-cream headache from too much 'sweet' in the garden. You crave a touch of the sinister. This is a counterpoint never hostile to its garden comrades, but like a good dijon mustard, sets the visual buds up, quickened and renewed." – Val Ward, Zone 5

EUPHORBIA
(Spurge) ☀ ◐

This huge group of plants includes the well-known Poinsettia. These all have colourful flower heads (bracts) that sit on top of the foliage. Milky sap can irritate the skin. The varieties listed are not invasive.

> "One of the best of all structural plants. It combines especially well with low ornamental grasses (*E. amygdaloides* 'Purpurea' with *Hakonechloa macra* 'Aureola' is a knockout). Use them almost anywhere in the garden for a striking moment." – Marjorie Harris, Zone 5

amygdaloides   ZONES 5–9

(Wood Spurge) Upright stems with a reddish tinge, supporting clusters of greenish-yellow flowers in late spring, produced on the previous year's growth. Plants are somewhat woody and should not be pruned back in spring. Recommended as a groundcover for partial shade, especially among trees or shrubs. Evergreen in milder areas. Prune lightly after blooming. May seed around a little.

HEIGHT/SPREAD:	30–45cm (12–18")/60cm (24")
LOCATION:	Average well-drained soil.
BLOOMS:	May–June
USES:	✄ ⋀▲ Massing, Shady borders

'Purpurea' (Purple Wood Spurge) Sometimes listed as **'Rubra'**. Beautiful mounding purple foliage nicely against the flowers.

robbiae (Purple Wood Spurge) Large lime-green flower heads, leathery dark-green foliage. Highly recommended as a groundcover for dry shady sites. Can become invasive in the border. Not quite as hardy as **'Purpurea'**.

characias wulfenii   ZONES 7–9

(Evergreen Spurge) Very bushy, upright growing variety for mild winter areas. The stems are surrounded with leathery blue-green leaves that remain evergreen. Huge clusters of greenish-yellow flowers open in very early spring. A unique, bold sculptural plant best used as a specimen. Also can be grown in a cool greenhouse.

HEIGHT/SPREAD:	120–150cm (4–5')/90cm (3')
LOCATION:	Average well-drained soil.
BLOOMS:	March–May
USES:	▲✄ 🌿 Specimen, Borders

dulcis 'Chameleon'   ZONES 4–9

Absolutely stunning burgundy-purple foliage, with a low mounding habit. Flower clusters are greenish-yellow with a purplish flush. Leaves become maroon in the fall, with fiery highlights. Best in semi-shade. Combine this with something in silver!

HEIGHT/SPREAD:	30–45cm (12–18")/45–60cm (18–24")
LOCATION:	Average well-drained soil.
BLOOMS:	April–May
USES:	✄ 🌿 Edging, Specimen

griffithii   ZONES 2–9

These make a large shrub-like mound of green leaves. Flame-orange bracts are showy over a long period. Superb plant. Fall foliage colour is often a good red.

HEIGHT/SPREAD:	50–90cm (20–36")/60cm (24")
LOCATION:	Average well-drained soil.
BLOOMS:	May–August
USES:	✄ Borders, Massing

'Dixter' Newer selection, similar to **'Fireglow,'** the foliage is dark bronzy green.

'Fireglow' The original Alan Bloom selection, fiery orange flowers.

Euphorbia amygdaloides 'Purpurea'

Euphorbia amygdaloides robbiae

Euphorbia dulcis 'Chameleon'

Euphorbia griffithii 'Fireglow'

Filipendula 'Kakome'

Filipendula vulgaris 'Flore-Pleno'

Fragaria 'Pink Panda'

Fragaria vesca 'Yellow Wonder'

myrsinites   **ZONES 5–9**

(Donkey-tail Spurge) A succulent, evergreen species with large steel-blue leaves arranged around the stem. This trails and flops in all directions, the ends of the stems producing clusters of sulphur-yellow flowers in spring. A unique rockery or wall plant. Extremely heat and drought-tolerant.

HEIGHT/SPREAD:	15–20cm (6–8")/45cm (18")
LOCATION:	Average to very dry soil.
BLOOMS:	May–June
USES:	▲▽🐝🌿 Edging, Walls

polychroma   **ZONES 2–9**

(Cushion Spurge) (= *E. epithymoides*) Forms a perfect dome of pale green leaves, covered by bright, chrome-yellow flower bracts in late spring. An unusual cut-flower. Foliage turns red in fall. Extremely drought-tolerant.

HEIGHT/SPREAD:	30–45cm (12–18")/45cm (18")
LOCATION:	Average well-drained soil.
BLOOMS:	May–June
USES:	▲▽✂🌿 Borders, Massing

FALLOPIA
(Knotweed) ☼ ◐

japonica compacta   **ZONES 3–9**

(Japanese Fleeceflower — Formerly *Polygonum cuspidatum* 'Compactum') A spreading groundcover with fairly invasive tendencies, best used for extensive massed plantings around shrubs or trees, or in tubs where it can be contained. Plants form an upright bushy green clump, with attractive beet-red stems and short spikes of rose-red flowers that are half hidden among the leathery leaves, followed by crimson seedheads. Foliage often has excellent red fall colour. Keep this out of the border.

HEIGHT/SPREAD:	60cm (24")/60cm (24")
LOCATION:	Average to moist well-drained soil.
BLOOMS:	August–September
USES:	◗◕🐝 Shrub borders, Median plantings

FILIPENDULA
(Meadowsweet, Queen-of-the-Prairie) ☼ ◐

Mostly large, upright plants for moist to wet soils. Showy clusters of flowers are similar to Spirea. Foliage is jagged and bold.

'Kakome'   **ZONES 3–9**

(Dwarf Pink Meadowsweet) A new dwarf selection from Blooms of Bressingham. Fluffy heads of rosy-pink flowers are held above the dark green lobed leaves. Likes a moist or wet site.

HEIGHT/SPREAD:	20–30cm (8–12")/30cm (12")
LOCATION:	Rich moist to wet soil.
BLOOMS:	July–August
USES:	✂ Edging, Waterside

purpurea 'Elegans'   **ZONES 4–9**

(Japanese Meadowsweet) Fragrant white flowers with showy red stamens. Excellent background plant or specimen, nice at the waterside.

HEIGHT/SPREAD:	90–120cm (3–4')/60cm (2')
LOCATION:	Rich moist to wet soil.
BLOOMS:	July–August
USES:	✂ Specimen, Borders

rubra 'Venusta'   **ZONES 3–9**

(Martha Washington's Plume) Bold accent plant, forms a sturdy bush. Large panicles of deep pink flowers. One of the showiest perennials for moist sites. This is a selection of a native North American wildflower.

"A real gem for those of us blessed with a garden site that is both sunny and moist! Beautifully textured compound leaves are topped with a pageant of peachy pink panicles. Impressive!"
– Suzette McDonnell, Zone 6

"Bold, yes, and beautiful, even the leaves. Moist soil it must have to flower well. Grew to five feet in my garden and was spectacular." – Margaret Burke, Zone 6

HEIGHT/SPREAD:	120–180cm (4–6')/90–120cm (3–4')
LOCATION:	Rich moist to wet soil.
BLOOMS:	July–August
USES:	✂ Specimen, Borders

ulmaria   **ZONES 3–9**

(European Meadowsweet) A taller form with the usual ferny leaves, topped with fragrant clusters of creamy-white flowers in summer. The species itself is not often grown, but several interesting selections exist. These prefer average to moist soils, the coloured-leaf forms growing best in part shade, otherwise they are prone to sunburn and spider mites. Some gardeners prefer to remove the flower stems as they appear, to maintain the attractive leaves. 'Variegata' has dark-green leaves with a handsome creamy-yellow blotch in the centre.

HEIGHT/SPREAD:	75–120cm (30–48")/45cm (18")
LOCATION:	Average to moist soil.
BLOOMS:	June–July
USES:	✂ Borders, Woodland gardens

vulgaris 'Flore-Pleno'   **ZONES 2–9**

(Double Dropwort) Preferring average to drier soils, unlike its taller cousins. Forms a low rosette of finely-cut ferny leaves that radiate out in a perfect circle. Long-lasting pure white flowers. Nice edging plant for the border.

HEIGHT/SPREAD:	30–45cm (12–18")/30cm (12")
LOCATION:	Average well-drained soil.
BLOOMS:	May–July
USES:	▲▽✂ Borders, Edging

FRAGARIA
(Strawberry) ☼ ◐

Garden strawberries, grown for their large fruit, are well known across the world. There are also a few unique forms that are grown primarily for their ornamental features. They adapt well to average garden conditions, and most are tolerant of part shade.

chiloensis 'Variegata'   **ZONES 3–9**

(formerly listed as *F. virginiana* 'Variegata') Unusual and showy deep green foliage, strongly variegated with creamy white. White flowers and small red fruit may be produced, but don't count on making jam. This variety will send out runners, but is not nearly as vigorous as 'Pink Panda'. Best in the rock garden or woodland.

HEIGHT/SPREAD:	10–15cm (4–6")/30cm (12")
LOCATION:	Moist, well-drained soil.
BLOOMS:	May–June
USES:	▲◗🐝 Woodland garden

✕ Hybrids   **ZONES 2–9**

A unique new group with large bright pink flowers that appear almost all season long. Ideal for edging or planting as a groundcover, also excellent in containers and hanging baskets. Tasty bright red fruits are of medium size. Plants send out lots of runners, spreading quickly just like any normal garden strawberry. Fairly shade-tolerant.

HEIGHT/SPREAD:	15cm (6")/30cm (12")
LOCATION:	Average to moist well-drained soil.
BLOOMS:	May–September
USES:	⚘△◈☀ Edible fruit. Hanging baskets

('Frel') Pink Panda The original pink strawberry! Large flowers in a beautiful rose-pink shade.

'Lipstick' New darker-flowered selection, more of a cherry red.

vesca   ZONES 2–9
(Alpine Strawberry) Runnerless, small-fruited strawberry. An everbearing type, with an excellent wild-strawberry flavour. Fruit and white flowers are also ornamental. Makes a unique edging.

HEIGHT/SPREAD:	15–25cm (6–10")/30cm (12")
LOCATION:	Average to moist soil.
BLOOMS:	May–October
USES:	△☀ Edible fruit, Edging

'Improved Rügen' The classic red-fruited European strain.

'Yellow Wonder' Bizarre creamy-white fruit. Unique and tasty!

FUCHSIA
(Fuchsia) ☼ ☾ ●

magellanica   ZONES 6–9
(Hardy Fuchsia) Truly a woody shrub, these associate well with perennials in the border, and benefit from a hard clipping back in early spring. Plants form an upright bush and bear many dangling tubular flowers, crimson with a purple centre. More delicate in appearance than the fancy hanging-basket types, but with a tougher constitution. Often winters in Zone 6 with a mulch.

HEIGHT/SPREAD:	60–120cm (2–4')/60–90cm (2–3')
LOCATION:	Prefers a rich, moist soil.
BLOOMS:	June–October
USES:	△☀ Borders, Containers

GAILLARDIA
(Blanket Flower) ☼

× grandiflora   ZONES 2–9
Brightly-coloured daisy flowers, often with a contrasting central eye. These are long blooming, excellent for cutting. Good choice for hot, dry areas, very drought-tolerant. Does well in containers. Cut back hard in early September; this forces new leaf growth and prevents plants from blooming to death.

SPREAD:	30cm (12")
LOCATION:	Well-drained soil.
BLOOMS:	June–September
USES:	✄☀✿❀ Borders, Meadows

'Burgundy' Deep wine-red flowers. HEIGHT: 60–90cm (2–3')

'Dwarf Goblin' Red petals with yellow tips. Compact habit. HEIGHT: 30cm (12")

'Golden Goblin' Solid yellow flowers. HEIGHT: 30cm (12")

'Mandarin' New selection from Blooms of Bressingham. Deep flame-orange petals with a touch of gold at the tips HEIGHT: 60cm (23")

'Monarch Strain' Mixed colours, yellow, orange, and red. A superb cutting strain. HEIGHT: 60–90cm (2–3')

GALIUM
(Sweet Woodruff) ☾ ●

odoratum   ZONES 3–9
(formerly *Asperula odorata*) Attractive, whorled green leaves set off the clusters of starry white flowers. Excellent fast-spreading groundcover, best in shady moist locations but will usually tolerate drier conditions under trees. Evergreen in mild climates.

Useful for planting over spring-blooming bulbs. Spreads quickly, but not terribly invasive. (See also under HERBS.)

> "The pretty little woodruff is in flower; what scent is so delicate as that of its leaves? They are almost sweeter when dried…it is a pleasant surprise to come upon these fragrant little stars between the leaves of a book." – Gertrude Jekyll, *Wood and Garden*

> "Why plant dark old vinca in the shade, when you could plant sweet woodruff? Sweet Woodruff is a lighter green and smells divine when you step on it. Northern Europeans may be reminded of their grandmothers by the fragrance, as I am. The dainty white flowers complement forget-me-nots gracefully."
> – Peggy Walsh Craig, Zone 3

HEIGHT/SPREAD:	10–20cm (4–8")/30–45cm (12–18")
LOCATION:	Average to moist soil.
BLOOMS:	April–May
USES:	◈▲☀ Woodland gardens

GAURA
(Gaura) ☼ ☾

lindheimeri   ZONES 5–9
(Butterfly Gaura) A North American wild-flower, only recently introduced into perennial borders. Plants bloom for many weeks, with loose sprays of white flowers, tinged with very light pink. In the breeze these move constantly, looking like a cloud of small butterflies. Trim plants lightly after their first flush of bloom is over. An interesting new cut flower. Very drought and heat tolerant. Plants may be short-lived in wet areas. A winter mulch is recommended in Zones 5–6. The straight species itself seeds freely, and even if the parent plants die out, new plants will often appear from seed and flower the same year.

> "Gaura is a fine plant to use as a "scrim." The term is borrowed from the theater, where it means a gauze curtain through which action on stage may be seen, but as if through a mist."
> – Allen Lacy, *The Garden in Autumn*

HEIGHT/SPREAD:	90–120cm (3–4')/60–90cm (2–3')
LOCATION:	Average well-drained soil.
BLOOMS:	June–September
USES:	✄✿ Borders, Meadows

'Corrie's Gold' Outstanding new variegated selection! Mid-green leaves are blotched with creamy-yellow. Flowers are white with a pale pink flush. Must be propagated by cuttings or division. HEIGHT: 60–90cm (2–3')

'Siskiyou Pink' Exciting new form with deep pink blossoms.

'Whirling Butterflies' A more compact selection, reported to be sterile and therefore flowers for a longer season. Must be propagated by cuttings or division. HEIGHT: 60–90cm (2–3')

GENTIANA
(Gentian) ☼ ☾

Best known are the dwarf, alpine varieties, with their bluer-than-blue trumpet-shaped flowers. This is a large group of plants; many of the taller species also are useful in the perennial garden, and are generally a lot easier to grow.

Gaillardia × grandiflora 'Dwarf Goblin'

Gaillardia × grandiflora 'Monarch Strain'

Gaura lindheimeri 'Whirling Butterflies'

Gentiana septemfida

Geranium 'Ann Folkard'

Geranium × *cantabrigiense* 'Biokovo'

Geranium dalmaticum

Geranium cinereum 'Ballerina'

septemfida   ZONES 2–9

(Every-man's Gentian) One of the easier Gentians, this species is a reasonable substitute if you can't seem to succeed with the alpine types. Plants form a sizable clump and are nice along the front of a border. Flowers are a good true blue, blooming in summer.

> "It is a beguiling little wonder at the front of the border, smothered for a long period in up-facing rich cobalt blooms — so exotic-looking yet so undemanding."
> – Cathy Forgie, Zone 4

HEIGHT/SPREAD: 15–20cm (6–8")/30–60cm (1–2')
LOCATION: Well-drained, humusy soil.
BLOOMS: July–September
USES: ◭ Edging, Walls, Slopes

GERANIUM
(Cranesbill) ☼ ☀

These are hardy relatives of the annual Geraniums (known botanically as Pelargoniums) that are so commonly used for summer bedding and window boxes. Cranesbills come in a wide range of heights, forms and colours, to suit most garden purposes, but for the convenience of designers they are indicated below as either alpine (short) or border (medium to tall) varieties.

All have similar divided or lobed leaves, forming a mound or mat of foliage. Cup-shaped or star-like flowers generally appear in early summer. Some types take on brilliant red foliage colouring in the fall.

'Ann Folkard'   ZONES 4–9

Alpine or Border type. Unusual chartreuse yellow foliage, contrasting against a display of magenta-purple flowers. Long-blooming hybrid. This is inclined to burn in full sun. Use this variety to weave in among other plants near the front of the border.

HEIGHT/SPREAD: 20–30cm (8–12")/30–60cm (12–24")
LOCATION: Average well-drained soil.
BLOOMS: June–August
USES: ◭∧⩊ Edging, Borders, Massing

'Brookside'   ZONES 4–9

Border type. Clumps of lacy green leaves, bearing large cup-shaped clear violet-blue flowers with a cream eye. A newer hybrid first discovered in England.

HEIGHT/SPREAD: 45–60cm (12–18")/60cm (24")
LOCATION: Average well-drained soil.
BLOOMS: June–July
USES: Borders, Massing

× cantabrigiense   ZONES 4–9

Alpine or Border type. This is a low-growing plant with trailing stems and glossy green, fragrant foliage. Flowers are sterile, and will repeat bloom for most of the summer. Shows much promise as a new groundcover plant. There are two colour forms.

HEIGHT/SPREAD: 20–30cm (8–12")/30cm (12")
LOCATION: Average well-drained soil.
BLOOMS: May–August
USES: ◭∧⩊ Edging, Borders, Massing

'Biokovo' A natural hybrid selection recently discovered growing wild in Yugoslavia. Large, showy, off-white flowers with a flush of pink in the middle.

'Cambridge' Bred at Cambridge University, bright pink showy flowers.

cinereum   ZONES 5–9

Alpine type. Dense, low mounds of foliage, with large flowers resting on the trailing stems all summer long.

Excellent in the rock garden, especially among dwarf conifers. The varieties listed have good vigour, preferring a gravelly soil, especially in areas with winter wet.

HEIGHT/SPREAD: 10–15cm (4–6")/30cm (12")
LOCATION: Very well-drained soil.
BLOOMS: May–September
USES: ◭∧⩊ Scree, Troughs

'Ballerina' Purplish-pink flowers with exotic dark veins and centre. Greyish leaves. A Bressingham Gardens selection.

Geranium cinereum 'Guiseppii'

'Guiseppii' Crimson-magenta flowers. Greyish foliage. Especially vigorous.

'Laurence Flatman' Deep pink flowers with dark crimson veining. Green leaves. From Blooms of Bressingham.

'Splendens' Dayglo magenta flowers with a dark eye.

clarkei 'Kashmir White'   ZONES 4–9

(Clarke's Cranesbill) Border type. Deeply-cut green foliage forms a low mound. Large cup-shaped white flowers have darker lilac veins, giving a luminescent effect. An excellent white form for general border use.

HEIGHT/SPREAD: 30–45cm (12–18")/45cm (18")
LOCATION: Average to moist well-drained soil.
BLOOMS: June–August
USES: Borders, Woodland gardens

dalmaticum   ZONES 3–9

(Dalmatian Cranesbill) Alpine type. Forms a low, glossy green cushion covered with clear shell-pink flowers. One of the best varieties. Good red fall colour.

HEIGHT/SPREAD: 10cm (4")/30cm (12")
LOCATION: Prefers a well-drained soil.
BLOOMS: May–July
USES: ◭∧⩊ Troughs, Scree, Walls

endressii   ZONES 3–9

Border type. Vigorous, dense mounds of shiny evergreen leaves, showy bright pink flowers in summer. Excellent groundcover. May need a hard clipping in midsummer.

HEIGHT/SPREAD: 30–45cm (12–18")/30–60cm (12–24")
LOCATION: Average well-drained soil.
BLOOMS: June–August
USES: ∧⩊ Borders, Edging

himalayense   ZONES 2–9

Border type. Mounding clumps of bold leaves and very large, deep violet blue flowers with a reddish-pink cast. Red foliage in fall.

HEIGHT/SPREAD: 30–45cm (12–18")/60cm (24")
LOCATION: Average well-drained soil.
BLOOMS: June–July
USES: Borders, Woodland gardens

'Plenum' (a.k.a. 'Birch Double') Fully double, lavender-violet flowers, tinged with pink. Long blooming and sterile. Not as vigorous.

× **'Johnson's Blue'**   **ZONES 2–9**
Border type. Most popular of all the blue selections. Large, lavender-blue flowers with a tinge of reddish-pink in midsummer. Sterile flowers, good vigorous habit.

HEIGHT/SPREAD:	30–60cm (12–24")/60cm (24")
LOCATION:	Average well-drained soil.
BLOOMS:	June–August
USES:	Borders, Massing

macrorrhizum   **ZONES 2–9**
(Bigroot Cranesbill) Border type. Extremely fragrant leaves form a dense, vigorous groundcover. Magenta pink flowers appear in early summer. Heat tolerant. This is the best species of Geranium for large groundcover plantings in sun or shade, even succeeding in the dry shade under trees. Good fall foliage colour. Several selections exist.

HEIGHT/SPREAD:	30cm (12")/60cm (24")
LOCATION:	Average well-drained soil.
BLOOMS:	June–July
USES:	⋀⋁ Borders, Massing

'Bevan's Variety' Deep magenta-pink flowers, bright and cheery. Selection from Blooms of Bressingham.

'Ingwersen's Variety' The most widely-grown form. Pale candy-floss pink flowers, light green foliage.

maculatum 'Chatto'   **ZONES 4–9**
(Spotted Cranesbill) Border type. Vigorous selection for late spring colour, with deeply divided green leaves. Pale lilac-pink flowers.

HEIGHT/SPREAD:	60–70cm (24–28")/60cm (24")
LOCATION:	Average to moist well-drained soil.
BLOOMS:	May–June
USES:	Borders, Massing

× **magnificum**   **ZONES 2–9**
(Showy Cranesbill) Border type. Abundant display of large violet-blue flowers with darker veins. Attractive divided green leaves with good red fall colour. Sterile.

HEIGHT/SPREAD:	45–60cm (18–24")/60cm (24")
LOCATION:	Average to moist well-drained soil.
BLOOMS:	June–July
USES:	Borders, Massing

oxonianum   **ZONES 3–9**
Border type. Broad mounds of glossy green leaves. Flowers are in various shades of pink with darker veins. These are vigorous selections, excellent for using on a large scale as a weed-proof groundcover or for mingling among other perennials towards the front of a border.

HEIGHT/SPREAD:	45–60cm (18–24")/60cm (24")
LOCATION:	Average to moist well-drained soil.
BLOOMS:	June–September
USES:	⋀▲ Borders, Massing

'A.T. Johnson' Bright pink flowers all season long. Good filler plant.

'Bressingham Delight' Lovely soft-pink flowers all summer. Selected by Blooms of Bressingham.

'Claridge Druce' Darker pink flowers, long-blooming.

phaeum   **ZONES 5–9**
(Mourning Widow) Border type. Unique dark maroon-purple nodding flowers, finely divided leaves. Good choice for moist shady areas, reported to also tolerate deep dry shade.

HEIGHT/SPREAD:	45–60cm (18–24")/60cm (24")
LOCATION:	Average to moist well-drained soil.
BLOOMS:	May–July
USES:	Borders, Massing

'Album' Large clear-white flowers.

'Lily Lovell' Beautiful violet-mauve flowers, light green leaves.

pratense   **ZONES 3–9**
(Meadow Cranesbill) Border type. Good show of large violet-blue flowers in early summer. Deadhead after blooming and plants may flower a second time. Has a tendency to self-seed.

HEIGHT/SPREAD:	60–90cm (2–6')/60cm (24")
LOCATION:	Average to moist well-drained soil.
BLOOMS:	May–June
USES:	Borders, Massing

psilostemon   **ZONES 4–9**
(Armenian Cranesbill) (= *G. armenum*) One of the tallest Cranesbills, this plant will be a focal point in the border when its black-centred, magenta flowers appear in early summer. Leaves are very large and deeply cut, with good red fall colour. Plants may require a little extra support and should be placed out of the wind.

> "Grow near *Gladiolus byzantinus* and tall shrub roses with similar flower colors."
> – Penelope Hobhouse,
> *Colour in Your Garden*

HEIGHT/SPREAD:	90–120cm (3–4')/90cm (3')
LOCATION:	Prefers a rich, moist soil.
BLOOMS:	June–August
USES:	Borders

'Bressingham Flair' Softer shade of rose-pink, not quite as brazen in the border. Selected by Blooms of Bressingham.

renardii   **ZONES 4–9**
Border or Alpine type. This species has quite unique foliage, sage green in colour with a bumpy puckered texture. Flowers are in clusters, white with bold stripes of violet purple. A little trickier to grow than some Cranesbills, with a need for excellent drainage and lean soil.

HEIGHT/SPREAD:	30cm (12")/30cm (12")
LOCATION:	Needs a very well-drained soil.
BLOOMS:	May–June
USES:	▲ Edging

sanguineum   **ZONES 3–9**
(Bloody Cranesbill) Border type. Low, spreading mat of finely-cut leaves. Flowers are a very showy, bright magenta-pink. Useful little groundcover or edging plant. Moderately drought-tolerant. HEIGHT: 30cm (12"). There are several selections.

SPREAD:	30cm (12")
LOCATION:	Average to moist well-drained soil.
BLOOMS:	June–August
USES:	▲⋀⋁ Borders, Massing

'Alan Bloom' New selection from Blooms of Bressingham. Long-blooming, bright pink flowers with subtle stripes. HEIGHT: 30cm (12")

'Album' Clear white flowers, loose habit. HEIGHT: 30–45cm (12–18")

'John Elsley' Low, trailing habit, bright pink flowers. New selection from Blooms of Bressingham. HEIGHT: 10–15cm (4–6")

'New Hampshire Purple' Deep magenta-purple flowers HEIGHT: 15–30cm (6–12")

striatum (= 'Lancastriense') Alpine type. Pale blush-pink flowers with dark crimson veins. One of the best! HEIGHT 10–15cm (4–6")

sylvaticum   **ZONES 4–9**
(Wood Cranesbill) Border type. Good in woodland conditions. Forms a broad clump of divided leaves, with upfacing cupped flowers. One of the earliest to bloom. Trim back foliage to 10cm (4") after flowering.

Geranium × 'Johnson's Blue'

Geranium × *magnificum*

Geranium psilostemon

Geranium sanguineum striatum

Geranium sylvaticum 'Album'

Geranium sylvaticum 'Mayflower'

Gypsophila paniculata

Goniolimon tataricum

HEIGHT/SPREAD: 45–60cm (18–24")/60cm (24")
LOCATION: Average to moist well-drained soil.
BLOOMS: May–June
USES: Borders, Woodland gardens

'Album' Large white flowers. Excellent.

'Mayflower' Violet-blue with a white eye.

'Silva' Bright pink with dark green leaves.

wlassovianum   ZONES 4–9

(Siberian Cranesbill) Border type. Interesting edging type, the foliage is velvety green with brown markings. Leaves develop good red and bronze tones in late summer and fall. Flowers are dark violet purple.

HEIGHT/SPREAD: 30cm (12")/30cm (12")
LOCATION: Needs a very well-drained soil.
BLOOMS: June–July
USES: Edging, Borders

GEUM
(Avens) ☼ ◑

These bright and cheerful perennials are always popular in the sunny border, and are valued for their long season of bloom. Branching stems of flowers rise up from a bushy clump of hairy leaves. Good for cutting. Protect from hot afternoon sun.

chiloense   ZONES 5–9

Well-branched stems of flowers are valuable for cutting. Nice filler plant in the summer border. These tend to be short-lived selections and also are not reliably hardy in all winters, but perform very well even if grown as annuals.

HEIGHT/SPREAD: 60–75cm (24–30")/30cm (12")
LOCATION: Well-drained soil. Dislikes winter wet.
BLOOMS: May–September
USES: ✂ Borders, Massing

'Lady Stratheden' Golden-yellow double flowers.

'Mrs. Bradshaw' Orange-red double flowers.

coccineum 'Borisii'   ZONES 2–9

(Dwarf Orange Geum) Bright orange, single flowers in late spring, often reblooming in fall. Compact tidy plants are very hardy and reliable. Clip off flower stems after blooming. This is an excellent low-maintenance plant and is grossly under-used. Evergreen foliage.

HEIGHT/SPREAD: 30cm (12")/30cm (12")
LOCATION: Prefers a rich, moist soil.
BLOOMS: May–July
USES: △✂▲ Borders, Edging

GILLENIA
(Bowman's Root) ◑

trifoliata   ZONES 4–9

Relatively unknown North American wildflower, useful in moist woodland situations. Low clumps of divided foliage are produced at the base, giving rise to tall branching stems of white star-like flowers that are held in wine-red cups or sepals. A delicate and airy-looking display.

HEIGHT/SPREAD: 60–120cm (2–4')/75cm (30")
LOCATION: Rich, moist woodland soil.
BLOOMS: July–August
USES: ✂ Borders, Woodland garden

GONIOLIMON
(German Statice, Dumosa) ☼

tataricum   ZONES 2–9

(formerly listed as *Statice*) Silvery-white flowers in a prickly, rounded panicle. Used mainly for cutting and drying, but also interesting as an edging plant. Prefers a hot sunny site. Excellent for drying.

HEIGHT/SPREAD: 25–40cm (10–16")/30cm (12")
LOCATION: Well-drained soil. Dislikes winter wet.
BLOOMS: July–August
USES: ✂ Edging, Borders

GUNNERA
(Gunnera) ☼ ◑

manicata   ZONES 7–9

(Giant Gunnera) Enormous rhubarb-like leaves rise from the ground on thick thorny stalks. Often seen in large gardens and parks at the West Coast. Bold feature plant for the waterside. Flowers appear in midsummer as bizarre bristly cones almost hidden at the base. In colder areas plants can be brought through the winter by covering with a very deep mulch piled inside a four-foot square wooden box in late fall.

HEIGHT/SPREAD: 1.8–3m (6–10')/1.8m (6')
LOCATION: Rich moist or wet soil.
BLOOMS: July–August
USES: Waterside specimen

GYPSOPHILA
(Baby's Breath) ☼

These all have the familiar misty clouds of flowers, but come in a variety of sizes and colours. They flower best in cool-summer areas, but are fairly carefree.

cerastioides   ZONES 4–9

(Alpine Baby's Breath) Well-behaved low species that is nice in the rockery or for edging. Makes a low mat of grey-green leaves with short-stemmed white or light-pink flowers in early summer.

HEIGHT/SPREAD: 10–15cm (4–6")/30–45cm (12–18")
LOCATION: Well-drained soil. Heat tolerant.
BLOOMS: June–July
USES: △⋀▼✂ Walls, Slopes, Edging

paniculata   ZONES 2–9

Widely grown cut flower, used by florists fresh or dried. Works well to fill gaps left by summer-dormant plants such as Bleeding Hearts or Oriental Poppies. Clumps resent being moved once established. They dislike winter wet.

In Manitoba this species has been placed on the bad list as a nuisance weed; mature plants can act as a tumbleweed and infest pasture land. However, this is highly unlikely to happen in an enclosed garden area. Double-flowered varieties rarely set seed.

> "If you want gypsophila to cover the bare places left by spring bulbs or vanishing Oriental poppies, a few strategically placed twiggy branches will guide the stems where they are needed."
> – Patrick Lima,
> *The Harrowsmith Perennial Garden*

SPREAD:	60–90cm (2–3′)
LOCATION:	Average well-drained soil.
BLOOMS:	June–September
USES:	✄ Dried Flower, Borders

'Alba' Single white flowers, very hardy. Grown from seed. HEIGHT: 90cm (36″)

'Bristol Fairy' Double white flowers, the best type for cutting. HEIGHT: 60–90cm (24–36″). Zones 4–9.

'Pink Fairy' Large, double light-pink flowers. Compact habit. HEIGHT: 30–45cm (12–18″). Zones 2–9.

repens   ZONES 2–9

(Creeping Baby's Breath) Low, creeping plants suitable for edging or rock gardens. Mats are smothered with flowers in early summer. Not invasive or weedy in any way. Moderately drought-tolerant.

'Alba' Pure white single flowers.

'Rosea' Light pink single flowers.

HEIGHT/SPREAD:	10–15cm (4–6″)/45–60cm (18–24″)
LOCATION:	Well-drained soil. Heat tolerant.
BLOOMS:	May–July
USES:	⚺⋀⋁☂ Walls, Slopes, Edging

HEBE
(Hebe, Shrubby Veronica) ☼ ◑

'Margret'   ZONES 8–9

A terrific new introduction from Blooms of Bressingham, growing especially well at the West coast. Plants form a low evergreen bush, with showy pointed spikes of bright blue flowers that fade to white as they age. Blooms all summer long. In colder regions this is worth a try in containers and window boxes, treated as an annual.

HEIGHT/SPREAD:	30–45cm (12–18″)/45–60cm (18–24″)
LOCATION:	Average to moist well-drained soil.
BLOOMS:	June–September
USES:	⚺⋀⋁☂ Borders, Edging

HEDYOTIS
See HOUSTONIA.

Helianthemum 'Firedragon'

HELENIUM
(Sneezeweed, Helen's Flower) ☼

Although relatively unknown in North America, these are valuable perennials for a late display of bright daisy-type flowers, and are also excellent for cutting. Widely grown in European gardens and commercially as a cut flower. Pinch plants back by half in early June to encourage bushiness. Staking may be required. These garden forms are descendants of native North American wildflowers.

autumnale Hybrids   ZONES 3–9

(Fall Helenium) Reliable performers for the late summer border. Large clusters of flowers are held on tall stems for an impressive background display. These are water-hogs, so give plenty of moisture in the summer. There are many named selections.

HEIGHT/SPREAD:	90–120cm (3–4′)/45–60cm (18–24″)
LOCATION:	Average to moist well-drained soil.
BLOOMS:	July–September
USES:	✄ ☙ Borders, Massing

'Bruno' Crimson-mahogany flowers. Late-blooming. Bred by Alan Bloom of Bressingham Gardens. 120cm (4′).

'Butterpat' Pure yellow flowers, tall and late-blooming. From Blooms of Bressingham.

'Coppelia' Another Blooms of Bressingham selection, with bright coppery-orange flowers.

'Flammenspiel' A new European selection with golden-orange flowers. Tall

'Red and Gold' Seed strain with a mixture of shades, including yellow, orange, red, and gold.

hoopesii   ZONES 2–9

(Orange Helenium) Bright yellow daisies with orange centres. Foliage is grey-green, glossy. Compact and early blooming.

HEIGHT/SPREAD:	60–90cm (2–3′)/45cm (18″)
LOCATION:	Average to moist well-drained soil.
BLOOMS:	June–August
USES:	✄ ☙ Borders, Meadows

HELIANTHEMUM
(Rock Rose, Sun Rose) ☼

Hybrids   ZONES 4–9

Versatile evergreen creepers, forming a low spreading mat of green or silvery-grey leaves. Flowers are like small roses, blooming over the summer months. Excellent choice for edging, rock gardens and walls, or in containers. Some varieties may survive to Zone 2 with adequate protection. These all require very good drainage to prevent rotting out in wet winters. Shear plants lightly after the first flush of bloom is over. Moderately drought-tolerant.

HEIGHT/SPREAD:	10–30cm (4–12″)/60cm (24″)
LOCATION:	Well-drained soil. Dislikes winter wet.
BLOOMS:	June–September
USES:	⚺⋀⋁☂ Walls, Slopes

'Annabel' Double, soft-pink flowers. Bushy form, green foliage.

'Double Apricot' Butterscotch flowers, an interesting peachy-orange shade, green leaves.

'Fireball' Double red flowers, green leaves.

'Firedragon' Single flame-orange flowers, excellent contrasting grey foliage.

'Henfield Brilliant' Large orange-red single flowers, grey foliage.

'Raspberry Ripple' Single crimson to rose with white streaks, upright grey foliage.

'Single Yellow' Large flowers, green leaves. Very vigorous and hardy.

'The Bride' Large single white flowers with a golden eye, silvery foliage.

'Wisley Pink' Large, single soft-pink flowers, grey leaves. Outstanding!

'Wisley Primrose' Pale yellow blooms over silvery-grey foliage.

Helenium 'Coppelia'

Helenium 'Butterpat'

Helianthemum 'Annabel'

Helianthemum 'Single Yellow'

Heliopsis helianthoides 'Loraine Sunshine'

Helleborus 'Atrorubens'

Helleborus niger

Helleborus orientalis

HELIANTHUS
(Sunflower) ☼

Hardy perennial relatives of the annual bird-seed and snack-food varieties. The varieties listed are happiest in a moist sunny location where they will form sizable non-invasive clumps. All are excellent for cutting.

decapetalus 'Plenus'   ZONES 4–9

Fully double golden-yellow daisy flowers, making an appearance from mid-summer on. Plants are upright and bushy, although staking may be necessary if soils are rich. These need a good moist site or powdery mildew may become a problem on the leaves.

> "…makes a fine background for white phlox and lingers long enough to flower alongside lavender-coloured hardy asters."
> – Patrick Lima,
> *The Harrowsmith Perennial Garden*

HEIGHT/SPREAD:	1.5m (5')/60–90cm (2–3")
LOCATION:	Prefers a rich moist soil.
BLOOMS:	August–September
USES:	✄ Borders, Meadows

salicifolius   ZONES 4–9

(Willow-leaf Sunflower) A most unique back-of-the-border subject that has been described as a giant asparagus fern. Stems are clothed in drooping, willowy leaves, with an almost tropical appearance. Single yellow daisies appear at the top in late fall and have a charm of their own. An interesting texture plant. Native North American wildflower.

> "This deceives people into thinking it a lily, while its mop-like growing point puts you in mind of a giant papyrus. Whatever it does or does not resemble, this is a most exciting and imposing plant."
> – Christopher Lloyd, *Foliage Plants*

HEIGHT/SPREAD:	180–240cm (6–8')/60cm (2')
LOCATION:	Prefers a rich moist soil.
BLOOMS:	September–October
USES:	✄ Specimen, Borders

'Compact form' Possibly a selection of *H. salicifolius* that is about half the height, with a nice display of yellow daisies with a green centre. Not sure yet what the correct name is for this one, but well worth growing in a sunny border.
HEIGHT: 90–120cm (3–4') SPREAD: 90cm (3')

HELIOPSIS
(False Sunflower) ☼

helianthoides   ZONES 2–9

The longest flowering of the tall daisy-flowered perennials, with large single or double golden daisies that bloom in succession over several months. Strong, sturdy stems are excellent for cutting. Terrific background plant for summer and fall colour. Reliable and long-lived. This is a selection from a native North American wildflower.

HEIGHT/SPREAD:	90–120cm (3–4')/45–60cm (18–24")
LOCATION:	Average well-drained soil.
BLOOMS:	June–October
USES:	✄ Borders, Massing

'Loraine Sunshine' New selection from Blooms of Bressingham. Outstanding for its variegated foliage, creamy-white with dark green veins. Large golden-yellow daisies. HEIGHT: 75cm (30")

'Midwest Dreams' A seed-grown mixture of yellow and orange shades, with large single daisies.

'Summer Sun' Semi-double golden daisies. A classic.

HELLEBORUS
(Hellebore) ◐ ●

Much sought-after by perennial enthusiasts everywhere, and almost always in short supply. These are invaluable for their mid-winter or early spring display of nodding, cup-shaped flowers. Although they grow best in Zones 6–9, Hellebores are worth a try in colder regions, where the blooming season will be delayed until March or April. A winter mulch of loose leaves or straw is not a bad idea in cold areas.

The different species all require moisture early in the year during their flowering period, but later in the year will tolerate moderate summer drought. Also in common, all species hate being disturbed once they are established; plants will sulk for six months or so just to let you know how unhappy they are. Starting with nursery-grown container plants should produce excellent results. You may even find that your own plants will self-seed!

> "Forget crocus and winter aconite as harbingers of Spring; my favorites are the Helleborus. Both *niger* and *orientalis* do well near Guelph. In late fall I provide a thick mulch of leaves, which are moved about March/April. I love the sturdy cup-shaped flowers and often look at them to remind myself that better weather is coming."
> – Dr. Virginia Hildebrandt, Zone 5

argutifolius   ZONES 6–9

(Corsican Hellebore) (= *H. corsicus*) A unique, apple-green flowered species. Forms an outstanding clump of grey-green, leathery foliage, coarsely toothed along the edges. More sun-tolerant than some of the other types. Do not trim until after flowering, if required.

HEIGHT/SPREAD:	45–60cm (18–24")/60cm (24")
LOCATION:	Well-drained loamy soil.
BLOOMS:	March–May
USES:	▲△♣✄ Specimen, Borders

'Atrorubens'   ZONES 5–9

(Purple Hellebore) A stunning plant when in flower, the blooms are deep maroon-purple, flowering in between the Christmas and Lenten Rose. Closely related to *H. orientalis*, it may benefit from trimming off the old foliage in late winter, just before blooming.

> "Something about hellebores suggests nostalgia. The rare 'Atrorubens', with its distinct mulled wine with pale green blooms, evokes the same sentiment as do fine handcrafted antiques — a very personal sense of deja vu; a familiarity of something you have never seen before. Place them in a natural-looking setting, but where they cannot be missed — they are invaluable for one of those throwaway 'Oh, that's just the Helleborus' kinds of lines!" – Val Ward, Zone 5

HEIGHT/SPREAD:	30–40cm (12–16")/30cm (12")
LOCATION:	Well-drained loamy soil.
BLOOMS:	February–May
USES:	▲△♣✄ Borders, Specimen

niger   ZONES 4–9

(Christmas Rose) This species is the one most well-known. Plants form a sturdy clump of leathery, evergreen leaves, not unlike a dwarf peony in appearance. Flowers are large and cup-shaped, pure white or sometimes tinged with pinkish green, appearing anytime from Christmas to Easter, depending on the climate. Plants sometimes even bloom under the snow! Slow to establish, but well worth the wait.

> "I always plant Christmas roses…in the near view, close to the house where I can enjoy the flowers from a window when cold weather hardly invites distant inspection." – Helen Van Pelt Wilson,
> *Helen Van Pelt Wilson's Own Garden and Landscape Book*

HEIGHT/SPREAD:	25–30cm (10–12")/40cm (16")
LOCATION:	Well-drained loamy soil.
BLOOMS:	December–March
USES:	▵▵⅍≺ Borders, Specimen

orientalis Hybrids ZONES 5–9

(Lenten Rose) Forms a tough clump of leathery, evergreen leaves. Flower stalks appear in early spring, holding large nodding flowers in shades of white, cream, pink, rose, red or maroon, often with contrasting spots. Blooms later than the Christmas rose, but considered by many gardeners to be the nicer of the two. Certainly the easiest species to grow, and very rewarding. Excellent under trees or shrubs. Cut off the old leaves in late winter if they look shabby.

HEIGHT/SPREAD:	40-60cm (16–24")/45cm (18")
LOCATION:	Well-drained loamy soil.
BLOOMS:	February–May
USES:	▵▵⅍≺▴ Borders, Woodland gardens

Hemerocallis 'Hyperion'

HEMEROCALLIS
(Daylily) ☼ ◑

Extensive breeding over the last fifty years has brought the Daylily to the top ranks of valuable garden perennials. Over sturdy clumps of grassy leaves, stems rise to hold large lily-shaped flowers that open in long succession, each lasting for about a day. By choosing varieties that bloom at different times you can extend the flowering season from May through late August. And there are plenty to choose from; over twenty thousand named varieties are registered with the American Hemerocallis Society at last count, with about 500 more added to the list each year.

Daylilies are suitable for planting in perennial and shrub borders, massing as a groundcover or landscaping plant, or for planting in large containers. All prefer full sun or part shade, and an average well-drained soil. They are very long-lived, and seldom need to be divided. Once established, Daylilies are also moderately heat and drought tolerant.

In addition to the named hybrids there are some excellent old species forms that are still of value in perennial gardens.

> "They are the most dependable of all perennials with handsome endearing foliage and in my experience they are absolutely pest- and disease-free. I grow them everywhere, even in a dim corner where an astounding red one lights up the darkness." – Helen Van Pelt Wilson,
> *Helen Van Pelt Wilson's Own Garden and Landscape Book*

citrina ZONES 2–9

(Citron Daylily) A very fragrant evening-blooming species. Large grapefruit-yellow flowers are held on stems above a sizable clump of dark green leaves. Not invasive. Nice to plant near a patio or deck to enjoy the scent.

HEIGHT/SPREAD:	90–120cm (3–4')/60cm (2')
LOCATION:	Average to moist soil.
BLOOMS:	June–July
USES:	⅍≺❦ Borders, Pots

fulva 'Kwanso' ZONES 2–9

(Double Orange Daylily) (also listed as 'Flore Pleno') This is the not-so-common double-flowered form of the wild orange Daylily that grows along the roadsides of eastern North America. While the wild form is a notorious spreader, this form spreads at about half the speed but still spreads to form a wide patch in time. Perhaps a bit too aggressive for the perennial border, but tolerant of difficult areas such as between or under trees and shrubs where little else will grow, or along steep slopes. Flowers are rusty orange, with twice the usual number of petals.

HEIGHT/SPREAD:	75–120cm (30–48")/60–90cm (2–3')
LOCATION:	Average to moist soil.
BLOOMS:	June–July
USES:	⋀◦❦ Massing, Slopes

lilioasphodelus ZONES 2–9

(Lemon Daylily) (formerly *H. flava*) An old-fashioned favorite, and always the first daylily to bloom. Flowers are lemon-yellow with a strong citrus fragrance, held on tall arching stems. Plants send out rhizomes and will slowly spread to form a colony.

HEIGHT/SPREAD:	75–90cm (30–36")/60cm (24")
LOCATION:	Average to moist soil.
BLOOMS:	May–June
USES:	⅍≺❦ Borders

NAMED HYBRIDS ZONES 2–9

This is but a short listing from the enormous number of named varieties in existence. In recent years there have been many new colour breakthroughs, particularly with whites, purple and pinks. Some breeders are working on more dwarf varieties with recurrent or continuous blooming, others are selecting for new flower shapes or markings. For those with a serious passion for Daylilies there are specialist nurseries in both the U.S. and Canada that carry the newest and latest (and most expensive!).

SPREAD:	60–90cm (2–3')
LOCATION:	Average well-drained soil.
BLOOMS:	Early – late June
	Midseason – mid July
	Late – August
USES:	⅍≺❦ Borders, Massing

Hemerocallis 'Siloam Ury Winniford'

Hemerocallis 'Bertie Ferris'

Hemerocallis 'Bejewelled'

Hemerocallis 'Catherine Woodbury'

Hemerocallis 'Cherry Cheeks'

Hemerocallis 'Flower Basket'

Hemerocallis 'Miss Tinkerbell'

Hemerocallis 'Buddah'

BICOLOR SHADES

'Cocktail Date' Pink and green blend, green throat. Early-midseason. 67cm (27")

'Eenie Allegro' Creamy-apricot with rose edges, miniature flowers. Midseason. 30cm (12")

'Little Audrey' Ruffled blossoms, butter yellow with a red eye. Miniature. Early/midseason. 50cm (20")

'Little Bumblebee' Soft yellow with a chocolate eye. Miniature. Early/midseason. 50cm (20")

'Little Rainbow' Pastel melon with orchid-pink. Fragrant. Early/midseason. 70cm (28")

'Magic Dawn' Light lemon yellow, maroon tips on every other petal. Midseason. 90cm (36")

'Siloam June Bug' Golden-yellow with a maroon eye and green throat. Miniature. Early/midseason. 55cm (22")

'Siloam Peewee' Unique creamy-white with a purple eye and green throat. Miniature. Early/midseason. 45cm (18")

'Siloam Ury Winniford' Creamy with a black-purple eye, sunfast. Award-winning. Midseason. 65cm (26")

GOLD & ORANGE SHADES

'Autumn Minarette' Gold with a reddish stripe. Very tall. Late. 100cm (40")

'Black-eyed Stella' The much talked-about offspring of 'Stella de Oro'. Bright golden-yellow flowers with a distinct red halo in the centre. Excellent constant flowering habit from June to frost. Early-midseason. 60cm (24")

'Bonanza' Light orange-yellow with a maroon-red blotch. Fragrant. Midseason. 85cm (34")

'Bertie Ferris' Persimmon-orange miniature flowers, ruffled. Award winning! Early. 50cm (20")

> "Intrigued by the 'persimmon' description, and unable to find that fruit's colour defined in the dictionary, I ordered this plant. Now I have seen persimmon and have found in the diminutive and elegant Bertie a friend for life."
> – Cathy Forgie, Zone 4

'Flaming Sword' Burnt orange-red, darker eye. Midseason. 75cm (30")

'Golden Prize' Very wide gold flowers. Tetraploid. Excellent foliage! Fragrant. Late. 65cm (26")

'Marse Connell' Frilly orange spider-type, petals tipped red. Midseason. 95cm (38")

'Miss Mary Mary' New selection from Blooms of Bressingham. Interesting introduction with small golden-yellow blooms very similar to 'Stella d'Oro' in the first flush, then becoming fully double when it reblooms. Compact and vigorous, with a constant-blooming habit. 40cm (16")

'Rocket City' Rich bittersweet orange, burnt-orange centre. Tetraploid. Midseason. 90cm (36")

'Stella de Oro' Very popular repeat-blooming dwarf. Small golden-yellow flowers with a darker throat. Fragrant. Blooms June–September. Excellent for edging or massing. Early-midseason. 30cm (12")

'Thundergold' Huge golden-yellow flowers. Midseason. 80cm (32")

LAVENDER & PURPLE SHADES

'Chicago Jewel' Tetraploid. Ruffled, deep lavender with creamy throat. Midseason. 62cm (25")

'Chicago Picotee Lace' Tetraploid. Pink with a purple throat. Midseason. 62cm (25")

'Chicago Royal Robe' Tetraploid. Rich plum purple. Midseason. 60cm (24")

'Grape Velvet' Deep purple, bright yellow throat. Midseason/Late. 60cm (24")

'Lady Eva' New selection from Blooms of Bressingham. Light violet-purple ruffled petals with a dark-purple eye-zone and yellow throat. Tetraploid. Large flowers and high bud count. Repeat-bloomer. 75cm (30")

'Little Grapette' Light grape-purple, miniature flowers. Repeat-bloomer. Award winning miniature. Early/mid-season. 30cm (12")

'Prairie Blue Eyes' Lavender with a bluish eye. Prolific bloomer, vigorous. Midseason. 70cm (28")

'Raspberry Pixie' Raspberry lavender blend, fragrant. Miniature. Midseason. 60cm (24")

'Russian Rhapsody' Plum-purple flowers, deep purple eye. Tetraploid. Midseason. 75cm (30")

'Silver Trumpet' Tetraploid. Lavender petals, creamy-pink ribs. Midseason. 65cm (26")

PINK SHADES

'Annie Welch' Solid soft pink, repeat bloomer. Midseason. 60cm (24")

'Bama Music' Pale pink, yellow throat. Midseason. 70cm (28")

'Bejeweled' Light lavender-pink. Midseason. 70cm (28")

'Better Believe It' Medium pink, bright red eye. Midseason. 60cm (24")

'Catherine Woodbury' Fragrant. Pale orchid-pink, lime-green throat. Midseason-late. 75cm (30")

'Cherry Cheeks' Tetraploid. Cherry-pink with a green throat. Early-midseason. 80cm (32")

'Chicago Rosy' Tetraploid. Dark rose flowers. Midseason. 62cm (25")

'Elaine Strutt' Salmon-pink flowers. Mid-season. 60cm (24")

'Evening Gown' Tetraploid. Melon-pink with peach petals, excellent flower. Late. 70cm (28")

'Fairy Tale Pink' Ruffled pink petals, green throat. Good heavy flowers. Award winner! Repeat bloomer. Midseason. 60cm (24")

'Flower Basket' Coral pink, semi-double flowers. Midseason. 60cm (24")

'Frosty Beauty' Orchid and rose blend, gold throat. Repeat bloomer. Midseason. 80cm (32")

'Hall's Pink' Light pink flowers, low-growing variety. Late. 50cm (20")

'Luxury Lace' Lavender-pink, ruffled edges. Repeat bloomer. Midseason. 80cm (32")

'Meadow Mist' Tetraploid. Light pink. Midseason. 65cm (26")

'Melon Balls' Orchid and melon-pink blend, small round flowers. Midseason. 80cm (32")

'Miss Tinkerbell' New selection from Blooms of Bressingham. Round, ruffled flowers, delicate pink petals with a rose-pink eye. Repeat-bloomer. Midseason. 45cm (18")

'Patricia Fay' Rose-pink, greenish throat. Midseason. 90cm (36")

'Pink Damask' Pink flowers. Midseason. 75cm (30")

'Vivacious' Silvery rose-pink, ruffled petals. Midseason. 50cm (20")

'Wayside Greenlamp' Tetraploid. Shell pink petals, ivory midribs. Late. 50cm (20")

RED SHADES

'Anzac' Red with a light yellow-green throat. Repeat bloomer. Midseason. 70cm (28")

'Baja' Tetraploid. Red with a green throat. Repeat bloomer. Early-midseason. 70cm (28")

> "More catalogue space should be devoted to the foliage of this family. 'Baja' remains green well into fall, and of course its huge velvety red blooms are irresistible and will repeat with dead-heading."
> – Cathy Forgie, Zone 4

'Baltimore Oriole' Tetraploid. Velvety-red with a green throat. Midseason. 65cm (26")

'Buddah' Black-red, gold throat. Repeat bloomer. Early/midseason. 75cm (30")

'Carey Quinn' Deep ruby-red, gold throat. Early/midseason. 75cm (30")

'Chicago Apache' Tetraploid. Fiery red, ruffled flowers. Fairly sunfast. Vigorous grower. Early/midseason. 70cm (28")

'Chicago Ruby' Tetraploid. Ruby-red, long flowering. Midseason. 105cm (42")

'Christmas Carol' Crimson red, green throat. Midseason. 85cm (34")

'Eenie Fanfare' Velvety red, green throat. Repeat bloomer. Miniature. Early/midseason. 30cm (12")

'Hearts Afire' Solid medium red. Midseason. 90cm (36")

'James Marsh' Tetraploid. Bright scarlet-red, large flowers. Early/midseason. 70cm (28")

'Little Winecup' Wine-red flowers, miniature. Repeat-bloomer. Early/midseason. 60cm (24")

'Pardon Me' Ruffled petals, bright red and fragrant. Repeat bloomer. Midseason. 45cm (18")

'Red Magic' Medium red, yellow throat. Early/midseason. 90cm (36")

'Summer Wine' Light wine-red with a green-yellow throat. Midseason. 60cm (24")

'Velveteen' Solid ruby red flowers. Repeat bloomer. Midseason. 75cm (30")

WHITE SHADES

'Gentle Shepherd' Lightly ruffled near-white flowers, green throat. Midseason. 73cm (29")

'Ice Carnival' Near-white with a green throat. Repeat-bloomer. Fragrant. Midseason. 70cm (28")

'Joan Senior' Large, ruffled creamy-white flowers, lime-green throat. Repeat-bloomer. Fragrant. Evergreen. Early-midseason. 60cm (24")

'Miss Amelia' New selection from Blooms of Bressingham. Small creamy-white flowers, delicately ruffled. Fragrant. Early. Repeat-bloomer. 75cm (30")

'White Formal' Ruffled off-white, chartreuse throat. Midseason. 75cm (30")

YELLOW SHADES

'Beloved Returns' Pale greenish-yellow, ruffled. Repeat bloomer. Midseason. 75cm (30")

'Buttercurls' Fragrant, soft lemon-yellow flowers. Midseason. 65cm (26")

'Buttered Popcorn' Tetraploid. Pale butter-yellow flowers, fragrant. Midseason/Late. 80cm (32")

'Daiquiri' Pale yellow blend, green throat. Repeat bloomer. Midseason. 80cm (32")

'Double Charm' Lemon yellow, double petals. Midseason. 60cm (24")

'Double Dream' Clear yellow flowers. Repeat bloomer. Early-midseason. 50cm (20")

'Eenie Weenie' Fragrant, light yellow with a green throat, lightly ruffled. Miniature. Repeat bloomer. Early-midseason. 25cm (10")

'Elfin Stella' A yellow-flowered version of the popular classic, with the same inclination to flower all season long. A superb landscaping Daylily! Blooms June–September. Miniature. Early-midseason. 28cm (11")

'Fanciful Finnery' Clear yellow, double petals. Midseason. 40cm (16")

'Girl Scout' Lemon-yellow, green throat. Midseason/Late. 85cm (34")

'Green Flutter' Canary yellow, green throat. Repeat bloomer. Late. 50cm (20")

'Happy Returns' Prolific canary-yellow flowers, fragrant. Tetraploid. Repeat bloomer, consistently blooms from May to frost! Early. 40cm (16")

'Holly Herrema' Yellow with a bright green throat, wide petals. Fragrant. Midseason. 70cm (28")

'Hyperion' Fragrant lemon-yellow flowers. Repeat bloomer. Still one of best. Midseason. 100cm (40")

'Mary Todd' Very ruffled solid yellow. Tetraploid. Award winning. Early. 65cm (26")

'Miss Victoria' New selection from Blooms of Bressingham. Clear lemon-yellow with a chartreuse throat, rounded ruffled flowers. Fragrant. Early. Repeat-bloomer. 55cm (22")

'Penny's Worth' Very small, light yellow flowers. Repeat bloomer. Very early. 25cm (10")

'Tetrina's Daughter' Tetraploid. Lemon-yellow, fragrant night-bloomer. Midseason. 125cm (50")

'Yellow Stone' Lemon yellow, green throat. Midseason. 90cm (36")

HESPERIS
(Sweet Rocket, Dame's Rocket) ☼ ◔

matronalis   ZONES 2–9
Heads of sweetly-scented purple, mauve or white flowers, resembling Summer Phlox. A real old-fashioned garden plant for the early summer border. Often performs as a self-seeding biennial. Naturalized throughout much of eastern North America.

HEIGHT/SPREAD:	60–90cm (2–3')/30cm (12")
LOCATION:	Average to moist soil.
BLOOMS:	June–July
USES:	✂ ❦ Borders, Meadows, Woodland

Heuchera 'Velvet Night'

HEUCHERA
(Coral Bells) ☼ ◔

A lot of breeding work is currently going on with the Coral Bells, and each year a dozen or more new selections seem to appear. The older types were grown primarily for their colourful early summer display of flowers, but many of the newer types have been selected more for their outstanding foliage, in previously unimagined shades of purple, brown, red and near-black, often with exotic metallic silver markings to rival the best Rex begonia!

All types are most effective when featured towards the front of a border or in a rockery where their delicate sprays of flowers or attrac-

Hemerocallis 'Pardon Me'

Hemerocallis 'Ice Carnival'

Hemerocallis 'Miss Amelia'

Hemerocallis 'Mary Todd'

Heuchera micrantha 'Bressingham Bronze'

Heuchera 'Checkers'

Heuchera 'Pewter Veil'

Heucherella 'Rosalie'

tive leaves can be seen from close range. Flowers are excellent for cutting.

americana hybrids   ZONES 4–9

The native North American species *H. americana* has given rise to an overwhelming number of new selections, grown primarily for their beautiful foliage, now in a wide range of colours, sizes and shapes. Flowers are usually greenish-white, held just above the leaves. These all dislike hot afternoon sun, but are tolerant of hot, humid summers. The exotic textures and deep colours seem to associate especially well with ferns and other woodland plants. Foliage stays near-evergreen in mild winter areas.

> "My favorite plants are the Heucheras.
> They are hardy, virtually disease and
> insect free, and associate beautifully with
> many plants. I plant them with Peonies
> and taller growing Sedums where the
> Heucheras fill the void in spring, provide
> tall airy blooms in summer, and continue
> to provide colour, texture and contrast
> until buried by snow."
> – Luba Taylor, Zone 4

> "All the great purple Heucheras: in sun or
> shade, used as edgers or specimens, there's
> nothing that these fabulous plants
> won't do." – Marjorie Harris, Zone 5

HEIGHT/SPREAD:	45–70cm (18–30")/30–45cm (12–18")
LOCATION:	Rich average to moist soil.
BLOOMS:	June–July
USES:	▲▲❦ Borders, Edging, Specimen

'Amethyst Myst' Deep amethyst-purple foliage with a silvery caste.

'Can-Can' The first ruffled typed with bright silvery-grey foliage, with darker green veining. The wine reverse peeks out from under the skirt in a teasing sort of way.

'Checkers' Silvery-metallic leaves, the added bonus of a showy display of large white flowers held well above the foliage.

'Chocolate Ruffles' Enormous ruffled leaves. Foliage is dark chocolate-brown on top, burgundy below. Flowers are creamy, held up on tall purple stems. Nearly evergreen in milder areas. Good heat tolerance.

> "The two-toned leaves create depth,
> shadow and, with even a light breeze,
> movement in your garden!"
> – Bruce Zimmerman, Zone 6

'Eco-Improved' A recent improvement on the older 'Eco-Magnififolia', which lacked vigour. Silvery-grey leaves with contrasting beet-red veining.

'Pewter Veil' New leaves are coppery pink, changing to silvery-pewter with darker veins. Large leaves. Outstanding!

'Plum Pudding' Rich plum-purple leaves with a shimmering metallic finish.

'Ring of Fire' Silvery leaves with purple veining, in late fall a distinctive bright coral edging appears and lasts through the winter months.

'Ruby Ruffles' Large burgundy leaves with superbly ruffled edges.

'Ruby Veil' Huge leaves, metallic ruby-violet with silvery-grey veins. Rich effect. Good sun tolerance.

'Smokey Rose' Smokey-bronze foliage with a ruffled edge. Nice display of rose-pink flowers in mid-summer. Heat tolerant.

'Stormy Seas' Ruffled leaves are a combination of pewter, silver, lavender and charcoal. Excellent vigour.

'Velvet Night' The darkest variety, huge near-black leaves overlaid with metallic purple-grey. Dan Heims, the originator, suggests planting this beside a gold-leaved Hosta.

Hybrids   ZONES 3–9

(*H. × brizoides*) This is a catch-all group that includes many of the older flowering garden forms, so popular for edging borders. Foliage is green, forming a low clump that gives rise in late spring to lots of waving stems with sprays of colourful bell-shaped flowers. Superb cut flowers. Divide plants every 2–3 years to maintain vigour.

SPREAD:	30cm (12")
LOCATION:	Average to moist well-drained soil.
BLOOMS:	June–July
USES:	✂❦ Borders, Edging

'Brandon Pink' Prairie-bred hybrid, hardy to Zone 2. Bright coral-pink flowers. HEIGHT: 45–60cm (18–24")

'Bressingham Hybrids' Attractive seed-grown mixture of pink, coral and red flowers, with the occasional white. Flowers vigorously. HEIGHT: 60–75cm (24–30")

'Northern Fire' Another prairie-hardy selection, from the Agriculture Canada Research Station at Morden, Manitoba. Rich scarlet-red flowers. Foliage is deep green, mottled with white. Zones 2–9. HEIGHT: 45–60cm (18–24")

micrantha   ZONES 4–9

The species itself is native to the West coast of North America, and from it some excellent purple-leaved selections have been made. Foliage is large and crinkly with an ivy or maple-leaf shape, in shades of deep purple-red. Stems of small whitish-pink flowers appear in early summer but are not very showy. Excellent at the border front, especially when massed. Evergreen in Zones 7–9.

HEIGHT/SPREAD:	30–60cm (12–24")/30–45cm (12–18")
LOCATION:	Average to moist well-drained soil.
BLOOMS:	June–July
USES:	✂▲❦ Borders, Edging

'Bressingham Bronze' An improvement on 'Palace Purple', with outstanding beet-red foliage, maintaining its colour reliably throughout the season. Excellent with blue fescue. A selection from Blooms of Bressingham.

'Palace Purple' A seed-grown strain, the foliage is deep purple in spring, fading to bronzy-brown for the summer. Plants maintain their colour best with afternoon shade. Rogue out any green-leaved seedlings that might appear. A former *Perennial Plant of the Year*.

sanguinea   ZONES 3–9

Among these are many of the excellent old garden forms, mostly of compact size, with a bright display of flowers in late spring. These are the best types for edging purposes, blooming slightly before most other types. Dead-heading faded flowers will encourage continual blooming. Divide every 2–3 years. Unfortunately, the variegated forms don't seem to be very vigorous.

> "I know. It's just plain old, green-leaved
> Coral Bells — but plant a big patch of it
> in view of the kitchen window. The
> opportunity to view hummingbirds will
> have your kids fighting over whose turn it
> is to wash the dishes! (Well, not really, but
> it's a nice thought…)"
> – Kevin Ward, Zone 5

HEIGHT/SPREAD:	30–45cm (12–18")/30cm (12")
LOCATION:	Average to moist well-drained soil.
BLOOMS:	May–July
USES:	▲✂❦ Borders, Edging

'Snow Storm' Extremely bright variegation, the near-white leaves are edged in green. Nicely ruffled. Flowers are cerise pink. Effective in groups.

'Splendens' Bright vermilion-red flowers. Good compact seed strain.

'Splish Splash' Outstanding variegated leaves, deep green heavily mottled with white. The leaf veins turn noticeably raspberry-red in colder months. Light pink flowers.

× HEUCHERELLA
(Foamy Bells) ☼ ◗

Hybrids   ZONES 3–9

Interesting hybrids between various *Heuchera* and *Tiarella* species. The result combines the dense foliage texture of Foamflower with the showier flowering habit of Coral Bells. Plants are generally vigorous and hardy. Outstanding in a woodland garden, appreciating part shade. Long flowering.

HEIGHT/SPREAD: 30–45cm (12–18")/30cm (12")
LOCATION: Rich, moist well-drained soil.
BLOOMS: June–July
USES: ⬜◣M◣◣ Edging, Borders

'Bridget Bloom' Mounding habit, great display of shell-pink flowers for many weeks. An older hybrid raised by Alan Bloom at Bressingham Gardens.

'Rosalie' Sometimes listed as *Tiarella* 'Rosalie'. A Canadian introduction featuring dark green leaves with a prominent bronzy-red centre. Rose-pink flowers appear for many weeks in late spring. Beautiful in a woodland setting. Compact habit.

HIBISCUS
(Rose Mallow) ☼

moscheutos 'Southern Belle'   ZONES 4–9

(Hardy Hibiscus) Large, shrub-like plants, similar to indoor Hibiscus. Dinner-plate sized flowers are red, rose, pink, or white, usually with a crimson centre. Needs lots of summer heat to bloom really well. Tolerates heat and humidity, but must not be allowed to dry out. A thick mulch for the first winter is advised, and planting before midsummer will increase survival. Selected forms may be propagated by cuttings.

> "I also found the *Hibiscus* 'Southern Belle' to be hardy in our area, once established, with no protection. It is a great accent plant, but I have a whole row of them backing a perennial bed. The plate-sized flowers start blooming in August and keep on coming till frost."
> – Dr. Virginia Hildebrandt, Zone 5

HEIGHT/SPREAD: 90–120cm (3–4')/60–90cm (2–3')
LOCATION: Rich, moist soil.
BLOOMS: July–September
USES: Borders, Specimen

HOLLYHOCK
See ALCEA.

HOSTA
(Hosta, Plantain Lily) ◗ ●

> There is nothing like a hosta emerging from the winter mulch — give them some age and they are like a bed of spikes. If only the slugs could be impaled instead of dining. – Bob Lilly, Zone 8

In ever-increasing demand are these first-class shade plants. Their lush clumps of bold, exotic leaves are the main feature, the stalks of mauve or white lily-like flowers an added bonus. Most varieties are easy reliable plants that adapt well even to densely shaded sites.

Both the foliage and flowers are of interest to floral designers.

With extensive breeding work still being undertaken there seems to be no end in sight to the number of Hosta varieties; well over a thousand are circulating among the specialists and collectors, from five-foot giants to 4-inch miniatures. Gardeners with a passion for these shade-lovers are advised to join their local chapter of the American Hosta Society.

Hosta are easily divided in spring or early fall but most varieties can be left for years before they become crowded and start to decline. Slugs and snails are often troublesome, particularly the monster slugs at the West coast. Aside from hand-picking, trapping or baiting slugs, an alternative approach is to select those Hosta varieties marked "slug-resistant"; these have especially thick and waxy leaves that slugs find difficult to eat. Using a mulch of gravel or coarse sand around your Hosta plants is reported to be a big help in deterring these voracious feeders.

LOCATION: Rich, moist but well-drained soil. Golden-leaved and variegated varieties are generally more sun tolerant than green or blue-leaved types.

USES: Each variety has been placed in one of the categories listed below. This should help you to choose the best Hosta for your landscape situation. As a general rule most varieties grow about as wide as the height of the foliage, or perhaps half again. See below regarding heights.

HEIGHTS given are for the *foliage*, the flower stems usually rising 30–45cm (12–18") above that. Each variety is placed into one or more of the following groups, largely based on height.

DWARF: 20cm (8") or less. Suitable for rock gardens or containers. Usually slow growing.

EDGING: 30cm (12") or less, vigorous growth.

GROUNDCOVER: 60cm (24") or less, very vigorous growth. Excellent for massed, low-maintenance plantings.

BACKGROUND: 75cm (30") or taller.

SPECIMEN: Good choice for a closely-viewed focal point. Interesting leaf texture, colour, shape, or flowers. Does not always indicate monstrous types.

HOSTA VARIETIES   ZONES 2–9

Included here is a good cross-section of some of the latest selections available, as well as the more standard older varieties. Hosta breeders are still very much at work all over the world, trying to come up with even more spectacular specimens, so keep an eye out

Hosta 'Bressingham Blue'

Hosta 'Francee'

Hosta sieboldiana 'Frances Williams'

Hosta 'Ginko Craig'

Hosta 'Golden Tiara'

Hosta 'Halcyon'

Hosta 'June'

Hosta 'Great Expectations'

for selections that may not be listed here. A word of warning is in order regarding prices: in general the newest and most exotic selections command a steep price for the first few years after they are released. Thanks to the modern technique of micro-propagation (also known as tissue-culture) many of these will become widely available and much more reasonable in price after just a few short years!

> "I've never seen a hosta I didn't like, but I do have some favorites. I'm especially partial to those with golden leaves, which pump color into dull and shady corners."
> – Allen Lacy, *The Garden in Autumn*

'Abiqua Drinking Gourd' SPECIMEN. Leaves are frosty blue in colour, the edges curling upwards into a cup that will actually hold water. Pale lavender flowers in July. HEIGHT: 45cm (18″) SPREAD: 35cm (14″)

'Allan P. McConnell' EDGING. Oval-shaped leaves are dark green with a clean white edge. Highly regarded edging variety. Purple flowers in July. HEIGHT: 20cm (8″) SPREAD: 45cm (18″)

'Antioch' GROUNDCOVER. Large light green leaves with a wide cream edge, forming large clumps. Pale lavender flowers in July. Outstanding. HEIGHT: 60cm (24″) SPREAD: 90cm (36″)

'August Moon' GROUNDCOVER. Large and deeply crinkled bright yellow leaves. Near-white flowers in July. Excellent, Award-winning. HEIGHT: 50cm (20″) SPREAD: 75cm (30″)

'Big Daddy' BACKGROUND. Huge, heavily quilted, deep blue leaves. Light lavender flowers in July. Slug-resistance is excellent! HEIGHT: 75cm (30″) SPREAD: 120cm (48″)

'Big Mama' BACKGROUND. Thick blue-green leaves, heavily quilted. Near-white flowers in July. HEIGHT: 70cm (28″) SPREAD: 100cm (40″)

'Birchwood Parky's Gold' EDGING. Compact golden mounds, bright gold in the fall. Showy mauve flowers in July. Sun-tolerant and fast-growing. HEIGHT: 35cm (14″) SPREAD: 75cm (30″)

'Blue Angel' SPECIMEN or BACKGROUND. Award-winning, enormous-growing selection with big powdery-blue leaves and a wide, mounding habit. Tall stems of near-white flowers late in the summer. Faster to mature than most other large blue varieties. HEIGHT: 90cm (36″) SPREAD: 120cm (48″)

'Blue Boy' EDGING. Rounded mound of small frosted blue leaves, rich texture. Nice for edging. HEIGHT: 35cm (18″) SPREAD: 50cm (20″)

'Blue Cadet' EDGING. Rounded leaves, intensely blue in colour, and so useful in this low-mounding selection. Good show of purple flowers. HEIGHT: 40cm (16″) SPREAD: 70cm (28″)

'Blue Dimples' EDGING. Thick-substanced, waxy leaves with an intense powdery-blue colour. Purple striped flowers in July. HEIGHT: 38cm (15″) SPREAD: 50cm (20″)

'Blue Mammoth' SPECIMEN. A highly-rated large, mounding selection with huge powdery-blue leaves. Good substance and slug resistance. Near-white flowers in midsummer. Heavily quilted texture. HEIGHT: 75cm (30″) SPREAD: 120cm (48″)

'Blue Umbrellas' SPECIMEN. Huge downward-cupping leaves, forming a giant mound, blue in spring later fading to green. Pale lavender flowers in June. One of the best blue-leaved monster Hostas. HEIGHT: 75cm (30″) SPREAD: 120cm (48″)

'Blue Wedgewood' EDGING or GROUNDCOVER. Good slug-resistance! Vigorous, grey-blue leaves with thick substance. Soft lavender flowers in July. HEIGHT: 35cm (14″) SPREAD: 60cm (24″)

'Blue Whirls' SPECIMEN. Narrow, pointed leaves are frosted blue-green in color. Leaves are arranged like spokes of a wheel when viewed from above. Vase-shaped habit. HEIGHT: 50cm (20″) SPREAD: 75cm (30″)

'Bold Ruffles' BACKGROUND. Large blue-grey leaves with ruffled edges. White flowers in July. Stiff, upright habit. Excellent slug-resistance. HEIGHT: 60cm (24″) SPREAD: 90cm (36″)

'Bressingham Blue' SPECIMEN or BACKGROUND. Deeply ribbed, powdery blue-green leaves, upwardly cupped. Tall stems of white flowers in June. HEIGHT: 60cm (24″) SPREAD: 120cm (48″)

'Brim Cup' EDGING. Unusual cupped habit, especially for a Hosta this small. Leaves are medium green with a wide creamy-yellow margin. Pale lavender flowers in July. HEIGHT: 30cm (12″) SPREAD: 38cm (15″)

'Canadian Shield' GROUNDCOVER. Discovered and recently introduced by Rainforest Gardens. This is a sport of 'Halcyon', featuring dark green shiny foliage and a very sturdy habit. Pale lavender flowers in August. HEIGHT: 45cm (18″) SPREAD: 75cm (30″)

> "The heavy veining and good substance of the leaf make it slug resistant. We feel it will hold up to any weather or soil conditions Canadian Gardens can throw at it!" – Elke Knechtel, Zone 7

'Candy Hearts' GROUNDCOVER. Perfectly rounded clump of grey-green heart-shaped leaves. Lavender flowers in July. HEIGHT: 45cm (18″) SPREAD: 70cm (28″)

> "A single specimen appears a soft green, but a mass planting takes on an incomparable opalescent, candied glow, thus explaining the first part of the name."
> – Cathy Forgie, Zone 4

'Chinese Sunrise' EDGING. Glossy, narrow foliage begins chartreuse-yellow, later becoming light green with a deep green margin. Good display of purple flowers in late summer. HEIGHT: 35cm (14″) SPREAD: 60cm (24″)

'Christmas Tree' SPECIMEN. Medium-sized clump of corrugated deep-green leaves with a creamy-white edge. Leaves continue up the flower stems. Lavender flowers in July. HEIGHT: 50cm (20″) SPREAD: 90cm (36″)

clausa **'Normalis'** EDGING. A low-growing selection that is ideal for edging or groundcover plantings, as the plants will spread to form a colony. Leaves are medium-green and oval in shape, giving rise to very showy dark lavender flowers in early summer. HEIGHT: 20cm (8″) SPREAD: 60cm (24″)

'Dorset Blue' EDGING. An outstanding dwarf blue type. Round, cupped powdery-blue leaves, lavender flowers in August. HEIGHT: 25cm (10″) SPREAD: 30cm (12″)

'El Capitan' GROUNDCOVER. Leaves of good substance, powdery sage-green centred with a golden margin, eventually forming a rather large mound. Edges are rippled. Lavender flowers in July. HEIGHT: 60cm (24″) SPREAD: 100cm (40″)

'Elisabeth' GROUNDCOVER. Popular form in Europe, especially valued for its outstanding display of purple flowers in late summer. Leaves are medium-green, oval shaped and ruffled. HEIGHT: 65cm (26″) SPREAD: 90cm (36″)

'Elvis Lives' SPECIMEN. Long, narrow blue-suede leaves are lightly ruffled along the edge. Lavender flowers in early summer. Gaining popularity quickly! HEIGHT: 40cm (15″) SPREAD: 90cm (36″)

'Emerald Tiara' EDGING. Leaf coloring is the reverse of 'Golden Tiara', bright golden centres with a mid-green margin. Lavender flowers in mid-summer. HEIGHT: 35cm (14″) SPREAD: 30cm (12″)

'Fall Bouquet' EDGING. One of the newer red-stemmed selections, with glossy dark-green leaves. Flowers are lavender, appearing in autumn, and held on deep-red stems. HEIGHT: 30cm (12″) SPREAD: 45cm (18″)

fluctuans **'Sagae'** SPECIMEN. Formerly known as *H. fluctuans* 'Variegated'. Very highly-rated among collectors, considered by many to be the finest variegated Hosta ever! Large grey-green leaves with wide, bright yellow margins. Forms a stunning upright mound. Lavender flowers in July. Find a prime spot for this baby. HEIGHT: 90cm (36″) SPREAD: 120cm (48″)

fortunei **'Albopicta'** GROUNDCOVER. Outstanding spring foliage, bright yellow with a dark green margin, fading to all green by mid-summer. Pale lilac flowers in late July. HEIGHT: 35cm (14″) SPREAD: 60cm (24″)

fortunei **'Aureomarginata'** GROUNDCOVER. Very popular form, attractive dark-green leaves with a strong yellow-gold edging. Pale violet flowers in July. HEIGHT: 40cm (16″) SPREAD: 60cm (24″)

fortunei **'Hyacinthina'** GROUNDCOVER. Silvery-green pointed leaves with a thin white pencil-margin, powdery white on the underside. Handsome upright mound. Pale purple flowers in July. HEIGHT: 45cm (18″) SPREAD: 60cm (24″)

'Fragrant Blue' DWARF. Heart-shaped powdery blue-green leaves, forming a small mound, and continuing to produce fresh blue foliage all season long. Pale lilac flowers are fragrant in warm-summer regions. HEIGHT: 20cm (8″) SPREAD: 30cm (12″)

'Fragrant Bouquet' SPECIMEN. Bright chartreuse-green leaves with a broad creamy-white margin. Outstanding display of large, fragrant pale lilac flowers in summer, held well above the leaves where they can be enjoyed. Vigorous habit. HEIGHT: 45cm (18″) SPREAD: 65cm (26″)

'Francee' GROUNDCOVER. Elegant mound of dark green leaves with a perfect white edge; refined and elegant. Lilac flowers in July. Award winning. HEIGHT: 60cm (24″) SPREAD: 90cm (36″)

'Frances Williams' SPECIMEN. Long considered to be one of the best Hosta of all time. Round, puckered leaves are blue-green with a wide yellow margin. Near-white flowers in July. Sometimes scorches around the edges unless grown in full shade. Spectacular! HEIGHT: 60cm (24″) SPREAD: 90cm (36″)

'Fringe Benefit' GROUNDCOVER. Large powdery blue-green leaves with a creamy-yellow margin. Good substance and a vigorous grower. Pale lavender flowers are held on tall stems. Fairly sun-resistant. HEIGHT: 60cm (24″) SPREAD: 90cm (36″)

'Frosted Jade' BACKGROUND. Powdery-green leaves with a rippled white margin, forming a large, broad mound. Pale lavender flowers in summer. Shade is best, to retain the powdery finish. HEIGHT: 75cm (30″) SPREAD: 90cm (36″)

'Ginko Craig' EDGING. Narrow lance-shaped leaves, green with a white edge. This fast-growing variety is excellent for edging. Medium purple flowers in August. HEIGHT: 30cm (12″) SPREAD: 50cm (20″)

'Gold Drop' DWARF. A well-known miniature variety that is excellent for edging. Heart-shaped leaves are thick in substance, chartreuse yellow. Near white flowers in July. HEIGHT: 15cm (6″) SPREAD: 30cm (12″)

'Gold Edger' EDGING. One of the best for edging, the heart-shaped leaves are reliably golden-green all season. Fast grower. Pale mauve flowers in July. HEIGHT: 30cm (12″) SPREAD: 70cm (28″)

'Gold Standard' GROUNDCOVER. All-green in spring, the leaves soon changing to bright yellow with a green margin, the centres near white by fall. Lavender flowers in July. Should receive a few hours of direct sun each day for best colouring to develop. HEIGHT: 60cm (24″) SPREAD: 90cm (36″)

'Golden Scepter' EDGING. An all-gold version of 'Golden Tiara', colours up early. Lavender-purple flowers in July. Vigorous grower. HEIGHT: 40cm (16″) SPREAD: 30cm (12″)

'Golden Sunburst' BACKGROUND. An all-yellow version of 'Frances Williams', best planted in the shade for bold effect. Huge leaves, good heavy texture. Near-white flowers. HEIGHT: 60cm (24″) SPREAD: 90cm (36″)

'Golden Tiara' EDGING. Perhaps the most popular edging variety. Light green heart-shaped leaves with a distinctive yellow edge. Fast grower. Purple flowers in July. HEIGHT: 35cm (14″) SPREAD: 30cm (12″)

'Grand Tiara' EDGING. Another variation on 'Golden Tiara', this time the leaves are gold with a small green-streaked centre. A unique variation, very eye-catching, same vigorous habit. Purple flowers in July. HEIGHT: 35cm (14″) SPREAD: 30cm (12″)

'Great Expectations' SPECIMEN. A stunning newer introduction that originated as a mutation of *sieboldiana* 'Elegans'. The deep blue leaves have an unusual bold centre variegation of golden-yellow, later changing to creamy-white. Truly exotic in appearance, a must for the collector. Near-white flowers in June. Needs some sun for best coloration. Slow grower. HEIGHT: 55cm (22″) SPREAD: 75cm (30″)

'Green Piecrust' SPECIMEN or BACKGROUND. Large olive-green leaves with unique heavily ruffled edges. Most effective when viewed up close. Lavender flowers in June. HEIGHT: 75cm (30″) SPREAD: 120cm (48″)

'Ground Master' GROUNDCOVER. Valued for its stoloniferous habit, this variety is excellent for mass planting as a ground cover. Leaves are medium-green with a creamy-yellow margin that later fades to white. Deep lavender flowers in August. HEIGHT: 30cm (12″) SPREAD: 50cm (20″)

'Ground Sulphur' DWARF. Low, dense mound of bright sulphur-yellow leaves. Appreciates some direct sun to bring out the colour. Lavender flowers in July. HEIGHT: 20cm (8″) SPREAD 50cm(20″)

'Hadspen Blue' GROUNDCOVER. Thick, powdery-blue leaves, perhaps the best of the smaller blue varieties, forming a dense mound. Excellent slug-resistance. Near-white flowers in July. HEIGHT: 30cm (12″) SPREAD: 45cm (18″)

'Halcyon' GROUNDCOVER. Deep blue-green leaves forming a dense mound. Thick substance means good slug-resistance. Tall stems of pale lavender flowers in August. HEIGHT: 50cm (20″) SPREAD: 100cm (40″)

'Honeybells' GROUNDCOVER. Fragrant pale-mauve flowers in August. Large light green leaves. Vigorous habit. HEIGHT: 60cm (24″) SPREAD: 120 (48″)

'Invincible' GROUNDCOVER. Pointed green foliage with a shiny, highly-polished finish. Sun-tolerant and some slug-resistance. An excellent choice for landscaping, with a showy display of fragrant lavender flowers in August. Flowers are occasionally double. Highly rated. HEIGHT: 50cm (20″) SPREAD: 100cm (40″)

'Janet' GROUNDCOVER. Bright gold-centred leaves with a green margin, the centre fading to white in summer. Pale lavender flowers in July. Highly rated, but a slow grower. HEIGHT: 40cm (16″) SPREAD: 60cm (24″)

'June' SPECIMEN. Much sought-after variegated form of 'Halcyon'. Leaves are chartreuse-yellow with a streaky blue-green margin. Needs some sun in spring to develop good coloration. Very highly rated! HEIGHT: 30cm (16″) SPREAD: 75cm (30″)

'Kabitan' DWARF. Long, narrow yellow leaves are edged in green and slightly ruffled. Rich purple flowers are a lovely contrast in July. Best with morning sun. Very bright and cheery. HEIGHT: 20cm (8″) SPREAD: 25cm (10″)

Hosta 'Krossa Regal'

Hosta 'Love Pat'

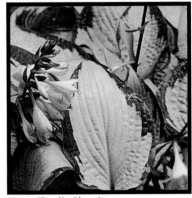

Hosta 'Paul's Glory'

Hosta 'Piedmont Gold'

Hosta sieboldiana 'Elegans'

Hosta 'So Sweet'

Hosta 'Summer Fragrance'

Hosta 'Sun Power'

'Krossa Regal' SPECIMEN. Upright vase-shaped habit. Outstanding powdery grey-blue leaves. Stems of lavender flowers in August reaching up to five feet! Good slug-resistance. Very highly rated. HEIGHT: 80cm (32″) SPREAD: 90cm (36″)

> "If only we could arrest the growth on this plant at unfurling stage. Those tall cones of green fluted flares call out for French vanilla and a cookie."
> – Bob Lilly, Zone 8

'Lancifolia' EDGING. Glossy dark green spear-shaped leaves, forming a tidy mound. Deep lilac-purple flowers in August. Tolerates drier, sunnier sites better than most other varieties. HEIGHT: 30cm (12″) SPREAD: 60cm (24″)

'Leather Sheen' EDGING. Lance-shaped leaves are dark green with the most amazing glossy, polished finish. This Hosta always sports the "wet look"! Lavender flowers in July. Said by many to be among the darkest-leaved selections. HEIGHT: 25cm (10″) SPREAD: 60cm (24″)

'Lemon Lime' EDGING or GROUNDCOVER. Small clumps of chartreuse-green leaves, vigorous habit. Good display of lavender-purple flowers in July, held well above the leaves. HEIGHT: 30cm (12″) SPREAD: 45cm (18″)

longissima DWARF. In Japan this is known as the Swamp Hosta, because it prefers a moist to wet soil. Very narrow leaves are shiny above, with almost a grass-like appearance. Good display of pale mauve flowers in summer. Worth a try beside a pond or in a bog garden. HEIGHT: 15cm (6″) SPREAD: 25cm (10″)

'Louisa' EDGING. Similar to *H. sieboldii* 'Alba', this form has green leaves with a white margin and a good display of white flowers in August. HEIGHT: 20cm (8″) SPREAD: 25cm (10″)

'Love Pat' SPECIMEN. Outstanding frosty-blue leaves, heavily quilted and cup-shaped. Very highly rated variety. Near-white flowers in July. Quickly becoming a classic! HEIGHT: 60cm (24″) SPREAD: 60cm (24″)

'Lunar Eclipse' GROUNDCOVER. Large, quilted bright yellow leaves, cleanly edged with white. Near-white flowers in July. Variegated form of **'August Moon'**. HEIGHT: 50cm (20″) SPREAD: 75cm (30″)

'Maraschino Cherry' GROUNDCOVER. Shiny, dark-green leaves, quickly forming a good-size clump. Lavender flowers appear in July, held well above the leaves on attractive purple-red stems. HEIGHT: 40cm (16″) SPREAD: 75cm (30″)

'Marilyn' GROUNDCOVER. Excellent golden foliage with wavy edges. Lavender flower in July. HEIGHT: 45cm (18″) SPREAD: 75cm (30″)

montana 'Aureo-marginata' SPECIMEN. Large, glossy leaves, deep green with irregular yellow margins, forming a wide mound. Outstanding all season long. White flowers in late July on very tall stems. Very early to emerge in the spring, may need some frost protection. HEIGHT: 68cm (27″) SPREAD: 100cm (40″)

montana macrophylla SPECIMEN. An enormous monster of a Hosta! Huge green leaves with prominent veins and an upright, arching habit. Even taller stems of white flowers in summer. As close to rhubarb as a Hosta can get. HEIGHT: 100cm (40″) SPREAD: 150cm (60″)

'Moonlight' GROUNDCOVER. Medium-green in spring, later changing to bright golden-yellow and later creamy-yellow with a white margin. Lavender flowers in July. Needs morning sun for best colouring to develop. HEIGHT: 60cm (24″) SPREAD: 90cm (36″)

'Night Before Christmas' SPECIMEN. Leaf centre is pure white, with a wide green margin, a most unusual variegation. Vigorous habit, and stunning in the garden. HEIGHT: 45cm (12″) SPREAD: 60cm (24″)

nigrescens elatior BACKGROUND. A Hosta of enormous proportions, with huge light green leaves, smooth in texture. Stems of lavender flowers have been known to reach seven feet! HEIGHT: 90cm (36″) SPREAD: 120cm (48″)

'Northern Halo' SPECIMEN. Heavily corrugated blue-grey leaves, thick creamy-white margins. This is a white-margined *sieboldiana* 'Elegans'. Slow to establish, but outstanding! White flowers in July. HEIGHT: 70cm (28″) SPREAD: 100cm (40″)

'On Stage' SPECIMEN. Much talked-about in Hosta circles! Bright yellow leaves with irregular green edging and streaking, later the centres fading to cream. Reported to tolerate full sun. Slow-growing and hard to come by. HEIGHT: 35cm (14″) SPREAD: 60cm (24″)

'Patriot' SPECIMEN. Truly one of the best variegated forms around, medium-green leaves are widely edged in white, with streaks towards the centre. Really stands out! HEIGHT: 60cm (24″) SPREAD: 90cm (36″)

'Paul's Glory' SPECIMEN. Another stunning newer introduction. Beautiful golden heart-shaped leaves, boldly streaked with blue-green on the margins, the centre later fading to parchment white. Flowers are lavender. HEIGHT: 55cm (22″) SPREAD: 90cm (36″)

'Pearl Lake' GROUNDCOVER. Profuse bloomer. Lavender flowers in July, over heart-shaped grey-green leaves. Vigorous grower. Award-winning. HEIGHT: 45cm (18″) SPREAD: 60cm (24″)

'Piedmont Gold' BACKGROUND or GROUNDCOVER. Large golden-yellow leaves with a powdery finish, handsomely quilted. Near-white flowers in July. One of the most impressive yellow varieties for lighting up a shady corner! HEIGHT: 50cm (20″) SPREAD: 100cm (40″)

'Pineapple Poll' GROUNDCOVER. Powdery mid-green rippled leaves, forming a dense mound. An improvement on 'Lancifolia'. Flower stems are leafy, with an appearance like the top of a pineapple, flowers lavender. HEIGHT: 45cm (18″) SPREAD: 45cm (18″)

'Pizzazz' GROUNDCOVER. Large heart-shaped leaves are frosted blue, with creamy-white wavy edging. Dense clusters of near-white flowers in July. HEIGHT: 30cm (12″) SPREAD: 45cm (18″)

plantaginea GROUNDCOVER or SPECIMEN. Very fragrant, huge white flowers in August are held just above the leaves, exceptionally showy. Shiny light-green foliage with good heat-tolerance. Also known as the old "August Lily", this is one of the original Hosta species first planted in North American gardens. Needs a warm summer climate to bloom reliably. HEIGHT: 60cm (24″) SPREAD: 75cm (30″)

'Regal Splendor' SPECIMEN. One of the most exciting newer introductions, a selection of 'Krossa Regal' with powdery grey-blue leaves, stunningly edged in creamy white. Tall stems of lavender flowers in August. Outstanding! HEIGHT: 80cm (32″) SPREAD: 90cm (36″)

'Royal Standard' GROUNDCOVER. Rich green, deeply-veined large leaves. Fragrant white flowers in August. Rated as the best fragrant white-flowered Hosta for general landscape planting. Fairly sun-tolerant. HEIGHT: 60cm (24″) SPREAD: 90cm (36″)

'Sea Dream' GROUNDCOVER. Leaves start out light green, later becoming yellow with a wide white edging. Lavender flowers in autumn. Regarded as one of the best white-edged yellows. HEIGHT: 30cm (12″) SPREAD 75cm (30″)

'Sea Lotus Leaf' GROUNDCOVER. Thick blue-green foliage, upwardly cupped like a lotus leaf. Arching vase-shaped mound. Very pale lavender flowers in July. HEIGHT: 50cm (20″) SPREAD 90cm (36″)

'Sea Octopus' DWARF or EDGING. Narrow mid-green leaves, heavily ruffled and rippled. A nice late show of mauve flowers. Most unusual! Grow on a ledge or in a trough so it can be easily seen. Should be divided every three years or so to maintain the ruffled appearance. HEIGHT: 20cm (8″) SPREAD: 35cm (14″)

'Sea Thunder' SPECIMEN. An outstanding newer selection with superb centre-variegation! Creamy-white, pointed leaves are bordered and streaked with dark green. Lavender flowers in July. Good vigour. HEIGHT: 30cm (12″) SPREAD 60cm (24″)

'Shade Fanfare' GROUNDCOVER. Soft golden-green leaves with a wide creamy-white margin. Popular variety, vigorous grower. Lavender flowers in July. HEIGHT: 40cm (16″) SPREAD: 45cm (18″)

'Sharmon' GROUNDCOVER. Creamy-white leaves are attractively edged with powdery dark green. Pale purple flowers in July. HEIGHT: 45cm (18″) SPREAD: 60cm (24″)

sieboldiana BACKGROUND. Large powdery grey-green leaves with attractive quilting and slightly wavy edges. Not to be confused with the blue form 'Elegans', listed below. Over the years this matures to form a very statuesque clump. Clusters of near-white flowers appear in mid-summer. HEIGHT: 60cm (24″) SPREAD: 90cm (36″)

sieboldiana **'Elegans'** SPECIMEN or BACKGROUND. The original, and still one of the best large-leaved true blue Hostas. Frosted powdery-blue leaves are heavily corrugated. Short stems of almost-white flowers appear in July. Slow to establish, but eventually becomes an enormous clump. HEIGHT: 75cm (30″) SPREAD: 120cm (48″)

sieboldii **'Alba'** EDGING. Formerly known as *H. minor* 'Alba'. An older variety that is still excellent for general groundcover use, as it spreads quickly to form a patch of lance-shaped green leaves. White flowers appear in August. HEIGHT: 20cm (8″) SPREAD: 25cm (10″)

'So Sweet' EDGING. Good display of very fragrant near-white flowers in late summer. Leaves are lance-shaped, green with a wide creamy-white edge and a glossy finish. Flowers better with a little sun. HEIGHT: 30cm (12″) SPREAD: 55cm (22″)

'Stiletto' DWARF. An outstanding dwarf selection, with narrow, grass-like foliage, green with a rippled white margin. Rich display of lavender-purple flowers in late summer. Good vigorous habit. HEIGHT: 15cm (6″) SPREAD: 30cm (12″)

'Sugar and Cream' GROUNDCOVER. Large wavy green leaves with white margins. Quickly makes a dense wide mound. Fragrant white flowers in August. This is the variegated form of 'Honeybells'. HEIGHT: 60cm (24″) SPREAD: 90cm (36″)

'Sum and Substance' SPECIMEN or BACKGROUND. Enormous golden-chartreuse leaves, the largest of any Hosta, forming a huge mound up to six feet wide, so be sure to give it room. Very highly rated. Pale lavender flowers in August. Slug-resistant. Sun tolerant. HEIGHT: 75cm (30″) SPREAD: 150cm (60″)

'Summer Fragrance' SPECIMEN or GROUNDCOVER. Quickly forms a large, upright mound of white-edged green leaves. Very fragrant lavender-purple flowers in August. Prefers a little sun. HEIGHT: 65cm (26″) SPREAD: 100cm (40″)

'Sun Power' BACKGROUND. Brilliant golden-yellow leaves, lightly ruffled and twisted. Rapid grower. A highly regarded gold form with an upright vase-shaped habit. Lavender flowers in July. HEIGHT: 75cm (30″) SPREAD: 90cm (36″)

'Sweet Susan' GROUNDCOVER. Large heart-shaped medium-green leaves. Fragrant flowers are purple with a white edge, appearing in early summer and sometimes re-blooming. HEIGHT: 45cm (18″) SPREAD: 75cm (30″)

'Tokudama' SPECIMEN. Thick, cupped foliage is an intense powdery-blue shade with attractive quilting. Still considered to be one of the best blue forms, but slow to establish. Near-white flowers in mid-summer. HEIGHT: 30cm (12″) SPREAD: 60cm (24″)

'Tokudama Aureo-nebulosa' SPECIMEN. Unusual centre variegation. Blue-green margins with a chartreuse and gold centre. Very choice, slow-growing variety for the enthusiast. Clusters of white flowers in July. Excellent slug-resistance. HEIGHT: 35cm (14″) SPREAD: 60cm (24″)

'Tokudama Flavocircinalis' SPECIMEN. Nearly round leaves, intense blue in the centre, with rich golden margins that sometimes streak towards the middle. Almost like a small form of 'Frances Williams. Near-white flowers. Slow to establish. HEIGHT: 35cm (14″) SPREAD: 60cm (24″)

'Undulata Albo-marginata' GROUNDCOVER. Slightly wavy leaves, two-tone green with a broad creamy-white margin. Lilac flowers in July. This is the old standard "variegated" hosta, especially valuable for mass planting. HEIGHT: 45cm (18″) SPREAD: 90cm (36″)

'Undulata' EDGING. (Sometimes listed as 'Variegata', 'Medio-variegata','Univittata') Wavy, twisted leaves are green with feathery creamy-white streaks in the centre. Lilac flowers in early July. This older, unstable variety will lose some variegation as plants mature in the garden. Divide every three years. HEIGHT: 35cm (14″) SPREAD: 45cm (18″)

ventricosa GROUNDCOVER. Sturdy, indestructible mounds of pointed green leaves, shiny on the underside. Good dense habit, tolerates very heavy shade. Flowers are showy deep-purple bells with light lavender stripes, appearing in July. Has a tendency to self-seed, and is the only Hosta that breeds true from seeds. HEIGHT: 60cm (24″) SPREAD: 90cm (36″)

ventricosa **'Aureo-marginata'** SPECIMEN or GROUNDCOVER. A highly regarded form. Leaves are deep green with irregular wide yellow to creamy-white margins. Showy bell-shaped purple flower in July. A must for the collector. HEIGHT: 55cm (22″) SPREAD: 90cm (36″)

'Wide Brim' GROUNDCOVER or SPECIMEN. Rounded green leaves with wide cream to gold margins, lightly quilted. Lots of pale lavender flowers in July. A highly-rated, award winning variety. HEIGHT: 60cm (24″) SPREAD: 90cm (36″)

'Zounds' GROUNDCOVER. Outstanding bright golden-yellow corrugated foliage, standing out like a beacon. One of the best gold-leafed forms for shady situations. Clean white flowers in late June. Good slug-resistance. HEIGHT: 50cm (20″) SPREAD: 90cm (36″)

HOUSTONIA
(Mountain Bluets) ☼ ◑

caerulea 'Millard's Variety'   ZONES 3–9
(formerly listed as *Hedyotis*) Low, creeping green mat of tiny green leaves, smothered by little blue star flowers in late spring. Easy rock garden perennial that will self-seed nicely. Likes a moist soil while blooming, but doesn't mind drying out in the summer. Dislikes lime. A native North American wildflower, but most gardeners are not familiar with it.

HEIGHT/SPREAD:	10–15cm (4–6″)/30cm (12″)
LOCATION:	Moist to wet lime-free soil.
BLOOMS:	April–June
USES:	⏶△∿ Waterside

HOUTTUYNIA
(Chameleon Plant) ☼ ◑

cordata 'Chameleon'   ZONES 4–9
Forms a thick patch of brightly-coloured leaves splashed with a bold combination of green, red, yellow and cream, and with an intense fragrance of tangerines that is not appealing to everyone. Plants spread quickly by underground rhizomes, especially in moist locations, and should be kept out of most borders. Flowers are insignificant. A useful groundcover although very late to come up in spring. Nice in

Hosta 'Frosted Jade'

Hosta ventricosa 'Aureo-marginata'

Hosta 'Wide Brim'

Houstonia caerulea 'Millard's Variety'

Houttuynia cordata 'Chameleon'

Humulus lupulus 'Aureus'

Iberis sempervirens 'Little Gem'

Incarvillea delavayi

containers or at the waterside. Plants will spread more slowly in dry locations. This is eaten as a vegetable in Japan and other Asian countries.

HEIGHT/SPREAD: 15–45cm (6–18″)/45cm (18″)
LOCATION: Prefers a damp to wet soil.
BLOOMS: August
USES: Mᵥ Waterside

HUMULUS
(Hops) ☼ ☀

lupulus   ZONES 2–9
Vigorous climbing vine, useful as a fast cover for a screen or fence. This can be trained up pergolas or trellises, or allowed to clamber up a tree. Cone-shaped dried fruits are used in beer making. Plants are herbaceous, growing back from the ground each year. Can become invasive, spreading quickly underground. Handsome lobed foliage. The gold-leaved form 'Aureus' is an outstanding garden plant and much less rampant, although it may be hardy only to Zone 4 or so.

> "As rampant as the species, this brightly coloured vine complements deep green evergreens, both shrubs and trees, as well as the better blue-foliaged evergreens. Don't be hiding that outhouse with plain old green Hops — let your guests know where it is by using this golden wonder!!"
> – Dr. Duncan Himmelman, Zone 3

HEIGHT/SPREAD: 3–6m (10–20′)/60cm (2′)
LOCATION: Prefers a rich, moist soil.
BLOOMS: July–August
USES: ꙮ Climbing vine

HYPERICUM
(St. John's-Wort) ☼ ☀

polyphyllum 'Grandiflora'   ZONES 5–9
Small, finely-textured leaves form a spreading clump set with large golden-yellow flowers in summer. Useful in the rockery, or over walls. Not evergreen like *H. calycinum*, which is listed under GROUNDCOVERS.

HEIGHT/SPREAD: 15–30cm (6–12″)/30cm (12″)
LOCATION: Average well-drained soil.
BLOOMS: June–August
USES: ⚇ Walls, Edging

HYSSOPUS
(Hyssop) ☼

officinalis 'Pink Delight'   ZONES 4–9
A selection of the normally blue-flowered herb (see under HERBS), this variety has spikes of shell-pink flowers in early summer for several weeks. Foliage is fragrant, and the plant can be used for flavouring, the same as any other hyssop. Plants are fairly woody and benefit from a hard pruning to 10cm (4″) in early spring to keep them dense and bushy. Very drought-tolerant.

HEIGHT/SPREAD: 60–75cm (24–30″)/60cm (24″)
LOCATION: Well-drained soil.
BLOOMS: July–August
USES: ✄⚇ Borders, Herb gardens

IBERIS
(Candytuft) ☼ ☀

sempervirens   ZONES 3–9
A spring-blooming favorite, usually seen cascading over rocks and walls or used as a groundcover. Evergreen foliage forms a compact mat or bush, smothered with white flowers for many weeks. Slightly drought-tolerant.

SPREAD: 30–90cm (1–3′)
LOCATION: Well-drained soil.
BLOOMS: April–June
USES: △Mᵥ▲ꙮ Walls, Slopes, Edging

'Dick Self' New large-flowered selection from Blooms of Bressingham. Pure white, exceptionally long flowering period. HEIGHT: 20–25cm (8–10″)

'Findel' Very big heads of snow-white flowers. A rare form, difficult for nurseries to produce, and worth seeking out! HEIGHT: 20–25cm (8–10″)

'Little Gem' Especially compact selection, very tidy. Masses of small white flowers. HEIGHT: 15cm (6″)

'Snowflake' Larger form, good for edging borders. Clean white flowers in medium-size clusters. HEIGHT: 25cm (10″)

INCARVILLEA
(Hardy Gloxinia) ☼ ☀

delavayi   ZONES 5–9
Large rose-purple, trumpet-shaped flowers above low clumps of bold dark green leaves. Winter protection is recommended in Zones 5–6. Worth growing as a container plant in Zones 1–4, bringing indoors for the winter, or treating as an annual. The fleshy roots are inclined to rot out where soils are heavy or stay wet in the winter. Excellent for cutting. 'Snowtop' is a beautiful new white-flowered selection.

HEIGHT/SPREAD: 45–60cm (18–24″)/30cm (12″)
LOCATION: Well-drained soil. Dislikes winter wet.
BLOOMS: May–July
USES: ✄⚇ Borders

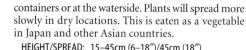

Iris setosa

IRIS
(Iris) ☼ ☀

A wonderful and diverse group of plants, with flowers in virtually every colour of the rainbow. Few gardens would be complete without at least one representative from the Iris ranks. All have grassy, sword-shaped leaves forming a clump. Most prefer a rich, well-drained soil with plenty of water during flowering.

Certain types, most notably the modern hybrid Bearded Irises, are susceptible to the Iris Borer. This nasty pest lays its eggs inside the leaves, which hatch and develop quickly into green worms that tunnel their way down to the fleshy rhizomes. See the section on PESTS & DISEASES at the end of this guide for more information.

ensata   ZONES 4–9
(Japanese Iris) (= *I. kaempferi*) Large, flat crepe-textured flowers appear over tall grassy clumps that

somewhat resemble cattails. These have been selected and bred in Japan for hundreds of years. Plants must have plenty of moisture until they bloom, followed by a drier period for the rest of the growing season. Also, they are not tolerant of lime soils or hot, dry conditions. Japanese Iris are set in their ways, and without the specific conditions just mentioned they will seldom thrive. There are now hundreds of named selections but growers often sell them by colour only, so try to buy plants in flower whenever possible to be sure of what you are getting. Flowers come in shades of blue, pink, purple and white, in both single and double forms.

HEIGHT/SPREAD: 60–120cm (2–4')/45cm (18")
LOCATION: Evenly moist rich soil, see above.
BLOOMS: June–July
USES: ✂ ⚘ Waterside, Borders

'Variegata' Grown more for its excellent foliage, boldly striped lengthwise with green and creamy-yellow, fading to green during the summer months. Flowers are violet-purple. Beautiful at the waterside.

foetidissima   ZONES 6–9
(Gladwyn Iris) An evergreen species, grown for its clusters of colourful scarlet fruit which look attractive in fall and winter, and are sometimes used in dried arrangements. Flowers are insignificant. Tolerates part shade. **'Variegata'** is exceptionally fine, the leaves striped lengthwise with green and white.

HEIGHT/SPREAD: 45–60cm (18–24")/45cm (18")
LOCATION: Prefers a rich moist soil.
BLOOMS: May–July
USES: ✂ Borders, Winter interest

× germanica Hybrids   ZONES 3–9
(Tall Bearded Iris) Familiar to everyone, these are the most popular and widely grown type. Their large satiny flowers put on a short but spectacular display in spring. Modern Bearded Iris flowers come in nearly every colour and combination imaginable, including blue, bronzy-brown, maroon-black, orange, peach, pink, purple, white, and yellow. There are over twenty thousand named varieties that have been selected over the last fifty years or so. Since most growers handle just a small selection of cultivars, gardeners wishing to build up a collection should consider joining one of the Iris societies or contact a specialist Iris grower who does mail-order.

> "I've also heard of a gardener who, every three years, rips out his iris beds and replaces his poor passé sorts with the latest developments, It is foolishness, I say, and not even gardening as I know it."
> – Patrick Lima,
> *The Harrowsmith Perennial Garden*

Bearded Irises are grouped into several categories from Tall (28" plus), down through Border, Intermediate, Standard Dwarf and Miniature Dwarf (the last two listed separately under *Iris pumila*). By far, the Tall Bearded group is the most popular, although these have a tendency to look tired after flowering and remain rather shabby for the rest of the season. They are heavy feeders, requiring additional fertilizer in early spring, again before blooming and once more in mid-August.

Divide plants every 3–4 years in July/August, making sure each division has at least one fan of leaves. Plant into rich well-prepared soil with excellent drainage and in a sunny location. It is very important that the top of the horizontal rhizome should be just showing at the surface of the soil, not too deep nor too shallow. Modern Bearded Iris are terribly overbred and seem to be susceptible to various insects and diseases, most notably Iris borers, aphids, various kinds

various kinds of leaf spots and rots. See the PESTS & DISEASES section for some ideas on controlling these.

HEIGHT/SPREAD: 70cm (28")/30–45cm (12–18")
LOCATION: Rich well-drained loamy soil, better on the dry side.
BLOOMS: May–June
USES: ✂ Borders

'Florentina' (Orris Root) Grown in gardens for centuries, the root of this Iris is dried and ground to produce Orris powder used in potpourri and perfume making. Looking like a typical Bearded Iris, the flowers are pale blue-grey with a yellow beard. HEIGHT: 45–60cm (18–24")

pallida   ZONES 3–9
(Sweet Iris) The species itself is seldom grown, but the striped forms listed below are very popular both for their handsome foliage, and showy lavender-blue flowers. Both forms are good for edging, or anywhere a splash of bright foliage would be effective in a border. These are reliable and disease-resistant. Evergreen in mild areas.

HEIGHT/SPREAD: 60cm (24")/30cm (12")
LOCATION: Average well-drained loamy soil.
BLOOMS: June–July
USES: ✂ ⚘ Borders, Edging

'Aureo-variegata' Attractive stripes of gold and bright green.
'Variegata' The more commonly seen form. Leaves are striped lengthwise with cream and grey-green.

Iris pseudacorus

pseudacorus   ZONES 2–9
(Yellow Flag Iris) Large cattail-sized clumps, attractive at the waterside but also happy in the border. Canary-yellow flowers put on a nice display. Naturalized in many parts of North America along lakes and rivers.

HEIGHT/SPREAD: 90–120cm (3–4')/60cm (24")
LOCATION: Rich average to wet soil.
BLOOMS: May–June
USES: ✂ Border, Waterside

'Flore Pleno' Twice the usual number of petals, flowers almost look like a Canna.
'Variegata' Handsome creamy-yellow stripes, fading at blooming time and then coming back in late summer.

× pumila Hybrids   ZONES 2–9
(Dwarf Bearded Iris) Included here are the Standard Dwarf and Miniature Dwarf Bearded Iris. These have a similar appearance, but both these groups bloom well before the main flush of Tall Beardeds. Their flowers bloom in a wide range of colours although there are not nearly as many named selections in existence; one advantage however is that as a group these are not nearly so overbred, and they naturally have a tougher constitution. Their preference is for a warm site and well-drained soil. Good choice for the rock

Iris ensata

Iris germanica

Iris foetidisima

Iris pallida 'Aureo-variegata'

Iris pallida 'Variegata'

Iris pumila

Iris sibirica 'Silver Edge'

Iris sibirica 'Ruffled Velvet'

garden, or grouped at the border front. These are much easier to grow than the Tall Bearded group, and are generally long-lived and pest free.

HEIGHT/SPREAD: 15–30cm (8–12″)/20–30cm (8–12″)
LOCATION: Average to dry well-drained soil.
BLOOMS: April–May
USES: ✄⊿ Borders, Edging

setosa   ZONES 2–9

(Arctic Iris) Compact, grassy foliage makes a nice edging. Good-sized lavender-blue flowers are similar in appearance to the Siberian Iris but plants are more compact. A very hardy species native to Siberia and Alaska. Could be massed effectively as a groundcover in Zones 2–6, much the way *Liriope* is used in the southern States.

HEIGHT/SPREAD: 15–30cm (6–12″)/30cm (12″)
LOCATION: Average to moist well-drained soil.
BLOOMS: May–June
USES: ⊿✄❦ Wildflower, Borders, Edging

Iris sibirica 'Dreaming Yellow'

sibirica   ZONES 2–9

(Siberian Iris) These have strong clumps of grassy leaves that remain attractive all season. Delicate-looking flowers rise above on slender stems in late spring. Tolerates shade better than most Irises as well as wet soils. Siberian Iris are very long-lived and need to be divided only when the flowers start to become small or few in number. Blooms are generally in shades of blue to rose, purple and white, with many named cultivars in existence. Flowers are nice for cutting, the seed-pods for dried arrangements.

> "Who doesn't love the flowers in June — in the garden and for cutting? The grassy leaves look fresh and verdant all season, and are a great foil for perennials of rounded clumping habit."
> – Ellen Eisenberg, Zone 5

HEIGHT/SPREAD: 60–100cm (24–40″)/60cm (24″)
LOCATION: Rich, average to wet soil.
BLOOMS: May–June
USES: ✄ Borders, Waterside

'Butter and Sugar' Award-winning selection in a soft white and butter-yellow combination. HEIGHT: 70cm (28″)

'Caesar's Brother' Deep violet-blue flowers. Excellent older selection. HEIGHT: 100cm (40″)

'Dreaming Yellow' Light yellow with darker yellow markings. HEIGHT: 75cm (30″)

'Ewen' Rich wine-red flowers with creamy markings. HEIGHT: 75cm (30″)

'Flight of Butterflies' Violet-blue flowers with intricate white veins, like a butterfly wing. HEIGHT: 90cm (3′)

'Papillon' Soft, light blue. HEIGHT: 90cm (3′)

'Persimmon' Rich mid-blue flowers. HEIGHT: 90cm (3′)

'Ruffled Velvet' Velvet-purple flowers with black and gold markings. HEIGHT: 60–75cm (24–30″)

'Silver Edge' Large sky-blue flowers, petals edged in silver. HEIGHT: 75cm (30″)

'Sky Wings' Light blue bicolour with yellow markings. HEIGHT: 90cm (3′)

'Snow Queen' Very tall white-flowered selection. HEIGHT: 100cm (40″)

'Sparkling Rose' Soft rosy-mauve, bronzy veining. HEIGHT: 90cm (3′)

unguicularis   ZONES 8–9

(Winter Iris) (= *I. stylosa*) Totally unlike any of the other Iris, this species opens its blossoms one by one from late fall to early spring. Plants make an evergreen grassy clump, the lavender flowers hiding among them for some extra protection. Prefers a hot, dry site, especially against a wall or house. Performs especially well at the West coast. Plants resent disturbance; divide or move only if absolutely necessary.

HEIGHT/SPREAD: 30–45cm (12–18″)/45cm (18″)
LOCATION: Average well-drained soil.
BLOOMS: December–March
USES: ⊿✄▲ Borders

versicolor   ZONES 2–9

(Blueflag Iris) Native to eastern North America, this species is like a blue-flowered version of *I. pseudacorus*. The bold, upright clumps of green foliage are attractive beside a pond or stream. Plants also adapt nicely to average border conditions.

HEIGHT/SPREAD: 90–120cm (3–4′)/60cm (24″)
LOCATION: Average to wet soil.
BLOOMS: May–June
USES: ✄ Wildflower, Borders, Waterside

ISOTOMA
(Blue Star Creeper) ☼ ◑

fluviatilis   ZONES 6–9

(formerly listed as *Laurentia fluviatilis*) Flat carpet of tiny, green leaves, smothered in light blue starry flowers all summer long. Ideal for planting between paving stones, will stand light traffic. Worth growing even as an annual in colder regions for its showy display. Proving to be hardier than first thought. May winter in Zone 5 with snowcover.

HEIGHT/SPREAD: 4cm (2″)/30cm (12″)
LOCATION: Average to moist well-drained soil.
BLOOMS: May–September
USES: ⊿⋀▲❦ Patios, Walkways

JASIONE
(Shepherd's Bit) ☼ ◑

laevis   ZONES 4–9

(= *J. perennis*) Violet-blue balls of flowers appear all summer. Nice frontal or edging plant. Related to the *Campanulas*, these are especially nice combined with summer-blooming heathers, enjoying similar conditions. Flowers are good for cutting.

HEIGHT/SPREAD: 25–45cm (10–18″)/30cm (12″)
LOCATION: Well-drained light soil, preferably acidic.
BLOOMS: July–September
USES: ⊿✄ Borders, Heather beds

KIRENGESHOMA
(Yellow Waxbells) ◑

HEIGHT/SPREAD: 90–120cm (3–4′)/60–90cm (2–3′)
LOCATION: Rich, moist woodland soil, preferably acidic.
BLOOMS: August–October
USES: ✄ Shady borders, Woodland gardens

koreana ZONES 5–9
Similar in effect to the species below, but more upright. Flowers are pale yellow bells held in upright spikes. Said to be slightly hardier. Both species require similar woodland conditions.

palmata ZONES 5–9
A first-rate foliage plant, with exotic-looking upright clumps of toothed green maple-like leaves. Flowers are pendulous yellow bells rising above on purple-black stems. Good candidate for a cool woodland garden. Somewhat slow to establish.

> "It is, *par excellence*, a subject for the foliage border, where its flowers will not be metaphorically killed by showy neighbours."
> – Christopher Lloyd, *Foliage Plants*

KNAUTIA
(Crimson Scabious) ☼

macedonica ZONES 4–9
(= *Scabiosa rumelica*) A bushy-growing border perennial, valued for its long succession of crimson red, double pincushion flowers. Excellent for cutting. This is a good "filler" plant for summer schemes, and one of the few perennials available in this rich shade of deep red. Sometimes performs as a biennial.

HEIGHT/SPREAD:	60–75cm (24–30″)/60cm (24″)
LOCATION:	Average well-drained soil.
BLOOMS:	June–September
USES:	✂◀▼ Borders

Kniphofia 'Royal Castle Hybrids'

KNIPHOFIA
(Red-Hot Poker, Torchlily) ☼
(formerly Tritoma) Tufts of sword-shaped leaves, forming a broad clump that remains evergreen in milder regions. Flowers are arranged in a bottle-brush shaped head, held on strong upright stems. Recent hybrids have extended the range of colours beyond the old red and yellow combination. In Zones 5–6 the leaves should be tied up and the plants mulched for the winter to protect the sensitive crown. Trim back any damaged leaf-tips in early spring. These demand excellent drainage, yet appreciate a good supply of moisture when blooming. Planting before midsummer is recommended.

Hybrids ZONES 5–9
Much breeding work and selection has happened over the last twenty years, aiming to produce a wider range of colours on sturdy cold-hardy plants. A great deal of variation in plant heights, blooming times, and hardiness has resulted. Moderately drought-tolerant.

SPREAD:	45cm (18″)
LOCATION:	Rich well-drained soil. Dislikes winter wet.
BLOOMS:	June–September
USES:	✂◀▼ Borders

'Bressingham Comet' Compact selection. Grassy foliage, flowers are a yellow and flame orange bicoloor. August–October. HEIGHT: 60cm (24″)

'Primrose Beauty' Flowers are soft primrose yellow, June–September. This stoloniferous variety seems to be hardy over a wide area. HEIGHT: 75–90cm (30–36″)

'Royal Castle Hybrids' Flowers are in various combinations of red, yellow and orange, heads often bicoloured. A seed-grown strain. June–August. HEIGHT: 90cm (3′)

'Shining Sceptre' Glowing golden-orange flowers. July–September. Another of the famous hybrids by Alan Bloom of Bressingham Gardens. HEIGHT: 100cm (40″)

LAMIASTRUM
(False Lamium, Yellow Archangel) ☼ ●

galeobdolon ZONES 2–9
Attractive groundcover plants for shady areas, the foliage remaining evergreen in mild winter regions. Small but showy yellow flowers appear briefly in the spring. Great in containers.

HEIGHT/SPREAD:	20–30cm (8–12″)/30cm (12″)
LOCATION:	Average to moist soil.
BLOOMS:	May–June
USES:	∿◀▼ Shady borders, Woodland

'Florentinum' (= 'Variegatum') Very fast-spreading mat of handsome green and silver striped foliage, the stems running and rooting where they touch the ground. Easily controlled by removing runners or clipping. An especially good groundcover for difficult shady areas, like under trees. Keep this out of the border. Beautiful bronzed appearance in winter.

'Herman's Pride' Pointed leaves, heavily veined with metallic silver. Forms a neat, non-spreading mound, well-behaved and excellent for edging.

> "It shimmers as it spills through even the deepest shade, and though not invasive, pretty much obviates the task of weeding throughout the season. It sculpts itself around the leaves of large Hostas and tumbles its way gracefully over the sides of raised beds and planters."
> – Cathy Forgie, Zone 4

LAMIUM
(Lamium, False Salvia) ☼ ●

maculatum ZONES 2–9
Handsome tidy groundcover plants, with small silver and green leaves. Clusters of flowers appear in spring and sporadically until late fall. Perfect for edging, walls, and in containers, but a bit too vigorous for the rock garden. Evergreen in mild regions. The various selections have become extremely popular in recent years, particularly for landscaping.

HEIGHT/SPREAD:	15–30cm (6–12″)/30–60cm (12–24″)
LOCATION:	Average to moist well-drained soil.
BLOOMS:	May–September
USES:	∿◀▼ Edging, Borders

Kirengeshoma palmata

Knautia macedonica

Kniphofia 'Bressingham Comet'

Kniphofia 'Shining Sceptre'

Lamium maculatum 'Aureum'

Lamium maculatum 'Chequers'

Lamium maculatum 'Shell Pink'

Lavandula angustifolia 'Blue Cushion'

'Aureum' Golden-yellow leaves, pink flowers. Will not tolerate direct sun, much less vigorous.

'Chequers' Very vigorous variety. Leaves are dark green with central silver stripes. Pink flowers throughout the summer. Will sometimes self-seed.

'Pink Pewter' Similar to 'White Nancy', but with clear pink flowers. Good vigour.

> "Lamiums are excellent, vigorous groundcovers, particularly in dry shade, an environment that can be challenging. 'Pink Pewter' has glistening silver and green leaves and shell-pink non-stop flowers. This is one of the great ones for brightening a shady corner."
> – Ellen Eisenberg, Zone 5

'Shell Pink' Green and white striped foliage, soft pink flowers.

'White Nancy' Leaves are almost completely silver, the clear white flowers appear to almost float on top. Excellent choice for covering large or small areas.

Lathyrus latifolius

LATHYRUS
(Sweet Pea) ☼

latifolius   ZONES 3–9
(Everlasting Pea) Trailing perennial vine, will climb on fences and trellises, or clamber over slopes. Flowers are in shades of rose, pink, and white. Good cut-flower, fresh or dried, but unfortunately lacking the fragrance of the annual Sweet Pea. This has naturalized throughout much of North America, but is not at all invasive in the garden.

HEIGHT/SPREAD:	30cm–2.4m (1–8')/30cm (12")
LOCATION:	Average well-drained soil.
BLOOMS:	June–September
USES:	✂ Slopes, Climbing vine

LAURENTIA
See ISOTOMA.

LAVANDULA
(Lavender) ☼

A group of low woody shrubs from the Mediterranean, often grown with perennials in borders and mixed plantings. Lavenders are native to areas with hot dry summers and mild winters, so they are extremely happy at the West coast, but there are some varieties of English Lavender that adapt well right across the country. All types have that same unmistakable sweet fragrance and spikes of showy flowers in summer. Shearing the bushes back lightly after flowering or in early spring will keep them

dense and compact. Most types are moderately drought-tolerant once established.

SPREAD:	30–60cm (12–24")
LOCATION:	Average well-drained soil.
BLOOMS:	June–August
USES:	✂◄▲▼☙ Dried, Borders, Edging

angustifolia   ZONES 4–9
(English Lavender) (formerly *L. vera*) Old-fashioned plant with a long history as a scented herb, but always appreciated for its showy spikes of flowers and attractive grey leaves. Lavender is especially effective when planted around shrub roses. Acting as an evergreen shrub in milder regions, Lavender can be used to make a low hedge. Mulch for the winter in cold areas. Several forms of this species exist.

'Blue Cushion' Excellent new dwarf selection from Blooms of Bressingham. Deep blue spikes of flowers appear freely over a long season. HEIGHT: 40cm (16")

'Hidcote Blue' Rich purple flower spikes, long blooming. Compact habit. A seed-grown strain. HEIGHT: 30–40cm (12–16")

'Jean Davis' Pale pink flowers, very unusual. Vegetatively grown. HEIGHT: 35cm (14")

'Munstead' Bright lavender-blue flowers. The most compact form and generally quite reliable. A seed-grown strain. HEIGHT: 30–40cm (12–16")

'Goodwin Creek Gray'   ZONES 7–9
Beautiful silver-grey foliage, slightly fuzzy and toothed along the edge. Spikes of lavender-blue over a long season. Excellent in a container. HEIGHT: 45–60cm (18–24")

× intermedia 'Provence'   ZONES 5–9
(Lavendin) Developed in France for the perfume industry, this hybrid is more vigorous and disease-free than the *L. angustifolia* types, and a little larger in habit. Light purple spikes held well above the olive-green foliage. HEIGHT: 45–60cm (18–24")

stoechas   ZONES 7–9
(Spanish Lavender) Plant habit is similar to English Lavender, but more tender. Spikes of mauve flowers are crowned by dark purple petals that wave like little flags. Unique and showy. Could be wintered indoors in colder areas. HEIGHT: 45–60cm (18–24")

LAVATERA
(Mallow) ☼

These are now all the rage in Europe but only starting to be widely seen in North American gardens. Their funnel-shaped flowers bring to mind a Rose-of-Sharon or a small single hollyhock, and all of these plants are close relatives. Lavatera are in constant bloom summer through fall, and combine effectively with so many other flowers. These are not long-lived plants but generally last three to five years before dying out.

Hybrids   ZONES 6–9
(Tree Mallow) Plants form a large mound of lobed grey-green leaves, covered in bright hollyhock-type flowers from midsummer to frost. These are actually woody shrubs that should be back hard each spring to 15cm (6"), forcing new bushy growth from the base. The various colour selections look equally at home with both perennials and shrubs. Planting before midsummer is recommended. Use a deep winter mulch in colder areas.

"Plant in a gray and pink color scheme; there are few pink-flowering shrubs so late in the season." – Penelope Hobhouse, *Colour in Your Garden*

HEIGHT/SPREAD:	1.2–3m (4–10')/1.5m (5')
LOCATION:	Average well-drained soil.
BLOOMS:	July–October
USES:	✄ Borders, Mixed plantings.

'Barnsley' White flowers with a red eye, fading to pink. Remove any stems that revert to pink. Reported to be hardy to Zone 5 with protection.

'Candy Floss' Pale pink flowers.

'Pink Frills' Ruffled flowers, soft pink with darker streaks.

'Rosea' Clear pink flowers, free-flowering.

LEONTOPODIUM
(Edelweiss) ☼

alpinum   ZONES 2–9
Well-known rockery plant from the Swiss Alps. Foliage is silver-grey, bearing woolly white flowers, sometimes used for dried arrangements. Best in a well-drained rock garden. Interesting and unique, particularly if you like the song. Extremely drought-tolerant.

HEIGHT/SPREAD:	15cm (6")/25cm (10")
LOCATION:	Very well-drained soil.
BLOOMS:	June–July
USES:	▲▲ Gravel gardens

LEPTINELLA
(Brass Buttons) ☼ ◐

potentillina   ZONES 5–9
(New Zealand Brass Buttons) (formerly *Cotula potentillina*) A flat, carpeting groundcover, the leaves are soft and feathery in texture. Green foliage develops some bronzy tones in cold weather. One of the best plants for between paving stones! Flowers are insignificant. Evergreen at the West coast.

HEIGHT/SPREAD:	5cm (2")/30cm (12")
LOCATION:	Evenly moist, well-drained soil.
USES:	▲△⋀▲ Between flagstones

LEUCANTHEMELLA
(Moon Daisy, Hungarian Daisy) ☼ ◐

serotina   ZONES 3–9
(formerly *Chrysanthemum serotinum*) This is a little-known daisy. Its large white flowers with a yellow eye put on an excellent display in late summer and fall. Plants are quite tall and bushy. Try combining this with some of the taller fall asters. Good for cutting.

HEIGHT/SPREAD:	1.2–1.5m (4–5')/70cm (30")
LOCATION:	Average well-drained soil.
BLOOMS:	August–October
USES:	✄🦋 Borders

Leucanthemum × superbum 'Alaska'

LEUCANTHEMUM
(Shasta Daisy) ☼ ◐

× superbum   ZONES 4–9
(Shasta Daisy) (formerly *Chrysanthemum maximum*) No sunny border would seem complete without these familiar, sturdy white daisies. Recent breeding has resulted in a good selection of flower types and plant heights. All bloom for many weeks beginning in mid-summer, especially when dead flowers are removed. Good drainage in winter is essential.

SPREAD:	30–45cm (12–18")
LOCATION:	Average well-drained soil.
BLOOMS:	June–September
USES:	✄🦋 Borders

'Aglaia' The true form has large, frilly double flowers with a crested white centre. Hardier than 'Esther Read'. Beware of single-flowered seed-grown impostors. HEIGHT: 60–75cm (24–30")

'Alaska' Classic single flowers. Hardy to Zone 3. HEIGHT: 60cm (24")

'Becky' From the southern U.S., this variety has quickly made the rounds and is receiving loud applause for its sturdiness and free-flowering habit, even in hot humid areas. Large single flowers, tall stems and fresh-looking foliage. HEIGHT: 90cm (3')

'Esther Read' Fully double flowers, almost like a florist's mum. Zones 5–9. HEIGHT: 30–60cm (12–24")

'Polaris' Very large single flowers. HEIGHT: 90cm (36")

'Sedgewick' (now *Leucanthemum vulgare*) Fully double flowers, spreading habit. This is likely a double form of Ox-eye Daisy. Zones 1–9. HEIGHT: 30–45cm (12–18")

'Silver Princess' Compact, mounded plants, the best compact seed-grown selection. Single flowers, long blooming. HEIGHT: 30cm (12")

'Snowcap' Excellent, compact selection raised by Blooms of Bressingham. Ideal for massing or edging along the front of the border. Large single white daisies all summer long. HEIGHT: 35cm (14")

'Snow Lady' Very dwarf habit, large single flowers. Award-winning, but noticeably lacking in vigour. HEIGHT: 25cm (10")

'Summer Snowball' Wonderful new double variety from Blooms of Bressingham. Round, fluffy flowers are pure white, the size of tennis balls. Great for cutting. HEIGHT: 75cm (30")

Lavandula × intermedia 'Provence'

Lavandula stoechas

Lavatera 'Rosea'

Leontopodium alpinum

LEWISIA
(Lewisia) ☼ ☀

cotyledon   ZONES 3–9

A challenging but rewarding plant for the rock garden, forming a flat rosette of evergreen foliage. Sprays of brightly-coloured flowers are held above in early summer. Modern hybrid strains produce both solid-coloured and striped flowers, from pink through salmon, orange, yellow and white shades. Lewisia demands perfect drainage, best achieved by placing plants almost vertically between rocks in a wall or planting in a scree garden. A mulch of gravel around the crown is required to keep plants high and dry. Very showy!

HEIGHT/SPREAD:	15–20cm (6–8")/15cm (6")
LOCATION:	Perfectly drained soil.
BLOOMS:	May–July
USES:	△▲❦ Troughs, Screes

Lewisia cotyledon

LIATRIS
(Blazing Star, Gayfeather) ☼

These are popular as commercial cut flowers for their tall, long-lasting spikes. Also excellent border perennials, and easy to naturalize in a meadow planting. Blazing Stars are tough, drought-tolerant North American native wildflowers.

spicata   ZONES 2–9

Plants form a low grassy clump of leaves, with tall spikes of rosy-purple flowers appearing in mid-summer. An easy, reliable border perennial. HEIGHT: 90cm (3')

SPREAD:	45cm (18")
LOCATION:	Well-drained soil. Dislikes winter wet.
BLOOMS:	July–September
USES:	✄❦❧ Borders, Meadows

'Floristan White' Spikes of fluffy white flowers, especially nice together with the purple. HEIGHT: 90cm (3')

'Kobold' Good compact habit, mauve flowers. Good height for the front or mid-border. HEIGHT: 45–60cm (18–24")

Liatris spicata 'Kobold'

LIGULARIA
(Ligularia) ☼ ☀

Bold background or specimen plants, these produce tall clumps of large, rounded leaves with upright spikes or clusters of yellow daisy flowers in summer. At their best in a cool, moist location, especially beside water. Avoid planting Ligularia under trees where they will have to compete for water. During periods of heat or drought the plants may look sad and wilted towards the end of the day, only to bounce back fresh and perky by morning. These are long-lived plants that seldom need dividing.

SPREAD:	70–90cm (30–36")
LOCATION:	Rich, moist to wet soil.
BLOOMS:	July–August
USES:	✄ Borders, Waterside, Specimen

dentata   ZONES 3–9

(= *L. clivorum*) The most commonly seen species with its large green, rhubarb-like rounded leaves that form a large clump. Tall spikes of golden-yellow flowers put on a great show at the back of a summer border. Excellent waterside specimen. Heat tolerant.

'Desdemona' Large handsome purplish leaves, contrasting branching heads of bright-orange daisies. An unforgettable combination! HEIGHT: 90–120cm (3–4')

Ligularia 'Desdemona'

Ligularia wilsoniana

"For sheer drama, this plant is invaluable. The huge clump of enormous leaves, with their deep mahogany-red stems and undersides and shiny, dark green upper surfaces are beautiful. The flowers — tall clusters of coarse orange 'daisies' in mid-summer — seem incongruous with the leaves, but, for its foliage alone, I would never be without this plant."
– Ellen Eisenberg, Zone 5

'Othello' Very similar, slightly earlier to bloom.

× hessei 'Gregynog Gold'   ZONES 3–9

Pyramidal spikes of golden-orange flowers over an impressive mound of large wavy green leaves. Nice for cutting. HEIGHT: 90–150cm (3–5')

stenocephala 'The Rocket'   ZONES 4–9

Purple-black stems ending in long bottle-brush spikes of yellow flowers. Leaves are deeply toothed or divided, lighter in form and reportedly slug-resistant. Excellent as a background plant. An Alan Bloom selection first introduced by Bressingham Gardens. HEIGHT: 120–180cm (4–6')

'Sungold'   ZONES 4–9

Recent Blooms of Bressingham selection with branching stems of golden-orange daisies and a good bushy habit. HEIGHT: 120–165cm (4–5.5')

wilsoniana   ZONES 2–9

Perhaps the best form of all for flower display, with very tall candelabra-like spikes of chrome-yellow daisies in mid-summer. Leaves are large and rounded, forest green. Extremely hardy. Blooms earlier than the rest. HEIGHT: 150–180cm (5–6')

Lilium 'Bolero' – Asiatic Hybrid

LILIUM
(Lily) ☼ ☀

Lilies can provide bold effect in the summer border with their large flowers. The various types offer a wide range of colours, shapes, and blooming times from which to choose. As cut-flowers they are strong stemmed and long-lasting. Divide the clumps every few years in late fall, separating the bulbs and replanting in a different site. Gardeners interested in building up a collection of lilies might consider joining one of the many Lily societies.

Asiatic Hybrids   ZONES 2–9

Easy to grow, early blooming and very hardy. Flowers open wide, either upfacing, outfacing, or nodding, in an incredibly wide range of colours and blends. Some of the newer selections are free of spots or have bold splotches (brushmarks) of a contrasting colour on each petal. The general range includes orange, pink, red, white, and yellow, with many pastels, bicolours and in-between shades available.

> "The garden that grows a crop of lilies cannot help making the transition from June's abundance to midsummer in the most beautiful way." – Patrick Lima, *The Harrowsmith Perennial Garden*

HEIGHT/SPREAD: 60–120cm (2–4')/30cm (12")
LOCATION: Average well-drained soil.
BLOOMS: June–July
USES: ✂❦ Borders, Massing

Aurelian Hybrids   ZONES 4–8
(Trumpet Lily) Immense flaring trumpet flowers, excellent as a background planting in the border or massed among shrubs. Strongly fragrant. These will require staking but otherwise are easy and trouble-free. The choice of named cultivars is not nearly as extensive as the Asiatics but includes a good range of colours, including shades of pink, apricot, orange, white, and yellow.

HEIGHT/SPREAD: 120–180cm (4–6')/45cm (18")
LOCATION: Average well-drained soil.
BLOOMS: July–August
USES: ✂ Borders

lancifolium   ZONES 2–9
(Tiger Lily) (formerly *L. tigrinum*) Out-facing or nodding orange flowers with black spots, held on strong stems in a long branching raceme. Petals curl back attractively behind the flowers. A classic old-fashioned flower, superb for cutting. The tiny little black bulbils held along the stems can be planted like seeds; these will form blooming-size bulbs in about three years.

HEIGHT/SPREAD: 120–150cm (4–5')/45cm (18")
LOCATION: Average well-drained soil.
BLOOMS: August–September
USES: ✂ Borders, Woodland gardens

Oriental Hybrids   ZONES 4–9
(Oriental Lily) Late-blooming and very fragrant, their large star-shaped flowers are superb for cutting. These deserve a place in every border. Oriental lilies have a reputation for being fussy and short-lived. They are often planted near Rhododendrons as the requirements for growing each are similar; light sandy-loam soils that are rich in compost or peat, preferably on the acid side. Gardeners in mild coastal climates most often succeed with these, but they are well worth trying in other areas. Winter mulching is recommended in Zones 4–5. There are many named selections of these but in a fairly small range of colour: mostly in shades of white, pink or red, sometimes attractively banded or spotted.

HEIGHT/SPREAD: 90–180cm (3–6')/45cm (18")
LOCATION: Well-drained lime-free soil. Dislikes winter wet.
BLOOMS: August–September
USES: ✂ Borders, Woodlands

speciosum 'Rubrum'   ZONES 4–9
(Red Japanese Lily) A late-blooming species with branching stems of fragrant ruby-red flowers with a white margin. An old-fashioned favorite for lime-free soils. Very popular flower in wedding bouquets. Prefers a cool exposure.

HEIGHT/SPREAD: 120–150cm (4–5')/45cm (18")
LOCATION: Well-drained lime-free soil.
BLOOMS: August–September
USES: ✂ Borders, Woodland gardens

LIMONIUM
(Sea Lavender) ☼

latifolium   ZONES 2–9
(Sea Lavender) Dainty lavender-blue flowers are borne in large panicles. Plants form a rounded bush, with up to a dozen flowering stems. This is a showy, attractive border perennial. Moderately drought-tolerant. Excellent for drying.

HEIGHT/SPREAD: 60–75cm (24–30")/60cm (24")
LOCATION: Well-drained soil. Dislikes winter wet.
BLOOMS: July–August
USES: ✂❦ Dried Flower, Borders

LINARIA
(Toad-flax) ☼

purpurea 'Canon J. Went'   ZONES 4–9
Short-lived species, but very long-blooming. Upright branching stems bear showy spikes of lavender-pink flowers, a little like miniature snapdragons. These love a warm, sunny site. Plants will usually self-seed.

HEIGHT/SPREAD: 60–90cm (2–3')/30–45cm (12–18")
LOCATION: Well-drained soil. Dislikes winter wet.
BLOOMS: June–September
USES: ✂❦ Borders

LINUM
(Flax) ☼

perenne 'Sapphire'   ZONES 2–9
(Blue Flax) Heavenly-blue flowers in early summer on an upright arching clump. Nice display when planted in groups. Prune hard after flowering to encourage a second flush. Needs excellent winter drainage. Short-lived, but readily self seeds. Very drought-tolerant. An old-fashioned favorite!

HEIGHT/SPREAD: 30cm (12")/30–60cm (1–2')
LOCATION: Well-drained soil. Dislikes winter wet.
BLOOMS: May–August
USES: ▲❦ Borders, Meadows

LIRIOPE
(Lily-turf) ☼ ◑ ●

Widely grown as a groundcover in the southern U.S., this is a sturdy group of plants valued for their heat-tolerance and resistance to pests and diseases. The grassy evergreen leaves form a dense clump or mat, with short spikes of showy flowers in late summer. Liriope prefer a shady exposure, particularly in hot summer areas. Although tolerant of a wide range of sites their preference is for a moist but well-drained soil with plenty of humus, preferably on the acid side. A light trim in early spring will tidy up any brown tips caused by winter winds. These perform surprisingly well in many parts of Canada and the northern U.S.

muscari   ZONES 6–9
(Blue Lily-turf) Plants quickly develop into dense evergreen clumps. Showy spikes of flowers are followed by black berries that remain through the winter. This is the species most used as a groundcover or edging, with close to one hundred named varieties in existence.

Lilium 'Casa Blanca' – Oriental Hybrid

Lilium – Trumpet Yellow

Lilium speciosum 'Rubrum'

Limonium latifolium

Liriope muscari 'Variegata'

Lobelia cardinalis

Lobelia – Fan Series Scarlet

Lobelia siphilitica

HEIGHT/SPREAD: 20–40cm (8–16")/30cm (12")
LOCATION: Average to moist well-drained soil, preferably acidic.
BLOOMS: July–September
USES: ◣△〰▲▼ Massing, Edging

'**Big Blue**' Large spikes of blue flowers, held well above the leaves.

'**Silvery Sunproof**' Green and white leaves.

'**Variegata**' Leaves brightly striped with green and cream. Lavender flowers.

Lithodora diffusa 'Grace Ward'

LITHODORA
(Lithospermum) ☼ ◑

diffusa 'Grace Ward'   ZONES 5–9
An excellent groundcover or rockery plant with brilliant sky-blue flowers all summer long. Foliage is evergreen, an attractive grey-green colour, forming a low creeping mat. Very popular at the West coast where it seems to grow especially well. Inclined to be fussy and short-lived in cold-winter areas; use a winter mulch in Zones 5–6. Must have acidic conditions and perfect drainage to thrive. '**Heavenly Blue**' is a very similar selection.

HEIGHT/SPREAD: 15cm (6")/30–45cm (12–18")
LOCATION: Well-drained acid soil. Dislikes lime.
BLOOMS: May–August
USES: △〰▲▼ Slopes, Walls

LOBELIA
(Lobelia) ☼ ◑
Showy late-summer blooming perennials with large upright spikes of flowers, not at all like the more familiar trailing annual types grown in hanging baskets. These short-lived perennials appreciate a moist site and look perfect growing beside a stream or pond where they will often naturalize by self-seeding. Flowers are excellent for cutting. Use a winter mulch in cold regions, or treat as annuals.

cardinalis   ZONES 4–9
(Cardinal Flower) A native wildflower over much of Eastern North America, growing alongside streams and ponds. Plants have bright green coarse foliage which forms a low clump, with upright spikes of scarlet-red flowers appearing in mid-summer. Typically this is a short-lived species which self-seeds in a good moist spot. Hummingbirds love it.

HEIGHT/SPREAD: 90–120cm (3–4')/45cm (18")
LOCATION: Rich moist, well-drained soil.
BLOOMS: July–September
USES: ✂▼ Borders, Massing

× speciosa   ZONES 6–9
(Hybrid Cardinal Flower) A hybrid group that includes a number of older selections that have traditionally been grown from cuttings and are seldom available in North America. Recent breeding work in Europe has resulted in some excellent new forms that offer a good range of colours with superior vigour. The clumps of bright green or bronze leaves have good strong stems. Hardiness is not yet widely tested but plants are expected to need a winter mulch in Zones 5–7. The long blooming season makes these useful even as bedding annuals.

SPREAD: 30cm (12")
LOCATION: Rich moist, well-drained soil.
BLOOMS: July–October
USES: ✂▼➤ Borders, Massing

Compliment Series Taller, large-flowered plants developed for the floral industry. Foliage is bright green with spikes of blue, deep red or scarlet. HEIGHT: 75cm (30")

Fan Series A compact bushy habit with spikes in shades of deep red, scarlet, deep cinnabar rose and soft orchid rose. Excellent for bedding. HEIGHT: 50–60cm (20–24")

'**Gladys Lindley**' Beautiful ivory-white flowers, large spikes. Zone 5. HEIGHT: 75cm (30")

'**La Fresco**' Jewel-like plum purple flowers. HEIGHT: 70cm (28")

'**Rose Beacon**' Incredible bright rose-pink. HEIGHT: 70cm (30")

'**Tania**' Magenta-purple blooms. Zone 4. HEIGHT: 90cm (36")

'**Wildwood Splendor**' Rich amethyst-purple flowers. Zone 4. HEIGHT: 90cm (36")

splendens 'Queen Victoria'   ZONES 7–9
(Red-leaved Cardinal Flower) Rich maroon-red foliage, contrasting with spikes of scarlet-red flowers. Superb for mass planting, or using in containers, this is widely considered to be one of the best perennials for foliage colour. Not reliably hardy in all areas, but worth growing even as an annual.

HEIGHT/SPREAD: 90cm (3')/30cm (12")
LOCATION: Moist but well-drained soil.
BLOOMS: July–September
USES: ✂▼➤ Specimen, Borders, Waterside

siphilitica   ZONES 4–9
(Giant Blue Lobelia) Stately upright spikes of flowers, from dark blue to white over leafy clumps of green foliage. Great for cutting. This is a native North American wildflower, easy to naturalize in any moist sunny area where it will happily self-seed.

> "The American Indians used this plant to cure syphilis. Gee, and you thought it was grown for its good looks."
> – Ellen M. Talmage, Zone 7

HEIGHT/SPREAD: 60–90cm (2–3')/30cm (12")
LOCATION: Average to moist or wet soil.
BLOOMS: August–October
USES: ✂ Borders, Waterside

LOTUS
(Golden Bird's-Foot) ☼

corniculatus 'Pleniflorus'   ZONES 2–9
A creeping green mat, smothered with double golden pea-flowers in early summer. Good groundcover for difficult sunny areas. Not overly invasive, tolerant of very poor soils.

HEIGHT/SPREAD: 10cm (4")/30cm (12")
LOCATION: Average well-drained soil.
BLOOMS: June–July
USES: △〰▲ Walls, Slopes

LUNARIA
(Money Plant, Honesty) ☼ ◑

annua   ZONES 2–9
(formerly *L. biennis*) Sprays of pretty purple or white flowers are followed by interesting coin-shaped seed-heads. The branches of papery dried pods are popular for indoor decoration. A self-seeding biennial, useful in the shade garden and not weedy.

HEIGHT/SPREAD:	60–90cm (2–3')/30cm (12")
LOCATION:	Rich average to moist soil.
BLOOMS:	May–June
USES:	✂ ☙ Woodland gardens, Meadows

LUPINUS
(Lupine) ☼ ◑

The tall spires of Lupines are an unforgettable sight in the late spring garden. Excellent for cutting, the flowers are available in a rainbow of colours. Plants grow best in a deep, rich soil on the neutral to acidic side. Good drainage is essential. Use a winter mulch in cold regions. Since Lupines are short-lived, renew plantings every other year. Cutting plants back to the base after blooming may encourage them to live an extra year. Lupines often look scruffy after blooming; plant something in front that will get big later in the summer to hide them. Aphids have a special liking for them.

Russell Hybrids   ZONES 3–9
Extensive breeding has created a choice of colours as well as plant heights. Spikes can now be had in shades of blue, pink, rose, red, white, or yellow, sometimes attractively bicoloured. Plants will self-seed if allowed but seedlings will usually revert to mixed colours. In recent years most nurseries are having a terrible struggle trying to grow Lupines due to the presence of a seed-borne disease that infects and kills the young plants. Better success might be had from starting Lupines from seed directly in the garden where they are to grow.

HEIGHT/SPREAD:	75–100cm (30–40")/30cm (12")
LOCATION:	Average to moist soil, preferably acidic.
BLOOMS:	June–July
USES:	✂ ➤ Borders

LYCHNIS
(Campion) ☼

Related to Dianthus, the Campions have flowers in bright pink, magenta, red or orange shades, mostly vibrant, hot shades that don't easily fit into soft pastel colour schemes. However, they are hardy, easy-to-grow plants, mostly for the summer border. Gardeners who develop a more daring sense of colour design will find these interesting and useful.

alpina   ZONES 1–9
(Arctic Campion) From short tufts of grassy leaves, clusters of bright pink flowers appear in late spring. Short-lived but readily self-seeds. An easy little rock garden plant, especially useful in brand-new rock gardens or walls.

HEIGHT/SPREAD:	10–15cm (4–6")/15cm (6")
LOCATION:	Average well-drained soil, preferably acidic.
BLOOMS:	May–June
USES:	◿ Walls

arkwrightii 'Vesuvius'   ZONES 3–9
Clusters of large scarlet-orange flowers, over a compact clump of burgundy leaves. Very showy for the border front. Not long-lived where drainage is poor. Nice for cutting.

HEIGHT/SPREAD:	30–45cm (12–18")/30cm (12")
LOCATION:	Average well-drained soil.
BLOOMS:	June–July
USES:	✂ Borders, Edging

chalcedonica   ZONES 2–9
(Maltese Cross) Very old-fashioned, long-lived cottage garden plants. Domed clusters of flaming scarlet-orange flowers are held aloft on strong stems. Excellent for cutting. Shear back hard (to 12 inches) after flowering to encourage a repeat bloom in fall. A unique salmon-rose shade ('Rosea') is seldom available but worth seeking.

> "…invaluable for its pure bright colour, and can be used in daring color schemes. Grow next to deeper reds, or experiment with neighbouring bronze and purple leaves which absorb some of the 'hot' color." – Penelope Hobhouse,
> *Colour in Your Garden*

HEIGHT/SPREAD:	90–120cm (3–4')/30cm (12")
LOCATION:	Average well-drained soil.
BLOOMS:	June–August
USES:	✂ Borders

coronaria   ZONES 3–9
(Rose Campion) Attractive rosettes of felty grey leaves. Branching stems of bright magenta-rose flowers bloom through the summer. Not a long-lived species, but readily self-seeds. Can be used for cutting. See below for other colour forms.

HEIGHT/SPREAD:	45–75cm (18–30")/30cm (12")
LOCATION:	Average well-drained soil.
BLOOMS:	June–August
USES:	✂ Borders, Meadows

'Alba' White-flowered form, excellent in pastel or white border schemes.

'Angel Blush' Flowers are a delicate soft-pink and white combination. Subtle.

LYSIMACHIA
(Loosestrife) ☼ ●

NOT the same as Purple Loosestrife. These true Loosestrife are all moisture-loving perennials, typically with short spikes of white or yellow flowers. They vary from low creeping types to taller border varieties. Most share the trait of spreading fairly quickly, so some extra consideration should be given to their placement.

ciliata 'Firecracker'   ZONES 3–9
(Fringed Loosestrife) (= *Steironema ciliata*) A species native to the eastern U.S., this select form has rich bronze-purple leaves, forming a loose upright clump. The nodding yellow flowers contrast beautifully. Although this spreads to form a patch it is not too invasive for the border.

> "Don't let this one's aggressive nature frighten you — plant it in a big container sunk into the garden, and you can enjoy its stunning bronze-maroon foliage without fear. By mid-summer, the foliage fades to olive-maroon, contrasting beautifully with the clear yellow flowers."
> – Kevin Ward, Zone 5

Lunaria annua

Lupinus – Yellow

Lychnis chalcedonica

Lychnis coronaria 'Angel Blush'

HEIGHT/SPREAD:	75–90cm (30–36″)/60cm (24″)
LOCATION:	Prefers a rich moist soil.
BLOOMS:	June–August
USES:	✄ Borders, Woodland gardens

Lysimachia ciliata 'Firecracker'

clethroides   ZONES 2–9

(Gooseneck Loosestrife) Unusual spikes of white flowers, bent just like a goose's neck, and highly valued by floral arrangers. Foliage can develop good red fall colour. Quickly spreads to form a patch and may swamp slower-growing neighbours. Best at the waterside or a similar moist location. Tolerates semi-shade. Great for massing.

HEIGHT/SPREAD:	60–90cm (2–3′)/90cm (3′)
LOCATION:	Rich, average to moist soil.
BLOOMS:	July–September
USES:	✄ Borders, Waterside, Woodland

ephemerum   ZONES 5–9

(Milky Loosestrife) A completely non-invasive species that is seldom seen in gardens. Forms a bushy, upright clump of powdery-green leaves and later tall tapering spikes of silvery-white flowers appear. Excellent for cutting.

HEIGHT/SPREAD:	90–120cm (3–4′)/60cm (2′)
LOCATION:	Rich, average to moist soil.
BLOOMS:	July–August
USES:	✄ Borders, Waterside, Woodland

Lysimachia ephemerum

nummularia   ZONES 2–9

(Creeping Jenny) Low trailing stems quickly form a bright green carpet. Golden-yellow flowers appear among the leaves from spring to fall. Also excellent in hanging baskets. Remains evergreen in mild climates. Can become invasive but runners are easily removed or weeded out. Quite tolerant of heavy shade.

HEIGHT/SPREAD:	5–10cm (2–4″)/45cm (18″)
LOCATION:	Prefers a rich moist soil.
BLOOMS:	May–August
USES:	∿▲❦ Lawn substitute, Waterside

'**Aurea**' Bright golden leaves make a glowing display. Must be planted in the shade to avoid scorching. Outstanding carpeter below blue *Pulmonaria*.

> "Adventurous souls might try this one with Heuchera 'Palace Purple', while conservative gardeners might be more comfortable teaming it with *Alchemilla mollis*. Either way, Golden Creeping Jenny's brilliant yellow foliage adds 'oomph' to garden-variety plants."
> – Kevin Ward, Zone 5

Lysimachia punctata 'Alexander'

punctata   ZONES 2–9

(Yellow Loosestrife) Upright, bushy clumps spreading to form a large patch. Star-shaped yellow flowers appear in leafy spikes in summer. Good waterside plant, but adapts well to the border and will even grow in shade under trees. Excellent for cutting.

HEIGHT/SPREAD:	45–90cm (18–36″)/60cm (24″)
LOCATION:	Prefers a rich moist soil.
BLOOMS:	June–August
USES:	✄ Borders, Woodland gardens

'**Alexander**' A recent arrival from England, this puts on an outstanding foliage display, the green leaves boldly edged with cream. Fresh growth is tinged with pink in the spring. Zone 4. HEIGHT: 45–60cm (18–24″)

> "Give this plant a nice warm summery spot and you will be rewarded with the soft green and palest of cream of an old pillow — too bad about the yellow flowers. Did we really wish for a variegated thug?" – Bob Lilly, Zone 8

Malva sylvestris 'Zebrina'

MACLEAYA
(Plume Poppy) ☼ ◑

cordata   ZONES 2–9

A giant background plant with handsome, deeply lobed blue-green leaves, topped in summer by cream-coloured plumes. Plants will spread fairly quickly to make a large patch and can become a tad invasive unless restrained each spring. Otherwise, this is a good bold specimen plant. *M. microcarpa* '**Kelway's Coral Plume**' is similar in stature, with slightly bluer leaves and plumes of bronzy-purple flowers.

HEIGHT/SPREAD:	1.8–2.4m (6–8′)/60–90cm (2–3′)
LOCATION:	Prefers a deep, rich soil.
BLOOMS:	July–August
USES:	✄ Borders, Specimen

MALVA
(Mallow) ☼

moschata 'Rosea'   ZONES 3–9

(Pink Musk Mallow) Satiny pink flowers, like a miniature Hibiscus. The deeply cut leaves give off a pleasant musky smell when crushed. Upright clumps, blooming for many weeks. Cut these back in late summer before they bloom themselves to death. Short-lived.

HEIGHT/SPREAD:	60–90cm (2–3′)/45cm (18″)
LOCATION:	Average well-drained soil.
BLOOMS:	July–September
USES:	✄❦ Borders, Meadows

sylvestris 'Zebrina'   ZONES 4–9

(Striped Mallow) Large bright rose-purple flowers, exotically striped with deep maroon veins. Often behaves as a self-seeding biennial or annual, sometimes lasting longer. An old European cottage garden plant. Blooms over a very long season, well into late fall.

HEIGHT/SPREAD:	60–120cm (2–4′)/45cm (18″)
LOCATION:	Average well-drained soil.
BLOOMS:	July–October
USES:	✄ Borders, Meadows

MAZUS
(Mazus) ☼ ◑

reptans   ZONES 5–9

(Creeping Mazus) Ground-hugging green mats are studded with yellow-spotted lavender flowers. Nice between paving stones or in the rock garden. Prefers a good moist location. Evergreen in Zones 8–9.

HEIGHT/SPREAD:	5–10cm (2–4″)/30cm (12″)
LOCATION:	Moist well-drained soil.
BLOOMS:	April–June
USES:	▲△∿▲ Between patio stones, Waterside

MENTHA
(Mint) ◑ ●

requienii   ZONES 7–9

(Corsican Mint) Tiny green leaves create a flat carpet with the fragrance of creme-de-menthe. Minute mauve flowers appear in July. Very nice growing in rock gardens and patio cracks, even as a self-seeding annual. Looks a bit like Baby-tears.

> "If you are a *laissez-faire* gardener with a shady piece of lawn that you don't treat with weed-killers, this is an ideal spot to introduce the creeping peppermint. As you tread and mow, a pungent waft from the plant will vie with the smell of oil and petrol fumes." – Christopher Lloyd, *Foliage Plants*

HEIGHT/SPREAD: 2.5cm (1")/15–30cm (6–12")
LOCATION: Likes a rich moist soil.
BLOOMS: July–August
USES: ▲△ⅿ⍦ Between patio stones

MERTENSIA
(Bluebells) ☼ ●

virginica **ZONES 3–9**
(Virginia Bluebells) A favorite woodland perennial, blooming in mid-to late spring and shortly thereafter setting seed and going completely dormant for the rest of the year. Flowers are large dangling sky-blue bells, held in a loose cluster over powdery blue-green leaves. In favoured sites the plants will increase by self-seeding. This plant is often harvested from the wild, so make sure the plants you purchase are nursery propagated!

HEIGHT/SPREAD: 45–60cm (18–24")/30cm (12")
LOCATION: Moist, rich woodland soil.
BLOOMS: April–May
USES: ▲ⅈ⋖Woodland gardens

MIMULUS
(Monkey Flower) ☼ ☼

Little-known in North America, aside from the seed-grown mixes usually sold in bedding packs in the spring. There are several excellent hybrids in existence, all of these grown from cuttings. Treat as a half-hardy perennial and winter indoors in a pot, except in mild regions. Constantly wet soils beside a pond or splashing fountain suit these perfectly.

'Puck' **ZONES 7–9**
New selection from England, this has bright yellow flowers tinged with nasturtium gold. Rich two-tone effect. Mounding, spreading habit.

HEIGHT/SPREAD: 15cm (6")/30cm (12")
LOCATION: Moist, rich soil.
BLOOMS: June–September
USES: ⅿ⍦Waterside, Containers

MONARDA
(Bee-Balm, Bergamot) ☼ ☼

Tall, bushy plants with aromatic mint-like foliage. Their bright shaggy flower heads attract bees and butterflies. Plants are suited to the border or wildflower garden, having been developed from native North American species. A good range of colours is available and there are some exciting new dwarf selections being developed that should become available in the near future.

Plants spread to form a vigorous patch that thins out in the middle; divide every other year and replant only the younger outside pieces. Powdery mildew on the foliage is often a problem. See the section on PESTS & DISEASES for some ideas on controlling this, or choose some of the resistant varieties.

didyma Hybrids **ZONES 3–9**
The varieties listed below are mostly tall growing, long-flowering and excellent for cutting. They grow best with a moist, rich soil and full sun. Mildew is often a sign of stress due to lack of water. Very attractive to hummingbirds and butterflies.

"Your bee-balm plants will flourish if you plant them in a sunny area near gravel. Mine 'reached' from their bed into nearby river stone, and multiplied by runners. New blooms appeared in late summer."
– Joan Nicks, Zone 6

HEIGHT/SPREAD: 75–120cm (30–48")/45cm (18")
LOCATION: Rich, moist well-drained soil.
BLOOMS: June–September
USES: ✂ ➤ ⍦ Borders, Woodland edge

'Adam' Large flowers, light red in colour.
'Beauty of Cobham' Lilac-pink flowers and purplish foliage.
'Gardenview Scarlet' An older variety but with good mildew resistance. Brilliant red flowers.
'Jacob Kline' Recent arrival, reported to be hands-down the most mildew-resistant red ever. Large scarlet heads, tall habit.
'Marshall's Delight' A newer hybrid from Agriculture Canada. Hot-pink flowers on good strong stems. Highly resistant to powdery mildew. Outstanding!
'Panorama Mix' Seed-strain with a nice range of scarlet, bright red, pink, salmon, and crimson shades.
'Petite Delight' Exciting new selection from Agriculture Canada. A real breakthrough, this is a dwarf selection with clear lavender-pink flowers, ideal for the front of the border or in pots! Good mildew-resistance. HEIGHT: 25–30cm (9–12")
'Prairie Night' ('Prärienacht') Very tall German selection, dark purple-lilac flowers.
'Snow White' ('Schneewittchen') Small creamy-white flower heads.
'Violet Queen' Deep purple-blue flowers.

MYOSOTIS
(Forget-Me-Not) ☼ ●

Few other flowers can match the true sky-blue of Forget-me-nots. Their long display combines perfectly with all sorts of spring-blooming bulbs and perennials. These are ideal "tuck-in" plants for the spring garden, self-seeding anywhere that pleases them.

scorpioides 'Spring Carpet' **ZONES 3–9**
(True Forget-Me-Not) (= *M. palustris*) A true perennial species that prefers a constantly moist or wet soil and a sunny site. Low, creeping stems form a low spreading patch. Flowers are bright blue with a yellow eye. Good waterside plant. Trim back lightly after blooming.

HEIGHT/SPREAD: 15–20cm (6–8")/20cm (8")
LOCATION: Moist to wet soil.
BLOOMS: April–June
USES: ⍦ Waterside, Wet sites

sylvatica **ZONES 3–9**
(Woodland Forget-Me-Not) The more commonly grown species, these always make a bright spring display. Widely used to underplant spring bulbs, especially tulips. This is a true biennial that will almost always perenniate by self-seeding. Fairly shade tolerant, especially below deciduous trees. There are strains available in various shades of blue as well as pink and white.

HEIGHT/SPREAD: 15–25cm (6–9")/15cm (6")
LOCATION: Average to moist well-drained soil.
BLOOMS: April–June
USES: ▲ⅿ⍦ Borders, Woodland gardens, Bedding

Mertensia virginica

Mimulus 'Puck'

Monarda 'Marshall's Delight'

Monarda 'Violet Queen'

Nepeta × 'Dropmore Blue'

Oenothera berlandieri 'Siskiyou'

Oenothera fruticosa 'Sonnenwende'

Oenothera pallida

NEPETA
(Catmint) ☼

Showy, fragrant relatives of the mints. These give us a good range of blues to use in the summer border, combining so nicely with the flashier border plants. Taller varieties are useful for cutting.

> "My cat ate the entire plant that first night. I hope at least his breath is fresher. It seemed to agree with him and did not make him sick. I think I will stick to my Basil, Oregano and Parsley."
> – Debby, Zone 8, via the Internet

× 'Dropmore Blue'   ZONES 2–9
A Canadian hybrid of high merit bred by Dr. Frank Skinner and introduced by him in 1932. Excellent choice for edging or mass planting, with masses of sterile bright blue flowers that appear throughout the summer. The dense fragrant grey-green foliage stands up well to heat, although plants often benefit from clipping back in early July. Great in containers. An effective companion to roses. Moderately drought-tolerant.

> "Some gardeners shear Dropmore Blue after blooming to encourage a second flush. Just once I tried this method, neighborhood cats immediately flattened my plants." – Joanne Baskerville, Zone 4

HEIGHT/SPREAD: 30cm (12")/30cm (12")
LOCATION: Average well-drained soil.
BLOOMS: June–September
USES: ❦❀ Edging, Borders, Massing

sibirica 'Blue Beauty'   ZONES 2–9
(Siberian Catmint) This variety is known in Europe as 'Souvenir d'André Chaudron'. Whatever you call it, this is a robust and long-blooming plant for the border. Spikes of fragrant tubular flowers are deep lavender blue, held above an upright clump of foliage. Inclined to spread a bit, but easily restrained with a spade. A little-known perennial, superb for cutting!

HEIGHT/SPREAD: 60–90cm (2–3')/45cm (18")
LOCATION: Average well-drained soil.
BLOOMS: June–August
USES: ✂ Borders

subsessilis   ZONES 4–9
(Chinese Catmint) A relative newcomer to the scene, this is a mounding species with glossy green foliage and large heads of lavender-blue flowers. Quite possibly hardier than listed.

HEIGHT/SPREAD: 45–60cm (18–24")/45cm (18")
LOCATION: Average well-drained soil.
BLOOMS: June–July
USES: ✂ Borders

NIPPONANTHEMUM
(Montauk Daisy, Nippon Daisy) ☼ ◑

nipponicum   ZONES 5–9
(Nippon Daisy, Montauk Daisy) (formerly *Chrysanthemum nipponicum*) A nearly shrubby type of daisy, with thick leathery green leaves. Plants grow fairly tall, and can be used to good specimen effect. Yellow-eyed white daisy flowers appear in fall. Prune plants back to 10cm (4") in spring, and pinch in midsummer if you want compact growth. Tolerant of ocean-side conditions.

HEIGHT/SPREAD: 60-90cm (2–3')/60cm (2')
LOCATION: Well-drained soil.
BLOOMS: September–October
USES: ✂❦❀ Specimen, Borders

OENANTHE
(Oenanthe) ◑

fistulosa 'Flamingo'   ZONES 4–9
(Flamingo Creeper) Recently brought over from Korea, this interesting foliage plant is related to parsley. The leaves are large and lacy, blue-green dappled with cream and lavender pink. Umbels of white flowers are held above. This forms a fast-spreading mat that roots wherever it touches the ground but can be easily controlled by clipping back the runners. Interesting in a hanging basket or window box.

HEIGHT/SPREAD: 10cm (4")/75cm (30")
LOCATION: Prefers a rich, moist soil.
BLOOMS: July–August
USES: ❧❀ Baskets

OENOTHERA
(Evening Primrose, Sundrops) ☼

Sun-loving plants, very tolerant of hot sites and lean dry soils. Flowers are poppy-shaped, with a soft satiny texture. Sundrops are daytime blooming, while Evening Primroses open late in the day and close before the next morning. All types are originally native North American wildflowers.

berlandieri 'Siskiyou'   ZONES 5–9
(Mexican Evening Primrose) A vigorous and extremely floriferous selection, with upfacing cup-shaped flowers in a beautiful light rose shade. This shows good potential as a landscaping plant with a long season of bloom. Foliage is olive green. Plants form a low mat. Because of its wandering habit, this should probably be restrained or edged regularly. Very drought-tolerant.

HEIGHT/SPREAD: 20–30cm (8–12")/60–75cm (24–30")
LOCATION: Needs a well-drained soil.
BLOOMS: June–September
USES: ❧❦❀ Edging, Massing

fremontii 'Lemon Silver'   ZONES 4–9
Beautiful new Canadian introduction that forms a low mat of silvery-blue leaves, bearing huge lemon-yellow crepe-textured flowers that seem to rest right on top. Blooms over a very long season. Similar to *O. macrocarpa*.

HEIGHT/SPREAD: 15cm (6")/30–45cm (12–18")
LOCATION: Average, well-drained soil.
BLOOMS: June–August
USES: ▲❦ Edging

fruticosa   ZONES 3–9
(Yellow Sundrops) (formerly listed as *O. tetragona*) Flowers begin as red buds, opening into lemon-yellow blossoms over several weeks. Plants eventually spread to form a wide patch. Divide every other year. These are reliable, long-lived garden perennials. Several named varieties exist. Very drought-tolerant.

HEIGHT/SPREAD: 45–60cm (18–24")/30–60cm (12–24")
LOCATION: Average well-drained soil.
BLOOMS: June–August
USES: ❦ Borders, Massing

'Sonnenwende' Excellent German selection. Bronzy-red tinged foliage forms a sturdy upright clump. Large, bright yellow flowers over a long season. A great improvement.

macrocarpa   ZONES 3–9
(Ozark Sundrops) (formerly listed as *O. missouriensis*) Large yellow blossoms with a crepe-like texture. With low, sprawling stems this is best suited to the rock garden or for edging. Very drought-tolerant.

HEIGHT/SPREAD:	15–30cm (6–12")/30cm (12")
LOCATION:	Deep, well-drained soil.
BLOOMS:	June–August
USES:	▲▼❦ Edging

pallida   ZONES 4–9

(White Evening Primrose) Large white crepe flowers, aging to shell pink. A short-lived perennial, but will self-seed if happy. Needs excellent drainage. Very drought-tolerant.

HEIGHT/SPREAD:	30cm (12")/30cm (12")
LOCATION:	Average to poor well-drained soil.
BLOOMS:	June–August
USES:	▲❦ Walls, Slopes

OPHIOPOGON
(Lilyturf) ☼ ☽

Many varieties of Lilyturf (or Mondo Grass) are used in the Southern U.S. as groundcovers. Generally not as hardy as the closely related Liriope, a winter mulch of evergreen boughs is recommended in Zones 5–6. These form evergreen grassy tufts, the small flowers almost hidden among the leaves.

planiscapus 'Niger'   ZONES 6–9

(Black Lilyturf) With its nearly jet-black leaves this makes a most unique specimen for edging or mass planting. Short spikes of pale pink flowers are followed by black berries in the fall. At its best when contrasted with yellow or silver foliage, such as *Lysimachia nummularia* 'Aurea' or *Lamium* 'White Nancy'. This is not a fast grower. Prefers a sheltered, partly shaded location.

> "The color is difficult to place in a garden, exotic and unusual but drawing the eye as firmly as a patch of red. Make a feature of it by emphasizing its dramatic potential with yet more deep purple foliage."
> – Penelope Hobhouse,
> *Colour in Your Garden*

> "One of the quotes I hear most frequently is that 'its black colour makes it hard to place in a garden…' Basic black is hard to place? Did all the rules just change?? Black goes with everything. Talk to Queen Street, Penelope!" – Val Ward, Zone 5

HEIGHT/SPREAD:	15–30cm (6–12")/20–30cm (8–12")
LOCATION:	Rich, moist well-drained soil.
BLOOMS:	July–August
USES:	▲⋀▲❦ Massing, Edging

OPUNTIA
(Prickly-pear Cactus) ☼

humifusa   ZONES 3–9

Lots of gardeners are surprised when they discover this hardy cactus for the first time. Not only a conversation piece, these are also beautiful in flower and nasty to weed around! Clumps form broad flat olive-green pads, with relatively few prickles. Large sulphur-yellow flowers are formed at the ends of the branching pads in summer, lasting for only a day or two before they shrivel up. Later in the fall rosy-pink fruits appear. Drought-tolerant, to say the least.

HEIGHT/SPREAD:	15–30cm (6–12")/20–30cm (8–12")
LOCATION:	Average to poor gravelly soil.
BLOOMS:	June–July
USES:	▲▲▼❦ Dry gardens, Edging

ORIGANUM
(Oregano) ☼

In addition to the more herbal, pizza-flavouring varieties, there are a few types of Oregano which are showy border perennials worthy of a bright sunny spot.

laevigatum 'Herrenhausen'   ZONES 4–9

Fragrant, bushy clumps bear many clusters of mauve-pink flowers through the summer. A recent German hybrid gaining much attention here. This is most effective when allowed to romp and trail through and over other border plants. Good for cutting.

HEIGHT/SPREAD:	30–60cm (12–24")/45cm (18")
LOCATION:	Average well-drained soil.
BLOOMS:	July–September
USES:	✂❦ Borders, Walls

vulgare 'Aureum'   ZONES 4–9

Excellent bright yellow foliage forming a low, spreading mat. A terrific edging plant in the border. Seems to colour up well in either sun or shade. Fragrant pale mauve flowers appear in early summer. Some gardeners prefer to keep this low throughout the season by clipping lightly every six weeks or so. This also serves to maintain the leaf colour into late fall. Nice on walls or slopes. 'Gold Tip' is similar, but with green foliage and bright golden-yellow tips it is even more handsome and effective.

> "A wonderful bright chartreuse-green ground cover, but watch it! It spreads."
> – Warren Hartman, Zone 6

HEIGHT/SPREAD:	15–30cm (6–12")/45cm (18")
LOCATION:	Average well-drained soil.
BLOOMS:	July–August
USES:	❦ Borders, Edging, Walls

PAEONIA
(Garden Peony) ☼

Old favorites for the late spring border, prized for their large satiny flowers, so superb for cutting. The handsome foliage remains attractive all season, particularly when hoops or rings are used to hold clumps together. Breeding has created thousands of named cultivars, many of which are available only through specialist growers. A small number of excellent varieties are listed below, offering a good starting point for newer gardeners.

Peonies prefer a deep, rich well-drained loamy soil and full sun exposure. New plants take several years to become established, and resent being disturbed at any time. Many years can go by before Peonies actually require dividing, as many as ten or fifteen. When necessary, divide plants in the early fall only; be sure that each division has several growth points or eyes, and that they are planted no deeper than they were originally growing. Established plants should be fertilized in the early spring and again immediately after blooming. Peonies can easily be damaged by rain, especially the double-flowered forms, unless adequately staked or grown in special peony hoops.

Ophiopogon planiscapus 'Niger'

Origanum laevigatum 'Herrenhausen'

Origanum 'Gold Tip'

Paeonia lactiflora 'Festiva Maxima'

Paeonia 'Monsieur Jules Elie'

Paeonia 'Nippon Beauty'

Paeonia 'Bowl of Beauty'

Paeonia tenuifolia

"As landscaping tools, peonies are more versatile than most perennials. In addition to spectacular blooms, the symmetrical yard-high growth of elegant, long-lasting leaves makes the plants naturals for focal points or massed display." – Patrick Lima, *The Harrowsmith Perennial Garden*

Peonies are fairly free of pests. Ants are often seen feeding on the sugar that coats the sticky flower buds, but they are in no way harmful or helpful. A fungal infection known as Botrytis can sometimes damage the flowers, turning them black. Thrips are occasionally a problem. See the PESTS & DISEASES section for information on controlling these.

lactiflora Hybrids   ZONES 2–9

(Common Garden Peony) The very large number of named cultivars have been categorized into Single, Japanese, Semi-double, and Double forms, each category basically having more petals than the one previous. Flowers vary tremendously in size, blooming time, and fragrance, with the range of colours including every shade of pink, magenta, red, white and cream imaginable. As some nurseries sell by colour only, it is wise to buy plants in flower whenever possible, or else look for named varieties.

HEIGHT/SPREAD:	75–100cm (30–40")/90cm (3')
LOCATION:	Rich, well-drained loamy soil.
BLOOMS:	late May–June, divided into early, middle and late.
USES:	✂ Borders, Massing

'Angel Cheeks' Double; soft pink, outer petals flecked with red; middle.

'Bowl of Beauty' Japanese; fuchsia-pink with creamy-white stamens; early.

'Catharina Fontijn' Double; soft pink with white blush; early.

'Claire de Lune' Single; creamy-yellow petals, fragrant; very early.

'Constance' Japanese; pink with yellow stamens; middle.

'Dia Jo Kuhan' Japanese; small-flowered, magenta with a pink edge, yellow stamens; middle.

'Duchesse de Nemours' Double; creamy-white with a yellow centre, fragrant; early.

'Festiva Maxima' Double; white with red streaks, fragrant; early.

'Henri Potin' Single; deep pink, tinted carmine, white stamens; late.

'Inspecteur Lavergne' Double; red with white petal edges; middle-early.

'Karl Rosenfield' Double; deep purple-red; middle.

'Laura Dessert' Double; creamy-white with a yellow flush; middle-early.

'L'Eclatante' Double; red flowers, yellow stamens; middle.

'Lou Schenk' Single; rose-pink, yellow stamens; middle.

'Monsieur Jules Elie' Double; large, light rose-pink flowers; early.

'Nippon Beauty' Japanese; dark red, yellow and red stamens; late.

'Okinawa' Japanese; carmine red, yellow stamens; middle.

'Prince of Darkness' Double; dark midnight-red; middle.

'Primavère' Double; incredible creamy-white outer petals, sulphur-yellow centre; early.

'Romance' Japanese; large pink flowers; middle.

'Sarah Bernhardt' Double; fragrant rose-pink favorite; late.

tenuifolia   ZONES 2–9

(Fernleaf Peony) Rare and much in demand. The finely-cut leaves make this quite unlike any other Peony. The delicate, crimson-red single flowers seem to rest on the leaves, appearing well before the main flush of Garden Peonies begins. Even more rare and expensive is the double red-flowered **'Plena'**, a collector's gem!

"It looks too exotic and delicate to be reliable in a northern garden, but is in fact iron-clad hardy, clumps up quite nicely and requires no special care. Don't be afraid of the price — this plant will outlive you." – Cathy Forgie, Zone 4

HEIGHT/SPREAD:	30–45cm (12–18")/30–45cm (12–18")
LOCATION:	Rich, well-drained loamy soil.
BLOOMS:	May–June
USES:	▲✂ Borders, Edging

Papaver orientale 'Allegro'

PAPAVER
(Poppy) ☼

Satiny poppy flowers are a traditional favorite. They are useful for cutting if picked in bud, the cut ends then seared over a flame. Good drainage is crucial, particularly where winters are wet. Most species are short-lived perennials that happily self-seed in any sunny border, the exception to this is the longer-lived Oriental Poppy. All species prefer lighter soils and a warm, sunny location.

alpinum Hybrids   ZONES 3–9

(Alpine Poppy) Short and graceful little poppies, in shades of yellow, orange, pink, and white, the petals sometimes intricately fringed. The ferny leaves form a low tuft. Short lived, but freely self-seeding into rock garden cracks and crevices. Moderately drought-tolerant. This species name is invalid, *P. burseri* currently is considered acceptable.

HEIGHT/SPREAD:	15–20cm (6–8")/15cm (6")
LOCATION:	Well-drained soil.
BLOOMS:	May–August
USES:	▲▼⚘ Screes, Troughs, Walls

atlanticum   ZONES 5–9

(Atlas Poppy) Low silvery-green tufts of hairy leaves are a pretty contrast to the soft sherbet-orange flowers. Short lived, but freely self-seeding. Nice scattered in a sunny border. The occasional double-flowered plant will show up unexpectedly from the seedlings.

HEIGHT/SPREAD:	30cm (12")/20cm (8")
LOCATION:	Well-drained soil.
BLOOMS:	May–August
USES:	▲✂ Borders, Meadows

nudicaule ZONES 2–9
(Iceland Poppy) Tufts of light-green leaves, with cheerful flowers in shades of yellow, orange, red, pink, or white, sometimes strikingly bicoloured. Long blooming season. Usually biennial but freely self-seeding. Many strains exist, each with a slightly different range of colours. Good for cutting if picked in bud. Moderately drought-tolerant.

HEIGHT/SPREAD: 30–45cm (12–18″)/30cm (12″)
LOCATION: Average well-drained soil.
BLOOMS: May–October
USES: △⌇✂ ✿ Borders, Walls

orientale ZONES 2–9
(Oriental Poppy) Large clumps of coarse, hairy foliage, producing enormous satiny flowers in late spring. Nice in the border, but because they usually go completely dormant after flowering, plant something nearby that gets bushy in the summer to fill in the gap. There are several good seed strains available in shades of orange, salmon and red, typically with a dark zone or eye in the middle. Many named hybrids also exist; these are propagated from root-cuttings and include both single and double-flowered forms in shades of orange, true pink, white, and deep red, sometimes bicoloured or with exotically fringed petals.

> "The two perennials that speak to me most strongly of early summer are lupins and oriental poppies. 'What about bearded irises?' you may well ask. Sad to say, I have grown out of them." – Christopher Lloyd, *Christopher Lloyd's Flower Garden*

HEIGHT/SPREAD: 75–100cm (30–40″)/60cm (24″)
LOCATION: Well-drained soil, preferably sandy loam.
BLOOMS: May–June
USES: ✂ Borders

'Allegro' Orange-scarlet blooms, compact. Seed strain. HEIGHT: 45–60cm (18–24″)
'Beauty of Livermere' Deep ox-blood red. Seed strain.
'Brilliant' Vivid, fiery scarlet. Seed strain.
'Carneum' Shades of salmon to flesh pink. Seed strain.
'Cedar Hill' Clear soft pink petals.
'Helen Elizabeth' Crinkled salmon-pink flowers, black centre.
'Perry's White' Large white flowers, black base spots.
'Picotee' Wide salmon-pink edges with a white base.
'Royal Wedding' White petals with a black centre. Seed strain.
'Türkenlouis' Fiery red with a black eye, unusual fringed petals.

PATRINIA
(Patrinia) ☀ ◐

scabiosifolia ZONES 4–9
A seldom-grown, yet worthwhile border perennial. Sprays of bright yellow flowers are held in branching heads, resembling dill at first glance. Useful as a filler among bolder flowering plants such as Summer Phlox. Try it in combination with *Verbena bonariensis*! Excellent for cutting.

HEIGHT/SPREAD: 90–120cm (3–4′)/60cm (2′)
LOCATION: Well-drained soil.
BLOOMS: July–September
USES: ✂ Borders, Massing

PELTIPHYLLUM
See DARMERA.

Penstemon barbatus 'Prairie Dusk'

PENSTEMON
(Beard-Tongue) ☀
A large and diverse group of plants, mostly wildflowers native to areas of North America with warm arid summers. Their showy, tubular flowers are usually held above the foliage in upright spikes. Taller types make excellent cut-flowers. Penstemon cannot tolerate wet feet, so very good drainage is a basic requirement for all types, especially so for the lower alpine species.

barbatus Hybrids ZONES 3–9
These are among the hardiest *Penstemon* available. Plants typically form a low mound of green foliage, with spikes of trumpet flowers rising above in early summer. Taller varieties are quite good for cutting. Divide plants every other year to keep them vigorous. Moderately drought and heat tolerant.

SPREAD: 30cm (12″)
LOCATION: Average well-drained soil.
BLOOMS: June–August
USES: ✂ ➤ ✿ Borders, Wildflower gardens

'Elfin Pink' Compact spikes of clear pink flowers. Good companion to 'Prairie Dusk', and equally as reliable. HEIGHT: 30–45cm (12–18″)
'Hyacinth Mix' The hardiest type, this seed strain produces compact clumps of flowers in a mixture of blue, lilac, pink, and scarlet. HEIGHT: 30cm (12″)
'Prairie Dusk' Strong stems of vivid purple flowers over a long season. Very effective in combination with *Achillea* 'Moonshine'. HEIGHT: 60cm (24″)

digitalis 'Husker Red' ZONES 4–9
A recent selection from the University of Nebraska. Attractive upright clumps of maroon-red foliage are a wonderful contrast in the border, retaining their colour all season long. Flowers are very pale pink, held on stems well above the leaves. Especially effective when mass planted. This is sure to become a popular variety in the near future. Selected as the 1996 Perennial Plant of the Year by the Perennial Plant Association.

HEIGHT/SPREAD: 75–90cm (30–36″)/30cm (12″)
LOCATION: Average well-drained soil.
BLOOMS: July–August
USES: ✂ Wildflower, Borders, Massing

fruticosus 'Purple Haze' ZONES 4–9
Introduced by the Native Plant Program at the U.B.C. Botanical Garden in 1992, this sub-shrub is native to the hot interior of British Columbia. Plants are smothered with showy lilac-purple flowers for several weeks in late spring. Foliage is evergreen, the plant forming a low bushy mound that will

Papaver orientale 'Carneum'

Papaver orientale 'Perry's White'

Papaver orientale 'Türkenlouis'

Patrinia scabiosifolia

Penstemon digitalis 'Husker Red'

Penstemon fruticosus 'Purple Haze'

Penstemon 'Garnet'

Perovskia atriplicifolia

cascade nicely over banks and walls. Suitable for rock gardens or edging. This plant will not be happy in heavy wet soils or with regular overhead irrigation. Very drought-tolerant.

> "Masses of tubular mauve-purple flowers overwhelm the foliage in late spring. Irresistible to neighbours and hummingbirds alike."
> – Joanne Baskerville, Zone 4

HEIGHT/SPREAD:	20cm (8")/60cm (24")
LOCATION:	Very well-drained soil.
BLOOMS:	May–June
USES:	△⋏⋎▲⋎ 🝔 Wildflower, Walls, Slopes

Hybrids   ZONES 8–9

(Hybrid Beard-tongue) The showiest varieties by far, these put on a terrific display of colour in the summer and fall border. Plants form a bushy upright clump, bearing several spikes of large trumpet flowers. Used in England for massed bedding. Unfortunately they are not reliably hardy and should be mulched even in mild winter areas, or treated as bedding annuals. Excellent in pots and tubs. Many named forms have been selected.

SPREAD:	45cm (18")
LOCATION:	Average well-drained soil.
BLOOMS:	June–October
USES:	✂⋎⋎ Borders, Massing

'Garnet' Wine red flowers. HEIGHT: 50cm (20")

'King George' Salmon-red with a white throat. HEIGHT: 60cm (24")

'Mother of Pearl' Very soft lilac-pink with red stamens. Blooms of Bressingham selection. HEIGHT: 60cm (24")

'Purple Passion' Bells of rich violet-purple. Blooms of Bressingham selection. HEIGHT: 60cm (24")

'Ruby' Bright ruby-red flowers, bushy growth. Blooms of Bressingham selection. HEIGHT: 50cm (20")

'Sour Grapes' Large, pale purple flowers. HEIGHT: 70cm (28")

'Snowstorm' Clean snow-white bells. Blooms of Bressingham selection. HEIGHT: 50cm (20")

PEROVSKIA
(Russian Sage) ☼

atriplicifolia   ZONES 4–9

Not really a sage at all, *Perovskia* forms an upright bush of fine-textured grey-green leaves that are pleasantly fragrant when rubbed. The plant becomes a haze of lavender blue by midsummer when spikes of tiny flowers appear. These continue to bloom well into the fall, contrasting beautifully with the various late-blooming Rudbeckias and other daisies in bloom then. Russian Sage is an excellent filler plant for the border, but can also make an effective display when mass planted on its own, or featured with waving ornamental grasses. Some of the woody stem must be left each year for new shoots to develop in the spring; prune plants back to 15cm (6") in late fall or early spring. Moderately drought-tolerant. A former Perennial Plant of the Year in 1995.

HEIGHT/SPREAD:	90–150cm (3–5')/60cm (2')
LOCATION:	Well-drained soil. Dislikes winter wet.
BLOOMS:	July–September
USES:	✂🝔 Borders, Massing

'Filigran' Hybrid selection from Germany. Foliage is even more lacy and finely cut, plants have a bushy upright habit. HEIGHT: 100cm (40")

Persicaria thunbergii 'Langthorn's Variety'

PERSICARIA
(Fleece-Flower, Knotweed) ☼ ◑

Formerly listed as Polygonum, these have recently been moved by botanists into Persicaria and Fallopia. A good number of these varieties are relatively new to North American gardens but can be depended on to create attention with their showy late summer and fall display. They all feature short spikes of pink or red poker flowers, usually held over top of the foliage.

affinis 'Dimity'   ZONES 3–9

(Dwarf Fleeceflower) (formerly *Polygonum affine*) Forms a low carpet of leathery green leaves, turning bronzy-red in fall. Short poker spikes of red flowers fade to pink as they age. A nice groundcover or rock garden plant, appreciating part shade. This form is more reliably perennial than some of the older ones. Extremely drought-tolerant. Flowers can be dried.

HEIGHT/SPREAD:	15–20cm (6–8")/30–60cm (12–24")
LOCATION:	Moist to average well-drained soil.
BLOOMS:	June–August
USES:	△⋏⋎🝔 Borders, Edging

amplexicaulis   ZONES 4–9

(Mountain Fleece) (formerly *Polygonum amplexicaule*) Quite new to North American gardens, these bushy plants are upright, ideal for massed landscape planting but yet not too invasive for the border. They are covered with showy poker flowers from midsummer on. Good choice for difficult wet sites. Nice for cutting, can also be dried.

> "An amazing plant, in beauty from the end of June until the frost of autumn."
> – Graham Stuart Thomas,
> *Perennial Garden Plants*

HEIGHT/SPREAD:	90–120cm (3–4')/60cm (24")
LOCATION:	Rich moist well-drained soil.
BLOOMS:	June–September
USES:	✂⋏⋎ Massing, Borders, Waterside

'Firetail' Bright salmon-red flowers, larger spikes. Selected by Blooms of Bressingham.

'Speciosa' Also known as 'Atrosanguinea'. An older selection with good deep red flowers.

'Taurus' Rich scarlet-red pokers on a fairly compact bush, excellent for cutting. A new hybrid from Blooms of Bressingham, and the best of the lot. HEIGHT: 90cm (3')

bistorta 'Superba'　　　ZONES 3–9
(Bistort) (formerly *Polygonum bistorta*) Large bright-pink spikes are held well above the dense green foliage. Another good perennial for mass planting, or in the border. Spreading but not invasive. Especially good for cutting.

    HEIGHT/SPREAD:　75cm (30")/60cm (24")
    LOCATION:　　　Average to moist well-drained soil.
    BLOOMS:　　　　June–August
    USES:　　　　　✂ Borders, Massing

campanulata　　　ZONES 5–9
(Bell-flowered Knotweed) Fluffy heads of dangling pink bell-shaped flowers appear for many weeks in high summer. Plants are bushy, upright and spread to form a clump. Prefers a moist site. **'Rosenrot'** is a selection with rosy-red flowers.

    HEIGHT/SPREAD:　90cm (3')/90cm (3')
    LOCATION:　　　Moist well-drained soil.
    BLOOMS:　　　　July–September
    USES:　　　　　✂ Borders, Massing

cuspidatum 'Compactum'
See FALLOPIA.

filiformis 'Painter's Palette'　　　ZONES 5–9
(Formerly listed as *Tovara virginiana*) Grown for its colourful foliage; the leaves are variegated with cream and green, with an unusual V-shaped chocolate-brown marking. Used as a groundcover for moist areas or as a bushy specimen plant. Sometimes tends to spread, sometimes not. Especially useful among shrubs. Airy sprays of greenish flowers change into deep red seed-heads in late fall. Seedlings may appear around the garden, many of them coming true.

    HEIGHT/SPREAD:　60–120cm (2–4')/60cm (2')
    LOCATION:　　　Prefers a rich, moist soil.
    BLOOMS:　　　　August–September
    USES:　　　　　◠● Massing, Waterside

polymorpha　　　ZONES 5–9
(White Fleeceflower) Recommended by designer Wolfgang Oehme as a well-behaved, non-spreading species with a long season of display. Upright, bushy plants bear big fluffy spikes of creamy-white flowers. Coarse in texture, but of interest particularly in the low-maintenance landscape. Hardiness is not yet fully tested. May be OK to Zone 4.

    HEIGHT/SPREAD:　90–120cm (3–4')/90cm (3')
    LOCATION:　　　Average to moist well-drained soil.
    BLOOMS:　　　　July–September
    USES:　　　　　✂ Borders, Massing

thunbergii 'Langthorn's Variety'　　　ZONES 6–9
A beautiful new foliage groundcover, pointy heart-shaped leaves are medium green with silvery and bronze v-shaped markings similar to a cyclamen leaf. Plants are creeping, the deep red stems rooting at the nodes where they touch the ground. Pale pink pom-pom flowers, a little bit like Baby's-breath. Shows great promise in containers and hanging baskets as well as under shrubs. Not widely tested yet for hardiness, possibly Zone 5 or colder. Can be invasive.

    HEIGHT/SPREAD:　10–15cm (4–6")/60–90cm (24–36")
    LOCATION:　　　Moist to average well-drained soil.
    BLOOMS:　　　　July–September
    USES:　　　　　◠◠● Borders, Edging

PETASITES
(Butterbur) ☀ ◑

japonicus 'Giganteus'　　　ZONES 4–9
(Giant Japanese Butterbur) A monster plant for the waterside, bearing enormous rounded leaves, not unlike rhubarb. Greenish flowers appear on naked stems in very early spring. This is a bold textural plant that looks great beside a pond or stream. Place carefully, as this is an aggressive spreader and difficult to eradicate. The leaf-stems are edible, if you are adventurous!

    HEIGHT/SPREAD:　120–180cm (4–6')/120cm (4')
    LOCATION:　　　Moist to wet soil, even in shallow water.
    BLOOMS:　　　　March–April
    USES:　　　　　Waterside specimen

PETRORHAGIA
(Tunic Flower) ☀

saxifraga　　　ZONES 2–9
(Formerly listed as *Tunica saxifraga*) A low-growing rock garden plant, producing a misty cloud of white or pale pink flowers similar to Baby's Breath. Easy and reliable. Blooms over a long season. Self-seeds prolifically.

    HEIGHT/SPREAD:　15–20cm (6–8")/15–30cm (6–12")
    LOCATION:　　　Average well-drained soil.
    BLOOMS:　　　　June–August
    USES:　　　　　◠● Walls, Edging

PHLOMIS
(Jerusalem Sage) ☀

tuberosa 'Amazone'　　　ZONES 4–9
Unknown in North American gardens, this is grown commercially in Europe as a cut flower. Forms a low mound of coarse dark green leaves, with tall spikes of rose-pink hooded flowers in the summer. Interesting in the middle of the sunny border.

    HEIGHT/SPREAD:　120–150cm (4–5')/60cm (2')
    LOCATION:　　　Average well-drained soil.
    BLOOMS:　　　　June–August
    USES:　　　　　✂ Borders

PHLOX
(Phlox) ☀ ◑

Among the most popular of garden perennials, these range in form from low creeping alpines to tall border plants. The flowers of most types have a heavy, sweet perfume, so the taller varieties are especially valued for cutting. All are selections or hybrids of native North American wildflowers.

× arendsii Hybrids　　　ZONES 3–9
(Hybrid Phlox) A small group of hybrids developed early the century, and similar in habit to Summer Phlox, but more disease-resistant for the most part. Blooming is a little earlier and plants are also shorter.

    HEIGHT/SPREAD:　60cm (2')/60cm (2')
    LOCATION:　　　Average to moist well-drained soil.
    BLOOMS:　　　　June–July
    USES:　　　　　✂ Borders, Meadow gardens

'Suzanne' White flowers with a contrasting red eye.

× chattahoochee　　　ZONES 4–9
(Chattahoochee Phlox) A chance hybrid found growing wild in northern Florida. This is an excellent newer variety suited to a lightly shaded woodland setting, but does equally well in full sun. Low, bushy plants are covered in brilliant blue flowers with a maroon-purple eye. Trim plants back lightly after flowering. May prove to be hardier.

    HEIGHT/SPREAD:　15–25cm (6–10")/30cm (12")
    LOCATION:　　　Prefers a rich, moist soil.
    BLOOMS:　　　　April–June
    USES:　　　　　◠● Edging, Woodland gardens

carolina Hybrids　　　ZONES 3–9
(Carolina Phlox) Similar to the Summer Phlox, these hybrids are less prone to powdery mildew and

Persicaria affinis 'Dimity'

Persicaria amplexicaulis 'Firetail'

Persicaria bistorta 'Superba'

Petasites japonicus 'Giganteus'

Phlox × chattahoochee

Phlox divaricata 'Louisiana'

Phlox douglasii 'Crackerjack'

Phlox paniculata 'Bright Eyes'

begin to bloom nearly a month earlier. Upright, bushy clumps. Dead-head after the first flush of flowers and they will usually re-bloom in the fall.

HEIGHT/SPREAD: 90cm (3')/60cm (2')
LOCATION: Average to moist well-drained soil.
BLOOMS: June–July
USES: Borders, Meadow gardens

'Magnificence' Good-size heads of magenta-pink flowers.

'Miss Lingard' Large heads of pure white flowers; early-blooming, extremely fragrant.

divaricata   ZONES 3–9
(Woodland Phlox) These medium-sized clumps are ideal for edging along a shady border. Loose clusters of flowers appear in spring. Nice groundcover under shrubs or trees, preferring partial shade. Shear plants lightly after blooming. There are a few named colour selections.

> "One of the prettiest flowers of April is the wild blue phlox. Along with the Virginia bluebell, it is one of the handsomest and showiest of American wildflowers." – Henry Mitchell, *One Man's Garden*

HEIGHT/SPREAD: 30cm (12")/30cm (12")
LOCATION: Moist, rich woodland soil.
BLOOMS: April–June
USES: Woodland gardens

'Louisiana' Purple-blue flowers with a dark eye. Early.

douglasii   ZONES 2–9
These are dwarf creepers, similar to *P. subulata* but even more compact, forming a dense, low carpet of evergreen leaves smothered with flowers in spring. Good choice for rock gardens or edging. More resistant to downy mildew and other disease problems that so often bother the *subulata* varieties. Best in full sun. Fairly drought-tolerant.

HEIGHT/SPREAD: 5–10cm (2–4")/30cm (12")
LOCATION: Well-drained soil.
BLOOMS: April–May
USES: Edging, Scree

'Crackerjack' Large flowers, intense carmine-red. Good grower!

'Red Admiral' Bright rose red flowers.

'Rose Cushion' Delicate soft baby pink. Very unusual.

maculata Hybrids   ZONES 3–9
(Meadow Phlox) This group of hybrid Phlox is often recommended as a substitute for Summer Phlox in areas where powdery mildew is a problem. Plants have a similar upright habit, but the foliage is darker green and the cone-shaped flower heads appear a little bit earlier. Flowers are fragrant, excellent for cutting. Though mildew-resistance is excellent, the choice of colours is more limited.

HEIGHT/SPREAD: 90cm (3')/60cm (2')
LOCATION: Average to moist well-drained soil.
BLOOMS: June–August
USES: Borders, Meadow gardens

'Natascha' Beautiful pink and white bicolor, candystripe effect.

paniculata   ZONES 3–9
(Summer Phlox, Garden Phlox) These luxurious panicles of bright flowers can be spectacular in the summer border. The many named selections offer a wide choice of colours to match any border scheme. Shorter plants should be placed in front of Summer Phlox, to hide the withering lower leaves at blooming time. Superb cut flowers.

Powdery mildew is often a problem, see the section on PESTS & DISEASES for some ideas on how to control it.

Simply growing Summer Phlox on a moist site or keeping it well watered will help to prevent mildew. Fertilize in early spring and again just before flowering as these are heavy feeders. Plants should be divided about every three years.

A great number of named cultivars have been developed over the years. These range in colour from pink through salmon, orange and red, to blue, mauve-purple and white. Some selections have a contrasting eye in the centre of each flower. A sampling of modern named varieties follows.

HEIGHT/SPREAD: 60–120cm (2–4')/60–75cm (24–30")
LOCATION: Rich, moist well-drained soil.
BLOOMS: July–September
USES: Wildflower, Borders

'Blue Boy' Bluish-mauve flowers, the closest to true blue. HEIGHT: 100cm (40")

'Bright Eyes' Pink with a red eye. Mildew-resistant. HEIGHT: 90cm (36")

'Darwin's Joyce' Variegated foliage, similar to and possibly identical to 'Norah Leigh'. HEIGHT: 75cm (30")

'David' A new white variety with very fragrant flowers, highly mildew resistant. HEIGHT: 90–100cm (36–40")

'Eva Cullum' Large heads, clear pink flowers with a dark red eye. Compact habit. Selected by Blooms of Bressingham. HEIGHT: 60–75cm (24–30")

'Fairest One' Good-size heads of shell-pink flowers. Compact. HEIGHT: 60cm (24")

'Franz Schubert' Lilac-blue flowers with a darker eye. Another long-blooming Blooms of Bressingham selection. HEIGHT: 90cm (36")

'Fuchsia' Deep purple-blue. HEIGHT: 90cm (36")

'Juliet' Pale-pink flowers, compact. HEIGHT: 60cm (24")

'Orange Perfection' The closest to a true orange. HEIGHT: 90cm (36")

'Norah Leigh' Until recently a hard-to-obtain variety, the leaves are strongly variegated with cream-yellow and green. Flowers are near-white with a pink eye. A little difficult to place in the border, but interesting all season long. HEIGHT: 75cm (30")

> "I really, really like this plant. I really, really don't know what to put with it." – Kevin Ward, Zone 5

'Shortwood' New selection from Blooms of Bressingham. Heads of pink flowers with a darker pink eye. A tall, mildew-resistant variety, good companion to 'David'. HEIGHT: 110cm (45")

'Starfire' Cherry-red flowers, bronzy green foliage. HEIGHT: 90cm (36")

'The King' Very deep wine purple, large trusses. HEIGHT: 60–75cm (24–30")

× procumbens 'Variegata'   ZONES 3–9
An outstanding variety, the foliage is strongly variegated with creamy-yellow and green. Mauve-pink flowers are held in upright clusters. A little gem for the woodland or rock garden, preferring part shade.

HEIGHT/SPREAD: 20cm (8")/30cm (12")
LOCATION: Well-drained soil.
BLOOMS: April–May
USES: Woodland garden

× 'Spring Delight'   ZONES 3–9
A late-spring blooming hybrid of medium height, with many clusters of rose-pink flowers. Vigorous habit, best in partial shade. Good for cutting.

HEIGHT/SPREAD:	30–50cm (12–16″)/30cm (12″)
LOCATION:	Average well-drained soil.
BLOOMS:	May–June
USES:	⚥⚔ Borders, Edging

stolonifera ZONES 2–9

(Creeping Phlox) A dense evergreen groundcover, tolerant of heavy shade. Small but showy clusters of flowers appear in late spring. Excellent under shrubs. Very different from the other spring-blooming varieties. Keep out of full sun. A former Perennial Plant of the Year.

HEIGHT/SPREAD:	15–30cm (6–12″)/30cm (12″)
LOCATION:	Rich, moist well-drained soil.
BLOOMS:	April–May
USES:	⚘△⋀▲ Edging, Woodland gardens

'Blue Ridge' Lilac-blue flowers.

'Bruce's White' White flowers with a yellow eye.

'Pink Ridge' Dark mauve-pink flowers.

'Sherwood Purple' Good strong purple-blue.

subulata ZONES 2–9

(Moss Phlox, Creeping Phlox) Low mats of evergreen leaves are smothered with flowers in spring. Very popular rock garden and edging plants. Not recommended as a groundcover for large areas as the plants thin out too quickly. Divide clumps every other year to maintain vigour. Shear plants lightly after blooming. Downy mildew is a common problem and is difficult to prevent; choosing a sunny well-drained site to begin with will help in avoiding it. Fairly drought-tolerant. Several colour selections are commonly available.

HEIGHT/SPREAD:	5–15cm (2–6″)/30–45cm (12–18″)
LOCATION:	Well-drained soil.
BLOOMS:	April–May
USES:	⚘△⋀▲⚔ Edging, Walls

'Apple Blossom' Lovely pale-pink blossoms.

'Atropurpurea' Rosy-red flowers.

'Benita' Lilac blue with a darker eye.

'Candy Stripes' A new variety with very attractive flowers; white and rose-pink stripes with a crimson eye.

'Ellie B.' Clear white star-shaped flowers. Tight habit.

'Emerald Cushion Blue' Pale lilac-blue flowers. Excellent foliage.

'Emerald Pink' By far the most widely grown variety, smothered with screaming pink flowers.

'Laura' Pale pink with a darker eye.

'Marjorie' Dark pink with a red eye.

'Oakington Blue Eyes' Lavender-blue flowers. Selected by Blooms of Bressingham.

'Rosette' Very compact and distinctly mound-forming. Rose-pink flowers.

PHYGELIUS
(Cape Fuchsia) ☼ ☽

Upright, bushy plants from South Africa, with tubular flowers similar to Fuchsia. They are perennial shrubs at the West coast, but also worth trying outdoors in the milder parts of Zone 5 and 6. Plants should be cut back hard to 15cm (6″) in early spring, and pinching occasionally through the season will maintain a more compact and bushy habit. Cuttings taken in fall will root easily in a greenhouse or under lights, providing a backup to plants wintering outside. These make excellent container plants for the patio or deck. Good for cutting.

HEIGHT/SPREAD:	90cm (3′)/45–60cm (18–24″)
LOCATION:	Average to moist well-drained soil.
BLOOMS:	July–October
USES:	⚥⚔ Borders, Tubs

aequalis 'Yellow Trumpet' ZONES 7–9

(Yellow Cape Fuchsia) Clusters of soft yellow hanging bells appear throughout the summer and fall.

capensis ZONES 6–9

(Orange Cape Fuchsia) Large orange-red flowers with a yellow throat. Reported to be the hardiest form. If left to get shrubby this may grow as tall as six or eight feet.

× rectus Hybrids ZONES 7–9

(Hybrid Cape Fuchsia) Recent crosses and hybrids, some of these are in interesting new shades, with especially large heads of flowers.

'Moonraker' Soft creamy-yellow flowers, dark green leaves.

'Winchester Fanfare' Deep salmon-pink with a yellow throat.

PHYSALIS
(Chinese Lantern) ☼ ☽

alkekengi ZONES 2–9

Showy scarlet-orange inflated pods appear in September, and are useful for dried arrangements. Flowers are insignificant. An aggressive spreader, best kept in the cutting garden or back lane, or allowed to naturalize at the edge of a woodland. Fertilize yearly for good-quality lanterns. For a little fun try tucking a vase full of the cut lantern stems next to a large gold-leaved hosta!

HEIGHT/SPREAD:	60–90cm (2–3′)/60cm (2′)
LOCATION:	Moist but well-drained soil.
USES:	⚥⚔ Cutting gardens, Not in borders

PHYSOSTEGIA
(Obedient Plant) ☼ ☽

virginiana ZONES 2–9

Another native North American wildflower. Tall wand-like spikes of flowers appear in midsummer, the common name comes from the fact that the individual flowers in the spikes will stay wherever you move them. Very useful as a background plant in the border or wild garden. Excellent cut flowers. These form a large clump that may be inclined to spread, but can be easily controlled with an edging spade. Several colour selections exist.

> "If you have nothing else to do, you can reposition the individual flowers, which are attached to their stems by the botanical equivalent of a ball-and-socket joint…" – Patrick Lima,
> *The Harrowsmith Perennial Garden*

SPREAD:	60cm (24″)
LOCATION:	Prefers a rich moist soil.
BLOOMS:	July–September
USES:	⚥⚔⚘ Borders, Woodland gardens

'Pink Bouquet' Bright pink flowers. HEIGHT: 90–120cm (3–4′)

'Summer Snow' Pure white flowers. Slower spreading. HEIGHT: 60–75cm (24–30″)

'Variegata' Green leaves are heavily blotched with cream. Lilac flowers. Much less aggressive, very choice! HEIGHT: 60–90cm (2–3′)

Phlox paniculata 'Norah Leigh'

Phlox stolonifera 'Sherwood Purple'

Phlox subulata 'Candy Stripes'

Physostegia virginiana

PLATYCODON
(Balloon Flower) ☼ ◐

Platycodon grandiflorus

grandiflorus   ZONES 3–9
These are a real novelty in the garden when their inflated buds actually "pop" open into star-shaped flowers. The long-lived plants form an upright clump in the border that seldom needs dividing, with flowers available in shades of blue, pink or white. Because Balloon Flowers are very slow to make an appearance in spring they can be easily damaged by early weeding or digging; you can mark the spot by planting crocuses or other small bulbs underneath them. Double flowered forms are sometimes available.

HEIGHT/SPREAD:	60–75cm (24–30")/60cm (24")
LOCATION:	Average well-drained soil.
BLOOMS:	June–August
USES:	✂ Borders

POLEMONIUM
(Jacob's Ladder) ☼ ●

Polemonium caeruleum 'Brise d'Anjou'

caeruleum   ZONES 2–9
These form lush clumps of fresh green leaves that can easily be mistaken for some kind of fern. Later in the spring the upright stems appear, topped with clusters of small bright blue or white bell-shaped flowers. Showy in the shade garden. Can be a prolific self-seeder unless the fading flower stems are removed.

HEIGHT/SPREAD:	45–90cm (18–36")/30cm (12")
LOCATION:	Average to moist soil.
BLOOMS:	May–July
USES:	✂▲ Borders, Woodland gardens

'Brise d'Anjou' An incredible new selection from Blooms of Bressingham. The ferny leaves are brightly edged in creamy-yellow, which makes for a completely new texture, delicate and lacy looking. Stems of violet-blue flowers are an added bonus, but the punch is really from the foliage alone. This is one of the most exciting finds of the last few years, sure to become a favourite for edging borders and shade gardens, also worth trying in containers. Best in part shade. HEIGHT: 60cm (24")

POLYGONATUM
(Solomon's Seal) ◐ ●

Polygonatum commutatum

Their graceful, arching stems add an exotic touch to the shade garden and are often described as being architectural. Delicate creamy bell flowers hang from the stems in late spring to be followed later by black berries. Solomon's Seal are the perfect woodland companions to Hostas, Astilbes, and ferns. These are highly regarded for cutting by flower arrangers. New plantings may take a year or two to become established.

LOCATION:	Moist woodland soil.
BLOOMS:	May–June
USES:	▲ Borders, Woodland gardens

commutatum   ZONES 3–9
(Giant Solomon's Seal) These bold, arching stems of green leaves can form a wide clump. This species is a North American wildflower that eventually needs lots of space or regular division.

HEIGHT/SPREAD:	90–120cm (3–4')/60–90cm (2–3')

Polygonatum odoratum 'Variegatum'

> "Not only does this plant give a wonderful green background in the summer months but as autumn arrives the leaves turn a bright yellow to gold."
> – Warren Hartman, Zone 6

falcatum 'Variegatum'   ZONES 2–9
Arching stems of green leaves, edged in creamy-white stripes. A compact form that is great for edging. HEIGHT: 45–60cm (18–24")

multiflorum   ZONES 2–9
(Many-flowered Solomon's Seal) The best species for flowering, with clusters of hanging bells all along the stem. 'Variegatum' has creamy-white leaf margins. HEIGHT: 60–70cm (24–30")

odoratum 'Variegatum'   ZONES 2–9
(Fragrant Solomon's Seal) Green leaves are edged with broad creamy-white stripes. Fragrant waxy bells appear in spring, followed by black berries. Brightens up a shady site. Slow to establish. HEIGHT: 60cm (24")

POLYGONUM
See PERSICARIA, FALLOPIA.

Potentilla megalantha

POTENTILLA
(Cinquefoil) ☼
Although the Shrubby Cinquefoils are familiar landscape plants, these herbaceous types are not nearly so well known. Their wild-rose shaped flowers appear in shades of red, orange, yellow, or white. Most are happy in average sunny border conditions.

megalantha   ZONES 2–9
(Woolly Cinquefoil) (formerly listed as *P. fragiformis*) Clumps of beautiful felty green strawberry-shaped leaves. Golden-yellow flowers are in clusters, blooming in early summer. Good rockery or edging plant. Excellent foliage.

HEIGHT/SPREAD:	30cm (12")/30cm (12")
LOCATION:	Average well-drained soil.
BLOOMS:	May–June
USES:	▲▼ Borders, Edging

nepalensis 'Miss Willmott'   ZONES 2–9
Scarlet-red single flowers, with a lighter pink centre. Good front-of-the-border or edging plant. Shear plants back after their first flush of bloom to keep them tidy and to encourage a second flush in the fall.

HEIGHT/SPREAD:	30cm (12")/30cm (12")
LOCATION:	Average well-drained soil.
BLOOMS:	June–September
USES:	▲ Borders, Edging

neumanniana 'Nana'   ZONES 3–9
(Alpine Cinquefoil) (formerly listed as *P. verna* 'Nana') A very low, non-spreading rockery plant. Single yellow buttercup flowers nestle on a compact evergreen mound. Very showy. Fairly drought-tolerant.

HEIGHT/SPREAD:	10cm (4")/15–30cm (6–12")
LOCATION:	Average well-drained soil.
BLOOMS:	April–June
USES:	▲▲♥⚘ Troughs, Walls

Primula × *bullesiana*

PRIMULA
(Primrose, Cowslip) ☿

Primrose flowers are a true sign of spring, associating well with all sorts of flowering bulbs. They are moisture-lovers, and seem to do best in cooler climates, particularly in coastal areas. Where winters are severe apply a thick mulch in late fall. Certain species are even hardy on the prairies.

> "No spring perennials bloom as long —
> a full five weeks on average — and no
> perennials at all, with the exception of
> bearded irises, display as wide and lovely
> a colour range as primroses."
> – Patrick Lima,
> *The Harrowsmith Perennial Garden*

auricula Hybrids   ZONES 2–9
(Auricula Primrose) (correctly *P.* × *pubescens*) Rosettes of waxy, evergreen leaves bear clusters of flowers in muted shades of yellow, mauve, pink, red and wine, usually with a contrasting eye. These were extremely popular in Victorian England where hundreds of named varieties were selected and collected.

HEIGHT/SPREAD:	15–20cm (6–8")/20–30cm (8–12")
LOCATION:	Well-drained moist soil.
BLOOMS:	March–May
USES:	▲▲♣✂⚘ Edging, Borders

× bullesiana   ZONES 4–9
(Hybrid Candelabra Primrose) A delightful hybrid group, generally grown from seed, that gives a mixture of yellow, violet and red shades. Flowers are held in whorls on upright stems. These are definitely vigorous moisture lovers.

HEIGHT/SPREAD:	50cm (20")/25cm (10")
LOCATION:	Rich moist soil.
BLOOMS:	June–August
USES:	✂△ Borders, Waterside

denticulata   ZONES 2–9
(Drumstick Primrose) Flowers are in a ball-shaped cluster, in shades of blue, lilac, pink, and white. These are vigorous, durable and tough garden plants; hardy almost anywhere with reliable snow cover or a light mulch.

HEIGHT/SPREAD:	30cm (12")/25cm (10")
LOCATION:	Rich moist soil.
BLOOMS:	March–May
USES:	✂△ Borders, Woodland gardens

× elatior Pacific Hybrids   ZONES 4–9
The best-known Primroses because they are so widely available, often sold at florists and grocery stores in late winter to be enjoyed indoors. These will survive outdoors and thrive particularly well in mild-winter areas where they pop into flower during warm spells from November through April. In colder regions these should be planted away from the cold north-west wind in a sheltered spot, and they will bloom through the cooler spring months. A huge range of colours and bicolours are available, including every shade of white, cream, pink, red, blue, purple, orange and yellow imaginable. Short-lived.

HEIGHT/SPREAD:	10–15cm (4–6")/15–20cm (6–8")
LOCATION:	Average to moist well-drained soil.
BLOOMS:	November–May
USES:	▲∿•▲⚘ Edging, Woodland gardens

florindae   ZONES 3–9
(Himalayan Cowslip) A late-blooming Primrose, sending up large umbels of fragrant, dangling yellow or orange flowers in the summer. Excellent for cutting. Long-lived if planted in a good moist site.

HEIGHT/SPREAD:	60–90cm (2–3')/30–60cm (1–2')
LOCATION:	Rich moist to wet soil.
BLOOMS:	June–August
USES:	✂ Borders, Waterside

japonica   ZONES 5–9
(Japanese Primrose) A candelabra-flowered type, with several whorls of red, pink or white blossoms on each upright stem. Leaves form a low, cabbage-like clump of fresh green. This species prefers a constantly moist soil, perhaps beside a stream or pond, but will adapt to a semi-shaded border. 'Miller's Crimson' has good medium-red flowers.

HEIGHT/SPREAD:	30–60cm (12–24")/30cm (12")
LOCATION:	Rich moist soil.
BLOOMS:	May–July
USES:	✂△ Borders, Woodland gardens

× juliae 'Wanda'   ZONES 2–9
(sometimes listed as *P. pruhoniciana*) An extremely popular, very old variety. Magenta-purple flowers smother the bright green leaves in early spring. Perhaps the toughest Primrose of all, the plants quickly form a dense patch. Divide plants every two to three years, right after blooming.

HEIGHT/SPREAD:	15cm (6")/30cm (12")
LOCATION:	Average to moist well-drained soil.
BLOOMS:	March–May
USES:	▲∿• Edging, Woodland gardens

'Lilac Wanda' A sport with lighter lilac-pink flowers. Not quite so shocking a colour.

'Wanda Hybrid Mix' A special seed-strain offering the same habit and vigour as the original 'Wanda' but in a wider range of colours, including yellow, red, pink and white.

vialii   ZONES 3–9
(Chinese Pagoda Primrose) Bizarre-looking rocket-shaped spikes of flowers in a dazzling mauve and scarlet combination. A short-lived summer bloomer, often self seeding when grown in a bright, cool woodland setting.

HEIGHT/SPREAD:	30–60cm (1–2')/20–30cm (8–12")
LOCATION:	Moist well-drained soil.
BLOOMS:	May–July
USES:	✂△ Woodland gardens, Borders

vulgaris Hybrids   ZONES 4–9
(Double English Primrose) These charming clusters of fully-double primrose flowers put on a tremendous display over the spring season. Double Primroses have been cherished in English cottage gardens for centuries. Thanks to modern tissue culture techniques these have been cleaned up of nasty

Primula florindae

Primula × *juliae* 'Lilac Wanda'

Primula vialii

Primula 'April Rose'

Primula 'Miss Indigo'

Pulmonaria 'Roy Davidson'

Pulmonaria rubra 'David Ward'

Pulmonaria saccharata 'Highdown'

viruses and are once again vigorous, healthy and available to today's gardeners.

As easy to grow as any other hardy *Primula*, these plants need a rich, moist soil with plenty of peat and well rotted manure. Choose a site that is protected from hot afternoon sun and can easily be watered during dry spells. Divide double primroses every two to three years to keep plants young and floriferous.

HEIGHT/SPREAD:	10–15cm (4–6")/20cm (8")
LOCATION:	Rich average to moist soil, preferably on the heavy side.
BLOOMS:	March–May
USES:	⚘△▲☗ Borders, Edging

'Alan Robb' Pale apricot.

'April Rose' Deep ruby red.

'Dawn Ansell' Clear white, interesting green cup holding each flower like a bouquet. Once called "Jack-in-the-Green".

'Granny Graham' Violet blue.

'Ken Dearman' Glowing salmon-orange.

'Lilian Harvey' Magenta-pink, flowers like little roses.

'Marie Crousse' Lilac-purple with a silvery edge.

'Miss Indigo' Deep purple with a white edge.

'Quaker's Bonnet' Lavender mauve, early. Very dainty.

'Red Velvet' Deep scarlet-red, leaves edged in bronze.

'Roy Cope' Crimson, fading to purple-red.

'Sue Jervis' Pale shell pink.

'Sunshine Susie' Bright golden-yellow.

'Val Horncastle' Pale sulphur-yellow.

PULMONARIA
(Lungwort) ☿ ●

Despite being stuck with such an unfortunate common name, these spring-blooming perennials are anything but unappealing. They create low mounds of handsome leaves, often heavily splotched or dotted with silvery-grey. Clusters of flowers are held above the leaves in various shades, from sky blue through to pink, red, and white. These look at home in a woodland setting, growing very well beneath trees and shrubs. Trim off any tired-looking leaves in very early spring. Any of these combine beautifully with spring-flowering primroses.

SPREAD:	30–45cm (12–18")
LOCATION:	Rich, moist woodland soil.
BLOOMS:	March–May
USES:	⚘≺△ⵕ▲☗ Edging, Massing, Borders

Hybrids   ZONES 3–9
Several newer American hybrids are now becoming available. These have been selected for superior form, leaf colour, mildew resistance and, of course, better flowers. Many more varieties are sure to come out of current breeding programs.

HEIGHT/SPREAD:	30–45cm (12–18")/30cm (12")
LOCATION:	Rich, moist woodland soil.
BLOOMS:	March–May
USES:	△▲☗ Edging, Massing, Borders

'Apple Frost' Chartreuse-green leaves with silvery frosting. Pink and blue flowers, compact and mildew-resistant. HEIGHT: 25cm (10")

'Berries and Cream' Unusual raspberry-pink flowers, leaves are wavy and shimmering silver. HEIGHT: 20cm (10")

'Excalibur' Leaves are all silver, with just an edging of dark green. Good mildew resistance. Rosy-purple flowers. HEIGHT: 30cm (12")

'Little Star' Large cobalt-blue flowers, long silver-spotted leaves. Compact. HEIGHT: 15–20cm (6–8")

'Roy Davidson' Powder-blue flowers, foliage long and narrow like 'E.B. Anderson'. HEIGHT: 35cm (14")

'Spilled Milk' Wide leaves, very silvered with a few blotches of green. Compact habit. Flowers begin pink fading to rose. Compact. HEIGHT: 15cm (6")

longifolia 'E.B. Anderson'   ZONES 3–9
(= 'Bertram Anderson') Leaves are long, narrow and pointed, with showy silver spots. Blooms appear a week or two later than other types, and are held in tight clusters. Foliage remains attractive all season long. HEIGHT: 25cm (10")

rubra 'David Ward'   ZONES 3–9
(Red Lungwort) This blooms in a deep coral-red shade with flowers appearing earlier than the other species. Foliage is bright green with remarkable ruffled white edges. Needs shade to prevent leaves from scorching. HEIGHT: 30–45cm (12–18")

> "Given to me as a gift, in honour of an uncle of the same name, this plant would merit garden space even without sentimental attachments. 'Uncle Dave's' crispy variegated foliage remains fresh and clear throughout the season — the innumerable watermelon-red flowers in the spring are an added bonus!"
> – Kevin Ward, Zone 5

saccharata   ZONES 2–9
(Bethlehem Sage) Low green foliage is usually heavily spotted with silver. Clusters of flowers open pink and soon turn to bright blue. Evergreen in milder areas. Still the most popular species. HEIGHT: 25cm (10")

'Argentea' Leaves are almost totally silver.

'Highdown' Good clear blue, leaves lightly spotted. Selection from Blooms of Bressingham.

'Mrs. Moon' An older variety, heavily spotted with silver.

'Pink Dawn' Flowers remain pink all spring.

'Sissinghurst White' Large white flowers, nice contrast to the blue forms.

PULSATILLA
(Pasque-flower) ☼ ☿

vulgaris   ZONES 2–9
(formerly listed as *Anemone pulsatilla*) A favorite early spring bloomer with violet-purple flowers like a Prairie Crocus. Showy in the rock garden or border, good for naturalizing. Occasionally there are other colour forms of this available in red, pink or white. Moderately drought-tolerant. **'Papageno'** is an interesting new strain in a mix of different shades, with the edges of each petal deeply fringed.

> "How can a flower seem both so elegant and so wonderfully silly at the same time? It's like a kid's crayon rendition of a flower — primitive, oversized, giddy-looking blossoms on fuzzy stems. Abounding for a very long spring season, the pretty lace foliage lasts through till fall." – Val Ward, Zone 5

HEIGHT/SPREAD:	15–30cm (6–12")/30cm (12")
LOCATION:	Well-drained soil.
BLOOMS:	March–May
USES:	△☃ Borders, Meadows

RANUNCULUS
(Buttercup) ☼ ◑

repens 'Pleniflorus'   ZONES 4–9
(Creeping Buttercup) Cheery late-spring display of button-sized bright yellow double buttercups. Plants have glossy fresh green leaves and form a low mat that spreads, the stems rooting where they touch the ground. This is maybe a little too rampant for the border, but a good choice as a groundcover in a sunny wet site.

HEIGHT/SPREAD:	15–20cm (6–8")/60cm (24")
LOCATION:	Rich, moist to wet soil.
USES:	∿ Waterside, Wet sites

RAOULIA
(Raoulia) ☼

australis   ZONES 5–9
(New Zealand Scab Plant) A little-known alpine from New Zealand. This forms an absolutely flat carpet of silver-grey foliage that will crawl in between and over rocks. An interesting choice for trough gardens and alpine screes. Flowers are tiny and insignificant. Must have perfect drainage.

HEIGHT/SPREAD:	1cm (1/2")/30cm (12")
LOCATION:	Very well-drained, gravelly soil.
USES:	▲▲▼ Troughs, Walls, Screes

RHEUM
(Rhubarb) ☼ ◑
There are several ornamental species, all of them related to the common edible back-yard rhubarb, but with more exotic-looking leaves. Impressive specimen plants for moist sites.

palmatum tanguticum   ZONES 3–9
(Ornamental Rhubarb) Large rhubarb leaves with pointy edges, almost like an enormous maple leaf. In the spring these are beautifully tinged with bronzy-red, later fading to dark green. Bizarre spikes of reddish-pink flowers appear in early summer on tall stems. An imposing specimen plant that looks great at the waterside. In warm regions this usually goes dormant by mid to late summer.

HEIGHT/SPREAD:	180cm (6')/90cm (3')
LOCATION:	Rich, moist soil.
BLOOMS:	May–June
USES:	✂▼ Specimen, Borders, Waterside

RODGERSIA
(Rodgersia) ☼ ◑
These make exotic bold-leaved clumps for the waterside or moist woodland areas. Fluffy plumes of flowers rise above in the summer. Unique specimen plants, but slow to establish, preferring the dappled shade of high trees.

SPREAD:	60–90cm (2–3')
LOCATION:	Rich, moist soil.
BLOOMS:	July–August
USES:	✂ Dried Flower, Borders, Waterside

aesculifolia   ZONES 3–9
(Fingerleaf Rodgersia) Leaves are large and shaped like those of the horse chestnut, dark green with some bronzy overtones. The creamy-white flowers are held above in a wide airy panicle, blooming later than the other species. HEIGHT: 90cm (3')

henrici   ZONES 4–9
(Bronze Rodgersia) Similar to *R. pinnata*, but the foliage is tinged with bronzy-purple, and flower heads are rose-pink. Sometimes listed as *R. pinnata* 'Superba'. HEIGHT: 90–120cm (3–4')

pinnata 'Elegans'   ZONES 4–9
(Featherleaf Rodgersia) Large upright clumps of compound leaves. Large heads of creamy-white flowers are held well above the foliage. Both the flowers and showy red seed heads are interesting for cutting. HEIGHT: 90–120cm (3–4')

sambucifolia   ZONES 4–9
(Elder-leaved Rodgersia) Open sprays of delicate creamy-white flowers in summer. Foliage is bold and coarse, dark green and compound, with leaflets like an Elder. HEIGHT: 90–120cm (3–4')

tabularis
See ASTILBOIDES.

ROSCOEA
(Roscoea) ☼ ◑
Exotic plants in the Ginger family, from the Himalayas. They bear short spikes of orchid-like flowers. The roots are easily stored for the winter like a Dahlia, or plants can be over-wintered outdoors in milder regions, although a thick mulch is recommended. Best in bright woodland conditions. These can winter in Zone 5, in a well-sheltered site.

> "…almost orchid-like flowers. Hardy in Zone 5 if planted deep and well mulched in winter. They need a rich, peaty soil and are happy with high shade."
> – Anna Leggatt, Zone 5

HEIGHT/SPREAD:	30–45cm (12–18")/30cm (12")
LOCATION:	Rich, moist woodland soil.
BLOOMS:	June–August
USES:	✂▲▼ Borders, Woodland gardens.

cautleoides 'Kew Beauty'   ZONES 6–9
(Yellow Roscoea) Blue-green sword-shaped leaves. Large primrose-yellow flowers make an attractive display.

purpurea procera   ZONES 6–9
(Purple Roscoea) Arching green leaves and large purplish-violet flowers. A vigorous form.

RUDBECKIA
(Cone-flower, Gloriosa Daisy) ☼
For a long display of bright colour in the late summer border it is hard to beat this tough group of plants, all of them descending from native North American wildflower species. The name "Black-eyed Susan" describes these coneflowers well, their large golden daisies centred with a deep brown or black eye. All varieties prefer a warm sunny location with rich moist soil. Superb cutting flowers, some also have attractive seed-heads for drying.

hirta Hybrids   ZONES 5–9
(Gloriosa Daisy) More or less biennial, these hybrids are best treated as self-seeding annuals in most regions. Their large flowers put on a constant display from midsummer to very late fall, and they will grow in hot locations with only the occasional deep soaking. Excellent as filler plants in the summer border, also a good choice for containers. Some unusual deep bronze colours are to be found among the modern tetraploid seed strains. Very drought-tolerant.

Pulsatilla vulgaris

Rodgersia pinnata 'Elegans'

Roscoea purpurpea procera

Rudbeckia hirta 'Indian Summer'

Rudbeckia fulgida 'Goldsturm'

Rudbeckia laciniata 'Goldquelle'

Rudbeckia maxima

Sagina subulata

> "If I were starting a garden from scratch in a sunny spot, wanted bright color quickly, needed a steady source of excellent cut flowers, and had no budget to speak of, there's no question about what I would plant — the hybrid rudbeckias called gloriosa daisies."
> – Allen Lacy, *The Garden in Autumn*

HEIGHT/SPREAD:	45–90cm (18–36")/30cm (12")
LOCATION:	Average to moist well-drained soil.
BLOOMS:	July–October
USES:	✂❅❦🦋 Borders, Massing

'Becky' A mixture with both solid and bronze-tinged shades, with large blooms. HEIGHT: 30–40cm (12–16")

'Double Gold' Extra-full golden-yellow flowers. The original Gloriosa Daisy. HEIGHT: 75–90cm (30–36")

'Indian Summer' Outstanding All America selection. Huge golden-orange daisies on tall stocky plants, blooming all season long. HEIGHT: 90–110cm (36–44")

'Irish Eyes' Single yellow flowers with green eyes. Charming selection. HEIGHT: 75cm (30")

'Rustic Mixture' Compact mixture of singles, in yellow, orange, bronze and deep, rich mahogany.

fulgida ZONES 3–9

A favourite perennial for the extremely long season of bloom. Plants have golden-orange daisies with a dark brown eye, and a bushy upright habit. Round black seed-heads can be left to stand for winter effect. Reliable and long-lived.

SPREAD:	45–60cm (18–24")
LOCATION:	Average to moist well-drained soil.
BLOOMS:	July–October
USES:	✂❅❦ Borders, Massing

'Goldsturm' The most familiar variety, widely used in low-maintenance gardens, especially popular for mass planting with ornamental grasses and *Sedum* 'Autumn Joy'. Rates among the top ten perennials of all time! HEIGHT: 45–70cm (18–28")

'Pot of Gold' A new dwarf Canadian introduction, very much like 'Goldsturm' but only half the size. HEIGHT: 30–40cm (12–16")

'Viette's Little Suzy' Another compact variety, very similar to 'Pot of Gold'. HEIGHT: 30–40cm (12–16")

laciniata ZONES 2–9

(Cut-leaf Coneflower) The species itself is seldom seen in gardens, but the two cultivars below are occasionally found. Plants are upright with bright green cut foliage and chrome-yellow daisies. They spread quickly underground and should be planted in a deep bottomless pail or controlled yearly with a spade to keep them put. An outstanding cut flower. Prone to powdery mildew.

HEIGHT/SPREAD:	90–100cm (36–40")/60cm (24")
LOCATION:	Average to moist well-drained soil.
BLOOMS:	July–September
USES:	✂❦ Borders

'Golden Glow' Lovingly referred to as the Outhouse Plant, this very old selection is extremely tall and rangy in habit, with the ability to make a huge patch after only a couple of years. Bright yellow double pompom flowers are terrific for cutting. Plants are very wind-prone and need to be staked. A MUST for the Victorian heritage garden! HEIGHT: 1.8–2.1m (6–7')

'Goldquelle' (Golden Fountain) A much more compact selection, half the height of 'Golden Glow' and self-supporting but with identical double yellow flowers. Spreads much less quickly. HEIGHT: 90–100cm (36–40")

maxima ZONES 4–9

(Giant Coneflower) This native of the southern states is quite new to gardens, but much hardier than everybody thought it would turn out to be. Plants first make a beautiful clump of powdery-blue basal leaves; then tall stems of drooping black-eyed Susan flowers appear in midsummer, making this a double-use plant. Good for cutting. Worth growing for the blue leaves alone!

> "*Rudbeckia maxima* is one of the silliest plants in my garden. Its extremely tall stems support bright yellow sombreros that wave about in the breeze."
> – Warren Hartman, Zone 6

HEIGHT/SPREAD:	1.8–2.1m (6–7')/60cm (2')
LOCATION:	Prefers a deep, rich moist soil.
BLOOMS:	July–September
USES:	✂❦ Specimen, Borders

nitida 'Herbstsonne' ZONES 2–9

(Autumn Sun Coneflower) Forms an enormous upright clump best suited to the back of a large border. The flowers are huge lemon-yellow daisies with drooping petals. Excellent for cutting. Appreciates a moist site. Long-lived.

> "The Godzilla of Coneflowers."
> – Geoff Lewis, Zone 4

HEIGHT/SPREAD:	1.5–2.4m (5–8')/90cm (3')
LOCATION:	Moist to average well-drained soil.
BLOOMS:	July–October
USES:	✂❦ Borders, Specimen, Waterside

SAGINA
(Pearl Wort) ☼ ◑

subulata ZONES 4–9

(Irish Moss) Creeping moss-like groundcover for small areas, sometimes used as a lawn substitute. Also nice between paving stones or in the rock garden. The bright green foliage is studded with tiny white flowers in summer. Evergreen in mild climates. Keep this out of hot afternoon sun. **'Aurea'** (Scotch Moss) has bright neon golden-yellow leaves.

HEIGHT/SPREAD:	2cm (1")/30cm (12")
LOCATION:	Prefers a moist well-drained soil.
BLOOMS:	June–August
USES:	⛰🏔🦋 Walls, Between flagstones

SALVIA
(Perennial Salvia, Sage) ☼

Some of these are valued for their long summer display of flowers, others more for their handsome foliage. Salvia is a large and diverse group of hardy and tender perennials that includes the familiar Common Sage and its many colour varieties (see HERBS). Almost all of these appreciate a warm sunny site and are fairly drought-tolerant. Salvias are currently gaining wide interest.

argentea ZONES 5–9

(Silver Sage) An unusual foliage plant, valued for its intensely silver, fuzzy leaves that are arranged in a low rosette. Spikes of yellowish flowers will rise above to about 120cm (4') but these are often removed. Plants are biennial or short-lived perennials. Place plants towards the front of the border where the impressive leaves can be easily viewed.

> "Coarse-textured; don't even try to blend or soften this in-your-face plant. Use it as a focal point!" – Bruce Zimmerman, Zone 6

HEIGHT/SPREAD:	30–45cm (12–18″)/40cm (16″)
LOCATION:	Needs a well-drained soil.
BLOOMS:	June–July
USES:	⚑▲ Specimen, Borders

azurea 'Grandiflora'   ZONES 5–9

(Azure Sage) (= *S. pitcheri*) Tall branching spikes of bright clear blue in late summer and fall. A native of the south-eastern U.S., tolerant of heat and humidity. These are fairly tall and may require staking. Some say this is the best hardy Salvia of all.

HEIGHT/SPREAD:	90–120cm (3–4′)/45cm (18″)
LOCATION:	Average well-drained soil.
BLOOMS:	August–October
USES:	✄ Wildflower, Borders, Meadows

officinalis   ZONES 4–9

(Common Sage) A favorite and familiar herb (see the Herb chapter, under SAGE), but equally at home in the perennial border. Leathery leaves are a muted sage-green in colour, bearing taller stems of rich violet-blue flowers in summer. Plants should be cut back to about 10cm (4″) in spring to keep a compact bushy habit. Makes good foliage for floral design. Fragrant. Drought-resistant once established.

HEIGHT/SPREAD:	30–60cm (12–20″)/30cm (12″)
LOCATION:	Well-drained soil.
BLOOMS:	July–August
USES:	✄▲⚑ Herb gardens, Edging

'Berggarten' A newer selection from Germany, featuring unusually large rounded leaves. Beautiful compact edging plant. Hardy.

'Icterina' (Also known as 'Aurea') Leaves are splotched in golden-yellow and green. Zone 6.

'Purpurea' Gorgeous violet-green leaves with dark purple stems. Zone 6.

'Tricolor' Dappled variegation of purple, pink, cream and green. Zone 7.

nemorosa Hybrids   ZONES 3–9

(Perennial Salvia) (formerly listed as *S. superba*) Dense spikes of flowers are held above low clumps of grey-green leaves. Very showy plants for the summer border often reblooming in the fall if deadheaded. Excellent for cutting. Fairly drought-tolerant. There are a good number of selections in existence.

HEIGHT/SPREAD:	45–60cm (18–24″)/45–60cm (18–24″)
LOCATION:	Average well-drained soil.
BLOOMS:	June–July
USES:	✄➤ Borders, Massing

'Blue Hills' ('Blauhügel') Closest to true blue, a German selection that is outstanding.

'Blue Queen' Rich violet-blue flowers.

'East Friesland' Dark violet-purple, compact habit.

'Lubeca' A taller hybrid with long lasting spikes of violet-blue flowers in summer. HEIGHT: 75cm (30″)

'May Night' ('Mainacht') Rich deep indigo-violet spikes. Selected as the 1997 Perennial Plant of the Year. HEIGHT: 45cm (30″)

'Plumosa' Distinctive spikes of feathery flowers, in a warm raspberry-violet shade, very unique. Terrific for cutting.

'Rose Queen' Distinctive rosy-violet. Inclined to be a bit floppy.

pratensis 'Indigo'   ZONES 4–9

(Meadow Clary) Branching stems with spikes of deep lavender-blue flowers in early summer, held well above sturdy low foliage. Especially good for cutting. May rebloom if cut back after flowering.

HEIGHT/SPREAD:	70cm (30″)/45cm (18″)
LOCATION:	Average well-drained soil.
BLOOMS:	June–July
USES:	✄ Borders, Meadows

verticillata 'Purple Rain'   ZONES 5–9

A unique selection from Europe that holds a lot of promise for North American gardens. Plants form a bushy mound of fuzzy green leaves. Arching stems rise above, holding rich violet-purple flowers that are held in clusters spaced evenly apart to the tip. Deadhead for continual bloom.

> "Although it will not winter over in my garden, this plant is well worth buying as an annual for the wealth of flowering and the richness of its colour that adds a dramatic contrast to companion plants in pink and silver. Good for picking too."
> – Margaret Burke, Zone 6

HEIGHT/SPREAD:	45cm (18″)/45cm (18″)
LOCATION:	Average well-drained soil.
BLOOMS:	July–September
USES:	✄ Massing, Borders

SANGUISORBA
(Burnet) ☼

obtusa   ZONES 4–9

(Japanese Bottlebrush) Forms a tough clump of elegant lacy leaves with a grey-blue powdery finish. Arching spikes of fluffy rose-pink flowers appear in mid-summer. Excellent for cutting. Tough and long-lived.

HEIGHT/SPREAD:	70–90cm (30–36″)/60cm (24″)
LOCATION:	Average well-drained soil.
BLOOMS:	June–July
USES:	✄ Borders

SANTOLINA
(Cotton Lavender) ☼

chamaecyparissus   ZONES 6–9

Low bushes of soft feathery silver-grey leaves, sometimes used as a miniature clipped hedge or edging. Yellow button-flowers appear in summer but are sometimes clipped off. The entire plant has a pleasant camphor-like fragrance. Evergreen in mild regions. Often treated as a bedding annual or used for carpet bedding. Give plants a good hard clipping to 10cm (4″) in early spring to keep them bushy. Very drought-tolerant.

HEIGHT/SPREAD:	30–45cm (12–18″)/30cm (12″)
LOCATION:	Well-drained soil. Dislikes wet feet.
BLOOMS:	June–July
USES:	⚑🌿 Dried Flower, Edging, Herb gardens

SAPONARIA
(Soapwort) ☼

The vigorous border species are best known, but there are also several cushion-forming types for the alpine enthusiast.

× 'Bressingham'   ZONES 4–9

Slowly spreads to form a dome of green foliage, studded with stemless bright pink flowers in late spring. A choice alpine variety for the rock garden or trough. Selected by Blooms of Bressingham.

HEIGHT/SPREAD:	5cm (2″)/15cm (6″)
LOCATION:	Gritty, humus-rich soil.
BLOOMS:	May–June
USES:	▲▲ Troughs, Screes

ocymoides   ZONES 2–9

(Rock Soapwort) Vigorous, trailing rockery or edging plant. The bright green foliage is smothered with pink flowers in late spring. Fine for tumbling over walls or slopes. Shear plants back hard after blooming. Fairly drought-tolerant.

Salvia azurea 'Grandiflora'

Salvia nemorosa 'Blue Hills'

Salvia nemorosa 'Blue Queen'

Saponaria × 'Bresssingham'

HEIGHT/SPREAD: 15–20cm (6–8″)/30–45cm (12–18″)
LOCATION: Lean, well-drained soil.
BLOOMS: May–June
USES: △⋏⊶▲Ἦ⅍ Walls, Slopes

officinalis 'Rosea Plena'   ZONES 2–9

(Double Pink Bouncing Bet) An old-fashioned perennial with a very long history in gardens. Its clusters of pale rose-pink double flowers are sweetly scented, similar to phlox. Plants form an upright clump, benefiting from a light pinching in May to encourage bushiness. Spreading but not invasive.

HEIGHT/SPREAD: 60–90cm (2–3′)/60cm (2′)
LOCATION: Average to moist well-drained soil.
BLOOMS: June–August
USES: ✂ Borders, Woodland gardens

Saxifraga × *arendsii* – Pink

SAXIFRAGA
(Saxifrage, Rockfoil) ☼

This huge group of plants includes many easy rock garden specimens, although some types are best left to the experienced alpine connoisseur. Their starry flowers are usually held in airy sprays during late spring. Rosettes of evergreen foliage develop into a neat clump. Most require excellent drainage and prefer a cool location, a rockery or scree providing the ideal conditions.

× arendsii   ZONES 4–9

(Mossy Saxifrage) Low cushions of bright green foliage with short stems of upfacing cup-shaped blossoms in shades of red through pink and white. Showy display in late spring. These require a cool, moist location and will not tolerate drought. Best in a shady rock garden or wall.

HEIGHT/SPREAD: 10–20cm (4–8″)/30cm (12″)
LOCATION: Moist, well-drained soil.
BLOOMS: April–June
USES: △▲Ἦ Walls, Troughs

'Cloth of Gold' Wonderful low mound of golden-yellow foliage, white flowers on short stems. Terrific edging selection.

'Bob Hawkins'   ZONES 5–9

(Variegated Saxifrage) Low mossy hummocks of ferny foliage, the tiny leaves striped with cream and green, which give an overall silvery-grey effect. Cup-shaped white flowers in spring. Needs even moisture and perfect drainage. Perhaps best in a trough garden.

HEIGHT/SPREAD: 5–10cm (2–4″)/15cm (6″)
LOCATION: Moist, well-drained lime-free soil.
BLOOMS: May–June
USES: △⅍✂▲Ἦ Walls, Troughs

Saxifraga × *urbium* 'Primuloides'

cotyledon   ZONES 3–9

(Pyramidal Saxifrage) Very wide, flat rosettes of grey-green leaves. Tall, branching panicles of white flowers in early summer, most attractive when arching out from a wall.

HEIGHT/SPREAD: 45–60cm (18–24″)/20cm (8″)
LOCATION: Moist, well-drained lime-free soil.
BLOOMS: June
USES: △⅍✂▲Ἦ Walls, Troughs

Saxifraga × *urbium* 'Aureopunctata'

fortunei 'Wada's Variety'   ZONES 5–9

(Red Rockfoil) A rare and highly prized rockfoil, this is quite unlike what is brought to mind when one thinks of Saxifrages. The glossy reddish brown leaves contrast wonderfully with the snow white flowers that are produced in late summer.

HEIGHT/SPREAD: 25cm (10″)/30cm (12″)
LOCATION: Average to moist well-drained soil.
BLOOMS: September–October
USES: △⅍✂Ἦ

Scabiosa columbaria 'Butterfly Blue'

paniculata   ZONES 3–9

(Encrusted Saxifrage) Clusters of grey-green rosettes form a neat tight mound, the leaf edges are trimmed with a curious silver deposit of lime. Short sprays of white starry flowers. One of the easiest types to grow in sun or part shade.

HEIGHT/SPREAD: 25cm (10″)/30cm (12″)
LOCATION: Average to moist well-drained soil.
BLOOMS: May–June
USES: △⅍◀▲Ἦ Walls, Edging

stolonifera 'Harvest Moon'   ZONES 6–9

(Strawberry Begonia) Familiar to many as a houseplant on Grandma's windowsill. This vigorous selection has bright golden-yellow rounded leaves, covered in red bristles. Plants form a small rosette and then send out runners like a strawberry with little plantlets on the ends. Sprays of pale pink flowers in fall. Terrific in the shady rock garden, in baskets or tubs, and of course as a houseplant!

SPREAD: 15–30cm (6–12″)
LOCATION: Average to moist soil.
BLOOMS: September–October
USES: △⋏⊶▲Ἦ Edging, Walls

× urbium   ZONES 4–9

(London Pride) Vigorous habit, spreading into low evergreen mats. Short stems of airy pale pink flowers in late spring. Excellent groundcover or edging plant for shady areas, even in dense shade under trees. There are a few selections available.

SPREAD: 15–30cm (6–12″)
LOCATION: Average to moist soil.
BLOOMS: May–June
USES: △⋏⊶▲Ἦ Edging, Walls

'Aureopunctata' (Golden London Pride) Leaves are heavily spotted with gold. Unique edging plant. HEIGHT: 20–30cm (8–12″)

'Primuloides' Miniature variety, with small rosettes of green leaves, for shaded rockeries. HEIGHT: 10cm (4″)

SCABIOSA
(Pincushion Flower) ☼

Popular old-fashioned favourites, especially valued for cutting. The round, flat quilled flowers appear over a long season. Dead-heading will encourage continued blooming well into the fall. Foliage is dark green and lacy. All are attractive to butterflies.

alpina   ZONES 4–9

(Dwarf Pincushion Flower) (= *Cephalaria alpina*) A cute little summer bloomer for the rock garden. Makes a mound of grey-green foliage, topped with mauve-blue pincushions.

HEIGHT/SPREAD: 15–20cm (6–8″)/30cm (12″)
LOCATION: Well-drained soil.
BLOOMS: May–August
USES: △Ἦ Edging

caucasica   ZONES 2–9

Large globe-shaped flowers, in shades of rich blue and lavender through white. Good strong stems. Flowers best in cool-summer regions.

HEIGHT/SPREAD: 45–75cm (18–30″)/30–45cm (12–18″)
LOCATION: Average well-drained soil. Dislikes winter wet.
BLOOMS: June–October
USES: ✂Ἦ Borders

columbaria   ZONES 3–9

Two new selections of this species have recently become available here in North America. These are creating quite a lot of excitement with their constant display of small pincushion flowers from late spring through fall. The effect is especially good when mass planted around shrubs or at the front of a border. Also worth a try in containers.

HEIGHT/SPREAD: 30–45cm (12–18")/30cm (12")
LOCATION: Average well-drained soil.
BLOOMS: June–September
USES: ✄ ☙ 🦋 Massing, Edging, Borders

'Butterfly Blue' Small lavender-blue flowers in profusion all season long.

'Pink Mist' Pale soft pink flowers, beautiful companion to the blue.

> [re: 'Butterfly Blue', 'Pink Mist' and *S. ochroleuca*] "Their basal foliage buried in snow, this pompom trio just kept on blooming, their heads intermingled atop the wiry stems — a very pleasing combination all season long."
> – Cathy Forgie, Zone 4

ochroleuca **ZONES 4–9**
(Yellow Scabious) An unusual colour for this genus, with round pincushion flowers in soft primrose yellow. Flowers are held above the foliage on wiry stems, appearing over many weeks. A short-lived perennial, but will often self-seed. Nice in combination with the crimson *Knautia macedonica*.

HEIGHT/SPREAD: 60–75cm (24–34")/60cm (24")
LOCATION: Well-drained soil.
BLOOMS: June–September
USES: ✄ ☙ Borders

SCHIZOSTYLIS
(Kaffir Lily) ☼

coccinea **ZONES 7–9**
Vigorous, grassy clumps of sword-shaped leaves, with a fall display of large starry flowers held in a spike well above the foliage. These have been described as looking like a daintier version of a gladiola. Recommended in milder regions, particularly at the West coast, for a burst of colour at the end of the season. Can be wintered in Zone 6 with a deep mulch or brought indoors in pots. Good for cutting. There are a few colour selections in existence, in shades of pink, salmon and white.

> "The silky, cup-shaped blooms of rich crimson with a coppery glint are held in slender spikes in September and October, just when such things are most welcome."
> – Graham Stuart Thomas,
> *Perennial Garden Plants*

HEIGHT/SPREAD: 30–60cm (1–2')/30cm (1')
LOCATION: Moist, well-drained woodland soil.
BLOOMS: September–December
USES: ✄ ☙ Borders, Tubs

'Snow Maiden' Clear white flowers.

SCROPHULARIA
(Figwort) ☼ ◐

auriculata 'Variegata' **ZONES 5–9**
A bold foliaged perennial, valued for its attractive green and creamy-white variegated leaves. Plants remain evergreen in milder areas. This does best in rich, moist soils, especially at the waterside. Flowers are insignificant and usually trimmed off. Worth trying in containers.

> "It is best in semi-shade and makes a splendid contrast with *Ligularia* 'Desdemona'." – Graham Stuart Thomas,
> *Perennial Garden Plants*

HEIGHT/SPREAD: 30–45cm (12–18")/30cm (1')
LOCATION: Rich, moist to wet soil
BLOOMS: June–July
USES: ☙ Borders, Waterside, Specimen

SEDUM
(Stonecrop) ☼ ◐

Fleshy, succulent plants, suited to the sunny rock garden or border; many will also tolerate partial shade. These offer the gardener an extensive choice of foliage types with clusters of starry flowers in many shades. Low mat-forming varieties are good ground-covers for hot dry slopes and other difficult sites. Taller cultivars are superb in the late season border.

DWARF VARIETIES **ZONES 2–9**
Most of these will form a thick evergreen mat, rooting into the ground as they creep. Fast-spreading types (marked "vigorous and spreading") can easily smother out slow-growing alpines if planted side by side. On the other hand, they might be worth considering as a groundcover or lawn substitute over large areas. The point is to choose varieties carefully to match your landscaping requirements. Extremely drought-tolerant.

SPREAD: 30–45cm (12–18")
LOCATION: Average to dry to soil.
BLOOMS: See variety description.
USES: ▲ ∧ ☙ 🏵 Edging, Slopes, Walls

acre **'Aureum'** (Golden Stonecrop) Ground-hugging carpet, bright golden-yellow in spring, later fading to light green. Yellow flowers June–August. Vigorous and spreading. HEIGHT: 8cm (3")

album **'Murale'** (Coral Carpet Stonecrop) Rounded green leaves, turning maroon in cold weather. Light pink flowers in summer. Vigorous and spreading. HEIGHT: 10cm (4")

album **'Murale Cristatum'** (Crested Stonecrop) Tiny, bright green leaves, good mulberry-red colour in cold weather. White flowers in summer. Vigorous and spreading. HEIGHT: 10cm (4")

anacampseros (Evergreen Orpine) Rounded blue-green leaves, clasping onto trailing stems. Non-spreading. Flowers dusky purple, in July–August. Deciduous. HEIGHT: 15–25cm (6–10")

'Bertram Anderson' An outstanding British selection. Low, spreading clumps of deep burgundy-black leaves with bright purple-red flowers in summer. Leaf colour is best in dry, sunny sites. Blooms July–August. HEIGHT: 20cm (8")

cauticola **'Lidakense'** Broad blue-green leaves, with a purple blush, non-spreading. Glistening deep-pink flowers from August–October. One of the best for late in the season. Deciduous. HEIGHT: 10cm (4")

cyaneum **'Rose Carpet'** ('Rosenteppich') Powdery blue-green leaves, showy clusters of rose-pink flowers in late summer. Deciduous. HEIGHT: 10cm (4")

divergens (Old-Man-Bones) Almost globular leaves like green pearls. Yellow flowers in summer. A North American native wildflower. Vigorous and spreading. HEIGHT: 10–15cm (4–6")

ewersii (Pink Stonecrop) Blue-green rounded leaves, non-spreading. Flowers rose-pink in late summer. Nice for edging. Deciduous. HEIGHT 15cm (6")

kamtschaticum (Russian Stonecrop) Scalloped green leaves, bright yellow flowers through the summer. One of the best for groundcover use or edging but not considered invasive. Prefers a moist site. Deciduous. HEIGHT: 15cm (6")

kamtschaticum **'Variegatum'** (Variegated Russian Stonecrop) Light green leaves, edged heavily with cream. Flowers are golden-orange. Very good for edging. Non-spreading. Prefers a moist site. Deciduous. HEIGHT: 15cm (6")

Scabiosa alpina

Schizostylis 'Snow Maiden'

Schizostylis 'Oregon Sunset'

Sedum 'Bertram Anderson'

Sedum oreganum

Sedum alboroseum 'Medio-variegatum'

Sedum spathulifolium 'Capa Blanca'

Sedum × 'Autumn Joy'

oreganum (Oregon Stonecrop) Thick shiny green leaves, like a tiny Jade plant. Bright red colour in dry, hot weather. Yellow flowers. A native North American wildflower. Not a fast spreader. HEIGHT: 15cm (6")

reflexum (Blue Stonecrop) Blue-green spruce-like foliage. Yellow flowers. Vigorous and spreading, outstanding groundcover. HEIGHT: 15cm (6")

sexangulare (Six-sided Stonecrop) Tiny bright green leaves spiral tightly on the stems. Yellow flowers in summer. Good winter effect. Vigorous and spreading. HEIGHT: 10cm (4")

sieboldii (October Daphne) Beautiful blue-green scalloped foliage, large heads of pink flowers appear in very late fall. Slightly fussy, dislikes winter wet. Zone 5. Deciduous. 'Medio-variegatum' is especially handsome, with a creamy-yellow blotch in the centre of each leaf. HEIGHT: 15–20cm (6–8")

spathulifolium Tight rosettes of fleshy leaves, taking on bright red colouring during hot dry weather. Yellow flowers in summer. Beautiful groundcover or edging but needs perfect drainage, especially in winter. Zones 5–9. HEIGHT: 10cm (4"). 'Capa Blanca' ('Cape Blanco') Intensely white-grey leaves. 'Purpureum' Unusual purplish-blue foliage. Nice contrast to 'Capa Blanca.'

spurium (Dragon's Blood) An easy and reliable group of Stonecrops. Thick, low mats of leaves and very showy flower clusters in pink, red or white, appearing in summer. These prefer a warm, moist site and tolerate part shade. Deciduous. 'Fuldaglut' has ruby-red flowers, orange-red foliage. 'Tricolor' with leaves variegated green, red and cream. Pinkish flowers. Remove any green shoots immediately or they will take over! HEIGHT: 15cm (6")

× 'Vera Jameson' Mahogany-red foliage, arching stems of dusky pink flowers. Better habit than the older 'Ruby Glow.' Excellent for edging, or in tubs. Flowers August–September. Needs excellent drainage. HEIGHT: 20cm (9")

BORDER VARIETIES   ZONES 2–9

More upright in habit, these are all late blooming perennials that provide outstanding fall colour with their large clusters of flowers. Suitable for mass planting, especially around shrubs or taller ornamental grasses. For the most part they prefer average to moist conditions but will tolerate short periods of drought. Many of these are excellent for cutting. Attractive to butterflies!

SPREAD:	30–45cm (12–18")
LOCATION:	Average to moist well-drained soil.
BLOOMS:	See each variety.
USES:	✂◀♥🌿🏵 Dried Flower, Borders, Massing

alboroseum 'Medio-variegatum' Similar to 'Autumn Joy' in stature, the leaves have a creamy-white blotch in the centre. Flowers are greenish-white with a touch of pink. Best in part shade. Any all-green shoots should be rogued out before they take over. Often listed as *S. spectabile* 'Variegatum' Blooms August–September. HEIGHT: 40–50cm (16–20")

× 'Autumn Joy' ('Herbstfreude') Massive heads of salmon-pink flowers, aging to bronzy-red. A favorite of bees and butterflies. Long considered to be one of the top ten perennials. Generally long-lived and trouble free. Flowers September–October. Seed heads remain effective for most of the winter. HEIGHT: 45–60cm (18–24")

> "The blossoms are creamy ivory at first, but there's a succession of colors that moves to pink, deep cherry-rose, russet, copper, and finally the dark mahogany of the seed heads, which remain handsome in winter, especially against a background of fresh-fallen snow." – Allen Lacy,
> *The Garden in Autumn*

'Mohrchen' A newer hybrid from Germany. Very deep bronzy-red foliage all season long, turning bright ruby red in late fall. Clusters of pink flowers appear in August–September. This promises to be an exciting border perennial for foliage contrast. HEIGHT: 45–60cm (18–24")

spectabile 'Brilliant' Very similar in appearance to 'Autumn Joy' but with flowers of a brighter mauve-pink. Keep these two away from each other, they clash terribly! Flowers August–October. HEIGHT: 45–60cm (18–24")

> "*Sedum spectabile* creates an absolutely delightful mega meal for butterflies as each flower head opens to reveal a multitude of nectar-rich blossoms…"
> – Suzette McDonnell, Zone 6

SEMPERVIVUM
(Hen and Chicks) ☼ ◑

Well-known succulents, with evergreen rosettes of leaves surrounded by smaller rosettes or "chicks". These are useful for edging borders, in rock gardens, walls, or container gardens. Tolerant of a wide variety of soils, even pure sand, their main requirement is good drainage. Starry flowers rise up on short stems in summer. In Europe these are often seen growing in the gravel on flat rooftops.

> "This is the only perennial that my grandfather still had growing in his yard when I was young. However, his attachment to this durable, self-sustaining species was unbending. I was taken by the star-shaped form and the sea-creature, hydra-like flowering stalks that arose in late summer. A creepy plant it was."
> – Dr. Duncan Himmelman, Zone 3

HEIGHT/SPREAD:	10–20cm (4–6")/15–30cm (6–12")
LOCATION:	Average well-drained soil.
BLOOMS:	June–August
USES:	⏸〰◢♥🏵 Edging, Troughs, Walls

Hybrids   ZONES 1–9

The selection of varieties available today is quite astonishing, especially if you are only familiar with the old green-leaved types. They now include both large and small rosettes, green, blue, red, grey, and multicoloured forms as well as various colours of flowers.

arachnoideum (Cobweb Hen and Chicks) Fine silvery hairs join together the leaf tips, like a tiny spider's web. A terrific novelty plant for children's gardens!

SENNA
(Wild Senna) ☼

hebecarpa   ZONES 4–9

(Formerly listed as *Cassia hebecarpa*) A sturdy upright-growing member of the pea family, native to eastern North America. The foliage is dark green, compound and lacy in appearance, forming a bushy mound topped with spikes of golden-yellow flowers in summer. A unique specimen or back-of-the-border subject. Drought-tolerant.

> "Creates a warm tropical effect that can be amplified by planting in combination with yucca, hardy cactus, and ornamental grasses." – Bruce Zimmerman, Zone 6

HEIGHT/SPREAD:	90–150cm (3–5')/90cm (3')
LOCATION:	Well-drained soil.
BLOOMS:	July–August
USES:	✂◀🏵 Borders

SIDALCEA
(Prairie Mallow) ☼ ◐

Hybrids   ZONES 4–9
Elegant long spikes of satiny pink flowers, like small single Hollyhocks. Clumps are upright and narrow, with long stems that are excellent for cutting. Cut back after blooming to encourage a second flush. Best in cool-summer areas. These dislike lime soils. There are several colour selections.

SPREAD:	30cm (12″)
LOCATION:	Rich well-drained soil, preferably acidic.
BLOOMS:	June–August
USES:	✄ Borders

'Brilliant' Deep rose flowers. HEIGHT: 60–75cm (24–30″)
'Elsie Heugh' Fringed pale pink flowers. HEIGHT: 90–120cm (36–48″)
'Party Girl' A seed mixture of various pink shades. HEIGHT: 60–90cm (2–3′)

SILENE
(Campion) ☼
These are similar to Lychnis, but the perennial species in cultivation are mostly low plants for rock gardens, walls or edging.

acaulis   ZONES 2–9
(Moss Campion) Flat green cushions are studded with tiny pink flowers through the summer. Not the easiest of alpines, grows best in well-drained, gravelly scree.

HEIGHT/SPREAD:	2.5cm (1″)/15–30cm (6–12″)
LOCATION:	Very well-drained, gravelly soil.
BLOOMS:	May–August
USES:	▲▼ Screes, Troughs

maritima 'Swan Lake'   ZONES 2–9
(Robin White-breast) Grey-green tufted foliage is similar to *Dianthus* in effect. Fully-double white flowers appear in summer, so full of petals they look like a ballerina's tutu! An easy rock garden plant for midsummer colour, this looks best hanging down from a wall.

HEIGHT/SPREAD:	15–20cm (6–8″)/30cm (12″)
LOCATION:	Average well-drained soil.
BLOOMS:	June–August
USES:	▲▼ Edging, Walls

schafta   ZONES 3–9
Starry rose-pink flowers, similar to creeping phlox. Plants form a loose carpet or mound. Good for late-summer colour in the rock garden, when little else is in bloom! Also nice for edging. Easy.

HEIGHT/SPREAD:	10–15cm (4–6″)/30cm (12″)
LOCATION:	Needs very good drainage.
BLOOMS:	August–September
USES:	▲▼ Edging, Walls

SISYRINCHIUM
(Blue-eyed Grass) ☼
Dwarf relatives of the Iris, forming low tufts of grassy leaves with clusters of small starry flowers. Plants will self-seed if the location suits them. Nice in the rock garden. We find these to be hardier than generally believed.

bellum   ZONES 4–9
Delicate violet-blue flowers in late spring. Neat clumps of grassy leaves are useful for edging. Will grow at the waterside. A pretty little wildflower native to North America.

HEIGHT/SPREAD:	15cm (6″)/15–20cm (6–8″)
LOCATION:	Average to wet well-drained soil.
BLOOMS:	May–June
USES:	▲▼ Waterside, Walls

striatum   ZONES 7–9
(Yellow-eyed Grass) Tufts of broad, grassy evergreen leaves resembling an Iris. Flowers are pale creamy-yellow, held in upright spikes that are useful for cutting. Slowly forms a large clump. This species is hardy only in mild areas, appreciating a sunny exposure. Will self-seed.

HEIGHT/SPREAD:	60–75cm (24–30″)/30cm (12″)
LOCATION:	Average to moist well-drained soil.
BLOOMS:	June–July
USES:	✄▲ Borders

SOLDANELLA
(Snowbell) ◐ ●

villosa   ZONES 4–9
(Pyrenean Snowbell) A charming little plant for the woodland garden or shaded rockery. Rounded, glossy evergreen leaves form a small patch. Stems rise above, holding clusters of nodding bell-shaped flowers, magenta pink with fringed petals. Very delicate, usually slow to establish.

HEIGHT/SPREAD:	10cm (4″)/20cm (8″)
LOCATION:	Prefers a moist soil.
BLOOMS:	April–May
USES:	▲▲▼ Troughs, Crevices

SOLIDAGO
(Golden-Rod) ☼ ◐
These species and hybrids are much superior to the common wild roadside types. Popular in Europe for years, they are finally gaining acceptance in North American gardens. Their branching clusters of golden flowers combine well with Asters in the fall border. Excellent for cutting. Goldenrod does not cause hay fever but always takes the blame.

graminifolia   ZONES 4–9
(Fine-leaved Goldenrod) A rather un-goldenrod looking species native over much of Eastern North America. Clumps of ferny green foliage are bushy and upright, eventually spreading to form a broad patch. Small clusters of bright yellow flowers appear at the ends of the branches in autumn. Shows great potential as a cut-flower. Worth trying in Zone 3 or colder.

HEIGHT/SPREAD:	90–120cm (3–4′)/90cm (3′)
LOCATION:	Average to moist well-drained soil.
BLOOMS:	September–October
USES:	✄🦋 Borders, Massing, Meadows

Hybrids   ZONES 2–9
The hybrids have been selected over the years by breeders in Europe, most notably Germany and England. As a group these are very useful to the late summer and autumn border scheme, forming wide leafy clumps that are full of colour for several weeks. They lack the invasive tendencies of our native species, so can be planted in the border with no fear of takeover. Powdery mildew is sometimes a problem, usually a sign that plants are under drought stress. All are excellent for cutting, and will not cause sneezing.

HEIGHT/SPREAD:	90cm (36″)/30cm (12″)
LOCATION:	Average to moist well-drained soil.
BLOOMS:	August–October
USES:	✄🦋 Borders, Massing, Meadows

Sempervivum – Hybrids

Sidalcea 'Brilliant'

Sidalcea 'Party Girl'

Sisyrinchium bellum

Solidago 'Crown of Rays'

Stachys byzantina

Stokesia laevis

Symphytum 'Goldsmith'

'Crown of Rays' ('Strahlenkrone') German selection with golden-yellow flowers held horizontally within the spikes; these have a mop-headed appearance. Bushy, compact habit. Early. HEIGHT: 70cm (28″)

'Praecox' An early-blooming variety, beginning in July. Flat golden-yellow heads.

rugosa 'Fireworks'   ZONES 4–9
A clumping variety selected in North Carolina, and recently introduced. Flowers are like exploding heads of golden yellow. An upright and bushy plant for the border.

HEIGHT/SPREAD:	90–120cm (3–4′)/70cm (30″)
LOCATION:	Moist to average well-drained soil.
BLOOMS:	August–October
USES:	✂ Ⓜ ❦ Massing, Borders

sphacelata 'Golden Fleece'   ZONES 4–9
Unusual heart-shaped leaves. A compact-growing selection with flowers quite unlike the more familiar large-headed varieties. Branching wands of little golden flowers are showy in late summer and fall. Especially effective when massed as a groundcover. Recently introduced by the Mt. Cuba Center in Delaware.

> "Its presence in your garden will always start a conversation. Combined with other hot colours (oranges, reds) it will add sunshine and fire to your autumn border."
> – Bruce Zimmerman, Zone 6

HEIGHT/SPREAD:	45cm (18″)/30–45cm (12–18″)
LOCATION:	Average well-drained soil.
BLOOMS:	August–October
USES:	✂ Ⓜ ❦ ❦ Massing, Borders

× SOLIDASTER
(Solidaster) ☼ ◐
Interesting hybrid between Aster and Solidago. Useful in the fall border.

luteus   ZONES 4–9
Starry yellow and pale cream flowers arranged in airy sprays. Popular with florists, and sold year-round for cutting. Nice filler in the late summer border. May require staking. Dislikes drying out.

> "When seen at a distance, it is the colour of butter, adding a pastel touch at a time of year when so many of the yellows are chrome. Well worth the trouble to pinch it back and stake it." – Cathy Forgie, Zone 4

HEIGHT/SPREAD:	60–75cm (24–30″)/30cm (12″)
LOCATION:	Average to moist well-drained soil.
BLOOMS:	July–October
USES:	✂ ❦ Borders, Meadows

'Lemore' Wide-branching panicles of soft primrose-yellow flowers. Late. HEIGHT: 75cm (30″)

STACHYS
(Lamb's-Ears) ☼ ◐

byzantina   ZONES 3–9
(= *S. olympica*) A popular edging plant valued for its low spreading mat of woolly grey leaves. Spikes of pinkish flowers appear in early summer but are often clipped off to keep plants short and tidy. Evergreen in milder regions. There are also some named selections, which must be grown from divisions. Moderately drought-tolerant.

HEIGHT/SPREAD:	30–45cm (12–18″)/30cm (12″)
LOCATION:	Average well-drained soil.
BLOOMS:	June
USES:	▲ Ⓜ ▲ ❦ Massing, Edging, Borders

'Helene von Stein' Also known as 'Big Ears' An incredible new variety that is twice the size of a normal Lamb's-ear. A strongly clumping habit and tendency to seldom flower makes this the best selection for edging purposes. Foliage is not quite as silver as the species, but an excellent texture plant nonetheless. HEIGHT: 30cm (12″)

> "Dramatic plant for a low accent. Soon forms a large, well-mannered clump. Particularly attractive dew-covered in the early morning." – Anna Leggatt, Zone 5

'Primrose Heron' Felty leaves appear golden-yellow in the spring, becoming light green later in the season. Magenta flowers.

grandiflora 'Rosea'   ZONES 2–9
(Sometimes listed as *S. macrantha*) Little-known variety, completely different in growth from Lamb's-ears. Foliage is bright green, a little bit like lemon-balm in appearance, with showy spikes of rose-pink flowers in early summer.

HEIGHT/SPREAD:	45cm (18″)/30cm (12″)
LOCATION:	Moist well-drained soil.
BLOOMS:	June–August
USES:	✂ Borders

STATICE
See GONIOLIMON, LIMONIUM.

STOKESIA
(Stoke's Aster) ☼

laevis   ZONES 4–9
A native North American wildflower. Flowers are lavender-blue, something like a double Shasta Daisy, beginning in midsummer and valuable for a late show. Excellent for cutting. Evergreen in milder regions. Resents winter wet. A winter mulch is recommended in Zones 4–5. Named selections exist with white or pale pink flowers.

HEIGHT/SPREAD:	30–60cm (1–2′)/30cm (12″)
LOCATION:	Moist but well-drained soil.
BLOOMS:	July–September
USES:	✂ Borders

'Blue Danube' Very large lavender-blue flowers.

SYMPHYTUM
(Comfrey) ◐ ●
Rugged, indestructible perennials with the same tough constitution as the common herb varieties. These are grown for their attractive clumps of bold, hairy leaves that quickly form a clump in early spring. The short spikes of bell-shaped flowers look similar in appearance to Pulmonaria. Best in a moist, rich soil where they will spread steadily.

SPREAD:	60cm (24″)
LOCATION:	Prefers a rich, moist soil.
BLOOMS:	May–July
USES:	Ⓜ Borders, Massing

grandiflorum   ZONES 4–9
(Large-flowered Comfrey) Low carpeting species, with pale creamy-yellow flowers in late spring. Good for use as a groundcover in dry shady areas. **'Goldsmith'** has beautiful variegated foliage, splashed with creamy-yellow and green. HEIGHT: 20cm (8″)

× rubrum   ZONES 3–9
(Red-flowered Comfrey) Clumps of dark-green foliage, clusters of dark red bell flowers in late spring. Excellent for massing as a groundcover among shrubs, spreads quickly. HEIGHT: 30–45cm (12–18″)

TANACETUM
(Tansy) ☼

Some members of the Chrysanthemum genus have now been moved here. These are all sturdy, summer-blooming daisies, and very hardy.

coccineum   ZONES 2–9
(Painted Daisy) (formerly *Chrysanthemum coccineum*) An old-fashioned cutting flower with large red, pink or white daisies on wiry stems. Plants form a clump of ferny green leaves. Deadhead regularly to encourage continued blooming. Short-lived unless divided every year or two. Although named selections exist in Europe, the forms grown here are mostly seed strains, but still excellent.

HEIGHT/SPREAD:	45–75cm (18–30")/45cm (18")
LOCATION:	Average well-drained soil.
BLOOMS:	June–July
USES:	✂ 🦋 Borders

'Extra Double Mixture' High percentage of double and semi-double flowers in a mixture of colours.

'James Kelway' Deep vermilion-red single flowers.

'Robinson Rose' Bright rose-pink, single flowers.

'Robinson Single Hybrids' Mixture of colours, large single flowers.

parthenium   ZONES 3–9
(Feverfew) (formerly *Chrysanthemum parthenium*) Branching sprays of small daisies, like little button mums, blooming for many weeks. Flowers are excellent for cutting. Foliage is bushy and aromatic. Plants will stay nice and compact if pinched back by half in May or June. These are short-lived perennials but readily self-seed and can then be moved to where you want them. Use a winter mulch in Zones 3–5. There are several selections. Also listed in the HERB chapter under FEVERFEW.

SPREAD:	15–20cm (6–8")
LOCATION:	Average well-drained soil.
BLOOMS:	July–October
USES:	✂ 🪴 Borders, Herb gardens

'Aureum' Beautiful chartreuse-yellow foliage, setting off single white flowers with a yellow eye. Stunning! HEIGHT: 30–60cm (1–2')

'Double White' Pure white button flowers. A taller form, the best for cutting. HEIGHT: 30–90cm (1–3')

'Golden Ball' Golden-yellow button flowers. Compact plants. HEIGHT: 30–45cm (12–18")

'White Stars' White daisies with yellow centres. HEIGHT: 30–45cm (12–18")

vulgare 'Crispum'   ZONES 2–9
(Fernleaf Tansy) Fresh deep green foliage, ruffled and curled like a parsley. Button-like yellow flowers appear in late summer and are excellent for cutting. This is a more ornamental selection of the common roadside variety, useful as a foliage accent in the border. Spreads quickly without becoming invasive. A very old plant of European cottage gardens. Moderately drought-tolerant.

HEIGHT/SPREAD:	75–90cm (30–36")/60cm (24")
LOCATION:	Average well-drained soil.
BLOOMS:	July–September
USES:	✂ 🪴 Borders, Herb gardens

TEUCRIUM
(Germander) ☼ ◐

Interesting foliage plants, well-suited to formal edging or mass planting. Their short spikes of mint-like flowers have a delicate effect.

chamaedrys 'Nanum'   ZONES 4–9
(Creeping Germander) Shiny green leaves form a low mound, spreading to form a patch. Short spikes of rosy-purple flowers in late summer. Small enough for the rock garden, excellent for edging. Evergreen in milder areas. Winter mulch is recommended in Zones 4–5. Reported to be attractive to cats. Moderately drought-tolerant. Often listed incorrectly as *T. canadense*.

HEIGHT/SPREAD:	15–25cm (6–10")/30cm (12")
LOCATION:	Well-drained soil.
BLOOMS:	July–August
USES:	△ ⋏ ▲ 🪴 Edging, Herb gardens

THALICTRUM
(Meadow-rue) ☼ ◐

Beautiful woodland perennials from various parts of the world, all of these have lacy foliage similar to a Columbine or Maidenhair Fern. The loose cloud-like sprays of flowers are useful for cutting. Although these are usually tall, their see-through appearance means they can be moved up toward the front of a border. All appreciate a cool woodland setting.

aquilegifolium   ZONES 3–9
(Columbine Meadow-rue) Very delicate mauve flowers held in a large spray. Plants form an upright clump of ferny heat-tolerant foliage. Fairly compact, early blooming. **'Thundercloud'** has darker purple flowers.

HEIGHT/SPREAD: 60–90cm (2–3')/60cm (2')

> "My most gratifying combination to date: wispy puffs of mauve-pink *Thalictrum aquilegifolium*, upright spires of purple-red lupines, great balls of *Allium aflatunense* — punctuated throughout with royal purple Columbine. Were it not in my own garden, I'd be envious!" –
> Kevin Ward, Zone 5

LOCATION:	Rich, moist woodland soil.
BLOOMS:	May–June
USES:	✂ Borders, Woodland gardens

delavayi 'Hewitt's Double'   ZONES 3–9
Large airy clouds of double mauve flowers, similar to Baby's Breath. Foliage is very lacy and fern-like. This variety gets fairly tall and may require staking. Plants increase slowly and are often difficult to obtain. Excellent for cutting, fresh or dried.

> "In my garden these have to be staked, but it's worth it for the cloud of mauve hovering over the smaller woodland plants." – Warren Hartman, Zone 6

HEIGHT/SPREAD:	120–150cm (4–5')/60cm (2')
LOCATION:	Rich, moist woodland soil.
BLOOMS:	June–August
USES:	✂ Borders, Woodland gardens

flavum glaucum   ZONES 4–9
Unusual powdery blue-green foliage, forming a good-size clump. Flowers are yellow, in good-size sprays. An easy and rewarding species for any shady border.

HEIGHT/SPREAD:	1.5–1.8m (5–6')/60cm (2')
LOCATION:	Rich, moist woodland soil.
BLOOMS:	July–August
USES:	✂ Borders, Woodland gardens

Tanacetum coccineum 'Robinson Single'

Thalictrum aquilegifolium

Thalictrum delavayi 'Hewitt's Double'

Thermopsis lanceolata

THERMOPSIS
(False Lupine, Golden Bean) ☼

lanceolata   ZONES 2–9

(Formerly listed as *T. lupinoides*) A North American native wildflower, similar in effect to a dwarf Lupine, with spikes of lemon-yellow flowers in late spring. Plants are long-lived and especially recommended for gardeners who can't seem to succeed with true Lupines. Use towards the front of a border. Resents being disturbed once established. Very drought-tolerant.

HEIGHT/SPREAD:	20–30cm (9–12″)/30cm (12″)
LOCATION:	Average well-drained soil.
BLOOMS:	May–June
USES:	△ ◢ ⚡ ⚔ ⚘ Borders, Meadows

Thymus praecox 'Purple Carpet'

THYMUS
(Thyme) ☼

Bushy or mat-forming herbs with small aromatic leaves and short spikes of flowers. Upright forms are good for massing or using as a low hedge. Creeping varieties make an attractive groundcover or lawn substitute for small areas, even tolerating light traffic. All prefer a sunny warm site. All are moderately drought-tolerant. Some of the most familiar garden forms have recently been reclassified.

× citriodorus   ZONES 4–9

(Lemon Thyme) A complex group of hybrids, most having extremely fragrant lemon-scented leaves. The habit, foliage colour and hardiness vary considerably between the named cultivars. The upright varieties are excellent cooking herbs.

SPREAD:	30cm (12″)
LOCATION:	Lean, well-drained soil.
BLOOMS:	July–August
USES:	△ ◢ ⚡ ⚔ ⚘ Edging, Herb gardens, Walls

'Bertram Anderson' ('E. B. Anderson') Dwarf carpeter. Good bright-golden foliage colour all winter and spring. Turns light green in summer. Seldom blooms. HEIGHT: 5cm (2″)

'Gold Edge' Delightful strong lemon fragrance. Green and yellow variegated foliage on an upright spreading bush. Pink flowers in summer. HEIGHT: 25cm (10″)

'Silver Queen' ('Argenteus') Silver Thyme. Bushy, upright variety. Leaves are light green, variegated with silver. Attractive ornamental, and one of the best for cooking. Lilac flowers. More tender than the others. ZONES 6–9. HEIGHT: 25cm (10″)

'Doone Valley'   ZONES 4–9

Fairly low creeping type. Dark-green foliage with bright gold tips in fall and spring, green in the summer. Good bronzy-red winter colour. Lavender flowers. HEIGHT: 10–15cm (4–6″)

HEIGHT/SPREAD:	10–15cm (4–6″)/45cm (18″)
LOCATION:	Lean, well-drained soil.
BLOOMS:	May–June
USES:	△ ◢ ⚡ ⚔ ⚘ Edging, Walls

'Moonlight'   ZONES 4–9

A delightful variety, forming a semi-upright bushy mound of grey foliage, with masses of light pink flowers in early summer. For rock gardens or edging. This may be a form of *T. leucotrichus* or *T. nitidus*.

HEIGHT/SPREAD:	10–15cm (4–6″)/30cm (12″)
LOCATION:	Lean, well-drained soil.
BLOOMS:	May–June
USES:	△ ◢ ⚡ ⚔ ⚘ Edging, Walls

praecox   ZONES 2–9

(Creeping Thyme, Mother-of-thyme) Very flat mats of tiny leaves, smothered with flowers in summer. Excellent between paving stones and in rock gardens. These form a very dense, long-lived carpet. Some of the varieties listed below are often included under *T. serpyllum*.

> "Collectors enjoy amassing the numerous named forms of garden thymes, but marvelous calico carpets can be woven simply by combining plants of mother of thyme." – Ann Lovejoy,
> *The American Mixed Border*

HEIGHT/SPREAD:	2–5cm (1–2″)/30cm (12″)
LOCATION:	Lean, well-drained soil.
BLOOMS:	June–July
USES:	△ ◢ ⚡ ⚔ ⚘ Edging, Walls

'Albiflorus' (White Moss Thyme) Very flat mat of light green leaves with clear white flowers. Slow to establish.

'Coccineus' (Red Creeping Thyme) Deep scarlet-purple flowers, very small dark green leaves.

'Elfin' A very compact variety for the rock garden. Low buns of tiny leaves bear soft pink flowers in summer. Not a fast spreader.

'Pseudolanuginosus' (Woolly Thyme) Fuzzy olive-grey foliage, with sparse pink flowers in summer. Perhaps the best for groundcover use, very vigorous habit.

'Purple Carpet' Similar habit to 'Coccineus', but flowers are a lighter mauve-purple. A chance seedling discovered and introduced by Valleybrook Gardens.

serpyllum   ZONES 2–9

(Mother-of-Thyme) Vigorous grower, bright green leaves and rose-purple flowers. This is a variable seed-grown variety, not nearly as refined as other creeping types, but very rugged and hardy. This could possibly be *T. pulegoides*.

HEIGHT/SPREAD:	15–20cm (6–8″)/30cm (12″)
LOCATION:	Lean, well-drained soil.
BLOOMS:	June–July
USES:	△ ◢ ⚡ ⚔ ⚘ Edging, Walls

TIARELLA
(Foamflower) ◐ ●

Closely related to Coral Bells, forming similar low clumps of leaves, with airy sprays of light pink or white flowers in late spring or early summer. The species are woodland plants native to North America, but several hybrid selections have been developed in recent years and some of these are now becoming widely available. There are both spreading and non-spreading forms.

Thymus 'Moonlight'

Thymus praecox 'Coccineus'

Tiarella cordifolia

Tiarella cordifolia 'Oak Leaf'

cordifolia   **ZONES 4–9**

This is a spreading species, best suited for ground-cover use or as a low edging in the shady border. Low clumps of hairy green leaves, spikes of white flowers in early summer. Excellent bronzy winter colour. Combines nicely with ferns and other woodland plants. Evergreen. *T. wherryi* is quite similar but forms a clump rather than a spreading patch, so it is better for use in rock gardens or as an edging. Most of the new hybrids listed below are also non-running.

> "This charming woodland species offers handsome evergreen foliage, topped with delicate spikes of creamy-white, fragrant flowers in May and June. In a moist, shady spot, it spreads enthusiastically (but not invasively), creating a lovely groundcover."
> – Ellen Eisenberg, Zone 5

HEIGHT/SPREAD: 15–30cm (6–12")/30cm (12")
LOCATION: Moist, rich woodland soil.
BLOOMS: May–July
USES: ⚘∧⋎▲ Edging, Woodland gardens

'Dark Eyes' Maple-shaped leaves, dark green with a maroon-black blotch in the centre. Semi-running habit.

'Filigree Lace' Deeply-cut lacy foliage with white flowers.

'Inkblot' Pale pink flowers contrasting against green leaves with a large inky-black splotch.

'Oakleaf' A stunning selection. Foliage is attractively lobed like an oak leaf. Deep red winter colour. Spikes of flowers are an unusual pale pink shade. A non-spreading clump form, excellent for edging and rock gardens.

'Skeleton Key' Very delicate-looking lacy foliage with a bronze flush.

TOVARA
See PERSICARIA.

Tradescantia × andersoniana 'Purple Dome'

TRADESCANTIA
(Spiderwort) ☼ ☽

× andersoniana Hybrids   **ZONES 3–9**
Grassy upright clumps with showy triangular flowers; these open over an exceptionally long season. Plants benefit from good clip after flowering to tidy them up and to encourage a fall bloom. Best in a moist location to keep the foliage from scorching. There are several named cultivars in various shades of light and dark blue, purple, pink, magenta and white.

HEIGHT/SPREAD: 30–60cm (1–2')/45–60cm (18–24")
LOCATION: Average to moist well-drained soil.
BLOOMS: June–September
USES: Borders, Waterside

'Charlotte' Clear pink flowers.

'Concord Grape' Exciting new selection. Frosted blue-green foliage with masses of deep purple flowers. Good rebloomer.

'Hawaiian Punch' Another new variety, with large magenta-pink flowers.

'Isis' White flowers with a flush of violet-blue in the centre.

'Little Doll' Light blue blossoms, a compact selection useful for edging. Narrow foliage.

'Purple Dome' Deep purple flowers.

'Rubra' Wine-red flowers.

'Zwanenburg Blue' Clear violet-blue.

TRICYRTIS
(Toad-lily) ☽

hirta   **ZONES 4–9**
(Japanese Toad-lily) A unique but easy plant for shady areas. Arching stems produce a fall display of bizarre white star flowers, heavily spotted with dark purple. Deserves a special spot where it can be seen up close. Subtle. Grown commercially as cut flowers. Several exciting selections have become available in the last few years.

> "The adjective that seems to be most common in describing the plant's flowers is "weird"; they look almost as though they evolved on some other planet."
> – Allen Lacy, *The Garden in Autumn*

HEIGHT/SPREAD: 60–90cm (2–3')/30–60cm (1–2')
LOCATION: Prefers a rich, moist soil.
BLOOMS: September–October
USES: ✂⋖△ Woodland gardens, Borders

'Hatatogisa' Pale blue flowers, white centre and purple spots.

'Shirohotogisu' Pure white flowers.

'Togen' Lavender-purple flowers with a white centre, no spots.

TRIFOLIUM
(Clover) ☼ ☽

Clover is most familiar as a hay crop or lawn weed, but there are a few ornamental types that are occasionally grown in gardens.

repens 'Pentaphyllum'   **ZONES 4–9**
(Black-leaved Clover) (Formerly listed as 'Atropurpureum') A handsome edging or ground-cover plant, the foliage is dark purple to black, with a green margin. Lots of lucky four-leaved clovers appear, and plants spread fairly quickly to form a dense patch. White flowers bloom in June. Evergreen in mild areas.

HEIGHT/SPREAD: 10cm (4")/30cm (12")
LOCATION: Average to moist well-drained soil.
BLOOMS: June
USES: ∧⋎⚘▲♥ Edging, Pots

TRITOMA
See KNIPHOFIA.

TROLLIUS
(Globeflower) ☼ ☽

× cultorum Hybrids   **ZONES 2–9**
(Hybrid Globeflower) Large round buttercup flowers rise above leafy clumps of deeply lobed foliage in late spring. These are popular for the early border, their showy flowers are sometimes used for cutting. Many named selections exist, all are in shades of yellow to orange, including some gorgeous pale forms. Plants can be sheared back in summer if they get tired looking.

Tiarella cordifolia 'Skeleton Key'

Tricyrtis hirta

Trifolium repens 'Pentaphyllum'

Trollius chinensis 'Golden Queen'

Trollius 'Orange Crest'

Trollius pumilus

Verbascum 'Helen Johnson'

Verbena bonariensis

"A plant always of interest in a semi-shade garden for the richness of its colour and the unusual shape of the flowers."
– Margaret Burke, Zone 6

HEIGHT/SPREAD: 60–90cm (2–3')/45–60cm (18–24")
LOCATION: Average to moist well-drained soil.
BLOOMS: May–June
USES: ✂ Borders, Meadow gardens

chinensis **'Golden Queen'** Deep golden-yellow flowers with a central tuft of deep orange. Late. HEIGHT: 90cm (36")

'Lemon Queen' Large clear yellow flowers. Vigorous. HEIGHT: 60cm (24")

'Orange Crest' Deep orange. HEIGHT: 75–90cm (30–36")

'Orange Princess' Orange-yellow. HEIGHT: 75–90cm (30–36")

pumilus ZONES 3–9
(Dwarf Globeflower) A rock garden or edging species, bright yellow open buttercups.

HEIGHT/SPREAD: 30cm (12")/30cm (12")
LOCATION: Average to moist well-drained soil.
BLOOMS: May–June
USES: ▲△✂ Rock gardens, Edging

yunnanensis ZONES 4–9
(Chinese Globeflower) Said to be the largest flow-ered Trollius, with glistening yellow buttercups on branching stems, held well above the leaves.

HEIGHT/SPREAD: 40–50cm (16–20")/30cm (12")
LOCATION: Average to moist well-drained soil.
BLOOMS: May–June
USES: ✂ Borders

TUNICA
See PETRORHAGIA.

VERBASCUM
(Mullein) ☼
Related to the common roadside Mullein, the garden forms are interesting and showy plants for sunny borders. All have upright spikes of flowers and leaves arranged in a low flat rosette. They are good cut flowers for those with a daring sense of design.

bombyciferum ZONES 4–9
(Giant Silver Mullein) Silvery-white felted leaves form a large rosette the first year, sending up tall stately spires of yellow flowers the following sum-mer. A spectacular specimen plant, usually treated as a biennial. Will self-seed.

"Elegant yellow spikes of an exotic nature give this plant an architectural quality."
– Warren Hartman, Zone 6

HEIGHT/SPREAD: 1.5–1.8m (5–6')/45cm (18")
LOCATION: Average well-drained soil.
BLOOMS: June–August
USES: ✂⛴ Specimen, Borders, Tubs

× Hybrids ZONES 5–9
(Hybrid Mullein) Showy, long-blooming varieties suited to the border. Branching spikes of flowers con-tinue blooming all summer if dead-headed regularly. These must be propagated by root cuttings. Foliage forms a low green rosette. Rarely seen in North American gardens.

HEIGHT/SPREAD: 90cm (3')/45cm (18")
LOCATION: Average well-drained soil.
BLOOMS: June–August
USES: ✂⛴ Specimen, Borders, Tubs

'Helen Johnson' Coppery-orange with a touch of cream.

'Pink Domino' Deep rose spikes.

phoeniceum ZONES 4–9
(Purple Mullein) Shorter spikes of flowers in a mix of purple, red, pink, or white. Showy when planted in groups towards the front of the border. Short-lived perennial, but self-seeds nicely. Special favorites can be grown from root-cuttings.

HEIGHT/SPREAD: 60–120cm (2–4')/30cm (1')
LOCATION: Average well-drained soil.
BLOOMS: May–July
USES: ✂ Borders

Verbena canadensis 'Homestead Purple'

VERBENA
(Verbena) ☼
Most of the perennial species of Verbena are generally on the tender side and are often grown as long-flowering annuals.

bonariensis ZONES 7–9
(Brazilian Verbena) Stiff, upright branching stems hold clusters of magenta-purple flowers from early summer through late fall. A large grouping makes an unforgettable display. Very heat tolerant. In many areas this is grown as a self-seeding annual.

"A single plant is curious, three together beautiful, and a large group is a splendid sight." – Graham Stuart Thomas, *Perennial Garden Plants*

HEIGHT/SPREAD: 90–120cm (3–4')/30cm (1')
LOCATION: Average well-drained soil.
BLOOMS: June–October
USES: ✂❦🐝 Massing, Borders

canadensis 'Homestead Purple' ZONES 7–9
(Clump Verbena) A low trailing perennial species native to the eastern U.S., this selection is a form recently discovered growing in a Georgia garden. Clusters of bright deep-purple flowers cover the plants for weeks on end. This requires good drainage and dislikes winter wet. Excellent in baskets and window boxes, worth considering as an unusual annual. Drought and heat-tolerant.

HEIGHT/SPREAD: 15–20cm (6–8")/45cm (18")
LOCATION: Well-drained soil.
BLOOMS: June–October
USES: ▲△M❦🐝🗲 Massing, Walls, Edging

VERNONIA
(Ironweed) ☼

noveboracensis ZONES 4–9
(New York Ironweed) In a sunny moist site this will form a bold, impressive clump of dark green leaves, with masses of magenta-purple flowers in late sum-mer and fall. A native to Eastern North America, this little-known perennial is especially useful in larger gardens.

HEIGHT/SPREAD:	1.8–2.1m (6–7')/90cm (3')
LOCATION:	Rich moist soil.
BLOOMS:	August–October
USES:	✄ Borders, Meadows

Veronica austriaca 'Trehane'

VERONICA
(Speedwell) ☼ ◐

Showy garden perennials, mostly with upright spikes of blue, pink or white flowers from early summer on. Taller varieties are excellent cut flowers. Shorter types put on a bright display in the rock garden.

allionii ZONES 2–9
(Alpine Speedwell) Very compact spikes of violet-blue flowers on a low mounded clump of evergreen leaves. Excellent edging plant.

HEIGHT/SPREAD:	15cm (6")/30cm (12")
LOCATION:	Average well-drained soil.
BLOOMS:	June–August
USES:	△△❦ Edging

austriaca ZONES 2–9
(Hungarian Speedwell) (Formerly listed as *V. teucrium*) An excellent edging plant, with spikes of blue flowers in early summer, plants forming a low clump. Trim back after flowering.

HEIGHT/SPREAD:	20–30cm (8–12")/30cm (12")
LOCATION:	Average well-drained soil.
BLOOMS:	May–July
USES:	△ Edging, Borders

'Crater Lake Blue' Intense gentian-blue flowers.

'Trehane' Bright golden-yellow foliage, compact habit. Unusual!

'Shirley Blue' Brilliant sky-blue flowers.

dabneyi ZONES 2–9
(Pink Speedwell) Bright green foliage forms a low clump, set with short spikes of pale pink flowers in late spring. Used in rock gardens and for edging.

HEIGHT/SPREAD:	15cm (6")/30cm (12")
LOCATION:	Average well-drained soil.
BLOOMS:	May–June
USES:	△ Edging, Walls

filifolia ZONES 4–9
(Fernleaved Speedwell) Quite unlike any of the other species. This is a little gem for the rock garden, and forms a low carpet of ferny green foliage set with large sky blue flowers in late spring. Not to be confused with the lawn weed *V. filiformis*.

HEIGHT/SPREAD:	5–10cm (2–4")/30–45cm (12–18")
LOCATION:	Average well-drained soil.
BLOOMS:	May–June
USES:	△∿▲❦ Walls, Edging

gentianoides ZONES 2–9
(Broad-leaved Speedwell) Leaves are light green, forming a low rosette. Upright spikes of light blue flowers rise above in late spring. 'Variegata' has leaves boldly splashed with creamy-white and green.

HEIGHT/SPREAD:	30–40cm (12–16")/30–45cm (12–18")
LOCATION:	Average well-drained soil.
BLOOMS:	May–June
USES:	✄ Massing, Borders

longifolia 'Blue Giant' ZONES 3–9
(Tall Speedwell) ('Blauriesin') The best of the bunch for cutting, this selection has fat spikes of lavender-blue flowers with nodding tips. Coarse green foliage. May need staking. Good at the back of the border.

HEIGHT/SPREAD:	90–100cm (36–40")/70cm (30")
LOCATION:	Average well-drained soil.
BLOOMS:	June–August
USES:	✄ Borders, Massing

peduncularis 'Georgia Blue' ZONES 4–9
Terrific new creeping selection from central Asia. Makes a low mat of small green leaves, studded with incredible true-blue upfacing flowers. Leaves turn bronzy-red during the colder months. An excellent cover for spring-blooming bulbs, especially Narcissus.

HEIGHT/SPREAD:	10cm (4")/60cm (24")
LOCATION:	Well-drained soil.
BLOOMS:	April–May
USES:	△∿▲ Walls, Edging

prostrata 'Heavenly Blue' ZONES 4–9
(Creeping Speedwell) Low, creeping mat of grey-green foliage, smothered by bright sapphire-blue flowers in late spring. A showy edging or rockery plant.

HEIGHT/SPREAD:	10cm (4")/30cm (12")
LOCATION:	Well-drained soil.
BLOOMS:	May–June
USES:	△∿ Walls, Edging

repens ZONES 2–9
(Creeping Speedwell) Makes a completely flat carpet of tiny green leaves, studded with little white flowers in late spring. Nice in the rockery, or between patio stones.

HEIGHT/SPREAD:	1cm (1/2")/15–30cm (6–12")
LOCATION:	Average well-drained soil.
BLOOMS:	May–June
USES:	△∿▲❦ Walls, Between flagstones

spicata ZONES 2–9
(Spike Speedwell) Bushy border plants, with upright spikes of violet-blue flowers for many weeks. Excellent for cutting. Many selections of this species exist, some with attractive pink or white flowers.

HEIGHT/SPREAD:	30–60cm (1–2')/30cm (12")
LOCATION:	Average well-drained soil.
BLOOMS:	June–August
USES:	✄ Borders, Massing

'Blue Carpet' ('Blauteppich') Very dwarf, deep blue flowers. HEIGHT: 5–10cm (2–4")

'Giles van Hees' Very tight-growing selection with clear rose-pink flowers. Long blooming season. HEIGHT: 20cm (8")

'Icicle' Good clear white spikes. Late.

incana (Woolly Speedwell) Silver-grey, woolly foliage, spikes of violet-blue flowers. Excellent foliage plant for edging or massing. Remove faded flower spikes to maintain foliage interest all season.

'Noah Williams' Variegated form of 'Icicle'. Leaf edges are toothed and blotched with creamy-white.

'Red Fox' Deep rose-pink flowers. Compact habit.

'Rosenrot' Rosy-pink, compact seed strain.

Veronica filifolia

Veronica gentianoides

Veronica longifolia 'Blue Giant'

Veronica peduncularis 'Georgia Blue'

Veronica spicata 'White Icicles'

Veronicastrum virginicum 'Album'

Viola cornuta 'Ardross Gem'

Viola cornuta 'Baby Lucia'

× 'Sunny Border Blue'   ZONES 3–9

This long-blooming hybrid features short spikes of deep violet-blue flowers all summer long. The bright green foliage is unusually crinkled and remains fresh-looking throughout the season, showing excellent mildew resistance. Plants have a dense and compact habit. Useful for massing or edging. A former *Perennial Plant of the Year.*

HEIGHT/SPREAD: 30–45cm (18–24")/30cm (12")
LOCATION: Average well-drained soil.
BLOOMS: July–September
USES: ✂❀ Massing, Edging, Borders

whitleyi   ZONES 3–9

(Whitley's Speedwell) An outstanding low edging or rockery plant! Forms a spreading mat of small grey-green leaves, absolutely smothered by soft blue flowers in spring with a few continuing all season long. This could also be used as a dense groundcover. This may be an incorrect species name.

HEIGHT/SPREAD: 5–10cm (2–4")/30–45cm (12–18")
LOCATION: Average well-drained soil.
BLOOMS: May–June
USES: △◭▲❀ Edging, Walls

VERONICASTRUM
(Culver's-root) ☼

Very closely related to Veronica, and sometimes included with them. These are native North American wildflowers of great garden value. They prefer a sunny location with a rich moist soil.

virginicum   ZONES 3–9

(=*Veronica virginica*) Forming impressive large clumps, these differ from *Veronica* in that the leaves are whorled, arranged on the stem like the spokes of an umbrella. Flowers are held in long wands that arch gracefully, appearing for several weeks in the late summer, excellent for cutting. Lots of moisture is needed for these to do their best.

HEIGHT/SPREAD: 1.2–1.8m (4–6')/90cm (3')
LOCATION: Rich moist soil.
BLOOMS: August–September
USES: ✂ Borders, Meadows

'Album' Clear white flowers, the most impressive.

> "Given plenty of head-room, a little morning sun, and rich, moist soil, Culver's Root makes a perfectly respectable substitute for a water feature — its gracefully arching branches tipped with white spires evoke images of water fountains — even those lacking in 'gardener's vision' can see the resemblance!" – Kevin Ward, Zone 5

'Lilac Carina' Unusual lavender-blue selection.

'Rosea' A very pale pink variety.

Viola cornuta – Mixed

VIOLA
(Violet, Pansy) ☼

This group includes the violets of woodlands and meadows as well as the small hardy garden pansies known as violas. All are of easy culture, preferring a cool partly shady location.

cornuta Hybrids   ZONES 4–9

(Perennial Pansy, Horned Violet) Also known as Winter Pansies, these are much hardier than annual pansies, being more tolerant of both summer heat and winter cold. Excellent for bedding, edging, rock gardens or containers. Use a winter mulch in Zones 3–5. These are excellent for massing with tulips and other spring bulbs, in containers or under shrubs. There are several good older seed strains in shades of apricot, yellow, blue, purple, bronzy-red, cream and white. The more modern **Princess Series** have dainty small flowers in several colours, and they are excellent performers. Some of the more unique varieties are noted below.

> "The horned violet…spills in cascades over the border's edge while lacing shoot after flower laden shoot as much as three feet long through taller plants nearby."
> – Ann Lovejoy,
> *The American Mixed Border*

HEIGHT/SPREAD: 10–20cm (4–8")/15–20cm (6–8")
LOCATION: Average to moist well-drained soil.
BLOOMS: April–October
USES: △◭▲❀ Massing, Edging, Borders

'Ardross Gem' Clear blue flowers with a gold flush. Grown from cuttings or division.

'Baby Franjo' Bright yellow miniature flowers. Compact.

'Baby Lucia' Small sky-blue flowers. Compact.

'Black Magic' Closest yet to jet black, with a charming yellow eye. Grown from cuttings or division.

'Purple Duet' Gorgeous, rich violet and mauve combination unlike any other.

'Purple Showers' Medium violet-blue, an excellent performer even during hot summers. Grown from cuttings or division

'Yellow Frost' Little yellow and blue flowers, whiskered.

labradorica   ZONES 4–9

(Purple Labrador Violet) Charming rock garden violet. Low tufts of purple-tinged leaves, with purple wild-violet type flowers. Blooms in spring and fall. Likes a cool, moist spot. A native North American wildflower.

"This charming little native excels as a ground cover in partial shade… the eye-catching, semi-evergreen deep purple heart-shaped foliage stops garden visitors in their tracks." – Joanne Baskerville, Zone 4

HEIGHT/SPREAD: 10–15cm (4–6")/15cm (6")
LOCATION: Moist, well-drained soil.
BLOOMS: May–September
USES: ▲△∧•♥ Woodland gardens, Borders

obliqua   ZONES 3–9
(Marsh Blue Violet) (Formerly listed as *V. cucullata*) Lush clumps of heart-shaped leaves are excellent for massing in the shade garden, though they tolerate sun with enough moisture. Large classic violet flowers are held just above the leaves. Flowers have a very slight fragrance. A native to eastern North America, some-times incorrectly listed as *V. odorata*. There are a few colour selections. Self-seeds prolifically.

HEIGHT/SPREAD: 15cm (6")/15–30cm (6–12")
LOCATION: Average to moist soil.
BLOOMS: April–June
USES: ∧•♥ Woodland gardens, Borders

'Royal Robe' Vibrant purple-blue flowers.

'White Czar' White flowers with a yellow centre.

pedata   ZONES 3–9
(Bird's Foot Violet) Another wildflower native to eastern North America, grown for its spring display of small violet-blue flowers and interesting divided leaves. Nice addition to a well-drained rock garden in part shade to full sun.

HEIGHT/SPREAD: 10–15cm (4–6")/20cm (8")
LOCATION: Needs a well-drained soil.
BLOOMS: April–June
USES: △ Borders, Edging

sororia   ZONES 3–9
(Woolly Blue Violet) Another species native to Eastern North America. Very similar in habit and flowering to *V. obliqua*, for spring flowering and a carpet of heart-shaped leaves all season long. Prolific self-seeder. Some interesting colour forms are listed below.

HEIGHT/SPREAD: 15cm (6")/15–30cm (6–12")
LOCATION: Average to moist soil.
BLOOMS: April–June
USES: ∧•♥ Woodland gardens, Borders

'Freckles' White flowers with lavender purple spots. Excellent in a children's garden! Degree of spotting varies in the seedlings.

priceana (Confederate Violet) Silvery-white flowers with blue blotches and veins.

'Rubra' Unusual wine-red flowers, truly unique.

tricolor   ZONES 2–9
(Johnny Jump-Up) Although usually treated as a bedding annual, Jump-ups will often overwinter or at least re-establish by self-seeding. Their tiny pansy flowers appear from early spring through late fall, especially when the nights are cool. Keep these out of the alpine garden to prevent seedlings from taking over.

HEIGHT/SPREAD: 10–15cm (4–6")/15cm (6")
LOCATION: Average to moist soil.
BLOOMS: April–October
USES: ♥ Massing, Borders, Edging

'Blue Elf' Bright violet-blue flowers. Very different!

'Helen Mount' The more traditional violet, yellow and mauve combination.

WALDSTEINIA
(Barren-Strawberry) ☼ ●

ternata   ZONES 4–9
This makes a low, dense mat of shiny semi-evergreen leaves that somewhat resemble those of a strawberry. A good low-maintenance groundcover, punctuated by little yellow flowers in the spring. Can be used to cover large or small areas, spreading by stolons but not considered invasive. Tolerates summer drought.

HEIGHT/SPREAD: 15cm (6")/30–45cm (12–18")
LOCATION: Average to moist soil.
BLOOMS: April–May
USES: ∧•▲ Massing, Edging

Zantedeschia aethiopica 'Crowborough'

ZANTEDESCHIA
(Calla Lily) ☼ ☼

aethiopica 'Crowborough'   ZONES 8–9
(White Calla) The hardiest Calla, overwintering outdoors at the West coast. Roots are easily stored indoors for the winter in colder regions, or can even be left in pots and stored in the basement. Tall clumps of broad, leathery leaves give rise to pure white flowers with yellow centres. Easy to grow in containers. Needs a dry period in winter.

HEIGHT/SPREAD: 90cm (3')/30–60cm (1–2')
LOCATION: Moist well-drained soil.
BLOOMS: June–October
USES: ✄♥ Specimen

Viola cornuta 'Black Magic'

Viola tricolor

Viola obliqua 'White Czar'

Viola sororia 'Freckles'

Ferns

Ferns are valuable garden plants of great dependability and beauty. Their leaves, known as fronds, can be lacy or leathery, plain green or variegated, and provide a long season of interest. Rarely suffering from pests and diseases, they offer trouble-free elegance.

Naturally inhabiting woodland areas, most ferns thrive in the shade and protection provided by trees. They perform best in a moist, well drained soil that is high in organic matter.

Ferns were tremendously popular in Victorian times, and many of the British well-to-do had ferneries — shady garden areas or whole greenhouses devoted to fern collections. As we become more aware of the value of foliage texture in modern landscaping, we are re-discovering the refreshing diversity of hardy ferns. Fortunately some of the best ferns have been introduced back into nursery production, so today's selection is much better than what was available even ten years ago.

There are numerous kinds of hardy ferns available in garden centres. While some species are deciduous, dying back to the ground for winter, others are evergreen, providing attractive winter foliage in the garden, especially in mild-winter areas. Ferns vary in texture and height as well, from low spreading mounds, to bold upright clumps. Even the smallest garden can have a woodland feeling by planting a few ferns along with other shade loving perennials such as Hostas, Primulas and Astilbes.

Try to start with vigorous container-grown plants which have been grown from spores or divisions, and which have had a chance to develop a strong healthy root system. A good many of the ferns (and other wildflowers) being sold today have been collected from the wild; buying such plants will only serve to encourage collectors to continue depleting our natural stands of native plants, some of them rare and endangered! When you buy any woodland wildflowers or ferns, be sure to find out whether or not they have been nursery propagated (as opposed to dug from the wild and then nursery grown in pots). All of the ferns listed here can be commercially grown from spores, with no need to obtain stock from the wild.

Tips on Planting and Care

Ferns require moist, humus-rich soil. To improve your soil, dig in 10–15cm (4–6″) of well-rotted compost, peat moss or other organic matter to increase its moisture holding ability.

Some ferns can grow well under trees, but tree roots tend to rob the soil of water and nutrients. Also, rain may not penetrate the canopy. You will have to provide regular watering to these areas if you want to grow ferns there, especially while plants are trying to get established. It is a good idea to mulch deeply around your ferns with compost or leaf litter once a year. This will improve the soil, keep roots cool and help to retain moisture.

If your ferns are forming large patches, or you wish to increase the size of your patch — perhaps even to trade with friends — you might want to tackle dividing your plants. This is very simple to do in early spring, and is exactly like dividing any other perennial that forms a clump or patch. One word of caution, however; don't try to divide a plant that has only one main crown with no smaller plants surrounding it. Wait a year or two and if you notice secondary shoots (called offsets) developing beside the main crown, carefully sneak these away in the spring using a sharp hand trowel.

Where winters are very cold, cover ferns with evergreen boughs or mulch with leaves in the fall to protect them. Any natural leaf-fall that accumulates should be left to decompose; the rich leaf-mould that results over many years is the best possible fertilizer for ferns and other woodland plants. Evergreen ferns may look somewhat tattered by late winter. If so, trim off any unsightly foliage in early spring. Varieties marked EVERGREEN should be so in Zones 7–9, but may become deciduous in colder regions or exposed windy areas.

Adiantum pedatum

Asplenium scolopendrium

Asplenium scolopendrium 'Kaye's Lacerate'

Athyrium f.f. 'Vernoniae Cristatum'

ADIANTUM
(Maidenhair Fern) ☼ ●

pedatum   **ZONES 2–9**

(Northern Maidenhair) Very delicate, fan-shaped fronds. Stems are shiny and black, with light green lacy leaves, turning bright gold in fall. Slowly spreads to form a rounded medium-sized clump. This fern is a real gem, and always in demand! Suitable for a rock garden, or among shrubs. Native. DECIDUOUS.

> "At first glance, it looks so vulnerable, its fragile leaves shivering in the slightest breeze. Be not fooled, for this fern sails through drought and harsh winters in both lime and acidic soil." – Cathy Forgie, Zone 4

HEIGHT/SPREAD: 30–60cm (12–24")/30–60cm (12–24")
LOCATION: Moist, humusy soil.
USES: △�◊

ASPLENIUM
(Spleenwort) ☼ ●
Valued for their symmetrical clumps of glossy fronds. This group is moderately easy to grow, best suited to a shady rock garden. They grow especially well on steep rocky slopes and walls, benefiting from extra-good drainage at the crown.

ebenoides   **ZONES 5–9**

(Dragon's-tail Fern, Scott's Spleenwort) Shiny green triangular fronds. A naturally-occurring hybrid native to eastern North America, sometimes classified as *Asplenosorus ebenoides*. Small, compact plant, best in a shaded rockery or trough garden where it can be seen. Also a good choice for indoor terrariums. EVERGREEN.

HEIGHT/SPREAD: 15–30cm (6–12")/20–30cm (8–12")
LOCATION: Moist, rich neutral to alkaline soil.
USES: △▲◊

scolopendrium   **ZONES 4–9**

(Hart's-tongue Fern) (synonym *Phyllitus scolopendrium*) A lime-tolerant species, moderately easy to grow. The shiny green strap-shaped fronds are not at all divided. Looks like a hardy Bird's-nest fern. Although native (and rare) in parts of eastern North America, the type being propagated in the trade is the European form, apparently much easier to succeed with in a garden setting. Even so, it demands excellent drainage. EVERGREEN.

'Kaye's Lacerate' (Crispy Hart's-Tongue Fern) Frond edges are ruffled or crimped, with bizarre forked ends. Very unusual.

HEIGHT/SPREAD: 30–40cm (12–16")/30–45cm (12–18")
LOCATION: Moist, well-drained alkaline soil or
                limestone rubble.
USES: △▲◊

ATHYRIUM
(Lady Fern) ☼ ●
Delicate and lacy-looking ferns, their triangular fronds divided into many small leaflets. These are all good garden performers of easy culture, forming dense low to medium-sized mounds that clump nicely, with no tendency to get out of control. Excellent for massing or edging. Best in a slightly acid, humus-rich soil that stays evenly moist.

filix-femina   **ZONES 3–9**

(Lady Fern) Lacy-looking fronds are bright green. Clumps are dense and mounded. An easy variety for any shady corner, this species will adapt to sunny sites that remain evenly moist. Great for massing. Many fancy cultivated types have been selected from the European forms of Lady Fern and were tremendously popular in Victorian England. DECIDUOUS.

'Vernoniae Cristatum' (Crested Lady Fern) Fronds have a crisped, tasseled appearance, the ends uniquely forked or crested.

HEIGHT/SPREAD: 30–60cm (12–24")/60cm (2')
LOCATION: Moist, humus-rich soil.
USES: ◊◊ Massing

niponicum 'Pictum'   **ZONES 4–9**

(Japanese Painted Fern) (syn. 'Metallicum') Arching fronds are olive green with a handsome metallic-grey and red sheen. Adds a bright touch to the shade garden. Easy to grow and very popular. Color may fade in direct sun. DECIDUOUS.

> "No other fern brightens a shady corner the way this one does!" – Marjorie Mason Hogue, Zone 4

HEIGHT/SPREAD: 30–60cm (12–24")/30cm (12")
LOCATION: Moist, humus-rich soil.
USES: △◊◊ Massing, Borders

otophorum   **ZONES 4–9**

(Auriculate or Eared Lady Fern) Emerging fronds are a pale silvery colour, turning dark glossy green as they mature. Stems are deep red. DECIDUOUS.

HEIGHT/SPREAD: 30–45cm (12–18")/45cm (18")
LOCATION: Moist, humus-rich soil.
USES: △◊◊ Massing

Blechnum spicant

BLECHNUM
(Hard Fern) ☼ ●

spicant   **ZONES 5–9**

(Deer Fern) One of the best-known species native to the Pacific Northwest. Forms a large low clump of leathery sterile leaves, with contrasting fertile fronds shooting straight up from the centre. This requires humus-rich acidic soils and shady conditions. Will handle full sun in wet situations. EVERGREEN.

HEIGHT/SPREAD: 45–90cm (18–36")/45–90cm (18–36")
LOCATION: Moist, humusy acidic soil.
USES: ◊▲◊◊ Massing, Borders

CHEILANTHES
(Lip Fern) ☼ ◑

An exception among ferns, this is a group of species that prefers sunny locations and is well-adapted to dry habitats. A sunny rock garden is the ideal location, the plants placed so that the roots are in a cool rock crevice or between boulders. Use a loose gravelly soil with plenty of humus and sandy grit for good drainage.

LOCATION: Well-drained, loose gritty soil.
USES: ⛰☮ Troughs

argentea   ZONES 5–9
(Silvery Lip Fern) A cute, low-mounding plant with interesting star-shaped fronds. Leaflets are green on top, the underside coated with a white wax that helps to retain moisture. Prefers limestone rocks and slightly alkaline soil. Grows well in walls. HEIGHT/SPREAD: 10–15cm (4–6")/20cm (8"). DECIDUOUS.

lanosa   ZONES 5–9
(Hairy Lip Fern) Low tufted clumps are made up of very finely divided dark green fronds, covered on both sides with soft rust-brown hairs. An easy grower in sunny to lightly shaded rock gardens with excellent drainage. US Native. HEIGHT/SPREAD: 15–30cm (6–12")/20cm (8"). DECIDUOUS.

Cyrtomium falcatum

CYRTOMIUM
(Holly Fern) ◑ ●

falcatum   ZONES 7–9
Beautifully glossy, wide, leathery leaflets make this species unique among hardy ferns. Tolerant of arid conditions, and much-used in the southern and south-western US. This species seems to prefer lime soils, and grows especially well beside a sidewalk or house foundation. Needs very good drainage. EVERGREEN.

HEIGHT/SPREAD: 30–45cm (12–18")/45–60cm (18–24")
LOCATION: Moist, well-drained lime soil.
USES: ⛰☮▲☮ Massing

DRYOPTERIS
(Wood Fern, Shield Fern) ◑ ●

Medium sized ferns, good for massing or groundcover plantings. Their broad, triangular fronds have the classic fern appearance, arranged in a strong-growing clump. Mostly native to northern temperate regions, many good garden ferns are represented in this group.

carthusiana   ZONES 2–9
(Toothed Wood Fern) (syn. *D. spinulosa*) Very easy fern. The tall, bright green fronds are widely used by florists for cut foliage. Good for naturalizing. Especially loves wet areas. A common native fern. DECIDUOUS.

HEIGHT/SPREAD: 60–90cm (2–3')/30cm (12")
LOCATION: Moist to wet humus-rich soil.
USES: ᐱ☮≺☮ Massing

celsa   ZONES 5–9
(Log Fern) A naturally occurring hybrid form, native to the southeastern US. The large fronds are triangular, with a shiny deep-green surface. A good larger fern. SEMI-EVERGREEN.

HEIGHT/SPREAD: 90–120cm (3–4')/60–90cm (24–36")
LOCATION: Moist, rich acidic soil.
USES: ☮☮ Massing, Specimen

× complexa 'Robusta'   ZONES 4–9
(Hybrid Robust Male Fern) (formerly listed as *D. filix-mas* 'Undulata Robusta') Vigorous, full clumps of arching green and lacy fronds. This form has outstanding drought-tolerance once established, making it useful for a wide range of garden conditions, or for naturalizing. SEMI-EVERGREEN.

HEIGHT/SPREAD: 60–90cm (24–36")/60cm (24")
LOCATION: Average to moist, humus-rich soil.
USES: ⛰☮☮ Massing, Borders

cycadina   ZONES 5–9
(Shaggy Shield Fern) (formerly listed as *D. atrata*) Light golden-green fronds with a stiff, leathery appearance. Leaf-stems are covered in dense black scales. Winter mulching is recommended. EVERGREEN.

HEIGHT/SPREAD: 30–75cm (12–30")/45–60cm (18–24")
LOCATION: Moist, humus-rich soil.
USES: ⛰▲ Massing, Borders

dilatata   ZONES 4–9
(Broad Buckler Fern) (formerly listed as *D. austriaca*) Graceful, wide-spreading dark green fronds. Tolerant of wet sites, but adapting well to drier conditions. This is a European species with many named selections, all of easy culture. SEMI-EVERGREEN.

'Jimmy Dyce' (Jimmy's Upright Broad Buckler Fern) Unique habit, the fronds are stiffly upright in habit, with a blue-green color. Excellent. HEIGHT: 60cm (24").

> "Here in the Pacific Northwest 'Jimmy Dyce' is gaining a reputation as a top notch landscape plant. Because of its stiffly erect habit and its attractively domed caudex complimentary plantings may be meshed right up to the crown and still be clearly visible." – Judith I. Jones, Zone 8

'Lepidota Cristata' (Lacy Crested Broad Buckler Fern) Very finely cut leaflets with lacy forked tips. Compact habit. HEIGHT: 30–60cm (12–24").

'Recurved Form' (Recurved Broad Buckler Fern) Large triangular fronds, quite lacy, each leaflet curling under. HEIGHT: 45–70cm (18–30").

> "All ferns do not have to be a mass of competing overlapping fronds going every which way to be good garden companion plants. It is high time gardeners learned to appreciate the open architecture of less substantially fronded forms." – Judith I. Jones, Zone 8

SPREAD: 60–90cm (2–3')
LOCATION: Moist, slightly acid, humus-rich soil.
USES: ⛰☮☮ Borders, Massed

Athyrium felix-femina

Athyrium niponicum 'Pictum'

Dryopteris dilatata

Dryopteris erythrosora

Dryopteris marginalis

Matteuccia struthiopteris

Polystichum acrostichoides

Polystichum braunii

erythrosora   ZONES 5–9

(Autumn Fern) Compact habit, nice in the rock garden. New young fronds are coppery-pink, contrasting well against the older green fronds. Glossy finish. Can be massed as a groundcover. Easy and adaptable. EVERGREEN.

HEIGHT/SPREAD: 30–60cm (12–24")/30–60cm (12–24")
LOCATION: Moist, humus-rich soil.
USES: △⋀⋆▲☙ Borders

filix-mas   ZONES 2–9

(Male Fern) One of the easiest and most common of the large woodland ferns. Elegant triangular fronds of lacy, dark green leaves are particularly effective in massed plantings. Will tolerate a fair bit of sun if the site is wet. Native. DECIDUOUS.

'Barnesii' (Barnes' Narrow Male Fern) Very slender upright habit with a distinctive appearance. An excellent specimen fern.

'Crispatissima' (Crinkled Male Fern) Ruffled edges on each leaflet, upright but compact habit. HEIGHT: 20–40cm (8–16").

'Grandiceps' (Crested Male Fern) Long, arching fronds with multiple forking crests on the end, leaflets are also crested.

'Linearis Polydactyla' (Slender Crested Male Fern) Very lacy, fine-textured fronds, forked or tasseled on the tip of each leaflet. Good with bold-textured companions.

HEIGHT/SPREAD: 75–120cm (30–48")/60–90cm (2–3')
LOCATION: Moist to wet, humus-rich soil.
USES: ⋀⋆☙ Massing, Borders

marginalis   ZONES 2–9

(Leather Wood Fern, Marginal Wood Fern) Another native species, recommended for the rock garden. Slowly forms a medium-sized clump of bluish-green fronds. An easy-to-grow species with a non-spreading habit. EVERGREEN.

HEIGHT/SPREAD: 45–60cm (18–24")/30–45cm (12–18")
LOCATION: Moist, well-drained soil.
USES: △△▲☙ Specimen

× remota   ZONES 4–9

(Scaly Buckler Fern) Graceful, arching fronds are lacy in appearance, with a contrasting golden midrib or stipe. A natural hybrid of European origin, forming a strong clump in the garden. May naturalize. SEMI-EVERGREEN.

> "This is one of my favorite ferns for the garden and is impressive-looking with its shaggy golden-scaled stipe and delicately cut blade… It is a strong grower and one of the few ferns to volunteer in my garden." – John Mickel,
> *Ferns for American Gardens*

HEIGHT/SPREAD: 60–90cm (24–36")/60–90cm (24–36")
LOCATION: Moist, well-drained soil.
USES: ⋀⋆▲☙ Specimen, Massing

wallichiana   ZONES 6–9

(Wallich's Wood Fern) Strongly upright clumps, becoming quite huge when the site is to their liking. Large triangular green fronds with a contrasting black stem. New growth is beautiful, the fiddleheads covered with dense maroon scales or hairs. Winter mulching recommended. SEMI-EVERGREEN.

> "This imposing goliath is a breath-taking vision with its uncoiling octopus-like fiddleheads." – Judith I. Jones, Zone 8

HEIGHT/SPREAD: 60–120cm (2–4')/60–90cm (2–3')
LOCATION: Moist, humus-rich soil.
USES: ▲☙ Massing, Specimen

MATTEUCCIA
(Ostrich Fern, Fiddlehead Fern) ☿ ●

struthiopteris   ZONES 1–9

This is the main species of fern harvested for its edible fiddleheads. Plants will form a wide-spreading patch of upright triangular green fronds. Perhaps the most common fern grown in gardens, easy to the point of becoming invasive! Good groundcover for steep slopes or damp areas. Native. DECIDUOUS.

> "I was given six plants, and fifteen years later these have given rise to more than seven hundred; and I give away one to two hundred each year! This is the sorcerer's apprentice of the fern world; the more of them you give away, the more are produced." – John Mickel,
> *Ferns for American Gardens*

HEIGHT/SPREAD: 90–120cm (3–4')/60–90cm (2–3')
LOCATION: Average to rich moist soil.
USES: ⋀⋆☙ Waterside, Specimen

Osmunda regalis

OSMUNDA
(Flowering Fern) ☼ ☿ ●

Several important native ferns species are included here, all of them having leafy green sterile fronds and bizarre-looking fertile fronds or sections of the sterile frond that bear spores and no leaves. These are tolerant of full sun conditions as long as the soil remains evenly moist.

cinnamomea   ZONES 2–9

(Cinnamon Fern) Large triangular sterile fronds are similar to the Ostrich Fern. Fertile fronds are leafless, shooting up from the centre of the clump in late spring, in an attractive cinnamon-brown shade. Prefers a lime-free acidic soil. Native. DECIDUOUS.

HEIGHT/SPREAD: 70–150cm (2.5–5')/90cm (3')
LOCATION: Rich, moist to wet acidic soil.
USES: ☙ Specimen, Borders, Waterside

regalis   ZONES 3–9

(Royal Fern) A truly unique and spectacular fern. This forms a large crown, sending out a ring of arching leathery green fronds. The fertile spore-bearing pinnae are clustered together at the ends of the fronds and mature to a rich golden-brown. Use this as a specimen plant, or for massing. Lime-tolerant, also sun-tolerant on wet sites. The form 'Purpurascens' has contrasting reddish stems. Native. DECIDUOUS.

"This is a fern of unparalleled mimicry with its sterile fronds copying the locust tree leaves and the fertile panicles echoing astilbe seedheads. In the spring there are curious woolly caps on the fiddleheads which detach as the unfurling progresses."
– Judith I. Jones, Zone 8

HEIGHT/SPREAD:	90–150cm (3–5')/90cm (3')
LOCATION:	Rich, moist to wet soil.
USES:	☙ Specimen, Borders, Waterside

POLYSTICHUM
(Holly Fern, Sword Fern, Shield Fern) ☼ ●
Mostly upright-growing ferns, with leathery fronds that are arranged in a formal-looking clump. Some of our best native ferns are among these.

acrostichoides   ZONES 3–9
(Christmas Fern) Leathery, dark green fronds were once used for decoration at Christmas. One of the most dependable evergreen ferns, particularly in eastern North America. Plants form a medium-sized clump that is the perfect size for a shady rock garden. Prefers a lime-free soil, and protection from winter winds. Native. EVERGREEN.

HEIGHT/SPREAD:	30–45cm (12–18")/30–45cm (12–18")
LOCATION:	Moist, humus-rich soil.
USES:	⛰⋀⋁☙ Massing, Borders

braunii   ZONES 4–9
(Braun's Holly Fern) Thick, dark green fronds, the stalks covered with contrasting golden-brown scales. This has a dense, upright and arching form, producing a single-crowned clump. Protect from late spring frosts with evergreen boughs or dry leaves. Native. EVERGREEN.

"This popular holly fern makes a beautiful crown of lustrous, bipinnate fronds and does very well in northern gardens. The fiddleheads… are spectacular with their dense covering of silvery scales, the scales becoming tan with age." – John Mickel, *Ferns for American Gardens*

HEIGHT/SPREAD:	30–75cm (12–30")/30cm (12")
LOCATION:	Moist, humus-rich soil.
USES:	⛰⋀☙ Massing, Borders

munitum   ZONES 6–9
(Western Sword Fern, Alaska Fern) Vigorous grower, native to the West coast. The leathery, dark green fronds form a bold clump that gets bigger each year. Although excellent for naturalizing in the Pacific Northwest, this is a poor performer in Eastern North America. EVERGREEN.

HEIGHT/SPREAD:	60–120cm (2–4')/60–120cm (2–4')
LOCATION:	Moist, humus-rich soil.
USES:	⛰⋀⋁☙ Specimen, Massing

polyblepharum   ZONES 5–9
(Japanese Tassel Fern) Wide-spreading, glossy dark green fronds with a tassel-like appearance as they emerge. Sensitive to late spring frosts. Medium size. Appreciates even moisture and partial shade. EVERGREEN.

HEIGHT/SPREAD:	30–60cm (1–2')/60cm (24")
LOCATION:	Moist, humus-rich soil.
USES:	⛰⋀⋁☙ Massing, Borders

setiferum   ZONES 5–9
(Soft Shield Fern) One of the most common garden ferns in Europe, with hundreds of selected forms named during Victorian times, most of these no longer available. Plants form a graceful arching mound of grass-green fronds that have an attractive, soft texture. Prefers high humidity and evenly moist soil. The form '**Congestum**' is about half the size of the species. SEMI-EVERGREEN.

HEIGHT/SPREAD:	30–60cm (12–24")/45–60cm (18–24")
LOCATION:	Moist, humus-rich soil.
USES:	⛰⋀⋁☙ Massing, Borders

tsus-simense   ZONES 6–9
(Korean Rock Fern) Neat, compact clumps of glossy, dark green, triangular fronds with black stems. New leaves have a purplish cast. Heat tolerant. Sometimes grown as an indoor fern. Good choice for the rock garden. EVERGREEN.

HEIGHT/SPREAD:	20–45cm (8–18")/30cm (12")
LOCATION:	Moist, humus-rich soil.
USES:	⛰⋀☙ Edging

Thelypteris decursive-pinnata

THELYPTERIS
(Beech Fern) ☼ ●

decursive-pinnata   ZONES 4–9
A handsome, medium-sized fern with narrow, triangular fronds that remain bright green all season long. In sunnier spots the colour changes to lemon-lime. Slowly spreads to form a small patch, without becoming invasive. Easy and vigorous. DECIDUOUS.

"This has to be one of the most well-behaved and spectacular species in a genus full of redundant-looking aggressive thugs (at least from a zone 8 perspective)."
– Judith I. Jones, Zone 8

HEIGHT/SPREAD:	30–60cm (1–2')/45–60cm (18–24")
LOCATION:	Rich moist soil, prefers slightly acidic.
USES:	⛰⋀⋁☙ Massing

Polystichum munitum

Polystichum polyblepharum

Polystichum setiferum

Polystichum tsus-simense

Grasses

Grasses can be used in so many ways for landscape design; from bold specimen subjects to large massed plantings waving in the breeze, as a low groundcover or edging, in the border, or growing in containers and tubs.

Some grasses are grown for their colourful foliage in green, gold, red, cream or white; sometimes even attractively striped or banded. Others may be valued more for their showy flower plumes, spikes or seed heads. Several types provide dramatic and lasting interest throughout the winter months. A few varieties can do all of these things!

Ornamental Grasses combine well with almost any kind of plant. Although they can be used in a special border devoted exclusively to grasses, the effect is usually more like a collection rather than a border, and is probably best suited to botanical or demonstration gardens. The most successful way to use grasses, in the smaller residential gardens that most of us have, is to integrate them in a mixed planting along with perennials, annuals, bulbs, deciduous shrubs and evergreens.

Grasses for every garden

The selection of grasses has never been better than it is today, with an astounding range of height, spread, colour and flowering times available. There should be room in every garden for a least one variety of ornamental grass, as they can fill such a variety of functions.

Tall, upright-growing types create linear (up-and-down) interest visually, especially when used towards the back of a border. Their bold lines break up space over a long season, some remaining attractive well into winter.

Medium-sized grasses may be effectively massed together, particularly in gardens with a low-maintenance emphasis. Spring flowering bulbs combine well with these for early season interest. They are often just the perfect size to integrate into a perennial or mixed border design without becoming the centre of attention.

Low-growing grasses are ideal for edging around shrubs or combining with spreading evergreens. When mass-planted, they can often form an attractive low-maintenance groundcover.

There are recommended varieties for every climate zone in North America, so gardeners in most regions can make use of ornamental grasses. Without question, milder climate zones have a larger palette of hardy grasses available, but some of the best grasses are fortunately very hardy and will withstand extremes of cold. There are attractive, worthwhile grasses available for Zones 2–9!

Grasses can be divided into two basic groups, based on their growth cycles:

Cool season grasses: These begin their growth in early spring, reaching their full size before summer heat hits. These are usually low to medium sized plants, and some types tend to brown out in hot summer weather. Clipping or mowing in July encourages lush regrowth for fall. Divide these in late summer or early spring. Several types remain evergreen in mild winter areas.

Warm season grasses: Among these are the stars of the late summer and fall border. Some form tall clumps, often with showy spikes or plumes of flowers. These grasses usually like plenty of light and hot summer weather. They should be pruned back in late winter before new growth begins in the spring. Divide warm-season grasses in early spring only.

Grasses for Special Uses

Showy seed-heads in late summer/fall:
Andropogon, Calamagrostis, Chasmanthium, Deschampsia, Erianthus, Miscanthus, Molinia, Panicum, Pennisetum, Stipa.

Grasses native to North America:
Andropogon gerardii, Andropogon scoparius, Bouteloua gracilis, Carex grayii, Carex muskingumensis, Chasmanthium latifolium, Panicum virgatum, Stipa tenuissima.

Grasses that spread invasively by underground rhizomes:
Arundo donax, Bromus inermis 'Skinner's Golden', Elymus racemosus, Glyceria maxima 'Variegata', Miscanthus sacchariflorus 'Robustus', Phalaris arundinacea, Spartina pectinata 'Aureo-marginata'.

Grasses that may self seed prolifically:
(Note: removing seed heads before they fully develop will prevent self seeding.) Alopecurus, Andropogon, Bouteloua, Briza, Bromus, Carex (non-variegated types), Chasmanthium, Deschampsia, Festuca, Milium, *Miscanthus, *Pennisetum, Stipa. (* seldom sets seed north of New York City)

Drought-tolerant grasses (once established):
Andropogon, Bouteloua, Erianthus, Festuca, Phalaris.

Grasses for moderately dry, well-drained sites:
Bouteloua, Elymus racemosus, Festuca, Helictotrichon, Pennisetum orientale, Sesleria caerulea, Stipa.

Grasses for damp or moist soils:
Acorus, Carex, Chasmanthium, Deschampsia, Glyceria, Luzula, Milium, Miscanthus, Molinia, Panicum, Pennisetum, Phalaris, Spartina.

Grasses for wet soils (waterside):
Acorus, Carex pendula, Chasmanthium, Deschampsia, Erianthus, Glyceria, Miscanthus, Molinia, Phalaris, Typha.

Shade-tolerant grasses:
Carex (many), Chasmanthium, Deschampsia, Hakonechloa, Luzula, Milium, Phalaris.

Acorus calamus 'Variegatus'

Acorus gramineus 'Minimus Aureus'

Andropogon scoparius

Arundo donax

ACORUS
(Sweet Flag) ☼ ☀

Not true grasses actually, these are in the Arum or Jack-in-the-Pulpit family, and form clumps of grassy, sword-shaped leaves. The fragrant roots of certain species have been used for centuries in perfume manufacture. These are happiest growing in wet or boggy sites, especially beside water.

calamus 'Variegatus'   ZONES 4–9
(Variegated Sweet Flag) This is a herbaceous species, dying back to the ground each year. Plants spread slowly to form a sizable clump, similar to a Japanese Iris, and strongly striped along the length with green and creamy yellow. Effective beside a pond, and will even grow directly in shallow water. Reported to tolerate shade.

HEIGHT/SPREAD:	60–90cm (2–3')/60cm (24")
LOCATION:	Rich, moist to wet soil.
BLOOMS:	July–August
USES:	✄◁☙ Waterside, Specimen

gramineus   ZONES 5–9
(Japanese Sweet Flag) Handsome evergreen clumps, most often seen planted in Japanese gardens. Plants can be effectively massed or used as an edging along paths or water features. As these are slow to establish, space closely at planting time to encourage a quicker fill-in. Foliage is fragrant when bruised. A winter mulch is recommended in Zones 5–6.

SPREAD:	30cm (12")
LOCATION:	Rich, moist to wet soil.
BLOOMS:	July–August
USES:	▲∿▲☙ Edging, Waterside

'Argenteostriatus' (Variegated Japanese Sweet Flag) Formerly listed as 'Variegatus'. Leaves are striped along their length with green and creamy-white. Best in part shade. Good for massing. HEIGHT: 20–30cm (8–12")
'Minimus Aureus' (Miniature Variegated Sweet Flag) Very dwarf form with all-gold leaves. Quite slow growing. HEIGHT: 7cm (3")

ALOPECURUS
(Meadow Foxtail) ☼ ☀

pratensis 'Aureovariegatus'   ZONES 4–9
(Golden Meadow Foxtail) (formerly listed as 'Aureus') Medium-sized clumps of yellow and green striped leaves, slowly forming a wide clump. Good for massing towards the front of a border. Short tan-coloured spikes in late spring. Remove seed heads to prevent self-sowing. Cool-season.

HEIGHT/SPREAD:	45–60cm (18–24")/30–60cm (1–2')
LOCATION:	Rich, average to moist soil.
BLOOMS:	May–June
USES:	∿ Borders, Massing

ANDROPOGON
(Blue Stem) ☼

Native North American grasses, originally covering large areas of the continent as a component of the prairie community, which has now largely disappeared. These are valuable grasses for late-season interest, developing warm rich foliage colours in the fall, as well as having beautiful seed-heads. Warm-season.

scoparius 'The Blues'   ZONES 4–9
(Little Bluestem) (= *Shizachyrium scoparium*) A selected form with especially good blue foliage and contrasting pinkish plumes. This clumping grass has a good compact habit that makes it well-suited for use in the border. Also effective for mass plantings or naturalizing. The ripening plumes develop a dark coppery-

brown colour, an excellent contrast to the foliage as it turns from green to bronzy-orange in the fall.

HEIGHT/SPREAD:	60–90cm (2–3')/30–45cm (12–18")
LOCATION:	Average well-drained soil.
BLOOMS:	August–September
USES:	✄☙ Borders, Meadow

Arrhenatherum bulbosum 'Variegatum'

ARRHENATHERUM
(Bulbous Oat Grass) ☼ ☀

bulbosum 'Variegatum'   ZONES 2–9
(formerly listed as *A. elatius bulbosum* 'Variegatum') Bushy, low clumps of cream and green striped leaves. Tan-coloured spikes in early summer. Combines nicely with bulbs in the spring garden. Plants usually brown out in July and should be clipped back to regrow for an attractive fall display. Drought tolerant once established. Cool-season.

> "This grass catches everyone's eyes in front of our barn with its striking starch white striping. Very refined clump former making an ideal subject with Hosta, Astrantia and ferns." – Elke Knechtel, Zone 7

HEIGHT/SPREAD:	30–45cm (12–18")/30cm (12")
LOCATION:	Average well-drained soil.
BLOOMS:	June
USES:	▲☙ Massing, Borders

ARUNDO
(Giant Reed) ☼

donax   ZONES 7–9
Truly imposing and enormous plants, in habit these fall somewhere in between herbaceous grasses and bamboos. Clumps spread underground from woody rhizomes to form a tall patch of stout, hollow canes. Leaves are blue-green, arching gracefully out in a layered manner. In colder climates these are most often used as a foliage focal point in annual bedding schemes, and potted up to winter indoors. Where hardy, they can be used as a fast-growing screen or windbreak. Heat tolerant. Warm-season.
'Versicolor' (Variegated Giant Reed) (formerly listed as 'Variegatus') Leaves of this form are strongly striped with creamy-yellow and green. Popular specimen plant in large parks.

> "Think about where you will put this monster... once you plant it, just sit back and watch it grow and hopefully you will never have to move it as you may need to use dynamite." – Elke Knechtel, Zone 7

HEIGHT/SPREAD:	1.8–3.5m (6–12')/90cm (3')
LOCATION:	Rich, moist soil.
BLOOMS:	September–October
USES:	☙ Specimen, Waterside, Screen

AVENA
see Helictotrichon.

BOUTELOUA
(Mosquito Grass) ☼

gracilis   ZONES 3–9
Another important native North American grass, this was a common component of the short-grass prairie plant community in the western plains. Mosquito Grass makes a low tuft of olive green leaves, with unusual spikes of bristly flowers that are held at an odd angle, somewhat resembling a flying insect. Well-behaved in the sunny border or rock garden. Drought-tolerant. Warm-season.

HEIGHT/SPREAD:	30–60cm (12–24")/30cm (12")
LOCATION:	Lean to average well-drained soil.
BLOOMS:	July–September
USES:	△⅜<🌼 Borders, Massing

BRIZA
(Quaking Grass) ☼

media   ZONES 5–9
Loose clusters of delicate heart-shaped flowers are used for fresh or dried arranging. Plants form a low green tuft of leaves. Effective when combined with heaths and heathers in a moor planting. Evergreen in milder areas. Cool-season.

HEIGHT/SPREAD:	25–45cm (10–18")/30cm (12")
LOCATION:	Lean well-drained soil.
BLOOMS:	July–September
USES:	△⅜<▲ Massing, Borders

CALAMAGROSTIS
(Feather Reed Grass) ☼ ◑

These are favorite grasses of landscape designers, who value the stiff, upright linear effect that Feather Reed Grass provides. Plants are often massed in great numbers, their wands of flowers waving in the breeze. They are equally effective used within a border in smaller groupings, remaining attractive well into the winter. Cool-season, but heat-tolerant.

SPREAD:	60cm (2')
LOCATION:	Average well-drained soil.
BLOOMS:	June–September
USES:	⅜<♥ Accent, Massing, Borders

× acutiflora 'Karl Foerster'   ZONES 4–9
(Foerster's Reed Grass) With its stiffly upright habit, this can be one of the most effective vertical elements in the summer and fall border. Narrow clumps of green foliage bear spikes of white flowers, first fading to rose then followed by tan seedheads. They begin blooming in early summer, remaining attractive well into the winter. Can be used as a specimen but most effective when planted in groups. HEIGHT: 120–150cm (4–5')

> "Any grass that is able to overwinter in a barrel by the side of a windswept road is a real winner!" – Marjorie Mason Hogue, Zone 4

> "Though recommended for mass planting, my solitary specimen stood like a beacon in the centre of a test bed, luring all who visited (and disappointing many, for I was sold out by the end of May)." – Cathy Forgie, Zone 4

'Overdam' (Variegated Reed Grass) A newer selection with foliage boldly striped in white and green. Spikes of gold flowers are a nice contrast. This is one of the most exciting grasses to come along in years, particularly effective in the spring and early summer garden. Excellent as a specimen. Slightly shorter, and not quite as hardy. Zones 5–9. HEIGHT: 90–120cm (3–4')

Carex comans 'Frosted Curls'

CAREX
(Sedge) ◑ ●

Though not true grasses, the Sedges are similar in appearance. Forming low to medium-sized tufts, they are frequently used for groundcover plantings, performing especially well in moist or wet areas. Flowers are usually insignificant. Most varieties benefit from a light clipping in early spring.

buchananii   ZONES 6–9
(Leatherleaf Sedge) Creates an arching, tufted clump of coppery-brown, hair-like foliage. Excellent for contrasting with dwarf conifers or other evergreens, especially in the winter garden. Also nice beside water. Ever-bronze.

> "Often mistaken for being dead, this sculptural grass adds a new colour dimension into a rockery or Mediterranean look garden… An added feature is the foliage is crimped and curled at the tips which shows up even more in the winter." – Elke Knechtel, Zone 7

HEIGHT/SPREAD:	45cm (18")/30cm (12")
LOCATION:	Prefers a rich, moist soil.
BLOOMS:	June–July
USES:	△▲♥ Borders, Massing, Waterside

comans 'Frosted Curls'   ZONES 6–9
(Frosted Curls Sedge) Unusual olive-green foliage that arches to form a mop-headed clump, the leaf-tips fading to near-white. Texture is fine and soft, like hair. Especially effective in containers.

HEIGHT/SPREAD:	20–30cm (9–12")/30–45cm (12–18")
LOCATION:	Prefers a rich, moist soil.
BLOOMS:	June–July
USES:	△▲♥ Borders, Massing, Specimen

dolichostachya glabberima
'Gold Fountains'   ZONES 5–9
(Gold Fountains Sedge, 'Kaga Nishiki') Recently arrived from Japan, this handsome form features slender gold-bordered foliage, remaining evergreen in mild winter areas. Not yet fully tested for hardiness. Best in part shade.

HEIGHT/SPREAD:	20–40cm (8–16")/30cm (12")
LOCATION:	Prefers a rich, moist soil.
BLOOMS:	May–June
USES:	△▲♥ Edging

flacca   ZONES 4–9
(Blue Sedge) (formerly listed as *C. glauca*) Leaves are steel blue, in a low tufted clump. An adaptable sedge, growing in most garden situations. Good groundcover. Mow or clip back hard in early spring. Evergreen.

Bouteloua gracilis

Briza media

Calamagrostis × *acutiflora* 'Karl Foerster'

Carex buchananii

Carex flacca

Carex morrowii 'Aureovariegata'

Carex siderostica 'Variegata'

Deschampsia caespitosa 'Goldstaub'

HEIGHT/SPREAD: 15cm (6")/15–30cm (6–12")
LOCATION: Prefers a rich, moist soil.
BLOOMS: May–June
USES: △⋀⋟ Massing, Edging

grayi   ZONES 3–9

(Morning Star Sedge) A native North American species, growing best beside water. Fresh green leaves are narrow and leathery, forming an upright clump. Insignificant flowers are followed by attractive, spiky star-shaped seed pods which are interesting to use in floral arranging.

HEIGHT/SPREAD: 60cm (2')/30cm (12")
LOCATION: Prefers a rich, moist soil.
BLOOMS: May–June
USES: ✂ Massing, Waterside

morrowii 'Aureovariegata'   ZONES 6–9

(Variegated Japanese Sedge) (= *C. hachioensis* 'Evergold') Compact, cascading tufts of creamy-yellow and green striped leaves. Excellent plant for brightening up damp shady areas. Terrific in containers. Try underplanting with masses of purple crocus. Evergreen.

HEIGHT/SPREAD: 20–30cm (8–12")/15–30cm (6–12")
LOCATION: Prefers a rich, moist soil.
BLOOMS: May–June
USES: △⋀⋟ Edging, Massing

muskingumensis   ZONES 4–9

(Palm Sedge) Another native North American species, though with an unusual tropical appearance. Plants form graceful clumps of divided leaves similar in effect to papyrus. Equally at home beside water or in a moist border. Best in part shade.

HEIGHT/SPREAD: 40–60cm (16–24")/30–45cm (12–18")
LOCATION: Prefers a rich, moist soil.
BLOOMS: July
USES: ✂ Massing, Waterside

ornithopoda 'Variegata'   ZONES 7–9

(Variegated Bird's-foot Sedge) Another very dwarf variegated selection that shines in the rock garden. Leaves are striped lengthwise with creamy-white in the centre. Prefers light shade and a rich humus soil. Evergreen.

HEIGHT/SPREAD: 10–15cm (4–6")/15–30cm (6–12")
LOCATION: Prefers a rich, moist soil.
BLOOMS: May–June
USES: △⋀⋟ Edging

pendula   ZONES 5–9

(Drooping Sedge) Evergreen in mild winter areas, this species forms an arching clump of wide green leaves with interesting spikes of flowers held well above in summer. Useful for floral arranging, and a nice waterside feature in the garden. Shade tolerant.

> "Drooping sedge is an effective accent plant along the water's edge, where the flowers and foliage can be reflected, or along a path or walk, where one can touch the drooping seed heads… The flowers are stunning in fresh and dried arrangements." – John Greenlee, *The Encyclopedia of Ornamental Grasses*

HEIGHT/SPREAD: 60–120cm (2–4')/30–60cm (12–24")
LOCATION: Prefers a rich, moist soil.
BLOOMS: May–June
USES: ✂ Massing, Borders, Waterside

siderostica 'Variegata'   ZONES 4–9

(Variegated Broad-leaved Sedge) On first viewing this is often mistaken for a narrow-leaved Hosta. The broad, sword-shaped leaves are bright green with a wide margin of creamy-white. Plants spread underground to form a loose clump or patch, so it can be used as a groundcover among taller woodland

plants. Foliage is deciduous, the fresh spring growth tinged with bright pink. Prefers dappled shade.

HEIGHT/SPREAD: 20–30cm (8–12")/30–60cm (12–24")
LOCATION: Prefers a rich, moist soil.
BLOOMS: June
USES: △⋀⋟ Borders, Woodland

'The Beatles'   ZONES 5–9

(Mop-headed Sedge) The perfect name for this low, clumping evergreen selection! Used as an edging to shady pathways, and short enough to use in between paving stones. Especially good interplanted with the smaller spring-flowering bulbs. Foliage is dark green and forms a dome-shaped clump.

HEIGHT/SPREAD: 10cm (4")/10–20cm (4–8")
LOCATION: Prefers a rich, moist soil.
BLOOMS: June
USES: △⋀⋟ Borders, Woodland

CHASMANTHIUM
(Sea Oats) ☼ ☽ ●

latifolium   ZONES 5–9

(Northern Sea Oats) One of the best grasses for shady sites. Upright clumps resemble a dwarf green bamboo. Gracefully arching stems hold dangling flower spikes that look and move like a school of little fishes. Great for cutting. May self-seed prolifically. Native wildflower. Warm-season.

> "Visitors to the shade garden always "ooh" and "aah" over this one! It's unlike any other plant in the shade repertoire."
> – Marjorie Mason Hogue, Zone 4

HEIGHT/SPREAD: 75–90cm (30–36")/30cm (12")
LOCATION: Prefers a rich moist soil.
BLOOMS: July–August
USES: ✂ Specimen, Massing, Borders

DESCHAMPSIA
(Tufted Hair Grass) ☼ ☽

caespitosa   ZONES 4–9

Clump-forming evergreen grass with symmetrical, tufted foliage. Airy sprays of delicate green flowers appear in early summer, maturing to deeper colours as summer goes on, and in such great numbers that the leaves become totally hidden below. Most effective when massed or allowed to drape over more substantial plants. Clip back hard in early spring. Fairly shade tolerant. Cool-season.

HEIGHT/SPREAD: 75–90cm (30–36")/30–45cm (12–18")
LOCATION: Prefers a moist, rich soil.
BLOOMS: May–August
USES: ✂ Massing, Borders, Meadows

'Bronzeschleier' (Bronzeveil Hair Grass) Flowers mature to a mass of bronzy-mustard. Early-blooming.

> "The frothy flowers are shimmery golden coloured and look wonderful against darker shrubs or a hedge."
> – Elke Knechtel, Zone 7

'Goldstaub' (Gold-dust Hair Grass) Sprays of bright golden-yellow flowers. Late-blooming.

ELYMUS
See Leymus.

ERIANTHUS
See Saccharum.

FESTUCA
(Fescue) ☼ ◑

Low tufted clump-formers, with fine-textured foliage from silver-blue to green. Fescues are widely planted as an edging or massed to create a low, hummocky groundcover. All are cool-season grasses, at their best in spring and early summer. Most remain evergreen in all but the coldest regions. Removing the faded flower heads will prevent self seeding.

filiformis   ZONES 3–9
(Fine-leaved Green Fescue) (formerly listed as *F. tenuifolia*) Low tufts of leaves like bright green hair. Effective on its own or in combination with Blue Fescue. Nice fresh colour in early spring, excellent cover for small bulbs. Also good in troughs.

    HEIGHT/SPREAD: 15–20cm (6–8")/20–30cm (8–12")
    LOCATION: Average well-drained soil.
    BLOOMS: May–June
    USES: △▲❦ Borders, Edging, Massing

gautleri 'Pic Carlit'   ZONES 5–9
(Dwarf Bearskin Fescue) (formerly listed as *F. scoparia*) Bizarre little mounds of evergreen leaves, stiff and sharp like a spruce needle. Flower spikes are held just above the leaves. A true alpine species, this appreciates a sunny location with the sort of cool, moist root-run that rocks can easily provide. Excellent in troughs.

    HEIGHT/SPREAD: 5–10cm (2–4")/20–30cm (8–12")
    LOCATION: Cool, moist well-drained soil.
    BLOOMS: May–June
    USES: △▲❦ Troughs, Edging

glauca   ZONES 3–9
(Blue Fescue) (formerly listed as *F. ovina glauca*) Valued for their low tufts of steely-blue foliage. Tan-coloured spikes rise on short stems in late spring. Clip seed heads off by mid-summer to tidy plants up. Nice in containers. Best in full sun.

    SPREAD: 20–30cm (8–12")
    LOCATION: Average well-drained soil.
    BLOOMS: May–June
    USES: △▲❦ Borders, Edging, Massing

'Elijah Blue' This is the best and brightest blue selection we have ever seen! Maintains its colour throughout the season. HEIGHT: 20–25cm (8–10")

'Sea Urchin' ('Seeigel') Fairly compact form, good metallic blue-grey colour. HEIGHT: 15cm (6")

'Skinner's Blue' Very hardy variety, selected in Manitoba. Colour is turquoise-green, not as intense as some, but better in cold winter areas where other varieties are short-lived. ZONES 2–9. HEIGHT: 30cm (12")

GLYCERIA
(Manna Grass) ☼

maxima 'Variegata'   ZONES 4–9
(Variegated Manna Grass) Similar in appearance to Ribbon Grass, with leaves striped green and creamy yellow. A spreading grass best planted at the waterside, or contained carefully in the border. Insignificant flower spikes.

    HEIGHT/SPREAD: 75–90cm (30–36")/20–30cm (8–12")
    LOCATION: Moist to wet soil.
    BLOOMS: June–July
    USES: ❦〜 Waterside

Hakonechloa macra 'Aureola'

HAKONECHLOA
(Hakonechloa) ◑

macra 'Aureola'   ZONES 5–9
(Golden Variegated Hakonechloa) One of the slowest grasses to establish, but well worth the extra effort to grow. Leaves are bright golden-yellow with narrow green stripes, arching all to one side like a waterfall. Airy flowers appear in late summer but are mostly hidden in the foliage. Fall colour is buff. This makes a fine specimen plant, especially near a patio or water garden, with a distinctly Oriental flavour. Excellent in large tubs.

> "Almost bamboo-like in appearance it is a real eye catcher in a dark shady spot in the garden. Slow to grow, making it perfect for the small garden where rampant plants are unwanted." – Elke Knechtel, Zone 7

    HEIGHT/SPREAD: 45–60cm (18–24")/60cm (24")
    LOCATION: Rich, moist well-drained soil.
    USES: △❦ Specimen, Woodland, Border

HELICTOTRICHON
(Blue Oat Grass) ☼

sempervirens   ZONES 3–9
Incredibly popular for its perfect, dome-shaped clumps of intensely blue leaves. This non-spreader is the best blue grass for general purpose border use. Tan spikes appear above on graceful arching stems. Evergreen. Cool-season. The selection **'Saphirsprudel'** ('Sapphire') is reported to have even better blue colour.

    HEIGHT/SPREAD: 60–90cm (2–3'/60cm (2')
    LOCATION: Average well-drained soil.
    BLOOMS: May–July
    USES: ❦ Border, Accent, Massing

HOLCUS
(Velvet Grass) ☼ ◑

mollis 'Albo-variegatus'   ZONES 5–9
(formerly listed as *H. lanatus*) Somewhat similar to *Arrhenatherum* in appearance, this forms a compact creeping patch of fine green and white striped leaves. Good for edging along the front of a border, or beside a water feature. At its best in the cooler months, expect Velvet Grass to brown out in summer heat.

    HEIGHT/SPREAD: 20–30cm (8–12")/30cm (12")
    LOCATION: Prefers a rich, moist soil.
    USES: 〜 Edging, Winter garden

Festuca gautleri 'Pic Carlit'

Festuca glauca 'Elijah Blue'

Festuca glauca 'Sea Urchin'

Helictotrichon sempervirens

IMPERATA
(Japanese Blood Grass) ☀ ☼

cylindrica 'Red Baron'   ZONES 5–9
An unusual and dramatic grass that slowly forms a medium-sized clump. Leaves are green at the base, and blood red at the top. Excellent for massing, and particularly effective with some clever backlighting. This can be slow to establish, and may not always predictably take to the site you have in mind; it seems to regard both hot, dry soils and heavy, wet soils with equal disdain. Warm-season.

HEIGHT/SPREAD:	45cm (18")/30cm (12")
LOCATION:	Moist but well-drained soil.
USES:	⚡⋏M⋅♛ Massing, Borders

Imperata cylindrica 'Red Baron'

JUNCUS
(Rush) ☀ ☼

effusus 'Unicorn'   ZONES 4–9
(Unicorn Spiral Rush, Corkscrew Rush) A brand new selection from the University of British Columbia Botanical Garden, a vast improvement on the older selection 'Spiralis'. Leaves are round and stem-like, with a unique corkscrew spiral all the way to the tip. This selection is tall and sturdy, deep green in colour and remains evergreen in mild winter areas. Has great potential in the florist market as a cut green! Flowers are brownish and insignificant. A superb choice for beside a pond or stream, or as a marginal water garden plant. Also excellent in pots.

HEIGHT/SPREAD:	60–100cm (24–40")/30–60cm (1–2')
LOCATION:	Moist to wet soil.
BLOOMS:	June–July
USES:	✂⋏▲♛ Waterside, Specimen

Juncus effusus 'Unicorn'

LEYMUS
(Lyme Grass) ☀ ☼

(formerly listed as Elymus) The various garden forms of Lyme Grass are almost all grown for their exceptionally beautiful steel-blue foliage. Most of them are invasive to the extreme, so some extra consideration in placing them is advised. Control the spread by planting inside a tile drain or bottomless plastic bucket sunk two feet down in the ground, or take advantage of the spreading nature to stabilize steep slopes. Large tubs or pots of Lyme Grass are very decorative. Warm-season.

arenarius   ZONES 4–9
(Blue Lyme Grass) Outstanding blue colour; foliage is beautiful in the garden or can be used for flower arranging. Quickly forms a large patch. Spikes of tan flowers appear in summer. Tolerant of salt spray. HEIGHT: 60–90cm (2–3')

'Findhorn' A little more compact in habit, exceptional blue colour. HEIGHT: 60–75cm (24–30")

SPREAD:	60–90cm (2–3')
LOCATION:	Poor to average well-drained soil.
BLOOMS:	July–August
USES:	✂M⋅♛ Massing, Naturalizing

LIRIOPE
See under Perennials.

LUZULA
(Wood Rush) ☼ ●

Grass-like plants, native to moist woodland sites, but tolerant of dry shade. They spread to form a low, dense ground cover of flat, softly hairy leaves. Although evergreen, these will need a light trim in early spring.

Leymus arenarius

Milium effusum 'Aureum'

nivea   ZONES 5–9
(Snowy Wood Rush) Upright, arching clumps of fuzzy grey-green leaves. Clusters of white flowers are showy in summer, good for cutting. Nice accent plant for the shade.

HEIGHT/SPREAD:	60cm (2')/30cm (1')
LOCATION:	Rich, average to moist soil, preferably on the acid side.
BLOOMS:	May–July
USES:	✂⋏M⋅▲ Accent, Massing, Borders

sylvatica   ZONES 4–9
(Greater Wood Rush) Dense clumps of shiny, tousled green leaves. Makes a thick spreading groundcover, but isn't invasive. Small clusters of brownish flowers. Grows well beneath trees and shrubs, even tolerating dry shade. The variety **'Marginata'** is especially worth seeking, the edges of each leaf blade trimmed in cream.

"The flush of new spring growth is both showy and enchanting, as the leaves catch and hold droplets of water, causing them to sparkle in bright spring light… Its ability not just to survive, but to thrive, in shade, in moisture, and in competition with tree roots makes it an invaluable plant for the woodland setting." – John Greenlee, *The Encyclopedia of Ornamental Grasses*

HEIGHT/SPREAD:	30cm (12")/30cm (12")
LOCATION:	Average to moist soil, preferably on the acid side.
BLOOMS:	May–June
USES:	⋏M⋅▲♛ Massing, Naturalizing

MILIUM
(Golden Grass) ☼ ●

effusum 'Aureum'   ZONES 5–9
A colourful little grass to lighten up a shady corner with its bright golden-yellow new growth in spring. Plants form a low clump of foliage mingled with delicate sprays of flowers. Most effective when mass planted in a cool moist location. Can be short-lived but will usually self seed. Cool-season.

HEIGHT/SPREAD:	30–40cm (12–16")/30cm (12")
LOCATION:	Prefers a rich, moist soil.
USES:	M⋅ Borders, Waterside

MISCANTHUS
(Miscanthus, Eulalia) ☀ ☼

Large, bold grasses suited to massed plantings in the low-maintenance garden and integrating into the perennial or mixed border. These are all warm-season grasses, tolerating heat and humidity very well. Flowers are in fan-shaped panicles, showy in the fall border, and sometimes used for cutting.

"As winter progresses, leaves drop from the stout culms, leaving a striking vertical skeleton. Truly dramatic when thrusting through the snow or backlit against a winter sky, giant Chinese silver grass is a constantly changing player in the garden." – John Greenlee, *The Encyclopedia of Ornamental Grasses*

floridulus   ZONES 4–9
(Giant Chinese Silver Grass) (sometimes listed as *M. giganteus*) Very tall clumps of green leaves, their tips arching gracefully in layers. Sometimes used to create a living screen or fence. Corn-like stalks remain upright through the winter. Reddish-pink flower spikes turn to silvery plumes as they mature. Tolerates shade

and poor soils. Lower leaves turn brown and dry in fall, giving the plant a "bare knees" look that can be avoided by planting something sizable in front.

HEIGHT/SPREAD:	3m (10')/90cm (3')
LOCATION:	Prefers a moist but well-drained soil.
BLOOMS:	September–October
USES:	Specimen, Screen, Living Fence

sacchariflorus 'Robustus'   ZONES 3–9

(Giant Silver Grass) Quickly forms a patch of tall, stout corn-like stems, clothed by gracefully arching foliage with a bamboo-like, tropical appearance. Silvery plumes turn reddish as they mature, and the foliage also has good red-orange fall colour. This plant will need to be contained to keep it in bounds as the roots have a terrible tendency to run. Recent trials in Minnesota have shown good hardiness in Zone 3.

HEIGHT/SPREAD:	1.8m (6')/90cm (3')
LOCATION:	Prefers a rich, moist to wet soil.
BLOOMS:	August–September
USES:	Specimen, Screen, Waterside

sinensis   ZONES 5–9

(Japanese Silver Grass) A superb group of grasses, versatile both as specimens or in massed plantings. All bloom in the fall, and hold their shape well into the winter, fading to shades of tan or cream and contrasting nicely with evergreens. Selections vary widely in leaf color, height, form and hardiness.

SPREAD:	90cm (3')
LOCATION:	Prefers a moist but well-drained soil.
BLOOMS:	August–October
USES:	✄❦⚘ Borders, Specimen, Massing

'Cosmopolitan' Similar to 'Variegatus' but leaves are twice as wide, creating a very bold white and green striped effect. Plants are self-supporting. Hardiness range is not yet fully determined, but probably Zones 6–9. HEIGHT: 1.8–2.4m (6–8')

'Goliath' (Goliath Silver Grass) Outstanding large-growing selection, forming a massive clump of foliage. Pinkish plumes in September. HEIGHT: 2.4–2.7m (8–9')

'Gracillimus' (Maiden Grass) Long, arching narrow green leaves, forming a large symmetrical clump. The best for formal plantings. Does not flower reliably in cool-summer areas. HEIGHT: 1.2–1.8m (4–6')

'Graziella' (Graziella Silver Grass) Slender green leaves, the large white plumes appearing early and held well above the foliage. Highly rated. HEIGHT: 1.5–1.8m (5–6')

'Grosse Fontaine' (Large Fountain Silver Grass) Arching foliage gives a cascading impression. Silvery plumes appear early. HEIGHT: 1.8–2.1m (6–7')

'Malepartus' (Red-flowered Miscanthus) Very hardy variety, with showy purple-pink plumes in late summer. Green foliage, becoming bronze in fall. Zones 4–9. HEIGHT: 1.5–1.8m (5–6')

'Morning Light' (Variegated Maiden Grass) Tightly rolled leaves similar to 'Gracillimus', but with a narrow band of white on the margin. The effect from several feet away is silvery and shimmering. Very late to flower with bronzy-red spikes. A recent introduction that is quickly becoming popular. HEIGHT: 1.5–1.8m (5–6')

'Nippon' (Nippon Silver Grass) Compact variety with fine-textured leaves, better suited to smaller gardens or containers. Fall colour is bronzy-red. HEIGHT: 1.2m (4')

'Puenktchen' (Little Dot Silver Grass) Gold-banded foliage, like 'Zebrinus', but with a more compact habit. HEIGHT: 1.5–2.1m (5–7')

purpurascens (Flame Grass) Early-blooming variety with spikes of rose flowers in August. Strongly upright clumps of green leaves, turning flame-orange and rust for the fall. Hardy to Zone 4. HEIGHT: 120–150cm (4–5')

'Rotsilber' (Red-Silver Maiden Grass) Compact German selection with outstanding large deep red plumes. Silvery foliage develops good fall colour as well. HEIGHT: 90–150cm (3–5')

'Sarabande' (Sarabande Silver Grass) Fine-textured silvery foliage, compact habit. Golden plumes in early fall. Hardy to Zone 4. HEIGHT: 120–150cm (4–5')

'Silberfeder' (Silver Feather Grass) An older selection, a refined version of the species, with shimmering silvery-white plumes appearing in late August, held up high above the foliage. Hardy to Zone 4. HEIGHT: 150–180cm (5–6')

'Silberpfeil' (Silver Arrow Miscanthus) Similar in appearance to 'Variegatus', with brighter variegation and a more upright habit. HEIGHT: 1.8–2.4m (6–8')

'Strictus' (Porcupine Grass) Bright green leaves with golden horizontal banding. Stiff, upright clumps that never require staking. Unique specimen plant. HEIGHT: 150–180cm (5–6')

> "The foliage and flowers of porcupine grass provide a dramatic garden accent. The column of banded foliage is particularly effective when backlit by early morning or late afternoon light."
> – John Greenlee,
> *The Encyclopedia of Ornamental Grasses*

'Undine' Selected for its low foliage, the showy silver-white plumes held well above in early fall. Good compact form that is in scale with smaller gardens. HEIGHT: 1.2–1.5m (4–5')

'Variegatus' (Variegated Silver Grass) Distinct green and white striped leaves in an arching clump. Creamy-pink plumes in late fall in warm-summer regions. Very bright and showy. HEIGHT: 1.5–1.8m (5–6')

'Yaku Jima' (Dwarf Maiden Grass) A newer, compact selection from Japan. Foliage is narrow, silvery green, similar to 'Gracillimus'. Silver plumes appear in August. Zones 6–9. HEIGHT: 90–120cm (3–4')

'Zebrinus' (Zebra Grass) Exactly like 'Strictus', but the plant habit is not quite as upright. May need support in shady exposures. HEIGHT: 1.5–2.1m (5–7')

MOLINIA
(Moor Grass) ☼ ◑

As a group, the Moor grasses have much to offer the gardener and deserve more consideration. All are clumping in habit, and have no inclination to seed about or spread in unwanted ways. Typically they have a low to medium-sized clump of foliage with wands of delicate flowers waving above in mid to late summer. Fall colour is usually excellent. Warm-season.

arundinacea 'Skyracer'   ZONES 4–9

(Tall Moor Grass) A tall-growing selection, which has been described as a "kinetic sculpture". Heads of flowers are in constant motion from the slightest breeze. Outstanding in front of a dark backdrop, used as a specimen or focal point.

> "In the fall this plant is the glory of the garden. The flower stalks turn bright golden yellow — in our dull autumns it's like a ray of sunshine." – Elke Knechtel, Zone 7

HEIGHT/SPREAD:	1.8–2.4m (6–8')/30–60cm (1–2')
LOCATION:	Prefers a rich, moist soil.
BLOOMS:	July–October
USES:	✄⚘ Specimen, Massing, Borders

Miscanthus sinensis 'Cosmopolitan'

Miscanthus sinensis purpurascens

Miscanthus sinensis 'Silberfeder'

Miscanthus sinensis 'Undine'

Molinia caerulea 'Variegata'

Panicum virgatum – flowers

Panicum virgatum 'Heavy Metal'

Pennisetum alopecuroides 'Hameln'

caerulea   ZONES 3–9

(Dwarf Moor Grass) A variable species that has produced a number of excellent cultivars. Native to moist, acid moors in northern Europe but readily adapts to garden conditions. Plants form a low to medium-sized mound that looks good either as a specimen or when mass planted in a border. Good fall foliage colour. Takes a year or two to get established.

SPREAD: 30–60cm (1–2')
LOCATION: Prefers a rich, moist soil.
BLOOMS: July–October
USES: ✄<☙ Specimen, Massing, Borders

'Moorhexe' ('Moor-witch') Compact habit. Leaves are dark green with some red tones in fall, with airy sprays of purple flowers. HEIGHT: 45–75cm (18–30")

'Variegata' An older selection, but still one of the best variegated grasses. Bright yellow-and-green striped leaves, medium-tall stems of purplish flowers. HEIGHT: 60–75cm (24–30")

OPHIOPOGON
See under Perennials.

PANICUM
(Switch Grass) ☼ ◑

Switch grass has made great strides in recent years, some of the newer selections becoming valued additions to perennial and mixed borders all over Europe and North America. Switch grass is native to North America and was an important component of the original tall-grass prairie.

virgatum   ZONES 3–9

(Red Switch Grass) One of the best grasses for multi-season interest, particularly for winter display. Plants form a wide clump of narrow green leaves, with airy clouds of flowers in July giving way to red seed heads in late summer. Outstanding yellow and red fall foliage colour, fading to tan in the winter. Drought and salt tolerant. Warm-season.

SPREAD: 60–90cm (2–3')
LOCATION: Average to moist fertile soil.
BLOOMS: July–September
USES: ✄<☙⚘ Borders, Massing

'Heavy Metal' Excellent newer selection. Bright metallic-blue foliage all season, developing yellow and red fall highlights. HEIGHT: 90–120cm (3–4')

'Prairie Sky' Brand new selection from Wisconsin, the most outstanding steely blue colour imaginable! More bushy and arching in habit than 'Heavy Metal'. Flower and seed heads are open and blousy. Good yellow fall colour. HEIGHT: 90–120cm (3–4')

'Rehbraun' Reddish-brown tinged leaves. HEIGHT: 90–120cm (3–4')

'Rotstrahlbusch' The best variety for deep red fall colour. HEIGHT: 90–120cm (3–4')

'Strictum' Tall-growing seed strain. Good blue-green foliage, stiff upright habit. HEIGHT: 120–180cm (4–6')

PENNISETUM
(Fountain Grass) ☼

A well-named grass, as the hundreds of soft bottlebrush flower spikes that arch out and move in the breeze do indeed resemble the spray of a fountain. The different species and selections now available vary greatly in hardiness, but most are quite effective even when treated as annuals in colder regions, especially in container plantings. Warm season.

alopecuroides   ZONES 5–9

Medium-sized clumps of cascading green leaves. Flowers are buff-coloured feathery spikes, held just above the leaves, followed by similar seed-heads. Excellent fall and early winter effect, foliage turns bright almond. Blooms best in a hot location. The species itself varies somewhat in height, flower colour and hardiness.

HEIGHT/SPREAD: 90–120cm (3–4')/60–75cm (24–30")
LOCATION: Average well-drained soil.
BLOOMS: August–October
USES: ✄<☙⚘ Borders, Massing, Specimen

'Hameln' (Dwarf Fountain Grass) Compact, earlier flowering selection. Excellent for massing and in containers. Reported to be the most reliably hardy variety in Zones 5–6. HEIGHT: 60–75cm (24–30")

'Little Bunny' (Miniature Fountain Grass) A miniature form, ideal for edging borders or in the rock garden. Also the perfect plant for children's gardens! HEIGHT: 30cm (12")

'Moudry' (Black-flowered Fountain Grass) Dark, near-black bottlebrush spikes in early fall. Self-seeding, it can be a bit of a nuisance in mild winter areas. Late to flower. Zone 6. HEIGHT: 75–90cm (30–36")

'Burgundy Giant'   ZONE 9

(Burgundy Giant Fountain Grass) Newer selection with similar uses to *P. setaceum* 'Rubrum', but quite distinct in appearance. The wide, arching leaves are deep beet-red in colour, and held in layers that give an exotic tropical feel to the plant. Rosy-purple flower plumes are held above in late summer. Plants will reach a large size in warm summer regions. Best used in containers so it can be wintered indoors. Protect from wind.

HEIGHT/SPREAD: 120–160cm (4–6')/60–90cm (24–36")
LOCATION: Moist, well-drained soil.
BLOOMS: August–October
USES: ✄<☙ Massing, Specimen, Borders

orientale   ZONES 7–9

(Oriental Fountain Grass) Unusual for its showy display of rose-pink flowers, blooming earlier and longer than other types as well. Great numbers of plumes are held well above the dense clump of grey-green foliage. Excellent medium-sized grass for the border.

"This grass looks like it is covered with giant fuzzy caterpillars. Nice cut flower."
– Elke Knechtel, Zone 7

HEIGHT/SPREAD: 60–75cm (24–30")/60–75cm (24–30")
LOCATION: Average to moist well-drained soil.
BLOOMS: August–October
USES: ✄<☙⚘ Borders, Massing, Specimen

setaceum   ZONE 9

(Tender Fountain Grass) Widely used in public gardens and civic plantings as a centre-piece to flowering annual beds. Plants make a large cascading mound of green leaves with showy rosy-pink plumes in late summer and fall. Although not hardy in most areas, this remains a favorite tender grass for its dependable display.

'Rubrum' (Purple-leaved Fountain Grass) Beautiful burgundy or wine-red foliage contrasts well against the pink bottle-brush plumes. Always welcome in the perennial border, and especially shines in container or tub plantings.

HEIGHT/SPREAD: 90–120cm (3–4')/60–75cm (24–30")
LOCATION: Average to moist soil.
BLOOMS: August–October
USES: ✄<☙ Massing, Specimen, Borders

PHALARIS
(Ribbon Grass) ☀ ◑

arundinacea   ZONES 2–9

Fast-spreading clumps of semi-evergreen leaves, brightly striped with various colours. Flowers are tan-coloured spikes. Useful groundcover, especially in wet areas, but can spread too quickly for the border unless contained. Excellent in pots and tubs. Cool-season.

HEIGHT/SPREAD: 60–90cm (2–3')/60–90cm (2–3')
LOCATION: Average to wet soil.
BLOOMS: June–July
USES: ✂◭M▾ Massing, Waterside

'Feesey' (= 'Tricolor') (Strawberries & Cream Ribbon Grass) Attractive stripes of pink, green and cream, most effective in the spring, later becoming white and green striped. Definitely an improvement on 'Picta', standing up better to summer heat and humidity, and remaining attractive all season long. Foliage is excellent for floral arranging. HEIGHT: 45–70cm (18–30")

'Picta' (Ribbon Grass, Gardener's Garters) The old-fashioned form, green and creamy white stripes. Needs a hard clip back in mid-summer.

SACCHARUM
(Plume Grass) ☀

This group of plants includes the Sugarcane, a tropical grass of great economic importance, and now also a hardy species is included here, formerly listed as Erianthus. Warm-season.

officinarum 'Pele's Smoke'   ZONES 9–10

(Red-leaved Sugarcane) An impressive large clump-forming selection, with dusky purple-red foliage and purple-black canes. This is a tropical grass that loves warm humid climates, and can reach quite a large size by the end of the season. Use as an accent in container plantings or in the border. Does not flower. Propagated by cane cuttings.

HEIGHT/SPREAD: 1.2–1.8m (4–6')/60–90cm (2–3')
LOCATION: Prefers a moist well-drained soil.
USES: ✂▾ Specimen, Borders

ravennae   ZONES 6–9

(Ravenna Grass, Northern Pampas Grass) (formerly listed as *Erianthus*) Large, stout clumps of grey-green leaves. Silvery plumes of flowers rise on very tall stems in late summer, lasting into the winter. Almost as dramatic in the landscape as true Pampas Grass (*Cortaderia*), but much hardier.

"In the fall, the foliage turns shades of orange, beige, tan, brown, and purple, often with multicolors blended throughout. The brown winter skeleton looks dramatic against a dark green or snowy background. Silvery flowers with purple tones emerge in August, maturing to fluffy, cream-colored panicles that persist into winter." – John Greenlee, *The Encyclopedia of Ornamental Grasses*

HEIGHT/SPREAD: 2.4–3.6m (8–12')/90cm (3')
LOCATION: Prefers a moist well-drained soil.
BLOOMS: August–October
USES: ✂ Specimen, Massing, Borders

SESLERIA
(Moor Grass) ☀ ◑

caerulea   ZONES 4–9

(Blue Moor Grass) A clump-forming grass with metallic blue-grey foliage. Spikes of purplish flowers appear in early spring. Compact clumps can be used as an accent or for massing. Tolerates wet sites. Cool-season.

HEIGHT/SPREAD: 20–45cm (8–18")/30cm (12")
LOCATION: Average to moist soil.
BLOOMS: April–May
USES: ◭M▾ Massing, Borders, Meadows

SPARTINA
(Cord Grass) ☀ ◑

pectinata 'Aureo-marginata'   ZONES 4–9

(Variegated Cord Grass) An upright grass, spreading quickly to form a patch or open clump. Stems are tall, the strongly arching foliage is bright green with a wide yellow margin. Most effective for massing, especially beside a pond or stream. Also nice at the back of the border. Good foliage for flower arranging. Drought-resistant once established. The species itself is native over much of North America.

HEIGHT/SPREAD: 1.5–2.1m (5–7')/90cm (3')
LOCATION: Average to moist soil.
BLOOMS: August–September
USES: ✂✸ Massing, Borders, Waterside

STIPA
(Feather Grass) ☀

Quite unique among grasses, Stipa are valued for their whiskered panicles or flower-heads. These are usually airy open sprays of tiny individual flowers held well above the leaves on the ends of graceful arching stems. Some types are especially valuable in hot, dry climates as they readily withstand drought. Warm-season.

tenuissima   ZONES 6–9

(Mexican Feather Grass) (= *S. tenuifolia*) Beautiful compact species, the fine hair-like bright green leaves forming a low clump. Spikes of bearded green flowers begin to appear in mid-summer, soon changing into handsome, golden-blond plumes. Even just a few plants will constantly be in motion from the slightest breeze. A unique flower for cutting, either fresh or dried. This may prove to be far hardier than first thought as long as plants have excellent drainage, or they may act as a self-seeding annual. Warm-season.

"Plant in a grouping to resemble rolling waves in an ocean. Incredible texture and added motion for the garden." – Elke Knechtel, Zone 7

HEIGHT/SPREAD: 45–60cm (18–24")/30cm (12")
LOCATION: Average to dry well-drained soil.
BLOOMS: June–September
USES: ✂▾✸ Massing, Borders

TYPHA
(Cattail) ☀

minima   ZONES 4–9

(Dwarf Japanese Cattail) This is like a miniature version of our native Cattail, on a scale more suited to the smaller garden. Narrow grassy leaves form a clump or small patch. Short, dark brown cattails appear in early summer. Prefers a wet to moist site, and is best at the waterside. Also worth trying in tubs or as a patio plant.

"Truly a fine plant for borders, it is underused in moist perennial borders. The foliage and flowers provide interest almost year-round and are beautiful in fresh and dried arrangements." – John Greenlee, *The Encyclopedia of Ornamental Grasses*

HEIGHT/SPREAD: 45–70cm (18–30")/30–60cm (1–2')
LOCATION: Moist to wet soil.
BLOOMS: June–July
USES: ✂▾ Waterside, Specimen

Pennisetum 'Burgundy Giant'

Pennisetum setaceum 'Rubrum'

Stipa tenuissima

Typha minima

Groundcovers

Groundcovers have become very important elements within the context of contemporary landscape design. For one thing, their ability to cover large areas quickly can significantly reduce the time, energy and cost that would otherwise be required to remove weeds. But there are other benefits to consider; dense groundcovers can act as a living mulch, helping to conserve water. For difficult sites, such as dense shade or steep slopes, there are groundcovers that will happily thrive where turf might fail or be too hazardous to maintain.

Also, there is more and more concern lately over the long-term environmental effects of maintaining huge areas of lawn. Certain groundcovers may be used effectively as alternatives to lawn monoculture, hopefully reducing the need for heavy doses of fertilizers and pesticides.

Planning & planting

From a design point of view, there are many interesting textural choices available among the various types of groundcovers. Some are evergreen, others deciduous. A few have showy fall or winter colour, some have bright berries that attract birds and other wildlife. Different regions of the country have their own ubiquitous, overused groundcover plants (Japanese Spurge, Periwinkle, Hypericum), but recently we are noticing a swing towards alternatives to these old standbys, and again this varies from region to region.

Whatever plants you select, if carefully chosen and properly installed, can last for many years with a minimum of care and attention. However, when badly chosen or poorly established, groundcover plantings can be a real eyesore, getting patchy and full of weeds. The extra time and cost involved in planning and preparing your site will pay off many times over the long term.

1. Eradicate all perennial weeds with a systemic, non-selective herbicide, or smother them out by using a black plastic mulch or thick layers of newspaper for a full year.
2. Look carefully at light, soil and moisture conditions first, and then try to find a plant that will tolerate what the site has to offer.
3. Modify the soil, if necessary, by adding plenty of weed-free organic matter. A loose, open soil is ideal for plants

to get rooted and establish quickly. Steep slopes may require stabilizing with wire mesh before planting.

4. Space plants closely enough to fill in completely within two or three growing seasons. Spacing them too far apart will allow weeds to become established. Each variety listed has a recommended number of plants per square metre (e.g. 5–9 plants/m^2). Roughly the same number per square yard should be used. Note that the cost of installation increases proportionately when you use more plants. In other words, certain groundcovers can be darned expensive to install!
5. Use an organic mulch, such as bark chips, to minimize future weed problems, but don't go more than about two inches thick if the plants you have chosen send out runners that want to root into the ground. In any case, hand weeding will still be required, especially during the first two years.
6. Water new plantings regularly for the first year. An oscillating sprinkler or soaker hose is ideal for this. Deep waterings every two weeks or so will help to encourage strong healthy roots. In subsequent years, groundcovers that have been well-chosen for the site should need watering only during extended periods of drought.
7. Fertilizing yearly in the spring will help to keep your groundcover thick and vigorous; a thin or patchy groundcover lets in weeds! Choose from the many organic or inorganic fertilizers available at your garden centre. Avoid lawn formulations with high nitrogen, and never use a Weed-and-Feed as it will kill or severely damage all groundcovers. Compost or composted manure is also excellent as an annual top dressing in the spring.

Check out these varieties…

These varieties, sometimes considered to be groundcovers, may be found listed under Perennials. In order to save space we have chosen not to list them twice: Aegopodium, Ajuga, Alchemilla, Artemisia, Cerastium, Ceratostigma, Chrysogonum, Convallaria, Coronilla, Dianthus, Epimedium, Fragaria, Galium, Geranium, Helianthemum, Hemerocallis, Hosta, Lamiastrum, Lamium, Liriope, Lysimachia, Mazus, Ophiopogon, Phlox, Saxifraga, Sedum,

Arctostaphylos uva-ursi 'Vancouver Jade'

Cornus canadensis

Calluna vulgaris 'Red Wings'

Erica carnea 'Loughrigg'

ARCTOSTAPHYLOS
(Bearberry, Kinnikinnick) ☼ ◑

uva-ursi   **ZONES 2–9**

Despite it being a native plant from coast to coast, Bearberry in not yet widely known and grown across the country. This will form a mat of glossy, evergreen foliage on low trailing stems. Pink bell-shaped flowers appear in spring, followed by bright red berries that remain showy for months. Foliage turns bronzy-red in cold winter areas. Fairly drought tolerant once established. Plantings seem to do best in sandy, acid soils with plenty of humus. Dislikes heavy wet soils. Prune tips lightly in mid-summer for the first 2–3 years.

'Vancouver Jade' An especially vigorous and disease-resistant selection from the west coast. Effective as a lawn substitute over large areas. Introduced by the U.B.C. Botanical Garden and registered with the Canadian Ornamental Plant Foundation. Recommended for Zones 4–9.

HEIGHT:	10–15cm (4–6″)
SPACING:	30–60cm (1–2′); 3–10 plants/m²
LOCATION:	Prefers an acid, well-drained soil.
BLOOMS:	April–June
USES:	⚘⟁〜▲▼🌿 Wildflower

Heather – a colourful groundcover

CALLUNA
(Scottish Heather) ☼ ◑

vulgaris   **ZONES 4–9**

A favorite late-summer and fall blooming dwarf shrub that performs especially well in maritime regions both at the east and west coasts. There are a tremendous number of named selections available in the nursery trade, the tiny bell-shaped flowers ranging in color from white through lilac, pink to near-red. Foliage color varies as well, from the standard green to golden yellow, silver or grey, and some varieties take on astonishing bronze or orange shades in the winter months. Heather is quite specific as to soil requirements: it MUST have a well-drained sandy loam on the acidic side or the plants will languish and die after only a year or two. Preference is for full sun and even moisture, but partial shade is usually tolerated. Plants need protection from cold dry winter winds. Water during periods of drought. Prune tips to just below the old flowers in spring to maintain compact plants.

HEIGHT:	15–30cm (4–6″)
SPACING:	30–60cm (12–24″); 4–10 plants/m²
LOCATION:	Well-drained, sandy or peaty acidic soil.
BLOOMS:	July–October
USES:	⚘⟁〜▲

CORNUS
(Dogwood) ◑

canadensis   **ZONES 1–9**

(Bunchberry) Native all across northern Canada, usually seen growing in bright, open deciduous or mixed woods. Plants creep to make a loose mat of pointed green leaves, developing deep bronze-red tones in the fall. Miniature greenish-white dogwood flowers appear in spring, later bearing showy clusters of scarlet-red berries. Plants dug directly from the wild seldom survive transplanting; look for strong container-grown plants to get off to a vigorous start. A slow-growing gem for neutral or acidic conditions. Best used to cover small areas only. No pruning required.

HEIGHT:	10–15cm (4–6″)
SPACING:	20–30cm (8–12″); 10–25 plants/m²
LOCATION:	Moist, sandy or peaty acidic soil.
BLOOMS:	May–June
USES:	⚘⟁〜 Woodland garden

COTONEASTER
(Cotoneaster) ☼ ◑

dammeri   **ZONES 5–9**

(Bearberry Cotoneaster) Fast-growing creeping shrub, excellent choice for slopes, walls or containers. Effective as a lawn substitute over large areas. Rounded leathery green leaves are evergreen in mild winter areas, otherwise deciduous. White flowers in early summer, followed by bright red berries that remain showy all winter. Prune tips lightly in mid-summer for the first 2–3 years.

> "Among the finest of evergreen ground covers, it is ideal for mass planting on a moderate to large scale where it blankets the soil and shuts out weed growth."
> – David S. MacKenzie,
> *Perennial Ground Covers*

HEIGHT:	15–30cm (6–12″)
SPACING:	60–90cm (2–3′); 2–3 plants/m²
LOCATION:	Average well-drained soil.
BLOOMS:	May–June
USES:	⚘⟁〜▲▼ Lawn substitute

ERICA
(Heath, Heather) ☼ ◑

Along with *Calluna*, this group of plants is now commonly referred to as Heather. These low shrubs are widely used in maritime climates in small gardens as well as for large massed groundcover plantings. There are several species or groups of these available, but the most common by far are the winter and early-spring blooming types listed below. They have soft needle-like evergreen foliage, and short spikes of papery bell flowers that are a favorite of bees. Hardiness is better than most people think; in Zones 4–6 choose a sheltered spot out of the north-west wind and hot afternoon sun. Prune tips lightly after blooming for the first 2–3 years.

carnea   **ZONES 4–9**

(Winter Heath, Spring Heath) (= *E. herbacea*) Usually considered the easiest type to grow, and the hardiest under cold-winter conditions. These will also put up with a much wider variation in soil conditions than other types of heathers. Many named selections have been developed, blooming in the January through May time-frame, depending where you live. Flower colour ranges from white through to lilac, rose, pink, to near-red. Like with *Calluna*, the foliage can be an outstanding feature as well, typically fresh green in colour, but sometimes golden or dark bronze in tone. Form is low and carpeting, the plants requiring little in the way of pruning or any other type of maintenance.

HEIGHT:	15–20cm (6–12″)
SPACING:	30–45cm (12–18″); 5–10plants/m²
LOCATION:	Average well-drained soil. Prefers acidic conditions.
USES:	⚘△〰▲♥ Walls, edging, mixed borders

× darleyensis   **ZONES 4–9**

(Hybrid Heath) More vigorous and bushy than the *E. carnea* types, these unfortunately have a reputation for being touchy in especially cold winters or under exposed conditions; these perform best in Zones 6–9, especially in coastal areas. Where they thrive, plants bloom for a very long season, sometimes from November to May! Tolerant of most soils. As with the other types, there are a great number of varieties from which to choose, both for foliage and flower colour.

HEIGHT:	30–45cm (12–18″)
SPACING:	45–70cm (18–30″); 3–5plants/m²
LOCATION:	Average well-drained soil. Prefers acidic conditions.
USES:	⚘△〰▲♥ Walls, edging, mixed borders

EUONYMUS
(Wintercreeper, Euonymus) ☼ ◑ ●

fortunei   **ZONES 4–9**

(Japanese Euonymus) A great many of the newer selections are grown these days as evergreen shrubs, particularly the variegated forms. While most of these could be trained as a creeping groundcover or even as a climber, they are seldom used in this way. A couple of older selections listed below are worth considering as tough groundcovers, particularly in urban situations. Prune tips lightly in mid-summer for the first 2–3 years.

'Coloratus' (Purple-Leaf Wintercreeper) The hardiest of the Winter Creepers, with spreading stems of leathery evergreen leaves of a coarse to medium texture. Foliage turns dusky purple in the fall, and may go deciduous in cold winter areas. Widely used for mass planting, especially in the eastern part of the continent. Plants will also climb walls, trees or rough fences. Hardy to Zone 3.

HEIGHT:	30–45cm (12–18″)
SPACING:	60–75cm (24–30″); 1–3 plants/m²
LOCATION:	Average well-drained soil.
USES:	〰▲♥ Climbing Vine

'Kewensis' (Miniature Wintercreeper) A delicate-looking little gem of a groundcover, with tiny green leaves and stems that hug the ground. Excellent for a fine-textured look over a smaller area. Apparently will also climb. Not commonly seen.

HEIGHT:	30–45cm (12–18″)
SPACING:	30–45cm (12–18″); 5–10 plants/m²
LOCATION:	Average well-drained soil.
USES:	⚘△〰▲

GAULTHERIA
(Wintergreen) ◑

procumbens   **ZONES 3–9**

(Wintergreen, Checkerberry) Beautiful little native North American groundcover flourishing in acidic peaty areas across northern Canada. Plants form a low mat of glossy dark green leaves, bearing pink bell-shaped flowers in early summer, followed by a crop of fat red edible berries in fall and winter. Widely planted as a groundcover at the west coast, but worth a try elsewhere in neutral to acidic conditions such as might be found beneath Rhododendrons. Slow spreading. Best used to cover small areas only. No pruning required.

> "Common Wintergreen is one of our most durable, aesthetically pleasing, and widely distributed natives; yet when it comes to intentionally planting it in our landscapes, most gardeners do not even consider it. Here is a classic example of America's fascination with the exotic to the exclusion of perfectly fine plants that grow right under our noses."
> – David S. MacKenzie,
> *Perennial Ground Covers*

HEIGHT:	15cm (6″)
SPACING:	20–30cm (8–12″); 10–25 plants/m²
LOCATION:	Moist, sandy or peaty acidic soil.
BLOOMS:	June-August
USES:	⚘△〰▲ Wildflower, Edible fruit

shallon   **ZONES 7–9**

(Salal) A Westcoast native species, particularly used for covering large areas and for erosion control. Foliage is oval-shaped, deep green and coarse in texture, the leafy branches used widely in the floral trade as a cut green. Pale pink bell-shaped flowers in spring are followed by a crop of edible black berries in fall. This rampant grower should be sited carefully so that the spreading roots will not become a nuisance. Drought-tolerant once established. Prune tips lightly in mid-summer for the first 2–3 years. Evergreen.

HEIGHT:	60–120cm (2–4′)
SPACING:	45–90cm (18–36″); 1–5 plants/m²
LOCATION:	Moist, sandy or peaty acidic soil.
BLOOMS:	May–June
USES:	⚘△〰▲♣ Wildflower, Edible fruit

GENISTA
(Broom) ☼

pilosa 'Vancouver Gold'   **ZONES 4–9**

(Vancouver Gold Creeping Broom) Fast-spreading evergreen shrub, forming a dense carpet of grey-green stems, smothered by golden yellow pea flowers in late spring. Good choice for slopes and effective over large areas as a lawn substitute. Fairly drought resistant. Prune tips lightly in mid-summer for the first 2–3 years. Introduced by the U.B.C. Botanical Garden and registered with the Canadian Ornamental Plant Foundation.

HEIGHT:	15–20cm (6–8″)
SPACING:	60–75cm (24–30″); 2–4 plants/m²
LOCATION:	Prefers a light well-drained soil.
BLOOMS:	May–June
USES:	⚘△〰▲♣ Lawn substitute

Cotoneaster dammeri

Gaultheria procumbens

Gaultheria shallon

Genista pilosa 'Vancouver Gold'

Hedera helix 'Hahn's'

Hedera helix 'Needlepoint'

Hypericum calycinum

Pachysandra terminalis

Hedera helix 'Glacier'

HEDERA
(Ivy) ☼ ◑ ●

A very well-known, popular group of evergreen vines. Of the hundreds of varieties in existence only a few are used outdoors as hardy groundcovers or climbers. Plants are generally vigorous, quickly spreading to form a dense patch, with the stems rooting where they touch the ground or forming aerial roots to climb up vertical surfaces. Cold dry winds or full sun may cause scorching in winter, so choose a sheltered site if your garden is in Zone 5 or 6. Ivy may be clipped back at almost any time if plants begin to get out of control.

helix   ZONES 5–9

(English Ivy) Vigorous evergreen groundcover or climbing vine. Creeping stems form a dense mat of dark-green leathery leaves. Very tolerant of shady sites. All varieties will either creep along the ground or climb by aerial roots, given some initial support. The various cultivars of English Ivy are currently in a rather mixed-up state within the trade, and sometimes even the descriptions in reference books disagree.

HEIGHT:	10–15cm (4–6")
SPACING:	30–60cm (1–2'); 3–10 plants/m²
LOCATION:	Prefers a rich, moist soil.
USES:	∿▲☗ Climbing vine, Lawn substitute

'Baltica' (Baltic Ivy) Medium-sized leaves, bright green in summer, dark green in winter or bronzy in colder areas. New growth is glossy. An excellent groundcover or climbing vine.

'Glacier' Leaves are small, dark green with grey-green and creamy-yellow margins. Freely branching, with a low, compact habit. Not a fast spreader. Beautiful with spring flowering bulbs. Also easily grown in pots to take inside for the winter. Zones 6–9.

'Hahn's' Bright green medium-sized leaves, the self-branching habit makes this a good groundcover selection. Zones 6–9.

'Little Diamond' Interesting diamond-shaped leaves without the usual ivy points at first. Habit is dense and bushy, colour is grey-green with a creamy-white edge. Zones 6–9.

'Needlepoint' A bushy, well-branched variety forming a dense mat of dark green birdsfoot-shaped leaves. Zones 6–9.

'Thorndale' Leaves are small, leathery, dark green with prominent white veins. This variety is often recommended as the hardiest type. Bronzy-red winter colour. Zones 5–9.

HYPERICUM
(St. John's-wort) ☼ ◑ ●

calycinum   ZONES 5–9

(Aaron's Beard, Rose-of-Sharon) Large golden-yellow flowers appear throughout the summer and fall, blooming more reliably in sunny exposures. Plants have upright stems of bright green leaves, forming a dense weed-proof patch. Tolerant of poor soils and moderately drought-tolerant. Especially good for stabilizing slopes. Widely used at the West coast. Prune tips lightly in spring for the first 2–3 years. Evergreen in Zones 7–9.

HEIGHT:	30–45cm (12–18")
SPACING:	30–45cm (12–18"); 5–10 plants/m²
LOCATION:	Average well-drained soil.
BLOOMS:	May–October
USES:	∿▲☗

Pachysandra terminalis 'Variegata'

PACHYSANDRA
(Japanese Spurge) ◑ ●

terminalis   ZONES 3–9

Dark green, glossy foliage forms a dense, spreading patch. White flowers appear briefly in spring. Very tolerant of poor soils and deep shade. One of the most reliable evergreen groundcovers, but notoriously slow to establish. 'Variegatus' and 'Silver Edge' have creamy-white leaf margins; they both grow at an extremely slow rate. No pruning generally required, but a little tidying up in the spring may be necessary.

> **"For a lovely infusion of tranquilizing lushness, try interplanting pachysandra with hostas, or cinnamon, lady, and royal ferns." – David S. MacKenzie,** *Perennial Ground Covers*

HEIGHT:	20cm (8")
SPACING:	15–30cm (6–12"); 10–40 plants/m²
LOCATION:	Prefers a rich, moist soil.
BLOOMS:	April–May
USES:	∿▲ Lawn substitute

Paxistima canbyi

PAXISTIMA
(Cliff Green, Ratstripper) ☼ ☾

canbyi   ZONES 2–9
Native North American evergreen shrub with small, glossy dark-green leaves, turning bronze in fall and winter. Fine-textured plant deserving of wider use. Excellent for underplanting trees and shrubs. Will spread slowly to form a dense patch. Best used to cover small areas only. Prune tips lightly in mid-summer for the first 2–3 years.

HEIGHT:	30cm (12″)
SPACING:	30–45cm (12–18″); 5–10 plants/m²
LOCATION:	Average well-drained soil.
USES:	◢△M⋎▲

Potentilla fruticosa 'Yellow Gem'

POTENTILLA
(Cinquefoil) ☼ ☾

fruticosa 'Yellow Gem'   ZONES 2–9
(Bush Cinquefoil) An outstanding groundcover selection introduced by the U.B.C. Botanical Garden. Large yellow flowers appear over many months on this low, spreading shrub. Excellent for edging, containers, or in mass plantings. Deciduous. Prune tips lightly in mid-summer for the first 2–3 years. Registered with the Canadian Ornamental Plant Foundation.

HEIGHT:	30–40cm (12–16″)
SPACING:	45–60cm (18–24″); 3–5 plants/m²
LOCATION:	Average well-drained soil.
BLOOMS:	May–October
USES:	◢△M⋎♊ Mixed borders

RUBUS
(Raspberry) ☼ ☾

calycinoides 'Emerald Carpet'   ZONES 7–9
(Taiwan Creeper) Low spreading, fast-growing evergreen groundcover. Rounded leaves are rough-textured and attractively scalloped. Edible golden berries appear in late summer. Effective as a lawn substitute over large areas. Fairly drought-tolerant.

HEIGHT:	10–15cm (4–6″)
SPACING:	60–90cm (2–3′); 4–9 plants/m²
LOCATION:	Average well-drained soil.
USES:	◢△M⋎♊ Lawn substitute

VACCINIUM
(Cranberry) ☼ ☾

vitis-idaea 'Minus'   ZONES 2–9
(Cowberry, Lingonberry) Low spreading bushes of rounded, shiny green leaves. Pale-pink bell flowers in late spring, followed by bright red edible berries. Very popular in Scandinavia for making jams and jellies. Also native to North America. Nice in cool, shady areas; good companion to Rhododendrons or Azaleas. Best used to cover small areas only. No pruning is required.

HEIGHT:	20cm (8″)
SPACING:	20–30cm (8–12″); 10–25 plants/m²
LOCATION:	Prefers a moist, acid soil.
BLOOMS:	May–June
USES:	◢△M⋎▲ Edible berries

VINCA
(Periwinkle, Myrtle) ☾ ●

minor   ZONES 3–9
Extremely popular groundcover, valued for its thick mat of glossy evergreen leaves, studded with periwinkle-blue flowers in spring. Very shade tolerant, even of dry shade, but tends to burn in full sun. Good reliable cover for large or small areas. Plants may be clipped back after flowering to encourage dense growth.

> "Periwinkle has one of those flowers that sets the stage for myth and magic."
> – Warren Hartman, Zone 6

'Atropurpurea' Deep wine-red flowers, green leaves.
'Ralph Shugert' Green leaves, edged in silver. Blue flowers. Excellent vigour.
'Sterling Silver' Leaves green, edged in silver. White flowers.
'Variegata' Roundish leaves, green with white edge. Blue flowers.

HEIGHT:	10–15cm (4–6″)
SPACING:	30–60cm (12–24″); 4–10 plants/m²
LOCATION:	Average to moist well-drained soil.
BLOOMS:	April–June
USES:	◢△M⋎▲♊ Lawn substitute

Rubus calycinoides 'Emerald Carpet'

Vaccinium vitis-idaea

Vinca minor 'Atropurpurea'

Vinca minor

Herbs

The word 'herb' has had many different meanings over time. Nowadays the definition has been broadened to include all plants that are of use to man for such diverse purposes as flavouring foods and beverages, for medicinal purposes, as pest repellents, room deodorizers, in perfumes and cosmetics, or for dying cloth and fibres.

Most of our common cooking herbs, like basil or parsley, have flavourful leaves. With chicory we can roast and grind the root as a coffee substitute. In the case of lovage and Florence fennel the stems may be eaten as a vegetable. The seeds of caraway and coriander are ground and used as a spice. Spices are usually dried parts of plants that can be stored for a long time. Some herbs, therefore, are also spices when they are used dried: oregano, rosemary, sage, and marjoram for example.

Growing Herbs

Any sunny garden that can successfully grow vegetables or geraniums should be an excellent site for most herbs. Direct sun all day long is recommended, but a site with full sun for only 3 to 4 hours, or even filtered sunlight all day should still give good results.

Growing herbs indoors is also possible with a sunny south window or fluorescent lights; they can be grown in pots of soil or even hydroponically. Good candidates for the house include basil, chives, dill, lemon balm, marjoram, mint, oregano, parsley, rosemary, sage, tarragon and thyme.

Almost all herbs prefer a warm site with excellent drainage. For general soil and site preparation please refer to the steps outlined in the front sections of this Gardening Guide; what works for a wide range of perennials will be ideal for herbs.

If you use fresh herbs a lot for cooking, try to choose a site that is convenient to the kitchen door so they can be picked just before using, ensuring optimum flavour and freshness. Raised beds are an excellent place for growing herbs, making them especially easy to harvest. Herbs with attractive foliage and flowers won't look out of place planted in a mixed border with annuals, perennials, bulbs, and even flowering shrubs.

Container gardening with herbs is especially successful. All kinds of pots, tubs, and baskets can be pressed into use as herbal containers, just make sure they have a drainage hole or two. Large half-barrels are especially good for containing various types of mint, to keep them from spreading all over the garden.

Planting & Maintenance

Please see the section near the front of this Gardening Guide for some basics on planting and maintenance.

Annual herb varieties will need to be replanted every year, or allowed to seed themselves. Sometimes they will self-seed in such numbers that they will need to be thinned. Just throw any unwanted seedlings on to the compost heap or pot them up to give to friends.

Biennial varieties, such as caraway, will not set seed until the second year. If you want a crop every year, be sure to do a new planting each spring or allow them to self seed.

Perennial herbs may need to be lifted every few years and divided to keep them vigorous and healthy. Spring is the best time to do this, before they get more than a few inches tall. In colder areas, some of the more tender perennial herbs will need a thick mulch in late fall in order to protect the plants for the winter. In the listing that follows, perennial varieties are indicated by the presence of hardiness zones.

Tender perennial herbs, like Pineapple Sage and Lemon Verbena, are best grown in a container so they can be easily moved indoors for the winter. Some people prefer just to take cuttings in late summer to start fresh plants indoors. This will help to avoid bringing in unwanted insect pests to your house plants.

Preserving the Harvest

Most of the common kitchen herbs can be preserved at home, in one way or another, for using all the year round. There are four basic methods commonly used: drying, freezing, preserving in oil, or making herbal vinegars.

Drying herbs

Drying your own herbs is easy to do. The resulting harvest, packed into airtight bags or jars, can be kept handy to add all kinds of interesting and exotic flavours to your cooking. Bunches of dried herbs are also attractive decorations for the kitchen, and can be turned into easy, inexpensive gifts from the garden.

Leaves: When harvesting the leaves, most herbs achieve their maximum flavour just before the plants flower, and first thing in the morning, so choose this time to pick the herbs whenever possible. Using garden shears or sharp scissors, cut nice long whole stems; flowers, leaves and all. Rinse them quickly in cold water to remove any dirt or insects, then shake dry. Tie the stems together in bunches of five to ten, and hang upside-down in a warm, dry place. A dark room is ideal, so long as there is good air circulation, but a brighter room will do so long as the herbs are kept out of direct sun. Some people prefer to tie a paper bag around the bunches to keep off dust and insects. Let the bundle hang for about two weeks to dry thoroughly. Then untie them, and separate the whole leaves from the stems. Pack leaves whole into jars or heavy zip-top freezer bags and store in a dark, dry place. For the best possible flavour, wait until you need to use the dried herbs before crumbling or crushing just enough for the recipe.

Seeds: Wait until the seeds begin to change colour from green to shades of medium brown, a sure sign of ripening. Gather the seeds by hand and put them into paper bags; this is a great job for kids! Don't worry about any stems or leaves that might fall in. Store the bags in a warm, dark room for at least a couple of weeks so they can finish ripening and drying. When dry, empty the contents onto a pie plate or cookie sheet. Pick out any stems, leaves or dirt. To get rid of small chaff, take the pie plate outside, shaking it back and forth while blowing gently across the seeds. The chaff should blow away, leaving a clean plate of seeds that are ready to store in clean jars or zip-top bags.

Freezing herbs

Certain herbs will lose their unique flavour when dried at home. Some of these are commercially freeze-dried (Chives, Tarragon), but for home-use plain freezing is the best alternative. For maximum flavour gather the herbs just before the plants flower, and first thing in the morning if possible. Rinse them quickly in cold water and shake dry. Simply pick off the leaves and chop coarsely on a cutting board, using a large sharp knife. Then place them in heavy zip-top bags and throw into the freezer. Some cooks like to freeze the herbs first on cookie sheets before packing, to keep the leaves separate. Use the same amount of frozen herbs as you would fresh. Herbs will usually freeze well for only four to six months before they dry out and lose their flavour.

Preserving herbs in oil

Certain herbs, most notably Basil and Tarragon, do not lend themselves well to drying because the flavours all but disappear. An alternative to freezing is this method of preserving in oil. Finely chop the herbs by hand, or use a food processor or blender, and put into a glass bowl. For every cup of chopped herbs add about two tablespoons of Extra-virgin olive oil, two teaspoons of salt, and mix well. Pack this into fairly small jars, leaving about an inch of headspace. Pour more oil in each jar, right to the top, and cover. Leave at room temperature for a few hours, top off the jars with more oil as needed, and refrigerate.

To use herbs, dig down below the oil with a spoon, pull out what you need, smooth the oil back over the top (adding a little more to cover if necessary) and put back in the fridge.

The idea here is that the oil keeps out air, which helps to prevent the herbs from spoiling, but for a maximum of two months in the refrigerator. Discard immediately if there are signs of surface mould, an off smell, or discoloration. Herbs in oil will keep very nicely in the freezer for a year or more.

Herbal vinegars

These flavoured vinegars are very handy for splashing over salad greens or adding to salad dressings and marinades. They are easy to make at home, and make attractive gifts, packed with the flavours of summer.

Begin with a good quality vinegar; apple cider and white wine vinegar are the best choices, but even regular white vinegar will do. Select the herb or combination of herbs that you wish to use, rinse in cold water, bruise with a kitchen mallet and place them whole (or coarsely chopped) into the bottom of a clean glass jar, bottle or crock. Pour the vinegar over, seal the top and leave to steep in a warm place (like on top of the fridge) for two to three weeks, shaking every once in awhile if you think of it. Taste the vinegar; if it seems strong enough continue on to the next step, otherwise leave to steep for another week. Strain the vinegar into a stainless steel or enamel pot, heat to boiling, pour into hot, sterilized bottles or jars, seal the tops and store in a cool, dark place. Some cooks skip this last step, but unpasteurized herb vinegar may not keep for as long.

The amount of herbs to vinegar can vary according to your taste, but a good ratio to begin with is ¼ to ½ cup (60–125ml) of fresh herbs to 2 cups (500ml) vinegar (or about a handful per pint). Choose single herbs or try a combination of different ones you like. To tint your vinegar deep pink use a generous amount of Purple Ruffles basil, chive blossoms or purple perilla leaves. Certain fruits might combine well with herbs to make vinegars; try raspberries, blackberries, blueberries or sour cherries. Some other potential garden or kitchen ingredients: nasturtium flowers and leaves, rose petals, calendula petals, violet flowers, fresh or dried chili peppers, ginger root, juniper berries, black pepper, chopped shallots.

Herbal infusions

A refreshing alternative to regular tea or coffee, limited in flavour only by your imagination. Serve them fresh-brewed and piping hot or chilled over ice, depending on your mood and the time of year. Certain herbal infusions are considered to have medicinal uses, but that sort of natural treatment should only be carried out under the guidance of a certified trained Homeopath, Naturopath, or Herbalist. Fortunately, many herbal infusions are quite harmless, in moderation, and can be made easily with your own home-grown herbs.

To make infusions fresh herbs, simply throw a couple of handfuls of chopped leaves and flowers into a tea pot, pour boiling water over and steep for five or ten minutes. Tasting part way through steeping is a good idea at first, until you get a feel for how much time is required, how many leaves to use, and which herbs you like. Frozen herbs will make acceptable herbal infusions.

Dried herbs can also be used, but in much smaller quantities because of their concentrated flavour. The rule of thumb is one teaspoon dried herbs per cup of water, increase to taste for milder-flavoured varieties. Honey, sugar, or lemon complement the flavours of most herbal infusions, but milk is not recommended.

Certain spices can be interesting in combination with fresh or dried herbs: try anise, cinnamon, cloves, coriander, ginger, lemon or orange peel. Commercial herbal infusions often include dried hibiscus flowers, strawberry, raspberry, blackberry or black currant leaves, rosehips, lemon grass, dried apples and other dried fruits; these can usually be found in bulk at health food stores if you want to try making your own personal blends.

Preserving Herbs

Herbs for home drying:
Bay Laurel, Caraway (seeds), Coriander (seeds), Dill (leaves & seeds), Fennel (leaves & seeds), Lovage (leaves & seeds), Marjoram, Mint, Oregano, Parsley, Rosemary, Sage, Summer Savory, Thyme.

Herbs that are better frozen than dried:
Basil, Chives, Garlic (whole cloves), Lemon Balm, Lemon Verbena, Parsley, Tarragon.

Herbs that can be preserved in oil:
Basil, Chervil, Coriander (Cilantro), Dill, Fennel, Garlic, Parsley, Sage, Sorrel, Tarragon.

Herbs for flavoured vinegars:
Basil, Bay, Borage, Burnet, Chervil, Chives, Dill, Fennel, Garlic, Lemon Balm, Lemon Verbena, Lovage, Marjoram, Mint, Parsley, Perilla, Rosemary, Sage, Thyme, Tarragon.

Herbs for infusing:
Anise-hyssop, Beebalm, Catnip, Chamomile, Lavender (flowers), Lemon Balm, Lemon Verbena, Marjoram, Mint (all types), Peppermint, Sage (especially Pineapple Sage), Thyme.

Anise-Hyssop

Bush Basil

Basil – Mixed

Bay Laurel

ANGELICA

(Angelica archangelica)   ZONES 2–9

A big, bold plant that may be biennial in habit, or a short-lived perennial. In the second year plants develop tall stems with a huge umbrella-shaped head of greenish-white flowers, later forming seeds. Stems have been candied and used to decorate cakes and pastries. Licorice-flavoured leaves are used in teas. Appreciates a rich, moist soil. HEIGHT: 1–2.4m (3–8′) USES: ✂ Borders, Waterside

ANISE

(Pimpinella anisum)   ANNUAL

Primarily grown for the ripe seeds harvested in late summer. Strong licorice flavour, used mostly in cookies, teas or to flavour liqueurs like anisette. Commercially, the oil is pressed and widely employed in the food industry. Fresh flowers and leaves can also be enjoyed in salads or to flavour soups. Plants somewhat resemble Queen-Anne's Lace, with ferny foliage and lacy umbels of whitish flowers. HEIGHT: 45–60cm (18–24″) USES: ✂ Borders

ANISE-HYSSOP

(Agastache foeniculum)   ZONES 2–9

Long spikes of lavender flowers are attractive to bees and excellent for cutting. Whole plant is strongly licorice scented and flavoured. Leaves may be used in teas and herbal jellies, edible flowers in salads. Mingles nicely with other summer-blooming perennials in the border. North American native wildflower. Anise-hyssop is not the same as Anise, see above. HEIGHT: 90–120cm (3–4′) USES: ✂ ❦ ❦ Borders

> "The tiny flowers of anise hyssop are so tasty that they give edible flowers a good name. With a flavor of anise, mint, and root beer combined, they are excellent in icy drinks, delicate desserts, and fancy tea breads." – Carole Saville, *Exotic Herbs*

BALM, LEMON
see LEMON BALM.

BASIL

(Ocimum spp.)   ANNUAL

One of the most widely-used herbs in all of its various forms. Especially valued in Italy and other Mediterranean countries for flavouring sauces, soups, pasta and tomato dishes, and vegetable salads, as well as meats and poultry. All Basils are very cold-sensitive, and should never be planted outside until late spring. Pinching off the flowers will encourage plants to keep producing leaves. Can also be grown successfully indoors over the winter in a sunny window. Basil is best used fresh; home-dried basil loses most of its flavour and is far inferior to fresh. Preserve or freeze it instead, for winter use. Unless otherwise noted, HEIGHT: 30–60cm (12–24″) USES: ❦ Borders

African Blue (*O.* 'African Blue') An exciting new hybrid selection with a most unusual fragrance that combines camphor and sweet basil. Coarse green leaves are attractively flushed with dark purple-blue, with blue stems and pinkish flowers. A superb container-garden ornamental, which deserves experimenting with in the kitchen! Outstanding in herbal vinegars. Vigorous and large in habit. HEIGHT: 90–120cm (3–4′)

Anise Basil (*O. basilicum*) A variety used in Asia, particularly in Thai and Vietnamese cooking. Sweet, exotic flavour with a hint of anise, purplish foliage. Worth experimenting with as a replacement to regular Sweet Basil. Same as Licorice Basil

Bush Basil (*O. basilicum minimum*) A compact, tiny-leaved dwarf basil, excellent for container growing or using as an edging. Very strong, spicy smell reminiscent of cloves. Good flavour, but no match for Sweet Basil. HEIGHT: 15–30cm (6–12″)

Cinnamon Basil (*O. basilicum*) Interesting cinnamon scent and flavour. Although this variety comes from Mexico, it seems to have an affinity for Middle Eastern and Italian meat dishes. Similar in appearance to Sweet Basil.

> "Inventive American chefs create tantalizing dishes with this spice-in-an-herb basil, and domestic cooks and home gardeners will find it to be as easily at home in a perfumed arrangement of ornamental flowers as it is in the kitchen." – Carole Saville, *Exotic Herbs*

East Indian Basil (*O. gratissimum*) A tall-growing species, the large leaves strongly pungent with a clove fragrance. Spicy flavour is appreciated in Indian cooking. In South America this is brewed into a hot or cold tea. HEIGHT: 1.2–1.8cm (4–6′)

Holy Basil (*O. sanctum*) (Sacred Basil) Very different from the other basils in appearance, taste and flavour. Leaves are downy, gray-green in colour. Very spicy taste and strong fragrance of cloves. Has religious uses in India, and is occasionally added to cold vegetable dishes or salads. Makes an unusual tea.

Lemon Basil (*O. basilicum citriodorum*) Intense lemon fragrance has a special affinity for fish and seafood dishes and herbal vinegars. Also nice in hot or cold teas. Bushy growth, medium-sized plant.

Lettuce-Leaf Basil

Lettuce-Leaf Basil (*O. basilicum* 'Crispum') A selected form of Sweet Basil with extra-large crinkly leaves. Good flavour. Produces the maximum amount of leaves in the smallest amount of space, with the least amount of effort! Terrific for making the ever-popular pesto.

Licorice Basil See Anise Basil.

Purple Ruffles Basil (*O. basilicum* 'Purple Ruffles') Very ornamental selection, the dark-purple leaves have a ruffled and crimped texture. Not always a vigorous grower, seems especially sensitive to cold spring weather. Used to make bright pink basil vinegar. The leaves turn green when added to hot foods.

Sweet Basil (*O. basilicum*) The traditional large-leaved variety. Still the most popular variety, grown for its pungent, slightly licorice flavour. The major ingredient in classic Italian pesto sauce.

BAY LAUREL

(Laurus nobilis)   ZONE 9

Evergreen shrub or small tree. Bay is best grown in a large pot or tub so it can be moved indoors to overwinter in a sunny window. The large, leathery leaves are used fresh or dried as a flavouring in soups, stews and meat dishes, especially in French cooking. Prune plants lightly in spring to keep them compact. Can be trained as a bush or standard. HEIGHT: 90–180cm (3–6') USES: ♥▲

BEEBALM

(Monarda didyma)   ZONES 2–9

Also known as Bergamot or Oswego Tea. Popular flowering perennial wildflower, the leaves and flowers may be used to make a delicious fragrant tea, or sparingly in salads. Fragrant and colourful ingredient for potpourri mixtures. Also listed in the PERENNIAL section under *Monarda*. HEIGHT: 90cm (3') USES: ⚘< ♥ ✈ Borders

BORAGE

(Borago officinalis)   ANNUAL

"Borage needs to be grown for the star-shaped blue flowers, not only as an herb. I've got mine in semi-shade and find it brightens up an area when planted *en masse*." – Dr. Virginia Hildebrandt, Zone 5

Young cucumber-flavoured leaves are used in salads. The star-shaped bright blue flowers are also fun to put in salads, or float in cold drinks. Adventurous bakers may like to have candied flowers on hand to decorate cakes and desserts. Older leaves are sometimes cooked as greens. An excellent plant for children's gardens, as it is fast to grow and practically foolproof. Borage usually self-seeds, so you only need to plant it once. Loved by bees. HEIGHT: 75cm (30") USES: ♥ Borders

BURNET, SALAD

(Sanguisorba minor)   ZONES 2–9

The lacy blue-green leaves are occasionally added to salads and sauces when young, lending a mild cool-cucumber taste. Sometimes minced with other *fines herbes* (chervil, parsley, tarragon, chives) and mixed into mayonnaise, sour cream, or quark cheese as a topping for boiled new potatoes. Also nice for flavouring vinegars, or floating as a garnish in cool drinks. Useful edging plant, remaining evergreen most winters. Crimson-red ball-shaped flowers rise up on stems in early summer. Benefits from cutting back after blooming. HEIGHT: 30cm (12") USES: ⚘<▲♥ Edging, Borders

CARAWAY

(Carum carvi)   BIENNIAL

Grown for its pungent seeds. These are commonly incorporated into breads (especially rye) and cheeses, and added to various foods as an important flavouring ingredient in several Northern European countries; sauerkraut, noodles, soups, cabbage and pork, for example. A few finely-chopped leaves can be added to salads or sandwiches. The carrot-like roots can be cooked and eaten as a vegetable. Plants have tall stems of lacy white flowers in their second year, followed by a heavy crop of seeds. These should be allowed to turn light brown before being harvested. HEIGHT: 90cm (3') USES: ⚘< Borders

Catnip & 'Marty'

CATNIP

(Nepeta cataria)   ZONES 2–9

Most cats love this plant fresh or dried, and a couple of plants in your garden will attract every cat in the neighbourhood. The leaves and flower heads can also be used to make a soothing bedtime tea for humans. Plants have a tendency to self-seed prolifically, and are not especially attractive in the border. A poultice of the mashed-up leaves is said to relieve the burn from stinging nettles. HEIGHT: 90cm (3') USES: Herb gardens, Back lanes

CHAMOMILE

German   ANNUAL

(*Matricaria recutita*) Grown for their pretty little white daisies, which are used fresh or dried to make a calming tea. Save any cold leftover tea; you can use it as a hair-rinse to bring out blonde highlights. Readily self-seeds. HEIGHT: 30cm (1') USES: Herb gardens

Roman   ZONES 4–9

(*Chamaemelum nobile*) Flowers are used exactly the same way as German Chamomile. The fragrant foliage is very dense, forming a fine-textured bright green mat. Has sometimes been used as a lawn substitute in hot, dry sites; will tolerate light foot traffic. There is an attractive double-flowered form, **'Flore Pleno'** HEIGHT: 15cm (6") USES: ∿♥ Edging, Lawn substitute

Beebalm

Borage

Chicory

Garlic Chives

Chives

Comfrey

Vietnamese Coriander

Dill

CHERVIL

(Anthriscus cerefolium)   ANNUAL

Has feathery green leaves that are used much the same way as parsley, but with a slight anise overtone in the flavour. One of the classic French *fines herbes*, and a favorite flavoring for tomato, egg and fish dishes. Often added to mayonnaise, butter, various sauces, soups and salads. Leaves must be used while young, as they turn very bitter with maturity. Preserve by chopping and freezing to retain flavour. Best to grow this in part shade. HEIGHT: 30cm (12")
USES: Herb gardens

CHICORY

(Cichorium intybus)   ZONES 2–9

Very young leaves may be used as a salad green. The roots of this variety are roasted until thoroughly dried, then ground as a coffee additive or substitute. Plants produce sky-blue daisy flowers all summer long in their second year, commonly seen on roadsides across the country, but pretty in the garden too. HEIGHT: 90cm (3') USES: Borders, Meadows

CHIVES

Common Chives   ZONES 1–9

(*Allium schoenoprasum*) One of the classic French *fines herbes*, and a good plant to have growing close to the kitchen door, handy for last-minute snipping into salads and sauces. A favorite addition to soups, egg or vegetable dishes, in herbal vinegars, and of course as a topping on baked potatoes, imparting a mild onion flavour. Attractive purple flowers appear in late spring, and these also can be eaten in salads or used as an edible garnish. See also the listing under *Allium schoenoprasum* in the PERENNIALS section. HEIGHT: 30cm (12") USES: ⚘ Borders

Garlic Chives   ZONES 2–9

(*Allium tuberosum*) Chinese Chives. Similar uses to Common Chives, and just as handy to have nearby the kitchen. Leaves are strongly flavoured with garlic, so use sparingly. Beautiful heads of white flowers appear in late summer and these are also edible. Remove faded flower heads to prevent self seeding everywhere. HEIGHT: 30–60cm (1–2') USES: ⚘ Borders

CILANTRO
See CORIANDER.

COMFREY

(Symphytum officinale)   ZONES 2–9

Bold-leaved, showy plants that fit well into the perennial border where their clusters of sky-blue or pinkish flowers are much appreciated. Comfrey was once used extensively in poultices on cuts, bruises, and broken bones, which explains one of its common names, Boneset. The presence of toxic alkaloids have made internal use of the leaves and roots no longer advisable. Plants are very tough and will survive for years without any attention. Cut plants right back to the ground in mid-summer as soon as you think they look a bit tired; fresh new growth will appear in no time. Bees love Comfrey flowers! Because of their extensive root system, plants are difficult to eradicate once established. HEIGHT: 90cm (3') USES: Borders

CORIANDER

Leaf Coriander, Cilantro   ANNUAL

(*Coriandrum sativum*) Chinese Parsley. Said to be the most widely-grown herb in the world. This is showing up in every green grocer and supermarket lately, so North Americans have quickly developed a taste for it. The fresh young leaves resemble parsley, and are used extensively as both a flavouring and garnish in foods from many diverse regions, including Asia, India, Latin America, Thailand, Mexico and the Middle East. Its pungent flavour is truly international! Pick the leaves before plants begin to flower. Later, the seeds can be harvested and dried when they begin to turn brown, and used to flavour curries and pickles. Roots are also edible and eaten as a vegetable. HEIGHT: 60–90cm (2–3') USES: ⚘ Herb gardens

Vietnamese Coriander   TENDER PERENNIAL

(*Persicaria odoratum*) Rau ram. Recently arrived in North America from south-east Asia. Foliage has a lemon-coriander fragrance and is used in various chicken and meat dishes, usually added at the end of cooking. Interesting to experiment with! Can be grown indoors on a sunny window sill or hanging basket. Prefers moist soil. HEIGHT: 10–20cm (4–8") USES: ⚘ Herb gardens

CUBAN OREGANO

(Plectranthus amboinicus) TENDER PERENNIAL

Thick, fleshy leaves are succulent, a little like a fuzzy jade plant. Most often grown in a pot to bring inside for the winter. The flavour is said to combine oregano, thyme and savory, and leaves are used in Cuba, Mexico and the West Indies where they are added to various meat and bean dishes. Also made into a tea to drink or used as a hair rinse. Outstanding ornamental. HEIGHT: 30–60cm (1–2') USES: ⚘ Fragrance gardens, Herb gardens

> "Cuban oregano is so decorative that it looks as if it could only be an ornamental. But when its velvet leaves are touched ever so lightly, you are overwhelmed by a resounding culinary oregano scent mixed with some other undefinable, exotic note, and you can almost taste the fragrance."
> – Carole Saville, *Exotic Herbs*

CURRY PLANT

(Helichrysum italicum)   TENDER PERENNIAL

Woolly silver-grey foliage with a distinctive scent of curry powder. Distilled oil is used in the commercial food industry. Although not traditionally used as a flavouring ingredient in Indian cooking, the fresh leaves are reported to lend a mild curry flavour to any rice or vegetable dish. Beautiful in tubs and containers. HEIGHT: 30–60cm (1–2') USES: ⚘ Fragrance gardens, Herb gardens

DILL

(Anethum graveolens)   ANNUAL

Commonly used in European and Middle Eastern cooking, both the fresh or dried leaves and seeds contribute their unique flavour to a variety of foods including pickles, marinated cucumbers, soups, sauces, fish dishes, and salad dressings. Dill will usually self-seed after the first year. HEIGHT: 90cm (3')
USES: ⚘ Herb gardens

ECHINACEA

(Echinacea angustifolia)   ZONES 3–9

(Narrowleaf Coneflower, Western Coneflower) Being widely promoted lately for strengthening the human immune system, and as an all-round tonic and blood purifier. Most health-food stores and pharmacies have reams of products containing *Echinacea*, usually derived from the dried and ground whole root. This species is said to be the most medicinally active. Flowers are very similar in appearance to the Purple Coneflower (see PERENNIAL section), but with paler, narrower ray florets. HEIGHT: 60–120cm (2–4′) USES: ✂ ⚘ Borders, Herb gardens

ELEPHANT GARLIC

See GARLIC, ELEPHANT.

Florence Fennel

FENNEL

(Foeniculum vulgare)

If you aren't familiar with fennel, try to imagine a dill plant that tastes mildly of anise or black licorice. The leaves of all varieties are very graceful and ferny, and can be used fresh or dried to impart their special flavour to fish or egg dishes, soups, salads, and stuffings. The seed is also dried and used in similar ways to Caraway or Dillseed. Plants are a favorite food for the swallowtail butterfly caterpillar. USES: ✂ ⚘ ⚘ Borders

Bronze Fennel   ZONES 6–9

('Purpureum') The most versatile Fennel, forming a large clump of ferny foliage that starts out dark purple, then matures to metallic bronze. An outstanding ornamental perennial, and useful kitchen herb as well. Self-seeds vigorously, if permitted. HEIGHT: 90–180cm (3–6′)

> "Bronze fennel is an exotic design feature in the garden. A large planting of the herb makes a dramatic stand that looks like glistening, fringed black feathers burnished with copper." – Carole Saville, *Exotic Herbs*

Florence Fennel   ANNUAL

(var. *azoricum*) As well as the leaves, this variety forms a swollen bulb of celery-like stems that are popular as a vegetable in Italy (known as *Finocchio*), where they are sliced and added to salads, baked with butter and garlic, or added to soups and stews. Harvest in late fall. HEIGHT: 90cm (3′)

Sweet Fennel   ZONES 5–9

(var. *dulce*) Common ingredient in German cooking, this is the variety generally grown for its seeds. Ferny foliage is attractive in the flower border. HEIGHT: 120cm (4′)

FEVERFEW

(Tanacetum parthenium)   ZONES 4–9

Clinical research has found this herb to be useful in treating migraine headaches in many people. Leaves are dried and processed into a wide variety of herbal products. Fresh leaves have an unpleasant taste and may cause mouth irritation. Consider growing Feverfew just for its pretty heads of white or yellow flowers, resembling a dwarf fall chrysanthemum. Plants are short-lived perennials that will self-seed year after year. **Golden Feverfew** ('Aureum') has beautiful dayglo yellow foliage and white flowers. Other selections are listed in the PERENNIALS section under *Tanacetum*. HEIGHT: 30–45cm (12–18″) USES: ✂ ⚘ Borders

GARLIC

(Allium sativum)   ANNUAL

Very well-known flavouring ingredient, used by nearly every cuisine of the world. Most often garlic is added to savory foods, including meat and vegetable dishes, soups, salads sauces and breads. Onion-like plants form a bulb which should be harvested in late summer. Proven to have an antibiotic effect, and widely sold in capsule form in the herbal trade. HEIGHT: 30cm (12″) USES: Herb or vegetable gardens

GARLIC CHIVES

See CHIVES, GARLIC.

GARLIC, ELEPHANT

(Allium ampeloprasum)   ZONES 4–9

Forms a monstrous bulb, but with a much milder flavour than regular garlic. Especially good roasted or grilled as a vegetable, developing a sweet, nutty taste. Children love this novelty! Attractive mauve flower heads appear in late summer. Harvest bulbs in the fall. HEIGHT: 30–90cm (1–3′) USES: ✂ Herb or vegetable garden

HYSSOP

(Hyssopus officinalis)   ZONES 4–9

An ancient, bitter herb that was once used extensively in Europe to mask the flavour of strong meat or game. Small amounts are said to aid digestion. The leaves taste slightly of pine needles, and can be finely chopped and added to salads, soups or stew in small quantities. Plants send up spikes of pretty blue flowers in summer, and these too are edible in salads. An excellent cut flower, pretty in the border and attractive to butterflies. Trim plants back to about 10cm (4″) in spring. Sometimes planted as a low clipped hedge around herbal knot gardens. The selection **'Pink Delight'** has soft pink flowers. HEIGHT: 60–75cm (24–30″). USES: ✂ ⚘ ⚘ Borders

Echinacea

Bronze Fennel

Feverfew

Hyssop

English Lavender

French Lavender

Spanish Lavender

Lovage

LAVENDER
(Lavandula spp.)

A group of herbs of ancient use, valued worldwide for their delightful sweet fragrance and attractive spikes of flowers. Some varieties are hardy perennial shrubs while others are best grown in pots for wintering indoors. In parts of Europe fields of lavender are still grown and harvested for the fragrant oil, an important ingredient in many fine perfumes. Fragrant potpourri, sachets, tussie-mussies and other gifts from the garden can be easily made at home. All varieties thrive in a warm sunny location and are moderately drought-tolerant. See also the listing *Lavandula* in the PERENNIALS section. USES: △▲▼❀✄✄

English Lavender   ZONES 4–9
(*L. angustifolia* 'Munstead') The hardiest and most popular type grown. Compact bushy plants with the classic deep-blue flowers and good strong fragrance. Occasionally used as a flavouring in herbal jellies, vinegars and syrups. Flowers make an attractive garnish. Often grown as a low clipped herbal hedge. HEIGHT: 30–60cm (1–2')

French Lavender   ZONES 8–9
(*L. dentata*) Also called Fringed Lavender. Uses are similar to English Lavender. Foliage is finer, silvery-grey in colour and finely toothed, with spikes of purple flowers. Not nearly as hardy, best grown in a pot and overwintered in a sunny window. Add a few sprigs to your bath! HEIGHT: 30–90cm (1–3')

Provence Lavender   ZONES 5–9
(*L. × intermedia* 'Provence') Also known as Lavendin. Apparently this is the form most often commercially grown in France for the high oil content. Plants are vigorous and more disease-resistant than English types. Taller in habit, with pretty purple spikes. HEIGHT: 45–90cm (18–36")

Spanish Lavender   ZONES 8–9
(*L. stoechas*) Also called Butterfly Lavender, or French Lavender. Spikes of dark purple flowers, with unique long bracts at the top that wave like little flags. Makes a terrific container plant! Foliage and flowers are used like English Lavender. **'Otto Quast'** is hardy to Zone 7 and grows a little larger, with silvery foliage. HEIGHT: 30–90cm (1–3')

LEMON BALM
(Melissa officinalis)   ZONES 4–9

With its shiny bright green foliage, Lemon Balm is an attractive low-maintenance groundcover as well as a useful kitchen herb. Easy to grow in shade or sun, preferring a rich, moist soil. The fresh leaves can be used to brew a deliciously lemon-flavoured and scented tea that is said to have a calming effect. Some cooks substitute finely chopped Lemon Balm leaves for the lemon in certain recipes or use whole sprigs as a garnish. Try a little scattered in a fruit salad or throw in a handful when poaching fish. Bees love the tiny nectar-filled flowers. Dried leaves are used in potpourri. HEIGHT: 30–60cm (1–2') USES: ⋔❀▼ Edging

LEMON VERBENA
(Aloysia triphylla)   ZONES 9–10

Grown as a tender perennial or sub-tropical shrub in most regions. An intensely lemon-scented and flavoured plant, just a few leaves will add zest to hot or cold desserts, sauces, rice, fish dishes, cold drinks and anything else you might use lemon with. Combines well with other tea herbs. Dried leaves are a fragrant addition to potpourri. Grow Lemon Verbena in a container and take indoors for the winter. Needs full sun. HEIGHT: 30–90cm (1–3') USES: ▼ Herb Gardens

LOVAGE
(Levisticum officinale)   ZONES 2–9

As common in European gardens as rhubarb is here. The entire plant smells and tastes strongly of celery, the leaves and stems are used (sparingly) to add their pleasant flavour to soups, stews and various meat, poultry or fish dishes, in stir-fries or vegetable salads. The seeds are also sometimes dried and ground, then sprinkled over biscuits, breads, roasting meats or added to cheese dishes. Tender young shoots are sometimes blanched and eaten as a vegetable. Next time you drink a Caesar, try using a hollow Lovage stem for a straw! Once Lovage settles in, it will be the giant of the herb garden, looking somewhat like a monstrous celery plant, but handsome enough to use in the back of a perennial border. Appreciates a rich, moist soil in part shade or full sun. HEIGHT: 1.5m (5') USES: ✄❀▼ Borders

MARJORAM
(Origanum spp.)

These are closely related to Oregano, and sorting out the differences can be confusing. They have a preference for sunny sites, and would not look out of place in a rock garden or edging a border. Marjorams have a fairly strong flavour that has sometimes been described as "perfumy," though it lacks the bite that makes Oregano the pizza herb. The various types can be used interchangeably for flavouring meats, poultry, sausages, stuffings, soup and stews, or in vegetable dishes, especially with tomatoes, squash or dried beans. Can be used to make a tea. USES: ▼ Edging, Rock gardens

Sweet Marjoram   ANNUAL
(*O. majorana*) The strongest-flavoured marjoram, and the one commonly sold in dried form. Add the fresh or dried herb towards the end of cooking time in order to preserve its flavour. Extensively used in Italian, French and Greek cuisine. Adds a nice flavour to herbal vinegars, oils, soaps and cosmetics. Definitely a tender annual, but also easily grown indoors for the winter. HEIGHT: 30cm (12")

Pot Marjoram   ZONES 6–9
(*O. onites*) Sometimes called Cretan Oregano. A hardier species with a slightly milder flavor, but said to be inferior to Sweet Marjoram. Mild enough to use in salads. HEIGHT: 20–30cm (8–12")

Variegated Marjoram   ZONES 7–9
(*O. vulgare* 'Variegatum') Mild flavor. Very attractive, heavily variegated green and white leaves. Low habit. An excellent edging plant for the herb garden or border, also attractive in containers. HEIGHT: 20cm (8")

MINT
(Mentha spp.)
Possibly the easiest of all the herbs to grow; in fact, mints are often accused of growing a little *too* well. Most varieties have a determined tendency to spread by sneaky underground stems or rhizomes. Mints can be easily controlled by planting in large tubs or containers — large square clay drain tiles, half-barrels, or deep plastic pots, for instance. Containers can be either free-standing or sunk into the ground, the method advised for cold winter areas. All varieties prefer a rich, moist soil in sun or partial shade. Divide plants every other year to maintain a good thick patch. Clip plants back when they flower to maintain a constant harvest until winter. One word of caution: don't unleash mint into the perennial border or anywhere else that you may regret it in a few years time. HEIGHT: Most types grow 30–60cm (1–2′) USES: ☙ Herb gardens

Spearmint is the variety most commonly used for cooking, but since all types share the same base menthol flavour, they can be used somewhat interchangeably. Mint adds a cool, refreshing flavour to fruit salads. Sprinkle finely chopped mint on cooked vegetables, peas, carrots, beets, or onions. Mint sauce is a classic finish to roast lamb. Used extensively in Indian, Thai, Vietnamese, Moroccan and Middle Eastern cuisines.

Apple Mint · ZONES 4–9
(*M. suaveolens*) Good flavour and strong green-apple fragrance; rounded, downy leaves. Excellent for cooking, especially fragrant in tea.

Chocolate Mint · ZONES 3–9
(*M. × piperita*) A special strain of peppermint with a subtle chocolate overtone in the fragrance. Foliage is very attractive, dark green with a bronzy cast.

Corsican Mint · ZONES 7–9
(*M. requienii*) Low, creeping variety mostly used as a groundcover. The tiny leaves smell and taste of creme de menthe, but are really too small to be of any culinary use. Excellent container plant, and grows well indoors. HEIGHT: 2cm (1″)

Ginger Mint · ZONES 3–9
(*M. × gracilis* 'Variegata') Especially attractive for garnishing, the leaves are streaked and dappled with golden yellow. Pleasant fruity scent. Said to be especially nice with melon and in fruit salad. Beautiful in pots.

> "A sliced fennel salad dressed with a light vinaigrette and strewn with chopped ginger mint leaves is a delightful combination, as is a cucumber and tomato sandwich with a lemony mayonnaise infused with ginger mint."
> – Carole Saville, *Exotic Herbs*

Grapefruit Mint · ZONES 2–9
A hybrid selection with an especially fruity fragrance, strongly reminiscent of grapefruit. Use like apple mint.

Orange Mint · ZONES 2–9
(*M. × piperita citrata*) Sometimes known as Lemon Mint or Eau de Cologne Mint. Foliage is slightly bronze in tone. Especially pleasant for tea. Also used in cooking, and for potpourri. Fruity citrus scent, with a hint of lavender.

Peppermint · ZONES 1–9
(*M. × piperita*) A strong-flavoured variety, used mostly for tea, candy and in liqueurs, otherwise a bit overpowering for most foods. True peppermint has reddish stems, smells and tastes exactly like a candy cane, and must be grown from divisions or cuttings as plants do not set seed. Watch out for impostors! **Variegated Peppermint** ('Variegata') is similar, but the leaves are attractively splashed with white streaks. Green shoots must be regularly removed. **Blue Balsam Mint** is a new variety with dark bronzy leaves and a strong flavour.

Silver Mint · ZONES 5–9
(*M. longifolia*) Especially fuzzy silver-grey leaves and large attractive spikes of mauve flowers. Used in Indian chutneys and Asian cuisines.

Spearmint · ZONES 1–9
(*M. spicata*) Pebbled, pointed leaves, and that familiar classic mint fragrance. This is the type most widely used for cooking, especially with lamb and in Middle Eastern cuisine. Also the key ingredient for a tall, cool Mint Julep. 'Kentucky Colonel' is a hybrid form with a high flavour content. 'English Mint' is a strain often recommended for mint jelly and traditional mint sauce.

Variegated Pineapplemint · ZONES 5–9
(*M. suaveolens* 'Variegata') Woolly leaves, with showy white and green variegation. The most attractive of the mints. Good flavour and a definite pineapple fragrance. Said to be less aggressive than other varieties.

ONION
(Allium fistulosum)
Welsh Onion · ZONES 2–9
Scallion, Spring Onion. Primarily used for early green onions, these are one of the first things to come up in the spring. A hardy perennial, slowly forming a clump of hollow green leaves, topped with showy heads of white flowers in early summer. Use the same as you would any regular green onion. Does not form a bulb. HEIGHT: 30–60cm (1–2′) USES: ✂ Borders, Herb garden

Oregano

OREGANO
(Origanum spp.)
Closely related to the Marjorams, but with a spicier flavour. Commonly used as an ingredient in pizza and pasta sauces, and other Italian dishes. Greek cooks add Oregano to marinades for meats, poultry and grilled vegetables, and to salad dressings. Also added to certain Mexican bean dishes, soups, meat and fish.

Corsican Mint

Apple Mint

Orange Mint

Golden Oregano

Curled Parsley

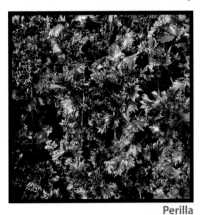
Perilla

Bush Rosemary

Rue

Oregano prefers a warm sunny site and a well-drained soil. The clusters of pretty pink flowers that appear in mid-summer make them suitable candidates for the perennial border. Bees and butterflies love the flowers. USES: ⅌< ♀ ☙ Borders, Herb garden

Common   ZONES 4–9
(*O. vulgare*) The most widely grown variety found in gardens, with a mild flavour when fresh, slightly stronger after the leaves are dried. HEIGHT: 30–45cm (12–18″). **'Dark Leaf'** Is a new cultivar, the leaves turning dark red in spring and fall, and said to have good flavour and fragrance. **Dwarf Oregano** ('Compactum') is a selection with a bushy, compact habit. Best choice for containers and indoors. Could be used as a low edging. HEIGHT: 15cm (6″). **Golden Oregano** ('Aureum') Forms a mat of bright golden-yellow leaves. Poor flavour, but really nice for edging or growing in tubs. Clip back hard in mid-summer to keep plants colourful and compact. HEIGHT: 30cm (12″). Also, see the listing under *Origanum* in the PERENNIALS section for several ornamental selections.

Greek   ZONES 5–9
(*O. vulgare hirtum*) Excellent strong oregano flavor, dark green leaves and white flowers. Perhaps the best for cooking. HEIGHT: 30–45cm (12–18″)

OREGANO, CUBAN
see CUBAN OREGANO.

PARSLEY
(Petroselinum crispum)
North Americans have finally taken a bite of the garnish and realized that parsley tastes good! There are such a multitude of uses for fresh parsley; it is commonly added to stews, soups, casseroles, egg and cheese dishes, chopped and sprinkled on cooked vegetables, meats, pasta, and many other savory foods. Different cuisines from all over the world make use of the fresh, somewhat peppery flavour.
Although biennial, parsley should be treated as an annual and planted each year, otherwise the plants bolt and go to seed in their second year and are of no culinary use anyway. The plants are fresh green and compact, and look right at home as an edging plant for general border use; no need to restrict parsley to the vegetable garden. Plants grown in pots may be brought indoors in the late fall for an indoor supply of parsley all winter. HEIGHT: 20–30cm (8–12″) USES: ♀ Edging, Herb garden

Curled   BIENNIAL
(var. *crispum*) The extra-curled type so familiar as a garnish. Perhaps the best general-purpose parsley. Especially attractive as an edging plant.

Italian   BIENNIAL
(var. *neopolitanum*) Many gourmet chefs swear that this plain-leaved type has a superior flavour, a bit stronger than regular curled parsley. Especially recommended for Italian and Middle Eastern cooking. Plants are not quite so compact.

PENNYROYAL
(Mentha pulegium)   ZONES 6–9
Closely related to mint, with a very strong wild-mint fragrance. The leaves were once used in small quantities to flavour puddings and sauces, however there may be some toxic effects so pregnant women should avoid eating it. Pennyroyal is now more commonly used to repel fleas and other flying insects, by simply rubbing some bruised leaves on the skin and clothing or on pets. Dried leaves are also used in potpourri. Plants will make a dense spreading groundcover for a moist partly shaded location. HEIGHT: 20–30cm (8–12″). **Carpet Pennyroyal** ('Nana') is a very compact selection, even better as a groundcover. HEIGHT: 10cm (4″) USES: ⋏⋎ ♀ Edging, Herb garden

PERILLA
(Perilla frutescens)   ANNUAL
Also called Beefsteak Plant. Known in Japan as *Shiso*, where both the red and green-leaved forms are used for a variety of things; garnishing, battered and fried as tempura, chopped finely to use in sushi, and to colour *umeboshi*, a salty plum pickle. The purple-leaved form is especially handsome in the border, in effect similar to a large purple basil. Excellent in containers, or massed for summer bedding. This is bound to catch on quickly as a multi-purpose garden plant. Self-seeds prolifically. HEIGHT: 45–60cm (18–24″) USES: ⅌< ♀ Massing, Borders

> "Perilla is also known as beefsteak plant either because of its use as a Japanese garnish or wrapping for beef or because of the similarity in color of the purple form's leaves to red meat — though to my eye it looks more like burgundy wine."
> – Carole Saville, *Exotic Herbs*

PINEAPPLE SAGE
See SAGE, PINEAPPLE.

ROSEMARY
(Rosmarinus officinalis)
Native to Mediterranean regions, Rosemary is an important flavouring herb, especially in Italy, France and Greece. The fresh or dried leaves are used in a wide variety of foods, especially chicken, lamb, pork, potato and other vegetable dishes, as well as many soups. The plants are evergreen, with needle-like leaves and pretty mauve flowers in early spring. Because they are tender in most parts of the country, a good solution is to grow in pots that may be taken indoors for the winter. Rosemary is actually a woody shrub and can be easily clipped or formed into various shapes or allowed to grow in a natural way. Plants appreciate full sun and a well-drained soil. USES: ▲♀🌠 Mixed borders, Herb gardens

> "In trendy restaurants, the presence of sprigs of rosemary infusing little puddles of extra virgin olive oil in which to dip crusty bread in place of butter attests to the herb's continuing popularity."
> – Carole Saville, *Exotic Herbs*

Bush   ZONES 8–9
The more popular upright form, easily maintained as a dense bush with a yearly clipping in late spring. Plants are sometimes trained as a standard or wreath. HEIGHT: 60cm (2′) or more. There are several named selections including: **'Arp'**, said to be hardy to Zone 7; **'Tuscan Blue'** with large leaves and deep lavender-blue flowers.

Trailing   ZONES 8–9

('Prostratum') Excellent rosemary for containers and hanging baskets, with a prostrate-to-cascading habit. HEIGHT: 15cm (6"). **'Irene'** is a newer selection with a more vigorous habit.

RUE

(Ruta graveolens)   ZONES 4–9

An ancient bitter herb, this once had great importance as a medicinal herb and as protection from witchcraft and evil in general. Although poisonous in large quantities, the leaves are used sparingly in salads or to flavour soft cheeses. It should not be eaten by pregnant women. Nowadays Rue is mostly grown in the border for its attractive blue-green foliage, or clipped as a hedge in formal knot gardens. The sap may cause serious skin irritation and blistering, when skin is exposed to sunlight. HEIGHT: 30–90cm (1–3') USES: ▲⚕☀ Borders, Herb gardens

SAGE

(Salvia spp.)

Some of the best garden flowers can be found among the ranks of this enormous group of plants, including several listed under *Salvia* in the PERENNIAL section. The herbal varieties of Sage bear fragrant leaves as well as showy flowers.

Common Sage   ZONES 4–9

(*Salvia officinalis*) A favorite flavouring for poultry stuffings, Sage can be easily grown in a sunny border where both its grey-green leaves and short spikes of violet-purple flowers are valued. The leaves are used sparingly, either fresh or dried, to flavour rich meats and stews, dried-bean dishes, in sausages and in cream cheese. Sage was an important medicinal herb, and many people still drink a cup of sage tea to ward off a sore throat. Plants should be pruned back to 15cm (6") in early spring so they stay compact. Flowers are attractive to bees and hummingbirds. HEIGHT: 45–75cm (18–30") USES: ✂◀▲⚕☀☼ Borders, Herb gardens

The unique selections of Common Sage listed below are well worth seeking. In addition to being useful kitchen herbs, they are extremely ornamental. Those that are slightly tender should be planted in a protected area, mulched for the winter or carried over in a coldframe.

Berggarten Sage

('Berggarten') Fat, tongue-shaped leaves in the classic olive-gray colour. Good hardiness, and excellent ornamental effect.

Dwarf Sage

('Compacta') A very bushy and compact form, reaching only 30cm (12") tall. The best for containers.

Golden Sage   ZONES 6–9

('Icterina') Leaves are strongly variegated with green and gold. Makes a nice edging. A favorite for containers.

Purple Sage   ZONES 6–9

('Purpurascens') Leaves are overlaid with a violet-purple cast, purple stems. Handsome.

Tricolor Sage   ZONES 7–9

('Tricolor') Foliage is boldly splashed with purple, pink, cream and green. Also useful for edging. The most tender cultivar and not as vigorous.

Pineapple Sage   TENDER PERENNIAL

(Salvia elegans) Tropical variety, grown as an annual or indoor/outdoor container plant. The hairy, bright green leaves smell strongly of pineapple with a mild, fruity flavour. Used finely chopped in salads, whole in jams, jellies, and cold drinks, or as a garnish for nearly anything. Also makes a refreshing hot tea. Over the course of one season this will form a substantial plant in a sunny site. Large, edible scarlet flowers appear very late in the fall when frosts stay away. HEIGHT: 90–120cm (3–4") USES: ✂⚕☀ Borders, Herb gardens. **Honeydew Sage** is an earlier-blooming selection, more compact and with a sweet melon fragrance.

SAVORY

(Satureja spp.)

Often added as a flavouring to dishes made with dried legumes, and sometimes referred to as "the bean herb". The fresh or dried leaves have a rich peppery flavour that can be overpowering in the wrong hands.

Summer Savory   ANNUAL

(*S. hortensis*) The milder-flavoured type, and favored by many cooks for this reason. Can subtly flavour egg dishes, tender summer vegetables, soups and stews, and a wide variety of other foods. Excellent used either fresh or dried. Summer Savory is an easy annual, growing in any average garden soil with a sunny exposure. HEIGHT: 30–60cm (1–2') USES: ⚕ Herb gardens

Winter Savory   ZONES 4–9

(*S. montana*) With a more pungent, stronger taste than Summer Savory, this is best used to flavour rich meats or stews, bean soups, casseroles and stuffings. Plants form a low evergreen bush that does not look out of place as either an edging or in the rock garden. Pale mauve flowers appear in summer. HEIGHT: 25cm (10") USES: ◢△ᴧᴧ◢▲⚕ Borders

Sorrel

SORREL, GARDEN

(Rumex acetosa)   ZONES 2–9

Also known as sour grass in Europe, where the leaves are widely used to make a delicious, tangy soup. The spinach-like leaves of Sorrel have a sharp sour-lemon flavour that is refreshing when added to other greens in a salad. Excellent cooked and pureed in sauces for broiled or poached fish. Tender young leaves will be produced all season long if flower spikes are faithfully removed. HEIGHT: 30cm (12≤) USES: Herb gardens

Golden Sage

Purple Sage

Tricolor Sage

Pineapple Sage

Southernwood

Alpine Wild Strawberry

Sweet Woodruff

French Tarragon

SOUTHERNWOOD

(Artemisia abrotanum)   ZONES 2–9

Also known as Old Man or Lad's Love. Plants form an upright bush of ferny grey-green leaves, with a spicy pine-orange fragrance. Has been used for centuries to repel moths from stored clothing, and as a popular ingredient of sachets and potpourri. Dried boughs add a nice aroma to a burning fire. Has been used medicinally. Try to locate this in the garden where passers-by will brush against it, releasing its fragrance into the air. Foliage is excellent for flower arranging. HEIGHT: 60–90cm (2–3') USES: ✂✓❦ Borders, Herb gardens

STEVIA, SUGARPLANT

(Stevia rebaudiana)   TENDER PERENNIAL

Gaining much media attention lately as a new wonder sugar substitute from Paraguay. Dried, powdered leaves are sprinkled over foods to sweeten, or mixed into baked goods and desserts. Although about 300 times sweeter than sugar, there is an accompanying bitter taste, so there needs to be a fair bit of experimentation to get it just right. Plants prefer a warm climate, good drainage and even moisture supply. Sensitive to frosts. Harvest just before plants bloom heavily in late summer. HEIGHT: 60–90cm (2–3') USES: Herb gardens

STRAWBERRY, WILD

(Fragaria vesca)   ZONES 2–9

Known as *Fraises des Bois* in France. Picking wild strawberries is a distant childhood memory for many people. Growing them in your own garden, however, can easily be an adult reality! Selected forms of wild strawberry offer larger fruit, easily twice the size of their wild cousins, but with that same special flavour that is definitely lacking in the larger commercial varieties. In addition, the plants are runnerless, forming compact clumps that don't spread all over. An excellent size for edging purposes. Leaves of wild strawberry can be steeped to make a soothing tea. HEIGHT: 20–30cm (8–12") USES: ❦ Edging, Borders

> "The aromatic berries are not widely available commercially… the small size of the fruit placed next to grand, fat strawberries doesn't lend to their marketing themselves too well, but discerning shoppers know the small size of fraises des bois belies their expansive taste, which causes a perfumed explosion in the mouth." – Carole Saville,
> *Exotic Herbs*

Alpine

('Rügen') Superb flavour. Showy, bright-red conical fruits. Everbearing.

Yellow Fruited

('Yellow Wonder') Pale creamy-yellow fruit, distinctive strawberry flavour with a hint of something else… apricot? A real novelty, especially nice growing next to the red-fruited form. Everbearing. An added feature of this variety is that birds won't steal the fruit because of the unusual colour.

Sweet Woodruff

SWEET WOODRUFF

(Galium odoratum)   ZONES 4–9

Becoming exceedingly popular as a groundcover for shady areas. Plants form a low mat of bright green leaves, studded with tiny white flowers in late spring. The stems and leaves, when dried, develop a wonderful aroma that is similar to vanilla or fresh-mown hay. A common use is in sachets, scented pillows and potpourri, where it also acts as a fixative. Sweet Woodruff is also the key ingredient for making German May-wine (*Waldmeister-Bowle*). HEIGHT: 20cm (8") USES: ⋀▲❦ Woodland gardens

French Tarragon

TARRAGON, FRENCH

(Artemisia dranunculus 'Sativa')   ZONES 4–9

True French Tarragon is unmistakable once you know the clue; a couple of fresh leaves when chewed should develop a strong licorice flavour. If not, you are dealing with the impostor, Russian Tarragon, a plant of no culinary value whatsoever! It is of the utmost importance in fine French cooking, being included among the four essential *fines herbes* (Chervil, Parsley, Chives and Tarragon). Tarragon is added to a wide variety of dishes, especially fish, shellfish, chicken, eggs, fresh tomatoes, and in green salads and dressings. Tarragon vinegar can easily be made at home.

The plant, for the most part, is rather unimpressive in appearance, with slender stems of narrow green leaves, forming a loose bush of medium height. Lacking vigour, it should be given a special spot with rich, well-drained soil, full sun, and a good supply of moisture. Divide plants every year or two to keep them young and healthy. HEIGHT: 45–60cm (18–24") USES: ❦ Herb gardens

THYME

(Thymus spp.)

There are a great many different kinds of Thyme, varying remarkably in their foliage and flower colour, habit, fragrance and flavour. See under *Thymus* in the PERENNIAL section for a more complete listing. The culinary varieties form semi-upright bushes of spicy-fragrant evergreen leaves. They prefer a well-drained, sunny location and are tolerant of hot, dry conditions once established. HEIGHT: 15–20cm (6–12″) USES: △ ⋀⋁ ▲ ▼ 🌿 Edging, Borders

Common Thyme

Common Thyme   ZONES 5–9

(*T. vulgaris*) This is the standard cooking thyme, the one dried and sold in packages at the supermarket. The grey-green foliage is pleasantly aromatic, and can be used fresh or dried to flavour meats, poultry, stews and soups, as well as a whole range of vegetable and dried-bean dishes. Needs excellent drainage, particularly through the winter months. It can also be grown in pots to bring indoors for the winter.

Lemon Thyme   ZONES 4–9

(*T. × citriodorus*) Delicious strong lemon fragrance, mild spicy thyme-citrus flavour. There are several forms of this around, the most ornamental kinds having bright gold-and-green variegated leaves. Before buying plants, be sure to test the fragrance first; don't settle for less than a big burst of fresh honey-lemon. Lemon Thyme can be used the same way as regular Thyme. Add a few sprigs to a pot of tea, or chop finely and sprinkle over baked fish, chicken or veal. Lemon Thyme should only be used fresh, and generally added at the last minute or its fragrance will be lost. **'Gold Edge'** has brightly variegated leaves in green and yellow and a strong lemon fragrance. **Silver Thyme** ('Argenteus') is said to be among the best-flavoured thymes for culinary use, and has brightly variegated white-and-green leaves.

Oregano-scented Thyme   ZONES 5–9

(*T. pulegioides*) A large-leafed variety, with good thyme flavor and fragrance, and just an overtone of oregano. Low creeping habit.

VALERIAN

(Valeriana officinalis)   ZONES 2–9

Also known as Garden Heliotrope, which describes the intensely fragrant clusters of white or pale-pink flowers. Plants form a tall upright clump of lacy leaves, blooming in the summer months. Said to attract cats. The dried, powdered roots of Valerian are included in a wide variety of herbal preparations for relieving pain, calming nerves, and as a sedative. Nice in the back of a perennial border, the flowers are good for cutting. HEIGHT: 1.2–1.5m (4–5′) USES: ✂ Borders

VERBENA, LEMON

See LEMON VERBENA.

WATER CRESS

(Nasturtium officinale)   ZONES 4–9

Not such an easy plant to grow in the average home garden, demanding a constant supply of moisture in a sunny or partly shaded location. In the wild it grows along the edges of slow-moving streams. It might be possible to succeed in growing Water cress if you have a pond, water garden, or even a large tub that is well aerated; plant in pots first, then submerge up to the rims. The peppery-flavoured leaves are a favorite spring salad green, also sometimes put in sandwiches or made into a French cream and potato soup. HEIGHT: 15cm (6″) USES: ⚑ Water gardens, Naturalizing

WOODRUFF

See SWEET WOODRUFF.

WORMWOOD

(Artemisia absinthium)   ZONES 2–9

An ancient bitter herb, used medicinally for hundreds of years to treat intestinal worms, and in soothing liniments. Also was once used as a flavouring ingredient in Absinthe, Vermouth, aperitifs and herbal wines. The presence of toxic compounds make it inadvisable for home culinary use. Plants form a fairly large bush of silvery-green ferny foliage, with a pleasant spicy fragrance. Sometimes included in sachets or potpourri. Trim back to 15cm (6″) in late fall or early spring. HEIGHT: 90cm (3′) USES: ✂ 🌿 Borders, Herb gardens

Lemon Thyme

Silver Thyme

Valerian

Water Cress

Pest Problems & Solutions

Prevention

Growing strong, healthy plants to begin with can do much towards preventing a buildup of pests. Unhealthy plants seem to give off visual signals of stress that attract a wide range of insect predators.

Siting & Spacing

Proper siting alone will meet the basic needs of many plants. Assess what kind of conditions exist in your garden before choosing the appropriate perennials. Getting a soil analysis done might be very helpful, any good garden centre will know how to go about this. A wider initial spacing of plants means that they will take much longer to become congested; when plants are packed closely together they have to compete for available moisture, nutrients and light, which leads to stress.

Maintenance

Regular fertilizing, watering and division of perennials, particularly in a closely-spaced border setting, will help them to stay healthy. See the Introduction for more details about these activities, and for initial soil preparation tips.

Good Hygiene

General garden hygiene is the key to preventing fungal and bacterial disease problems. Remove and dispose of diseased plant material promptly by putting it in the garbage; don't put it in the compost heap or the problem may eventually spread all over the garden. Clean up the dead tops of perennials in late fall or early spring and put them on the compost. This activity does for the border what flossing does for your teeth: it removes the opportunity for insects and diseases to hide and possibly spread to living plants.

Monitoring

Throughout the season, keep an eye out for plants that don't look quite right. Examine them for signs of insects or disease and remove the affected part immediately or treat as required before the problem spreads. If you know of certain plants that are particularly prone to aphids or mildew, for example, develop a regular routine of checking them every week or two for signs of trouble. Usually the worst problems develop as weather warms up, especially in humid regions. Early June is an excellent opportunity to prevent a disaster from happening in early July.

Diseases

Much more mysterious than insects, fungal diseases often seem to suddenly appear from nowhere. They are a problem on certain perennials in some years yet don't seem to appear in others. We can blame some of this on the weather conditions that promote the germination and growth of spores that happen to land on the appropriate host plants. Cleaning up garden debris and weeds will help to eliminate many of the fungus spores and bacteria that might be lurking around your healthy plants.

LEAFSPOT: Brown or black spots on leaves. Leaves may drop off.
Damage: Unsightly. May slightly weaken plant.
Recommended controls: Sanitation; remove infected leaves, clean up around plants in fall. Usually worse in warm humid weather. Good air circulation may help in prevention.
Plant hosts: Wide range of perennials and other plants. Peonies, Foxglove.

POWDERY MILDEW: White powdery-looking coating on the upper surface of leaves. Usually apparent in late summer or fall.
Damage: Leaves may drop or be unsightly. Severe, recurrent infestation can weaken and kill plant.
Recommended controls: Increase air circulation. Use a preventative fungicidal spray. Select a resistant variety.
Plant hosts: Wide range of perennials, especially Asters, Phlox, Delphinium, Monarda, Solidago.

RUST: Orange or red spots, usually on the underside of leaves.
Damage: Unsightly. Can weaken plant if severe.
Recommended controls: Sanitation; remove infected leaves. Clear weeds in the vicinity. Use a recommended fungicide.
Plant hosts: Wide range of perennials, especially Hollyhocks, Sidalcea, Lavatera, Heuchera, Helenium, Helianthus, Monarda.

VIRUSES: Wide range of symptoms. Look for stunted, unhealthy-looking plants. Most plant viruses are spread by insect pests.
Damage: Yellowing or mottling leaf colour, crinkled, twisted or distorted leaves, flattened and weird-looking multiple stems (especially lilies).
Recommended controls: Destroy and discard all infected plants. Control insect infestations. No cure. Plants usually wane and die.
Plant hosts: Wide range of perennials, especially Chrysanthemum, Primula, Delphinium.

WILTS: Arching or withered shoots and leaves. Sudden collapsing of infected plants, not due to lack of water. Rather mysterious.
Damage: Shoot or whole plant usually dies.

Recommended controls: May be caused by a fungal or bacterial wilt infection. Destroy and discard infected plants. Wilts are soil-borne so avoid putting another plant of the same kind in the vicinity.

Plant hosts: Wide range of perennials, Asters, Chrysanthemum, Helianthus, Peony Foxglove.

Insects

The list of creepy-crawly things that generally affect perennials is not a long one. Hopefully the descriptions of insects and damage symptoms below will help to identity most of the common insect pests you are likely to encounter. If you are unsure, take a sample to your local garden centre for identification; they can also recommend specific insecticides and other recommended controls for your region.

APHIDS: Small green or black soft-bodied insects; in clusters on stems, buds or under leaves. They usually secrete a sticky substance.

Damage: Deformed leaves, shoots or flowers. Can spread viral diseases.

Recommended controls: Hose off with water. Spray with insecticidal soap. Remove affected shoots. Sprinkle with diatomaceous earth. Release ladybugs as natural predators. Use a recommended insecticide.

Plant hosts: Wide range of perennials. Especially Delphinium, Coral-bells, Oriental Poppies.

BEETLES, LEAF: Hard-shelled medium to large beetles. Various colours.

Damage: Chew holes in leaves.

Recommended controls: Hand pick. Use a recommended insecticide.

Plant hosts: Wide range of perennials, varies from region to region.

CATERPILLARS: Crawling worm-like, many legs. Smooth, spiny or hairy. Often green or brown but can be many colours. The adults are butterflies and moths.

Damage: Holes in leaves, sometimes severely chewed.

Recommended controls: Hand-picking. Spraying with B.T. (an organic bacterial spray that only affects caterpillars). Use a recommended insecticide.

Plant hosts: Wide range of perennials. Especially grey-leaved plants.

EARWIGS: Long, narrow hard-shelled brown bugs with what looks like a mean pincer on one end. Usually seen at night; they hide under debris during the daytime.

Damage: General leaf-eating and skeletonizing, especially on newly planted perennials, annuals, vegetable and herb seedlings.

Recommended controls: Aluminum tart shells half-filled with soya sauce and a thin layer of vegetable oil, sunk down to ground level; this actually works! Trap under boards and hand pick. Use a recommended insecticidal bait (but they usually don't work well).

Plant hosts: Wide range of perennials.

IRIS BORER: Large worm that feeds inside the rhizome. Starts out as a small worm inside the leaf and works its way down.

Damage: Tunneling inside roots. Plants often develop a mushy rot at the base causing the leaf fans to fall over. A serious pest of iris that can destroy the plant.

Recommended controls: Sanitation; remove all dead or discoloured leaves. Lift affected clumps; divide and soak rhizomes in a strong bleach solution or kill worms by poking with a piece of wire. Replant in a new location.

Plant hosts: Iris, especially Bearded Iris, occasionally other types.

JAPANESE BEETLE: Large, hard-shelled iridescent beetle, usually seen from June to September. Not a problem west of the Rockies, on the prairies or in the maritime provinces.

Damage: Feeding on flowers and leaves.

Recommended controls: Hand picking. Use a recommended insecticide.

Plant hosts: Wide range of plants, especially roses and wild grapes.

LEAFHOPPERS: Small fast-moving green diamond-shaped bugs. Usually hiding under leaves; brush plants to make them hop. Often a problem in rural areas or next to meadows, natural areas.

Damage: These bugs suck plant juices from leaves, causing discolored yellow or dead areas. Can spread viruses.

Recommended controls: Sprinkle diatomaceous earth. Use a recommended insecticide. Keep grassy or weedy areas mowed.

Plant hosts: Wide range of perennials, especially bushy or leafy ones.

LEAFMINERS: Tiny little worms that feed and tunnel inside leaves.

Damage: White, yellow or brown blotches on leaves, tunnels or trails can be easily seen.

Recommended controls: Sanitation; remove and discard affected leaves. Mulching with gravel under the plants may help. Cut back foliage to force attractive fresh leaves. Can be prevented by using recommended insecticides.

Plant hosts: Columbines, Chrysanthemum, Delphinium, Euphorbia, not many others.

NEMATODES: Tiny microscopic worms that usually feed on plant roots.

Damage: Stunted growth, not caused by lack of water or fertilizer. Galls may be present on roots.

Recommended controls: Destroy infected plants. Avoid planting the same species in that spot. Chemical controls are costly and impractical for home gardeners. French marigolds are said to kill nematodes.

Plant hosts: Wide range of perennials. Chrysanthemum, Peony, Delphinium, Poppies, Aconitum. Likely much more prevalent than most people realize.

PLANT BUGS: Smallish yellow-green oval-shaped bugs, sometimes striped.

Extreme slug damage on Hosta.

Damage: Distorted leaves, stem tips or buds. Spots on leaves.
Recommended controls: Diatomaceous earth. Use a recommended insecticide.
Plant hosts: Wide range of perennials.

SLUGS & SNAILS: Yucky soft-bodied, slimy rounded or long mollusks, big or small. Not an insect. Snails have a hard spiral-shaped shell.
Damage: General feeding on leaves, rasping holes.
Recommended controls: Clean up garden debris where they like to hide. Pick off by hand on overcast days or in early morning. Stale-beer bait stations. Use a recommended pesticide.
Plant hosts: Wide range of perennials, but especially hosta, hellebores, primula, delphiniums, hollyhocks, viola. Slugs love shady places.

SPIDER MITES, MITES: Tiny spider-like bugs, usually red, yellow or brown, on the underside of leaves. Fine webs may be visible to the naked eye on close inspection.
Damage: Pale yellow-looking leaves, distorted growth, stunting, silver or white spots on leaves.
Recommended controls: Insecticidal soap, recommended insecticide. Cut back affected shoots.
Plant hosts: Wide range of perennials, especially those in the rose family and daylilies.

SPITTLEBUG: Foamy, frothy white stuff that looks like spit; this covers and protects the little greenish-brown bugs.
Damage: Mainly looks gross. They suck on plant juices.
Recommended controls: Ignore. If prominent, use a recommended insecticide.
Plant hosts: Wide range of perennials.

THRIPS: Very small, narrow winged insect, a bit like a miniscule mosquito.
Damage: Sucks plant juices, causing brown streaks or white spots on flowers or leaves, sometimes distorted growth. Can spread viruses.
Recommended controls: Destroy affected plant parts. Sulphur dust. Diatomaceous earth. Use a recommended insecticide.
Plant hosts: Wide range of perennials. Gladiolus, Daylilies, Lilies, Iris.

WHITEFLY: Tiny triangular soft-bodied flies, powdery white. Will fly up in a mass when disturbed.
Damage: Suck plant juices. Yellow leaves, sometimes a stunted appearance.
Recommended controls: Insecticidal soap. Recommended insecticide.
Plant hosts: Wide range of perennials. Fuchsia, Impatiens, many annuals.

A Note Regarding Botanical Name Changes

The job of the botanist is to figure out the relationships between living plants, catalogue them and organize the information into a form that can be stored in books. They have been at this science now for several hundred years, and by and large they are pretty good at it!

We, as gardeners, often feel the victims whenever the botanists as a group change their collective minds about something or other, especially when it involves changing the names of plants that are familiar to us. What we have been calling *Chrysanthemum*, with seemingly little warning suddenly is re-classified as *Leucanthemum*. Or a species name like *Oenothera missouriensis* we are told had been superceded by *Oenothera macrocarpa*. Well, in the Big World of Science it seems that we gardeners have little collective clout when it comes right down to it, and eventually the new names filter into to the reference books, catalogues and our own notes and conversations.

For this guide, the standard reference used for botanical nomenclature is the 1995 version of *Naamlijst van Vaste Planten* (List of Names of Perennials), a standard listing used by the nursery industry in Europe, and recently adopted by the Perennial Plant Association. This booklet is produced and updated every five years by the Horticulture Research Station in Boskoop, Holland. In some cases, we used various other botanical references when any of the newer plants were not contained in the Naamlijst, or when we just simply disagreed.

Quotes & References

The following publications and individuals are quoted throughout this book:

Reference Books

The following books have been quoted in the Perennial Gardening Guide and are recommended for further reading:

Greenlee, John; *The Encyclopedia of Ornamental Grasses*; 1992; Rodale Press, PA; ISBN 0-87596-100-2

Hobhouse, Penelope; *Color in Your Garden*; 1989; Little, Brown & Co., Boston; ISBN 0-316-36748-6

Jekyll, Gertrude (editor Penelope Hobhouse); *Gertude Jekyll on Gardening*; 1985; Vintage Books/Random House, NY; ISBN 0-394-72924-2

Lacy, Allen; *The Garden in Autumn*; 1990; The Atlantic Monthly Press; ISBN 0-87113-347-4

Lima, Patrick; *The Harrowsmith Perennial Garden*; 1987; Camden House Publishing; ISBN 0-920656-74-9

Lloyd, Christopher; *Christopher Lloyd's Flower Garden*; 1993; Dorling Kindersley, London; ISBN 0-7513-0023-3

Lloyd, Christopher; *Foliage Plants*; 1985; Viking/Penguin Books, Markham, ON; ISBN 0-670-80197-6

Lovejoy, Anne; *The American Mixed Border*; 1993: MacMillen Publishing; ISBN 0-02-575580-3

MacKenzie, David S.; *Perennial Ground Covers*; 1997; Timber Press, Inc., Portland OR; ISBN 0-88192-368-0

Mickel, John; *Ferns for American Gardens*; 1994; Macmillen Publishing Company, NY; ISBN 0-02-584491-1

Mitchell, Henry; *One Man's Garden*; 1992; Houghton Mifflin Co., NY; ISBN 0-395-63319-2

Saville, Carole; *Exotic Herbs: a compendium of exceptional culinary herbs*; 1997; Henry Holt and Company, NY; ISBN 0-8050-4073-0

Thomas, Graham Stuart; *Perennial Garden Plants*; 1982; J.M. Dent & Sons, Toronto; ISBN 0-460-04575-X

Wilson, Helen Van Pelt; *Helen Van Pelt Wilson's Own Garden Book*;1973; Weathervane Books, NY; ISBN 0-517-191458

Commercial Nurseries

Davidson, Larry; **Lost Horizons**; R.R.#1, Acton, ON, L7J 2L7; (519) 853-3085; Catalogue: $3 (Zone 5)

Forgie, Cathy; **Lang Village Gardens**; 878 Lang Rd., R.R.#3, Keene, ON, K0L 2G0; (705) 295-6118; (Zone 4)

Jones, Judith I.; **Fancy Fronds Nursery**; 1911 4th Ave. West, Seattle, WA 98119-2610; (360) 793-1472; Catalogue: US$2 (Zone 8)

Knechtel, Elke; **Rainforest Gardens**; 13139 224th St., Maple Ridge, BC, V2X 7E7; (604) 467-4218; Catalogue: $4 (Zone 7)

Mason Hogue, Marjorie; **Mason Hogue Gardens**; R.R.#4, 3520 Durham Rd. 1, Uxbridge, ON, L9P 1R4; (905) 649-3532; Catalogue: $2 (Zone 4)

Talmage, Ellen M.; **Talmage Farm**; 2975 Sound Ave., Riverhead, NY 11901; (516) 727-0124

Ward, Val; **Buds**; 21 Vaughan Rd., Toronto, ON; (416) 658-9429; (Zone 5)

Gardeners and Writers

Adams, Denise; Doctoral Student (Horticulture), Ohio State University; Lithopolis, OH (Zone 5)

Baskerville, Joanne; Garden Consultant, Designer and Writer, Merritt, BC (Zone 4)

Burke, Margaret; Professor of Drama in Education; Brock University, St. Catharines, ON (Zone 6)

Craig, Peggy Walsh; Executive Director, COPF; North Bay, ON (Zone 3)

Eisenberg, Ellen; Garden Writer, Consultant; North York, ON (Zone 5)

Harris, Marjorie; Garden Writer, Editor, Gardening Life Magazine, Toronto, ON (Zone 5)

Hartman, Warren; Professor of Art History and Theatre, Brock University; St. Catharines, ON (Zone 6)

Hildebrandt, Dr. Virginia; V. Hildebrandt Plant Laboratory (tissue culture); Cambridge, ON (Zone 5)

Himmelman, Dr. Duncan; Horticulture Instructor, Olds College; Olds, AB (Zone 3)

Leggatt, Anna; Gardener, Chair, Ontario Rock Garden Society; Toronto, ON (Zone 5)

Lewis, Geoff; Horticulture Consultant, Vancouver, BC (Zone 8)

Lilly, Bob; Plantsman, Seattle, WA (Zone 7/8)

McDonnell, Suzette; Gardener, Garden Consultant (NPSH); Niagara Falls, ON (Zone 6)

Nicks, Joan; Professor of Film Studies, Brock University; St. Catharines, ON (Zone 6)

Schwartz, Bobbie; Bobbie's Green Thumb, Shaker Heights, OH (Zone 5)

Taylor, Luba; Gardener, Member of Aurora Horticulture Society; Sutton West, ON (Zone 4)

Vandenberg, John; Parks & Recreation Foreman, Town of Niagara-on-the-Lake, ON (Zone 6)

Ward, Kevin; Garden Writer, Gardener Extraordinaire; Baltimore, ON (Zone 4)

Zimmerman, Bruce; Garden Broadcaster and GWAA member, St. Catharines, ON (Zone 6)

Index

A Note Regarding Type & Other Production Stuff

The typefaces used in this book are Adobe Minion™ and Adobe Myriad.™ Minion is a 1990 Adobe Originals typeface by Robert Slimbach. It is inspired by classical, old style typefaces of the late Renaissance, a period of elegant, beautiful, and highly readable type designs. Myriad is an Adobe Originals typeface designed by Carol Twombly and Robert Slimbach in 1992. Myriad, a multiple master typeface, is a sans serif design that allows the generation of thousands of individual fonts from one master typeface by interactively varying the design attributes of weight and width.

This entire book was created digitally on an Apple Power Macintosh™ G3 computer.

Page layouts were made with Quark XPress.™ Photographs were scanned from 35mm slides using Polaroid's SprintScan™ slide scanner and Kodak's PhotoCD™ service. Colour separations and corrections were made using Adobe PhotoShop.™

Digital colour proofs were output on a Lexmark Optra C colour laser printer and a Xerox Splash colour proofer. Film was output on an Agfa Avantra 44s imagesetter and laminated film proofs made with the 3M Matchprint system.

The book is printed on Luna Gloss on a Solna C96 web press by Mitchell Press in Vancouver, British Columbia. The cover is printed on Warren Flo Brilliant Gloss on a Mitsubishi 6-colour 40″ sheet-fed press.